Virtuosity in Business

Virtuosity in Business

Invisible Law Guiding the Invisible Hand

Kevin T. Jackson

PENN

UNIVERSITY OF PENNSYLVANIA PRESS

PHILADELPHIA

Published by
University of Pennsylvania Press
Philadelphia, Pennsylvania 19104—4112
www.upenn.edu/pennpress

Printed in the United States of America on acid-free paper

10 9 8 7 6 5 4 3 2 1

Library of Congress Cataloging-in-Publication Data
Jackson, Kevin T.
    Virtuosity in business : invisible law guiding the invisible hand / Kevin T. Jackson.
— 1st ed.
        p.   cm.
    Includes bibliographical references and index.
    ISBN 978-0-8122-4376-5 (hardcover : alk. paper)
    1. Business ethics.   2. Industrial management—Moral and ethical aspects.   3. Organizational behavior—Moral and ethical aspects.   4. Goodwill (Commerce).   I. Title.
HF5387.J297155   2012
174'.4—dc23
                                                                        2011030430

Contents

Preface

We shall judge the work of art as the living vehicle of a hidden truth to which both the work and we ourselves are together subject, and which is the measure at once of the work and of our mind. Under such circumstances we truly judge because we do not set ourselves up as judges but strive to be obedient to that which the work may teach us.
—Jacques Maritain, *The Range of Reason*

ASSUMING A PHILOSOPHICAL perspective on the field of business ethics reveals pressing and universal issues that, although connected to business and economics, are neither exclusively economic, nor completely related to business in their nature and origin. One of the principal concerns in this book is with the moral and intellectual health of the wider culture within which the global economy and today's business enterprises operate.

It is within this spirit that *Virtuosity in Business* undertakes to show that inattention to ethics has been the overriding problem for business and that attention to it is the only enduring solution. The target of my concern is real, full-blooded ethics. The brand of moral realism that I set forth is opposed to relativism and its postmodern next of kin. Throughout the text I affirm this thesis, defend it, and seek to bring out its far-reaching implications for a broad range of topics in the face of scientism and other current intellectual ills. I draw inspiration not just from Aristotle and other ancients, but also from Aquinas and fellow propounders of the natural law tradition, existentialism, legal studies, and various other disciplines extending from economics and political philosophy all the way to musicology. My aim is to deepen the reader's awareness of how ethics is crucial to virtually everything that business touches.

In some parts of the book I highlight the importance of the intellectual and moral formation of businesspeople and other professionals who are closely connected to them. I believe that the task of educating future business leaders is severely hampered by widespread intellectual weaknesses not only in schools of business but in other institutions of learning as well. These weaknesses are simultaneously causes and effects of various intellectual vices, methodologies, and ideologies that are hostile to, and incompatible with, a proper understanding of human nature and its relationship to business and economics.

At the same time, the concept of virtuosity developed in this book extends boldly beyond the sometimes pedantic treatment of moral virtue delivered by academics who are perhaps well trained in moral philosophy yet nevertheless uninformed about or excessively skeptical of how virtue realistically applies in the highly competitive world of business. Virtuosity, I maintain, is not simply about exhorting business actors to display excellence in "doing the right thing." When considered in the context of a market economy, virtuosity is equally connected with performance, competition, success, and the creation of value for oneself and others. For this reason, at various junctures the book presents the model of musical virtuosity as an analogy for deepening our understanding of, and quest for cultivating, virtue in business.

The book pays homage to the worth and dignity of philosophy not only for understanding the significance of business as a human endeavor but also for conducting business successfully. It is an exhortation to businesspeople of all kinds and in all countries to think more broadly, to think bigger and deeper. By stressing the profound importance of philosophy for business and economics, I insist on the role of the field of business ethics as a scholarly and intellectual discipline that must be firmly rooted in questions of truth, goodness, and even beauty.

I am seeking to promote a proper understanding of the relationship between business and the wider moral and intellectual culture not primarily for the sake of solving an intriguing intellectual problem but because in a very real way the salvation of our civilization is at stake. It is of vital importance that business ethics be equipped to vigorously defend the ability of human reason to know the truth. A firm confidence in reason has been an integral part of the Western philosophical tradition, but it stands in special need of reaffirmation today. I believe that at least part of the reason for this is connected with the global financial crisis. In general, economic crises tend to be accompanied by disturbing perplexity regarding values, not only financial ones but moral, epistemological, and aesthetic ones as well. This feature renders such crises particularly disquieting not just within financial institutions, but throughout the wider culture as well. Accordingly, it is understandable that people would look to philosophy, which examines fundamental assumptions, in an effort to restore their basic sense of comprehension about the world. In the face of widespread and fundamental doubt about financial affairs, we begin to reconsider what the twentieth-century American composer (and life-insurance entrepreneur) Charles Ives saw as perennial issues of our existence, the unanswered questions: Who am I? Where I did come from? Why are we here? Where ought we to be going?

A lack of confidence in one's ability to know the truth has serious consequences both for our economic life and for the wider culture. Without objective truth, people are simply adrift. Given human weakness and the strength of human passions, this understandably ushers in crisis and tragedy. The recent global financial crisis has been due in no small part to reason basically abandoning the pursuit of ultimate and objective truth. The result has been a pervasive skepticism and relativism, which, if not stemmed, will lead not to the advancement of humanity but, instead, to yet more of the despair and irrationality that has attended the catastrophic erosion of economic value.

I believe that the widespread misunderstanding of the relationship between economics (ultimately anchored in truth), ethics (ultimately anchored in goodness), and culture (ultimately anchored in beauty), particularly among those primarily responsible for teaching business, weakens the ability of both business schools and business organizations to cultivate and transmit authentic human values. The "ethics" that corporations and business schools attempt to transmit, when they badly misunderstand the relationship, is "business ethics" only in a weak and defective sense. For example, it may be an agenda for political correctness (motivated from either end of the political spectrum), or it may amount to an effort at "window dressing" to serve the narrow interests of the organization.

I wish to stress the role of philosophy in the theory and practice of business and the need for businesspeople and business academics to be trained rigorously in philosophy. But I do not mean philosophy in the narrow sense that many departments of philosophy take it to be, detached from a broader understanding of human culture. It is not conceptual puzzles and brain-teasers, but rather wellsprings of wisdom that need to be integrated into business education. A syncretic understanding of philosophical thought can help one in constructing a holistic worldview. We ought to be alarmed that indispensable philosophical work is widely neglected—both in business research and in the formation of business leaders—in favor of mathematical and financial modeling approaches to economics; such technocratic approaches are often reductionist and incompatible with the humanistic enterprise of business in whose service they are putatively placed. This is not to say that nonhumanistic fields lack legitimacy, autonomy, and importance as intellectual disciplines in their own right, but rather that there is a threat of possible corruptions of these fields that render them incompatible with the proper end of the economy, which is to serve humanity and not the other way around.

The first of these potential dangers is that the legitimate autonomy of the science of economics can be misinterpreted as liberating it from the overarching requirements of morality—the higher, invisible law that philosophy seeks to reveal (no matter how controversial our interpretations of it may be). What may be termed a scientistic (as opposed to scientific) mind-set can lead people to falsely reckon that if some innovation in business is technically possible, then it is therefore morally permissible.

The second possible danger concerns scientism—a philosophical notion that refuses to accept the validity of any form of knowledge besides positive science. Scientism deems values to be mere by-products of emotions and relegates the question of the meaning of life to the land of the irrational or illusory. The growing presence of scientism in economic thought reveals both the possibility of philosophical error and the fact that economic philosophy can turn, as it were, antiphilosophical. The positivism at the core of scientism was embraced by philosophers as part of their philosophical mission to instrumentalize reason, to place reason in servitude to the passions. In this manner, positivism attempted to reinvent philosophy, not as the pursuit of wisdom, what we may term the *quest for sapiential knowledge*, but as a purely analytic kind of venture.

As rationalism took root within Western philosophy, a decoupling of reason and faith ensued, culminating in various forms of nihilism that are prominent within contemporary thought and culture. Nihilism is characterized by an abandonment of meaning and rejection of the objectivity of truth. Life is taken to lack any objective purpose, meaning, or intrinsic value. According to moral nihilism, morality does not exist, and any established moral values are abstract contrivances. In place of objective morality the utilitarian goals of pleasure and power are glorified. Subsequently there are no moral values with which to uphold a rule or logically prefer one action over another. Accordingly, people are viewed as objects that may be manipulated instead of as persons possessing inherent dignity to be honored. Nihilism is seen throughout contemporary culture: in art, entertainment, music, and literature. To transcend nihilism, however, philosophy must return to its initial status as both an analytic and sapiential endeavor.

What does all of this have to do with business ethics? In order to assist in moving economics and business back to playing a more constructive part in the human enterprise, not only must philosophy be restored to its Socratic roots, but also it must help to revivify business ethics in partnership with the panoply of worldly concerns that have attended the economic crisis: restoration of faith in the market, respect for human rights, environmental sustainability, and so on. Ultimately, the global economy has a stake in the renewal of philosophy in both its analytical and sapiential aspirations.

More than one philosophical system can be valuable in the pursuit of both the truth and the understanding of virtuosity within invisible law. While it is true that many scholars of the natural law tradition would grant pride of place to the thought of Thomas Aquinas and other prominent thinkers within that tradition, it is not necessary to confer standing upon any one thinker or group of thinkers as embodying the one true philosophy of natural law. That is so because no historical form of philosophy can legitimately claim to embrace the totality of truth, or can claim to be the complete explanation of the human being, of the world, and of the human being's relationship to the eternal. It is for this reason that I present the broader notion of "invisible law" as a way of avoiding disputes about the "correct" understanding of "natural law." Competing accounts of natural law theory have arisen in part from political and religious agendas seeking to claim legitimacy from it. It is not the aim of this book to advance any such agendas.

Although diverse philosophical systems may legitimately be embraced by an orientation toward invisible law, and while various systems can contribute to understanding virtuosity, my view of philosophy is not a relativistic one. Neither is it inclined toward ethnocentrism, moral absolutism, and other views that would deny the need for moral conversation, reflection, and analysis. There are false and destructive philosophies, false and dangerous philosophical claims. I would count among them not only scientism and nihilism but also views that ignore the logical requirement of internal coherence and the principle of noncontradiction; ideological intolerance, which brushes aside without reasoned debate all moral standpoints other than one's own; and "vulgar utilitarianism" that sacrifices moral principle to perceived interests and expediency.

Philosophical errors are possible in part because of the weakening of reason itself, by its neglect of virtuosity—that is, the neglect of maintaining the proper balance between truth, beauty, and goodness. In the absence of virtuosity, even those aspects of the moral life that can, in principle, be grasped and understood by reason—for instance, those aspects stressed by a legalistic mind-set—remain hidden from view to some extent. Reason needs virtue to illuminate even those truths to which it has access. But virtue also needs reason.

Many conventional approaches to business ethics tend to make the reading and exegesis of purported norms of business ethics the sole criterion of economic morality. Such approaches offer ever more lists of rules of ethics for guiding business conduct. In consequence, ethics in business is identified with conventional moral rules alone, thus eliminating the role of virtuosity and the need for reflection on the moral life as something that transcends mere collections of rules. The "supreme rule of virtuosity" derives instead from a unity among truth, goodness, and beauty in a reciprocity, which means that none of the three can survive without the others.

Philosophy and other forms of rational inquiry are often indispensable to understanding the full implications of propositions of business ethics. Absent philosophy's contribution, it would in fact be next to impossible to undertake any meaningful and systematic treatment of ideas such as the moral law, conscience, freedom, guilt, and individual responsibility, which are in part disambiguated by philosophical ethics. One cannot simply look up the answers to these questions in a code of conduct. To achieve an adequate understanding of business ethics, one must advert to philosophical truths.

To be effective, business cannot do without philosophy. Philosophical reflection on economic data is often necessary. The human capacity to reason and think abstractly is an extraordinary endowment. Human beings are capable of obtaining true knowledge concerning themselves and the world in which they live. Humans have an innate desire to know the truth about themselves. It is vital that they seek truth. It is only by making a choice to live according to true values that mankind can remain true to its nature and discover genuine happiness. The need to come to terms with the ultimate questions in life is unavoidable. Following in the spirit of ancient philosophy, we can define the human being as that being which seeks truth. Since business is first and foremost a human endeavor, we ought to recognize that *homo economicus* is not sufficient unto himself, and to set our sights higher, to *homo verus*.

Although a great deal has been written about the necessity of trust for attaining success in business and other practical affairs of life, there is a much more fundamental way in which we require trust: it is essential that we place trust in other people in our shared quest for such ultimate truths about our existence. We rely on others for knowledge of every kind. It is impossible for anyone to personally examine and verify the truth of everything we depend on to get by in life. From the heritage of innumerable historical facts and scientific experiments to day-to-day practical details communicated from person to person, we must place our trust in others and learn to believe what others tell and teach us, even though not all that we are told and taught is true. In the course of our interactions with others we develop the ability to entrust ourselves to them. For me to be able to believe anything I must be able to place my trust in you. I trust that what you are telling me is the truth. In this way, our beliefs and our knowledge are ultimately grounded in interpersonal relationships of trust.

In his meditations concerning the virtue of faith, Aquinas depicts faith as an intellectual virtue. What he means is that we have a habit of mind according to which we tend to accept some things as true from a variety of grounds: sometimes our acceptance is on the basis of authority, other times we accede because we don't have time to check for ourselves, or because we aren't equipped with the necessary scientific wherewithal from which to obtain the knowledge firsthand.

It is a characteristic of our human nature that we are in pursuit of truth. More than that, we have an inherent need for others. And we depend on a culture to help us on our voyage toward these realities. This goes to show why so much of the financial crisis—which involved such a widespread crippling of confidence in others who were relied upon to provide the truth, for instance about the value of assets—necessarily merges into a wider intellectual and moral crises.

When deeply rooted in experience, cultures show forth the human being's openness to the universal and transcendent. They offer different paths to the truth, which assuredly serve men and women well in revealing values that can make their life ever more human. Insofar as cultures appeal to the values of older traditions, they point—implicitly but authentically—to a vision of things that are enduring in the human spirit. Just as faith cannot do without philosophy, it cannot do without cultures—which are particular and limited. People understand, appropriate, and live the truths of faith in light of particular cultures. Faith is mediated by and through cultural structures even as it necessarily transcends every culture. Truth is both universal and universally longed for. Since the finite reality that we inhabit is incapable of giving us an adequate response to our quest for the meaning of life, we are prompted toward the ideas of beauty, truth, and goodness. Art, music, literature, and philosophy all have a role to play in penetrating the world of appearances to reveal timeless truths. In every human heart there is a desire to know truth, as Socrates said to "know thyself," to arrive at a fullness of truth about ourselves and others.

Introduction

> Good people do not need laws to tell them to act responsibly, while bad people will
> find a way around the laws.
> —Plato

THE FINANCIAL CALAMITIES of recent years offer strong evidence that
there is such a thing as immorality in the market economy and that it is
very destructive. In this book I aim to present a new approach to business
ethics, based on objective morality, which exposes and revivifies the implicit
and broad cultural understandings of the meaning of moral excellence. The
conception of *virtuosity* that I present is, in a sense, quite idealistic. However, business needs to be, and needs to be seen as, a noble activity. Business
ethics can play an important role in providing a broader, deeper, and more
systematic account of business than many current discussions allow. It is in
light of the imperative of nobility in business that the notion of virtuosity
provides, or ought to provide, both a source of vision and a standard of excellence for market participants, whether they are individuals or organizations operating locally or globally.

By *market participants* I mean to include more than just for-profit enterprises and the people running them. Many not-for-profit enterprises,
whether they are houses of worship, public arts organizations, housing co-
operatives, or charitable foundations, are truly "businesses" in the wider
sense. They must operate according to the same standards of diligence and
discipline as for-profit businesses in order to attain their objectives. Conversely, many for-profit enterprises often benefit financially by operating as
if they were nonprofit concerns, that is, by acting not purely for the pursuit

of profit but rather with the expectation of profit coming about as an off-shoot of attaining excellence and contributing to social betterment.

Cultivating cultures of virtuosity within our economic communities, and honoring the often unspoken timeless cultural understandings about the nature and importance of goodness, truth, and even beauty, provides the moral glue for such communities; this is how, I believe, many of the problems facing business ethics can be fruitfully addressed. Further, I think that confronting such challenges requires the engagement of a deeper and universal "invisible law" superseding not only written legal codes and the visible legal orders that enforce them, but also superseding parochial ethical standards established by organizations that are normally assumed to specify the obligations of business.

Consider how odd it would be to speak of the accomplishments of a virtuoso musician apart from any regard for her mastery of any particular music, that is, in isolation from any structure or form imposed by the "rules" of composition. Such rules, of course, are behind any great composition and even provide a necessary background for meaningful improvisation. If one were to counter that so-called free-form music arises from a conscious disregard for any compositional format laid down through rules, my response is to agree wholeheartedly; I would say in reply that the vapidity of such music (which typically caters to and sanctifies the spontaneous whims of a performer yet fails to enrich or inspire listeners) is a good example of what is missing in business ethics when we strip moral virtue away from its primordial grounding in norms and the guidance they provide.

Virtuous conduct, in business and elsewhere, does not take place in a vacuum. Particularly in the world of business, which operates in the shadow of law and its many institutions, norms provide an intricate web within which moral actions make their moves. It would be a grave error to suppose that, working as an investment banker, one can simply be admonished to "be courageous" while remaining oblivious to the finely textured normative matrix that rules and principles establish. At the same time, deliberation and judgment with those norms require virtue, along with some grasp of the broader meaning of the moral life beyond technical legal compliance. One does not know whether a compass functions well and points true apart from the pull of the invisible magnetic field. One cannot say whether a person is virtuous apart from the promptings of the invisible moral order.

Accordingly, I term the approach that combines the quest for moral and performative excellence in business culture together with these deeper and broader kinds of philosophical considerations grounded in human nature *virtuosity: the invisible law guiding the invisible hand.*

The portrait I render in *Virtuosity in Business* blends conceptual colors extracted from the virtue tradition with intellectual hues drawn from the natural law tradition. The resultant chromatic mixture is intended to afford a nuanced picture of business ethics to be painted, one that is equally attuned to questions of virtue, disposition, authenticity, and character, on the one hand, and matters of moral law, justice, human rights, and sage corporate governance, on the other. Since these seemingly disparate facets of virtue and law are in fact deeply interwoven, a broadened sapiential approach such as the one offered here holds promise to illuminate the kind of discussions of business ethics needed to meet the challenges the postcrisis, globalized economy poses for business today.

Virtuosity in Business seeks to explore ways that our thinking about business and economics can be illuminated with the help of a quartet of bold images:

1. *The market participant as virtuoso artist.* So conceived, the businessperson's or business firm's competitive performance, like that of a musician, is dictated by creativity, authenticity, self-knowledge, inner discipline, and a relentless pursuit of excellence. Such characteristics cannot be prescribed by rules or regulations, nor can they be effectively instilled simply by threats of sanctions for noncompliance, but instead require an engagement with higher and more noble ideals that spring from our nature as humans in search of fulfillment.

2. *Business as an existential human endeavor respective of freedom and authenticity.* We cannot hope to understand business unless we understand the human condition, since that is the wellspring from which all relationships of commerce and trade ultimately flow. Whether one is a disciple of, say, J. Paul Sartre, one the one hand, or J. Paul II,[1] on the other, one must confront fundamental questions of free choice, reason, and authenticity of character. In today's globalized world, where the corporation often arrogantly asserts its metaphysical stature as a distinctive "person," seeking to earn (if not downright command) our trust, even while frequently violating it, we ought to have some notion of just what such an extension of trust might mean, what the stakes are, and whether we are prepared to

abdicate our own human moral responsibility while ceding authority to corporations in the pursuit of ever greater technological and material conquests, as individuals and as a society.

3. *The juxtaposition of metaphorical types of capital alongside the familiar notion of financial capital: cultural capital and reputational capital.* Such metaphors help us to see connections between economic value and moral value. The metaphors express the economic significance attached to intangible assets such as character, honor, and virtue, which are preconditions of business success, yet at the same time they have intrinsic worth that, somewhat paradoxically, must be honored in order to trigger that success. The way that our culture fosters (or fails to promote) such intangible assets profoundly influences whether business within our culture flourishes or decays. Conversely, the way business fosters (or fails to promote) these intangible assets will profoundly influence whether our culture will flourish or decay.

4. *Adopting a sapiential outlook on business ethics that embraces both virtue and the moral law.* As virtue theory is asserting itself in business ethics as a moral tradition as worthy as legalistic approaches, it is important to guard against polarization. So I seek to give voice to the possible harmonization of these traditions.

Virtuosity in Business does not aim to supplant but rather to honor ancient wisdom about the primacy of virtue, seeking at the same time to rekindle our passion for pursuing it and for engaging it in our approach to contemporary economic ethics. While the book acknowledges that significant differences exist between cultures of virtue that arise from different societies separated through historical time and geographical space, it recognizes the moral authority of key transcultural truths, for example, the idea that human beings everywhere are deserving of dignity and basic human rights, and that by their nature all humans seek happiness.

The concept of invisible law that I expound throughout the text follows in the footsteps of Aristotelian philosophers who, like Thomas Aquinas, assert that an objective moral order exists. Although the moral order is not directly visible with our eyes, it can be seen with our mind's eye, by human reason. Moreover, we possess, according to our human nature, the free will either to follow it or to abandon it. Proceeding from the ancient Greek notion of the well-ordered soul, I would argue that, guided by reason, virtue is master over emotivism and noncognitivism (to modify Plato's charioteer allegory) as a reliable guide for ethics.[2] Skeptics hailing from various camps—nihilism, postmodernism, and ethical relativism, to name a few—will of course demur. In a departure from Aristotle's moral realism, such theorists maintain that although the world may supply us with objective facts to discover, the world does not furnish us with any objective values. Rather, values are the product of our own creation. Consequently, for these skeptics we are not able to extract an "ought" from an "is"; we cannot formulate moral prescriptions concerning what ought to be just by observing states of affairs as they actually are. What that means is that no ready-made, objective basis can be given for why you ought to pursue some given aim over any other—choosing the aspirations of being a solitary drunk in preference to the ambitions of a leader of nations, to use Sartre's example. For such a worldview, reason remains simply an instrument placed in the service of any passion or desire that happens to float your boat. As Hume famously put it, "Reason is, and ought only to be, the slave of the passions and can never pretend to any other office than to serve and obey them."[3]

However, if we cannot point to any rational ground for choosing some purposes instead of other purposes, what becomes of the possibility for the human exercise of authentic freedom of choice? We are instead left with an amoral fatalism that explains human behavior, on putatively empirical grounds, in terms of multifarious causal influences like oxytocin deficiencies, DNA, an excess of Twinkies, or anything else that might preordain you to opt for a vocation of, say, entering bars (as a self-absorbed drunkard) on the one hand, or passing bars (as a civic-minded attorney) on the other. Thus, I argue in this book that one can look to either rationally based and freedom-respecting theories (such as the virtuosity model, albeit Kantian and other deontological approaches would fill the bill as well) to drive our understanding of and participation in business ethics, or we can abandon the field to irrationally based subjectivist, relativist, and deterministic approaches. In this sense, as well as many others, philosophical currents that originate within the broader intellectual culture feed directly into our understanding of business and economics, even though traditional economic theory and even some current schools of management claim that their disciplines have an exceedingly narrow scope that effectively quarantines them from moral life.

Some approaches to business ethics—utilitarian, econometric, contractuarian, and compliance-driven legalistic theories tend to deliver a relentlessly narrow and negative message about business and economic life. Owing in part to their origins in the tradition of analytical philosophy, there is seldom any effort to provide a synthetic view of what the world means for us, what characterizes our human nature, and how human beings figure into the commercial realm.

Such theories of business ethics fail to render any satisfactory account of what Aristotle referred to as *eudaimonia,* which designates an especially deep form of happiness, and the principal exemplar of the common good. *Eudaimonia* is a state that we will attain only through association with others. Accordingly, there is a need to put culture in the picture, to establish connections between business and the broader culture.

As cultural understandings change, so too do the challenges for business. The expected standards of excellence for business performance today derive from a different set of concerns than have ever existed before. These stepped-up expectations are apt to trigger reputational sanctions and rewards that often attach directly to the moral probity of market participants. Today, reputational penalties and benefits are as important, if not more significant, than legal penalties that were predominant in previous decades. In the aftermath of the recent financial crisis and the rash of corporate scandals leading up to that crisis, broad shifts of moral viewpoints toward business have occurred. In wide-ranging shifts across continents, social investment funds, employees, customers, corporate executives, elements of global civil society such as activists and NGOs, as well as members of the general public have dramatically recalibrated their interpretations of what virtue and excellence means for businesspeople today and, correspondingly, what the underlying moral responsibilities of business enterprises are.

Not so long ago, companies were basically expected to focus on producing goods and services at reasonable prices. In contrast, today we find corporations being held responsible for a host of moral issues encompassing environmental rectitude, human rights, alleviation of poverty through entrepreneurship, and quality of life. In companies throughout the world, sustainability issues, gender issues, diversity issues, and questions of the clash between work and family are all included in the agenda of corporate social responsibility.

Among the challenges that I take on in *Virtuosity in Business* is crafting a narrative that reaffirms the ancient notion of virtue as something built into human nature together with the confirmation of objective moral precepts that demand respect for human dignity, being just and fair, and advancing the common good. Yet I acknowledge the reality that cultivating virtue in the competitive world of business and wisely applying open-textured precepts is an ongoing process, requiring commitment by reasonable people of good will who are sincerely motivated to seek excellence in themselves and others. I believe that the task of undertaking such commitments is assisted when people are able to live in a culture that keeps faith with time-honored values, fundamental truths, and settled wisdom even while confronting complex situations that severely test fidelity to those philosophical constants and would have perhaps been incomprehensible to ancient philosophers. *Virtuosity in Business* provides such a portrait.

The concepts that inform *Virtuosity in Business* are at once simple and complex. The simple idea is that both moral virtue and moral law constitute the basic operating system of business ethics. Without knowing core moral rules and principles (norms) it is not possible to distinguish what matters and what doesn't ethically in a specific business context. However, just knowing what the rules are is insufficient. Just as genuine virtuoso artists are driven by their desire for self-imposed excellence and their inclinations for musicality, authentic virtuoso businesspeople will pursue fineness and possess a disposition to be ethical, to want to do the right thing for its own sake. Our determinations about whether we trust businesspeople and the companies within which they work enough to want to do business with them, and on what terms, are in large part based on our judgments about their character and sincerity, their display of honesty, and many other virtues upon which we depend. These very simple ideas, however, require elaboration and justification. Hence, *Virtuosity in Business* is framed within a more complex rationale and set of concepts. The book's architectonic is constructed as follows.

Chapter 1 ("Virtue and Character") begins with a conception of the human person as a rational being, and this discussion forms a point of departure for examining how such a being attains virtue and character Anchoring the analysis in ancient thought, including ideas from Confucius, Lao Tse, Plato, and Aristotle, the chapter extends insights about moral virtue and the character it produces to contemporary concerns raised by the recent economic crisis, such as executive compensation and the choice of a meaningful career path.

Chapter 2 ("Authenticity and Freedom") expands and deepens this discussion with a conception of persons as rational beings endowed with existential freedom. This chapter shows how notions of authenticity and freedom derived from Sartrean existentialism can provide an illuminating and useful point of view on the nature of the moral character of businesspeople in the contemporary world. In spite of all that may undermine or seduce us, in spite of inevitable ambiguity, we are required to take responsibility for our character and actions and to make decisions in view of our own projects and that of others, and other broad concerns. However, in doing this, we often find traditional sources of moral guidance unhelpful or incomplete. Nevertheless, it would be a mistake to suppose that there are never any good reasons for making a big existential choice. For instance, sometimes deciding to be this rather than that sort of a person is morally wrong. The chapter shows how a Sartrean perspective offers some important insights about the way our roles, and this includes the roles we occupy in business organizations, can be implicated in bad faith.

Chapter 3 ("The Art of Business") augments the analysis with a conception of rational and free persons as creative artisans. However, rather than painting an idealistic, Quixote-like portrait, this chapter seeks to come to terms with the practical implications of taking virtue seriously in the hardnosed world of competitive business, an environment that often threatens to "crowd out" the virtues. Just how far can the metaphor of artistic excellence take us in a field where the relentless pursuit of profits seems to be the order of the day? Some commentators, particularly Kantians, are perplexed by the assertion that a businessperson or firm can choose something both for its own sake and for the sake of something else. Can a businessperson or company authentically choose to conduct an honest transaction for its own sake—because it's the right thing to do—and also for the sake of boosting its reputation with clients, thus enhancing its profitability both in the near- and long term? I argue that choosing a virtuous action for its own sake and for the sake of other ends makes sense at face value, given that the pursuit of those further ends does not undermine the choice of the virtuous act undertaken in the first place. The plausibility of this account is maintained once we place profitability in proper perspective. That is, we must recognize that for the virtuous businessperson or firm, profitability, albeit an important goal, is not the narrow sine qua non of all business activity that some extremists tout it to be. Instead, profitability is a reasonably predictable result flowing from the pursuit of virtuosity—excellence in providing a valuable good or service for the common good.

Chapter 4 ("Trust, Personhood, and the Soul of an Enterprise") augments the conception of moral personhood with that of the business enterprise as a moral actor. This chapter shows how, due to legal and regulatory issues of corporate responsibility, and as an outgrowth of motivational and marketing tools, our traditional analysis of conduct and character has been shifting from the individual level to the corporate one. The chapter explores questions raised by that trend: If a corporation is capable of assuming a real personality, assembled by artful PR specialists, then is the signal being sent that the people working in the firm do not have to act like real or ethical people? What happens if people begin to act in the image of the invented corporate person to diffuse and limit responsibility?

These discussions set the stage for Chapter 5 ("Discerning a Higher Law"), which examines the challenges of interpreting ethical pronouncements for business enterprises and the people in them as conceptually derivative from an objective moral law. Arguments from a moral realist frame of reference are put forward for the idea of a higher moral law from which obligations to honor human rights and other moral precepts specified in corporate and international instruments can be drawn. Replies are given to the views of moral skeptics, relativists, and nihilists who oppose the robust brand of moral realism that I offer.

Chapter 6 ("Polycentered Phronēsis") is orchestrated with the help of metaphors from music theory, with the aim of showing how many ethical issues facing the leaders of multinational corporations are polycentric in nature. That is, they involve a number of distinct centers, each of which defines rights and obligations of a multiplicity of affected parties, and resolving matters around one center typically creates unpredictable repercussions around one or more of the other centers. Polycentricity is a normative phenomenon especially unsuited for adjudication, often requiring recourse to alternative processes of contract (or reciprocal adjustment) and managerial direction. The chapter explores how such concerns about the limits of adjudication (and its various moral counterparts) apply to virtuosic decision making connected to human rights obligations of multinational companies. The focus is on ethical scenarios, such as controlling child labor in less developed countries such as Bangladesh, India, and Pakistan, setting wages in developing countries like Honduras, and conducting business transactions with rights-violating regimes, such as the government of Sudan.

Chapter 7 ("Moral-Cultural Undertones of the Financial Crisis") begins with a brief account of the emergence of the financial crisis, drawing on the received views of leading economists, businesspersons, and legal experts. It offers a critical exegesis of the three chief conceptual models that have framed these received reactions to the calamity: the paradigms of economics, business management, and legal regulation. Second, it argues that in light of the limitations of these three mental models, an alternative moral mental model is of particular importance. Third, it applies the book's moral framework, based on virtue, dignity, and the common good, to the financial crisis, distinguishing that framework from mainstream "business ethics" models. Current business ethics models are deficient for dealing with the financial crisis for these reasons. First, they tend to be based on the idea that if it's not illegal, it's acceptable. Second, they fail to seriously engage moral right and wrong because of their immersion in moral relativism. Third, they are dominated by window dressing, political-correctness, and antibusiness agendas. The chapter continues by identifying the existence of a moral-cultural malaise lurking beneath the financial crisis. This general condition is characterized by a postmodern moral relativism and rejection of traditional values (both economic and moral), a rise in speculative culture, and egoistic individualism. Moral reform focused on virtue, dignity, and the common good, rather than legal regulation, is the appropriate response to these factors. The chapter also introduces the concept of *market ecology* and relates it to the idea of the common good. I highlight a number of key moral malfeasances connected to the financial crisis to illustrate the harm such practices inflict on the ecology of the market so conceived. The chapter concludes that instead of looking only to the adoption of new legal regulations, visionary corporate governance ought to take greater cognizance of cultivating virtuous, dignity-respecting behavior directed at the common good, which will create favorable background moral conditions for sustaining the ecology of the market.

In Chapter 8 ("Symphony of Soft Law"), I argue that corporate governance must focus on the role of soft law in today's global environment. Soft law is a novel mechanism for constraining corporate behavior. In reconciling financial and social imperatives, firms must consider its impact on reputation capital. I analyze the emergence of the corporate social responsibility (CSR) paradigm and its connection to global corporate governance. By examining its history, I first illustrate how the CSR movement has rendered firms' reputations accountable to the movement's demands, and then I trace the conceptual expansion of CSR to the related notions of "corporate social responsiveness" and "corporate social performance." I examine alternative conceptual models of global corporate governance including the "monophonic" model, the "polyphonic" model, the "integrative social contracts" model, and finally, the "reputational capital" model. I also examine specific types of global civil regulations in detail, and I discuss the bases for why global corporations accept the emerging soft-law regime. After highlighting the chief characteristics of civil regulations in light of the underlying regulatory aim to bind firms and markets to worldwide norms, I discuss the dominant forms of civil regulation within the triad of voluntary self-regulation, interfirm and cross-industry initiatives, and coregulation and multistakeholder partnerships. I then build on these discussions to analyze the role that reputation-accountability mechanisms play in securing firms' compliance with global civil regulations. After distinguishing reputation accountability from legal accountability, I explain the operational components of reputation accountability, the process by which key constituents of transnational firms enforce the "rule of reputation," and the strategic and operational implications firms face as a result of such enforcement. Finally, I take on arguments in opposition to the emerging paradigm of global civil regulation.

There are serious questions concerning what endures morally. Assuming that there is merit to the philosophical accounts of human nature about rationality, freedom, creativity, and sociability—and therefore about virtuosity as well—we are faced with significant challenges going forward. What sort of position are we in to evaluate the possible future cultures and political and economic arrangements into which we are evolving without knowing what it will be like to live in them? It is hard enough to figure out what tradition teaches us for today. It is far harder to figure out what valuable lessons tradition has for tomorrow. So Chapter 9 ("Theme and Variations") and the Conclusion wrap up the book's performance with a discussion of economic culture and the transgressive influence it has on market ecology, in an attempt to take these interpretive challenges into account.

Thus, I offer *Virtuosity in Business* as a means to highlight the significance of emerging expectations for industries, corporations, and other market participants, even as it qualifies such expectations. While predicated on moral objectivity, *Virtuosity in Business* recognizes variety in individual and cultural values and preferences. The challenge is to find the right balance between a conception of virtue as universal and global, while recognizing the relevance of local cultural moral understandings and practices. Once again, the music analogy is helpful. Although music is often described as a "universal language," which we find "spoken" in all cultures, significant differences exist among the types of music that cultures create and the variant modes through which they perform it.

Many of the same qualities that sanctify the performance of a virtuoso musician on the stage turn out to sanctify the ostensibly much different kind of performance of a virtuoso businessperson or business enterprise. Remaining mindful of the many aspects in which musical and business performances remain (appropriately) dissimilar, however, should not deter us from reflecting on some of the striking points of similarity. One of the chief reasons for undertaking this kind of comparison is that it helps us to envision businesses and businesspeople in a new light, something sorely needed in these times of profound disillusionment with economic institutions and actors. It would be a stretch to suggest that the more mundane aspects of doing business, say, running a convenience store, are tantamount to delivering an aria at the Met. To think this way, however, is to miss the point, and those too quick to dismiss the value of positing a virtuoso metaphor for economic life, perhaps deeming business to be utterly irredeemable, pass up an opportunity to gain deeper insight into what business might be if we changed our thinking about it and began to see it as a human endeavor ordained to the common good, instead of as the ruthless profit-maximizing war of all against all that business is often taken to be.

Putting the doubts of detractors aside for a moment, what points of comparison can we make between the art of music and the art of business? In both instances we can discern a pursuit of excellence in the face of fierce competition, the need for discipline, the self-governing spirit that eludes capture by any excessively legalistic regime of rules, the heavy dependence on reputation; qualities such as these are characteristic of successful musical flourishing (indeed, enduring artistic achievement in general), and they are intricately woven throughout the business world as well. These are the components of what I call *virtuosity*, which provides the warp and woof of economic life. Turning our attention to these human-centered features promises to provide a fresh dose of inspiration that, given the current unease about business within contemporary culture, we cannot afford to miss. It is my wish that not only business ethicists but market participants of all kinds, from rank-and-file employees to managers and executives, who are working within any firm, industry, or national economy will benefit from the reflections provided here.

This, then, is the "invisible law" that guides the "invisible hand" of business in a free-market economy.

Chapter 1

Virtue and Character

Man looks in the abyss, there's nothing staring back at him. At that moment, man finds his character. And that is what keeps him out of the abyss.
—*Wall Street* (20th Century Fox, 1987)

APART FROM PROFOUNDLY disrupting the functioning of the economic system, the financial crisis has soured the reputation of the free-market economy and called into question the moral standing of business enterprises and the character of the people who run them.

Postcrisis angst can be seen in expressions of concern like these:

· immersion in contemporary business culture seems to lead many people away from fulfillment and well-being and instead diverts them toward vice, making them greedy, materialistic, and avaricious;
· such vice is seen in many corporate leaders, such as narcissistic "rock star" CEOs of distressed firms;
· the free market appears to sometimes lead to gross unfairness, as witnessed in outrage over excessive executive pay, particularly when lavished upon lackluster and, in some cases, seemingly talentless, chiefs of enterprises; and
· toiling away in today's vicious bureaucratic ethos may place the authentic human self in jeopardy, crowding out existential and social values that might otherwise promote responsible business conduct.

If allegations like these hold water, why would anybody contemplate pursuing a life in the business world (even if you get a corner office)? Indeed, coming to terms with such deep moral qualms about business culture requires turning attention to ideas from ancient wisdom. Perhaps the notions of virtue and character as understood in early philosophical thought will provide a good place to begin finding a path toward reclaiming faith in business, or at least gaining a keener understanding of what is at stake in the effort to do so.

Ancient Roots of Virtue

Turning the clock back quite a bit, we find an idea in Confucian and Taoist philosophies that virtue is a precondition for harmonious living. The premise that human society is built upon a foundation of virtue is expressed eloquently in the following passage from the Great Learning (*Daxue*):

> Things have their root and their branches. Affairs have their end and their beginning. To know what is first and what is last will lead near to what is taught in the Great Learning.
>
> The ancients, who wished to illustrate illustrious virtue throughout the kingdom, first ordered well their own states. Wishing to order well their states, they first regulated their families.
>
> Wishing to regulate their families, they first cultivated their persons. Wishing to cultivate their persons, they first rectified their hearts. Wishing to rectify their hearts, they first sought to be sincere in their thoughts. Wishing to be sincere in their thoughts, they first extended to the utmost their knowledge. Such extension of knowledge lay in the investigation of things.
>
> Things being investigated, knowledge became complete. Their knowledge being complete, their thoughts were sincere. Their thoughts being sincere, their hearts were then rectified. Their hearts being recti-fied, their persons were cultivated. Their persons being cultivated, their families were regulated. Their families being regulated, their states were rightly governed. Their states being rightly governed, the whole kingdom was made tranquil and happy. From the Son of Heaven (the emperor) down to the mass of the people, all must consider the culti-vation of the person as the root of everything else. When the root is neglected, what should spring from it cannot be well ordered. It never

has been the case that what was of great importance has been neglected, or that what was of minor importance has been cared for greatly.[1]

Simply put, in order to attain excellence, and to place everything in a well-ordered state of peace, you must begin by rectifying your own heart.

We find a similar pronouncement in the *Tao Te Ching*:

Let the Tao be present in your life
and you will become genuine.
Let it be present in your family
and your family will flourish.
Let it be present in your country
and your country will be an example
to all countries in the world.
Let it be present in the universe
and the universe will sing.

How do I know this is true?
By looking inside myself.[2]

These eloquent passages imply that the most significant task a leader can undertake is to cultivate virtue. Virtue is cultivated not for the leader's own sake, not for her own glory, but for that of others. Listen to Lao Tse:

The Master has no mind of her own.
She works with the mind of the people.[3]

Perhaps we can distill these ancient insights into a terse message for those holding themselves out as business leaders today: stop acting as if it's all about you and your big ego; get your own act together, then help your people do the same; everyone will be better off as a result.

Moving thousands of miles away from ancient China to the origins of philosophical thought in Greece, we find Aristotle asserting something very similar. Aristotle does not separate living a life that is good for oneself from living a life that is good for one's community, for human beings are by their nature communal creatures.

Let's explore in detail the thought process by which Aristotle, one of the greatest philosophers of all time, establishes this viewpoint.

Aristotle

Aristotle's moral thought is aimed at human happiness. By offering a universal account of happiness, or flourishing, Aristotle stresses the importance of practicing virtue, that is, persistently behaving in a way that satisfies our highest potential.

Pursuant to their nature, people are drawn to demonstrate virtues such as courage, generosity, self-control, prudence, and wisdom, whether inside or outside the sphere of business. Yet virtues are not exercised to reach monetary triumph. Indeed, financial achievement is taken to mean that which is needed to underwrite the life of virtue.

For Aristotle, leaders of associations are among those exemplifying virtuous life.

An Aristotelian approach to business—a virtuosity mind-set—shows that business will rise to the highest moral level by having virtuous leaders, not only at the top, although that is necessary, but at all levels of the enterprise. In turn, such leaders will, by exercising virtue, foster ethical economic cultures.

It is good to keep two points in mind. The first is that the relative degree of prosperity generated by today's market economies accords a substantial amount of time for leisure, offering contemplative opportunities to a larger segment of the populace than existed in Aristotle's time. The second point is that today's business organizations all around the world offer a more extensive assortment of opportunities for leadership as compared to ancient times, when an elevated governmental position would have provided the only real chance to direct a sizeable outfit.

Adopting an Aristotelian outlook on leadership means enabling people to know themselves. It means helping people understand that a vast gulf separates merely living from living well. Virtue comes into the picture the moment we deliberately choose to seek excellence. You display virtue insofar as you opt to cultivate your distinctive talents and abilities, especially your higher-level capabilities of thought and feeling. Should you have the good fortune to hold a position as head of an organization, you display virtuosity to the degree that you are able to assist others to attain happiness and to realize their own human excellence.

When you think about it, we are all, in a real way, already leaders, or could develop into leaders. We just don't realize it. If we consider that parents are "leaders" of their children, and that those who occupy even foundation-level positions in organizations of any size face countless opportunities on the frontier of day-to-day interactions with others (customers, colleagues, supervisors) to set a nobler example, to point to a higher path through excellence and virtuous conduct, then everyone is, from a broadened perspective, truly a leader.

Virtue and the Good Life

Aristotle launched his study of the nature of morality in *Nicomachean Ethics* with the observation that all paths ultimately lead to the good: "Every art and every inquiry, and similarly every action and pursuit, is thought to aim at some good; and for this reason the good has rightly been declared to be that at which all things aim."[4] He seeks to establish that the good at which all of our actions are aimed is happiness. This strikes us modern readers as odd. Normally we speak about happiness and morality in starkly different terms. We praise someone for acting on moral principle even if they suffer personal hardship as a result. To Aristotle, however, happiness is not the same thing as enjoying a pleasant frame of mind. Otherwise, we would have to reach the conclusion that someone stays happy even while fast asleep. As he puts it:

> With those who identify happiness with virtue or some one virtue our account is in harmony; for to virtue belongs virtuous activity. But it makes perhaps no small difference whether we place the chief good in possession or in use, in state of mind or in activity. For the state of mind may exist without producing any good result, as in a man who is asleep or in some other way quite inactive, but the activity cannot; for one who has the activity will of necessity be acting, and acting well. And as in the Olympic Games it is not the most beautiful and the strongest that are crowned but those who compete (for it is some of these that are victorious), so those who act win, and rightly win, the noble and good things in life.[5]

For Aristotle, the idea of *eudaimonia*, normally translated into English as "happiness" or "flourishing," refers to activity that puts our capacities to correct use. Being in a state of happiness is tied to a way of living, that is, acting pursuant to our proper end as human beings. According to Aristotle, it is implicit in the logic of choice that whatever we are choosing to do, we are doing so to bring about an end.

Ordinarily, the nearest objective we are considering turns out to be, when we think about it, advancing some other objective. And that further end itself turns out to be sought for the sake of yet some other thing. By continuing to scrutinize all of our objectives like this, eventually we reach an end that is not leading us beyond itself to anything else. That is going to be what we pursue for its own sake, which is to say, the good life.

As Aristotle explains:

> If, then, there is some end of the things we do, which we desire for its own sake (everything else being desired for the sake of this) and if we do not choose everything for the sake of something else (for at that rate the process would go on to infinity, so that our desire would be empty and vain), clearly this must be the good and the chief good. Will not the knowledge of it, then, have a great influence on life?[6]

Because all human choice inevitably points this way, getting clear about what happiness entails constitutes the essence of ethical reflection. Indeed this focus on happiness is foundational for the structure of decent human associations.

Happiness Is Social

For Aristotle, happiness is not an exclusively individual affair; I can be happy only by living in a web of relationships with other people. In the eyes of Aristotle, humans are social and political creatures. People are inclined to live and to work collectively, and they do so not just from basic instinct, or because they need to, or because it's easier that way. Rather, nature disposes us to be social with an eye to our *telos* (end), which is coextensive with our perfection as human beings. Our flourishing entails living agreeably in a sociable community. There is reciprocity. You benefit your friends, family, and neighbors while they bring you benefits in return. Living in society completes us.

> The proof that the state is a creation of nature and prior to the individual is that the individual, when isolated, is not self-sufficing; and therefore he is like a part in relation to the whole. But he who is unable to live in society, or who has no need because he is sufficient for himself, must be either a beast or a god: he is no part of a state. A social

instinct is implanted in all men by nature, and yet he who first founded the state was the greatest of benefactors. For man, when perfected, is the best of animals. . . . [7]

Thus, Aristotle maintains that it is not sufficient just to have the ability to reason. Nor is it sufficient to cultivate our reason. To be truly virtuous we also need to apply our reasoning ability toward the service of human communities. To grasp the significance of this for our look at virtue in business life, it is necessary to consider what Aristotle means by activities such as "philosophy" and "politics."

To Aristotle's mind, those activities that are most distinctly human are politics and philosophy. Because these endeavors involve maximum use of abstract thinking, they are of the highest order. But the realm of "philosophy" is quite broad, encompassing what we today consider to be the arts and sciences, together with all learned professions. Alongside this wide sense of philosophy, virtuous people are also active in the practical realm of politics. By "politics" Aristotle means not just elected officials, but something much more expansive that would certainly include people occupying positions of leadership in business enterprises.

From an Aristotelian perspective, what is most significant is not some particular job description or career path. What matters instead is how you go about putting upper-level mental potentialities to use. Accordingly, the rank-and-file employee that is enlisted to solve company problems may be using the same high-order capacities as one of the firm's executive. Nevertheless, Aristotle endorses a hierarchy. At the apex are people with the highest inborn ability as well as those who cultivate their own abilities most completely. To be sure, this way of thinking seems totally out of sync with today's emphasis on equality. It is congruent, however, with how many economists analyze things and with the vertical structure that many business organizations are patterned upon. For this reason Aristotle's thought is particularly germane to contemporary concerns about what those at the top of organizations deserve or do not deserve.

What we are seeing today is an odd juxtaposition of two things. On the one hand, there is the phenomenon of the "rock star" CEO. The cult of leadership personalities, such as Jack Welch and "J4M" who supposedly embody virtues for which extraordinary economic value is assigned, is reflected in the eye-popping ratios of monetary compensation when compared to the lowest-ranking members of a firm. On the other hand, there is the perception that if overvalued personalities are "bubbles" that have burst in the wake of a widespread crisis of moral authenticity maybe we ought to carefully scrutinize individual moral accountability at all levels of business organizations. In other words, we need to foster virtuous "leaders" not just at the top but in the middle and at the bottom of organizations as well. This entails rethinking business management. The virtuous leader is able to deliberate well and is curious, rational, introspective, and self-critical. Aristotle is dubious about whether one will long be successful in business matters absent such traits. Practical and virtuous individuals pose hard questions regarding what is good. Through habitual questioning of this sort, they arrive at an understanding of that which is right for not only for themselves, but also for their business and for their communities.

Aristotle states that deliberative people will opt to restrain their wealth. However, this does not mean that he is delivering a condemnation of business entrepreneurship or calling on the wealthy to relinquish all of their possessions. The point is not that the creation of wealth is inherently evil, but rather that it is good to seek moderation.

Considering commonly held views on happiness, Aristotle concludes they are reducible to a triad of pleasure, politics, and contemplation. "To judge from the lives that men lead, most men, and men of the most vulgar type, seem (not without some ground) to identify the good, or happiness, with pleasure; which is the reason why they love the life of enjoyment. For there are, we may say, three prominent types of life—that just mentioned, the political, and thirdly the contemplative life."[8] We shall consider each of these kinds of life in turn.

The Life of Pleasure

> Gimme the loot, gimme the loot.
> —Notorious B.I.G.

The way of pleasure is devoted to sensual satisfactions and to distractions of the mind that cause our most elevated intellectual abilities to lay fallow. Pursuing a pleasure-filled life means amassing creature comforts, enjoying culinary pleasures, inhabiting an enormous residence, and so on. The vast majority of people, observes Aristotle, cling to this ideal of happiness. Yet he rejects straightaway the hedonistic lifestyle sought by most people on the grounds that dwelling on sensual satisfaction places us on par with non-human creatures. "Now the mass of mankind are evidently quite slavish in their tastes, preferring a life suitable to beasts, but they get some ground for their view from the fact that many of those in high places share the tastes of Sardanapallus."[9]

In today's world, business is of course deeply engaged in catering to, indeed fueling, such an ideal of a life of pleasure, both through encouraging mass consumption of goods and services and enlisting as employees people whose main objective in work is making enough money to fund that way of life. A materialistic culture is most "successful" when people's conception of themselves is dictated by how much money they possess and, accordingly, how much they are capable of consuming. Paul Nystrom coined the phrase "philosophy of futility" to denote a disposition triggered by the boredom attending the industrial era for people to pursue gratification from shallow aspects of life such as fashion. As Nystrom puts it:

> One's outlook on life and its purposes may greatly modify one's attitude toward goods in which fashion is prominent. At the present time, not a few people in western nations have departed from old-time standards of religion and philosophy, and having failed to develop forceful views to take their places, hold to something that may be called, for want of a better name a philosophy of futility. This view of life (or lack of a view of life) involves a question as to the value of motives and purposes of the main human activities. There is ever a tendency to challenge the purpose of life itself. This lack of purpose in life has an effect on consumption similar to that of having a narrow life interest, that is, in concentrating human attention on the more superficial things that comprise much of fashionable consumption.[10]

The Life of Politics

The next account of happiness that Aristotle examines, the life of politics, seems at first glance to be disconnected from the life of business. But Aristotle believed that the life of politics mainly is about the governance of people with an eye to gaining honor, or stated in modern parlance, an outstanding reputation. "A consideration of the prominent types of life shows that people of superior refinement and of active disposition identify happiness with honour; for this is, roughly speaking, the end of the political life."[11] So it is not much of a stretch to connect the life of politics in Aristotle's sense to the life of business. The structure of many of today's business firms parallel governmental organizations. Within such top-to-bottom structures managerial and executive positions empower people to govern substantial numbers of other individuals. In the course of exercising their power, business leaders are as quick to seize opportunities for burnishing their reputations as politicians are. Just think about the eagerness of corporate CEOs to get in the limelight on CNBC to brag about themselves and their firms.

The Life of Contemplation

The life of contemplation is the third of Aristotle's alternatives. Concerning distractions of the mind, Aristotle reckons it is ludicrous to labor for the sole purpose of paying for diversions. "Now to exert oneself and work for the sake of amusement seems silly and utterly childish."[12] Today most of us would agree. After all, what would you think of a person who told you that their sole objective in slaving away at their job was to pay for video games, trips to amusement parks, and visits to comedy clubs? To Aristotle's way of thinking, it is more reasonable to see amusements as recreation that revivifies us while on the way to more important endeavors. "But to amuse oneself in order that one may exert oneself, as Anacharsis puts it, seems right; for amusement is a sort of relaxation, and we need relaxation because we cannot work continuously. Relaxation, then, is not an end; for it is taken for the sake of activity."[13] Although Aristotle accords merit to the acclaim people seek from governing others, ultimately he deems such a pursuit as deficient because it makes people dependent on others' opinions. We should not deem something a supreme good if it remains outside our influence. Plus, Aristotle notes that people who are ostensibly pursuing public approval are actually seeking to have their virtues acknowledged. For Aristotle, this shows that virtue lies at the heart of the good life. He writes:

> A consideration of the prominent types of life shows that people of superior refinement and of active disposition identify happiness with honour; for this is, roughly speaking, the end of political life. But it seems too superficial to be what we are looking for, since it is thought to

depend on those who bestow honour rather than on him who receives it, but the good we divine to be something proper to a man and not easily taken from him. Further, men seem to pursue honour in order that they may be assured of their goodness; at least it is by men of practical wisdom that they seek to be honoured, and among those who know them and on the ground of their virtue; clearly, then, according to them at any rate, virtue is better.[14]

In Aristotle's view:

If happiness is activity in accordance with virtue, it is reasonable that it should be in accordance with the highest virtue; and this will be the best thing in us. Whether it be reason or something else that is this element which is thought to be our natural ruler and guide and to take thought of things noble and divine, whether it be itself also divine or only the most divine element in is, the activity of this in accordance with its proper virtue will be perfect happiness. That this activity is contemplative we have already said.[15]

Quite a number of thinkers in the Western tradition, from Socrates and the Stoic philosophers to Schopenhauer and Adam Smith, espoused the notion that some form of deliberation constitutes the supreme good of life. In Eastern thought, one sees this view endorsed in the Buddhist, Confucian, Zen, and Taoist quest for a tranquil state of mind. Lao Tse's query runs:

Do you have the patience to wait
till your mud settles and the water is clear?[16]

Aristotle's ideas about contemplation resemble the Zen-like state creative artists experience when, intensely focused, ordinary thought is suspended. In this state, troubles seem to disappear. The artist Botero said he only started existing when working in his studio, a refuge from the world's violence. He felt superb fulfillment, finding harmony in precise form coupled with correct color. A profound joy he likened to lovemaking issued from a magical, unexpected moment. A sense of peace pervaded the canvas and his heart.[17]

How about the quest for riches? Aristotle dismisses this pursuit with the claim that we do not go after money for its own sake. What people genuinely want is not wealth as such. They seek to get at something else by means of their wealth. As Aristotle states, "The life of money-making is one undertaken under compulsion, and wealth is evidently not the good we are seeking; for it is merely useful and for the sake of something else."[18] What a person is truly after will fall into one of three categories: pleasure, recognition, or using the intellect in leisure. A skeptic might argue that Aristotle is overlooking the possibility that one might gleefully go after treasures, reveling in the hunt itself, as one might enjoy fishing or hunting. Acquiring immense wealth is like a game, a critic might say: the more money you make, the higher your score. We've all heard the line, "The one with the most toys at the end wins." Yet this view is implicit in Aristotle's observation that "some men turn every quality or art into a means of getting wealth; this they conceive to be the end, and to the promotion of the end they think all things must contribute."[19] To be sure, Aristotle has a ready response. Someone chasing money for sport is in fact most interested in showing how great they are in winning the money game. On this point, Aristotle has the winning argument. He shows that, in the end, virtue is actually the good. Taking another swipe at the obsession for money grabbing, Aristotle claims that it not only saps our opportunity for engaging in leisure, it also tends to make us forget that, after all, wealth is not itself an end, but rather a means to attain the end of happiness. In Aristotle's words, "Some persons are led to believe that . . . the whole idea of their lives is that they ought either to increase their money without limit, or at any rate not to lose it. The origin of this disposition in men is that they are intent upon living only, and not upon living well; and, as their desires are unlimited, they also desire that the means of gratifying them should be without limit."[20]

Many people get trapped in a vicious cycle: unaware of the endless futility that occurs when no matter how much you get, you only want more. So Aristotle's thinking equips us with a way of understanding our own greed beyond that which our culture provides. Aristotle's thought gives a powerful vantage point from which to look at contemporary business. Consider the claim that some business practices leave people endlessly treading a hamster wheel. Aristotle is not averse to one's acquisition of goods from the natural world, as in farming, fishing, or hunting.[21] Likewise, he is not against acquiring goods through exchange where such is required to satisfy a demand for goods (for example, shoes) that can be produced with greater efficiency by others (shoemakers). Here, the process of exchange serves to correct natural inequality in distributions of resources and talent, reallocating them in accordance with the natural arrangement of human wants. Aristotle makes the point as follows:

> For example, a shoe is used to wear, and is used for exchange; both are uses of the shoe. He who gives a shoe in exchange for money or food to him who wants one, does indeed use the shoe as a shoe, but this is not its proper or primary purpose, for a shoe is not made to be an object of barter. The same may be said of all possessions, for the art of exchange extends to all of them, and it arises at first from what is natural, from the circumstance that some have too little, others too much.[22]

The moral difficulty comes when we enter into the business of trade, where exchange is undertaken solely for financial reward. Yet this is precisely how a lot of business is conducted in the modern capitalist economy. Since there are no built-in limits to how much accumulation can result from trade (as distinct from the sort of exchange mentioned above, where natural wants impose constraints), Aristotle claims that involvement in trade leads us to harbor an illusion of unlimited accumulation of wealth. Rather than working cooperatively, assisting others in realizing their human capabilities, the enterprise of trade pits us in competition with each other. Consequently, we start to see other people as mere opportunities for amassing more and more profit. As Aristotle puts it, "There are two sorts of wealth-getting, as I have said; one is a part of household management, the other is retail trade: the former necessary and honourable, while that which consists in exchange is justly censured; for it is unnatural, and a mode by which men gain from one another."[23] Compounding this moral problem, for Aristotle, is the practice of money trading over time. In other words, extending loans—with interest. The proper end for money lies in facilitating exchanges of goods, not in concocting yet more money. Thus, as Aristotle says:

> The most hated sort [of wealth-getting], and with the greatest reason, is usury, which makes a gain out of money itself, and not from the natural object of it. For money was intended to be used in exchange, but not to increase at interest. And this term interest, which means the birth of money from money, is applied to the breeding of money because the offspring resembles the parent. Wherefore of all modes of getting wealth this is the most unnatural.[24]

But how realistic is it to abide by a stricture against lending money with interest in today's economy? After all, how would firms ever obtain the financial backing to get off the ground? Plus, we'd have to gut our savings to buy big-ticket items like cars, houses, and appliances. However, for Aristotle, there is a different priority at stake in commercial life: it falls on virtue to oversee the quest for wealth. Because it is the highest good, virtue is not to be sacrificed to pursue affluence. The true moral objective in life is lurking within the quest for the *summum bonum* driving the most virtuous elite. In other words, true happiness is not found in the preoccupation with creature comforts so characteristic of the masses.

To grasp how Aristotle reaches this conclusion, bear in mind that he considers happiness an activity. His notion of happiness does not exactly match our modern understanding. For Aristotle, a person is not happy if they are not performing well, regardless of what they are doing. To say something is performing well, for Aristotle, is to say that it is fulfilling its function or role. The function of a violin is to produce musical sounds. We would say that a violin that satisfies that function well is an excellent violin. Similarly, we all have some notion of what is means for a person to be an outstanding business executive, or a fine chef, or a superb musical conductor. And yet it will not suffice to just turn to conventional social roles to ascertain the broader meaning of satisfying a role or function with excellence. After all, ethics concerns what it is that leads human beings to be happy. Ethics is not about the narrow question of what renders this or that person happy. Thus, reasons Aristotle, we need to arrive at some understanding of the function or role of humans as such:

> Since happiness is an activity of soul in accordance with perfect virtue, we must consider the nature of virtue; for perhaps we shall thus see better the nature of happiness. The true student of politics, too, is thought to have studied virtue above all things; for he wishes to make his fellow citizens good and obedient to the laws. . . . And if this inquiry belongs to political science, clearly the pursuit of it will be in accordance with our original plan. But clearly the virtue we must study is human virtue; for the good we were seeking was human good and the happiness human happiness. By human virtue we mean not that of the body but that of the soul; and happiness also we call an activity of soul. [25]

In the same way that we might best allocate tasks amongst people according to their differences, the function of humans should be picked out according to what distinguishes humans from all other beings. Humans share something in common with animals and plants alike: they are inclined toward nutrition and growth. And just like animals, humans are directed by appetite and able to perceive objects around them. What sets human beings apart, says Aristotle, is this: our souls possess a rational principle. This equips us to comprehend universal concepts, decide among different courses of action, and discipline our appetites.

> There are two parts of the soul—that which grasps a rule or rational principle, and the irrational; let us now draw a similar distinction within the part which grasps a rational principle. And let it be assumed that there are two parts which grasp a rational principle—one by which we contemplate the kind of things whose originative causes are invariable, and one by which we contemplate variable things; for where objects differ in kind the part of the soul answering to each of the two is different in kind, since it is in virtue of a certain likeness and kinship with their objects that they have the knowledge they have. Let one of these parts be called the scientific and the other the calculative; for to deliberate and to calculate are the same thing, but no one deliberates about the invariable. Therefore the calculative is one part of the faculty which grasps a rational principle.[26]

Since the distinctly human function is found in the use of cognitive capabilities, Aristotle concludes that virtue consists of reason being used with excellence.

> Now if the function of man is an activity of soul which follows or implies a rational principle, and if we say 'a so-and-so' and 'a good so-and-so' have a function which is the same in kind, e.g., a lyre-player and a good lyre-player, and so without qualification in all cases, eminence in respect of goodness being added to the name of the function (for the function of a lyre-player is to play the lyre, and that of a good lyre-player is to do so well): if this is the case, [and we state the function of man to be a certain kind of life, and this to be an activity or actions of the soul implying a rational principle, and the function of a good man to be the good and noble performance of these, and if any action is well performed when it is performed in accordance with the appropriate excellence: if this is the case,] human good turns out to be activity of

> soul in accordance with virtue, and if there are more than one virtue,
> in accordance with the best and most complete.[27]

Yet virtue does not, by itself, ensure happiness. In contrast to Stoic philosophers, who maintained that having virtue alone is pretty much enough, Aristotle believes that virtue is rightly accompanied by other goods apart from
the mind.

> It is impossible, or not easy, to do noble acts without the proper equip-
> ment. In many actions we use friends and riches and political power as
> instruments; and there are some things the lack of which takes the lus-
> ter from happiness, as good birth, goodly children, beauty; for the man
> who is very ugly in appearance or ill-born or solitary and childless is
> not very likely to be happy, and perhaps a man would be still less likely
> if he had thoroughly bad children or friends or had lost good children
> or friends by death. As we said, then, happiness seems to need this sort
> of prosperity in addition; for which reason some identify happiness
> with good fortune, though others identify it with virtue.[28]

Having monetary resources is needed before one can even think about
undertaking some virtuous actions, among them generosity. Conversely,
being short on financial resources ushers in temptation to defraud and
steal.

Virtue and pleasure are linked insofar as the ethical individual will feel
good by doing the right thing. Aristotle expresses the point well:

> Now for most men their pleasures are in conflict with one another
> because these are not by nature pleasant, but the lovers of what is noble
> find pleasant the things that are by nature pleasant; and virtuous ac-
> tions are such, so that these are pleasant for such men as well as in their
> own nature. Their life, therefore, has no further need of pleasure as a
> sort of adventitious charm, but has its pleasure in itself.[29]

In the world of business, virtue in and of itself will not console someone
whose 401(k) has been ravaged by the economic downturn, or who has been
terminated from his or her employment or driven into bankruptcy. On the
other hand, virtuous people will possess sufficient fortitude to ride out turns
of misfortune. As Aristotle explains:

Now many events happen by chance, and events differing in importance; small pieces of good fortune or of its opposite clearly do not
weigh down the scales of life one way or the other, but a multitude of
great events if they turn out well will make life happier (for not only are
they themselves such as to add beauty to life, but the way a man deals
with them may be noble and good), while if they turn out ill they crush
and maim happiness; for they both bring pain with them and hinder
many activities. Yet even in these nobility shines through, when a man
bears with resignation many great misfortunes, not through insensibil-
ity to pain but through nobility and greatness of soul.[30]

But, as Aristotle notes, "Many changes occur in life, and all manner of
chances, and the most prosperous may fall into great misfortunes in old
age."[31] So if our hardship is substantial, or sustained, or turns up at a point in
life where it's hard to bounce back, a person's fortitude is tested: "For neither
will he be moved from his happy state easily or by any ordinary misadven-
tures, but only by many great ones, nor, if he has had many great misadven-
tures, will he recover his happiness in a short time, but if at all, only in a
long and complete one in which he has attained many splendid successes."[32]
Living the ethical life does not necessarily equate to business success. But
Aristotle suggests that due to its durability, virtue lends sustainability to a
person's life:

No function of man has so much permanence as virtuous activities
(these are thought to be more durable even than knowledge of the
sciences), and of these themselves the most valuable are more durable
because those who are happy spend their life most readily and most
continuously in these; for this seems to be the reason why we do not
forget them. The attribute in question, [durability] then, will belong to
the happy man, and he will be happy throughout his life; for always, or
by preference to everything else, he will be engaged in virtuous action
and contemplation, and he will bear the chances of life most nobly
and altogether decorously, if he is 'truly good' and 'foursquare beyond
reproach.'[33]

A message that can be gleaned from this—particularly in these times of
postfinancial crisis anxiety—is that no matter how bad it seems, it's best
to keep to the virtuous route, cling to the hope that the link between good

actions and happiness will reappear, bringing an upturn in fortune that will help you spring back.[34]

Virtues

Cardinal Virtues

The cardinal virtues are courage, justice, temperance, and practical wisdom (*phronēsis*) or prudence.[35] What do we mean when we say these characteristics are virtues? A musician might claim that her violin possesses the virtue of keeping in tune. In this way, she is describing her violin in terms of its usefulness to her. (She doesn't have to retune it often.) Keeping in tune is a useful characteristic of a musical instrument that players have an interest in. But in talking about a person having virtue, we don't mean that she is useful. First and foremost, we are pointing out that she possesses dispositions conducive to the pursuit of human well-being, in particular to her own flourishing. To be sure, all of us keep our eyes on one another's character. However, your dominant interest looks toward developing your own character, and the sorts of things that you set out to accomplish in your life and career on the basis of it. You discriminate between your vices and virtues, knowing that your moral habits impact the nature of your private and cherished understanding of who you are. At the same time, not only do your first-rate inclinations draw you closer to achievements, but also they accord you inner harmony and serenity.

Aristotle reckoned this way too. Granted, the archaic world of the Greek city-state out of which Aristotle's thinking emerged was in some respects a far cry from the world inhabited by today's global business enterprises. The *oikonomia* of the ancient world was centered on home management and agriculture and the political sphere involved persistent threats of Athenian invasion from Persian neighbors. Yet Aristotle's line of reasoning touches what is unchanging about our essential nature as human beings. His philosophy is directed at uncovering what we need in order to live well today, at illuminating the moral features we draw upon in all facets of life that enable us to attain the excellence and state of flourishing for which we are destined by our design. As we saw in our earlier discussion of Aristotle, virtues are dispositions, acquired in part through emulation and practice, yet ultimately engaging the whole person in a dynamic deeper than just a Pavlovian stimulus-response mechanism.

As a person of virtue, not only are you developing greater discipline, but also you are cultivating better and more satisfying moral motives. What makes you a courageous person is not a developed ability to simply mimic the conduct of a courageous individual. Imitating some virtuous person's actions doesn't cut it because you cannot possibly know beforehand what any such person's actions would require you to do. When you are a genuinely courageous individual, your soul is stirred by the yearning for honor and excellence, irrespective of the toll to personal comfort and security. One of the things that is so striking about virtue is the dependability it carries. In large part, what makes you a person that others can place their trust in is that you have the right sorts of motivations and dispositions to act in certain ways. When dangerous circumstances arise, others will turn to you—the person of courage—because they place confidence in your deep disposition to elevate concern for the common good over narrow worries about self-protection.

Moral Virtues

Reason carries an intellectual part together with a component governing the appetites. Hence, Aristotle differentiates two kinds of virtue. On the one hand are intellectual virtues, connected to the ways the soul arrives at the truth through activity that uses reason's apprehensive strength. On the other hand are moral virtues associated with regulating desire.

> Virtue . . . is distinguished into kinds . . . for we say that some of the virtues are intellectual and others moral, philosophic wisdom and understanding and practical wisdom being intellectual, liberality and temperance moral. For in speaking about a man's character we do not say that he is wise or has understanding but that he is good-tempered or temperate; yet we praise the wise man also with respect to his state of mind; and of states of mind we call those which merit praise virtues.[36]

Among the moral virtues are courage, temperance, self-discipline, moderation, modesty, generosity, friendliness, truthfulness, honesty, and justice. Rather than just learning the moral virtues, Aristotle says that we acquire them from persistent practice. Laying stress on the requirement of relentless rehearsal to produce virtuosity brings to mind the gag about the disoriented

Manhattan visitor who asks how to get to Carnegie Hall and is bluntly admonished "practice, practice, practice!" "The virtues we get by first exercising them, as also happens in the case of the arts as well. For the things we have to learn before we can do them, we learn by doing them, e.g., men become builders by building and lyre-players by playing the lyre; so too we become just by doing just acts, temperate by doing temperate acts, brave by doing brave acts."[37] It is optimal if such practice is started when young, continuing to the point of becoming habitual and second nature. As Aristotle puts it, "It makes no small difference then, whether we form habits of one kind or of another from our very youth; it makes a very great difference, or rather *all* the difference."[38] Because there are persistent temptations toward vice, however, Aristotle claims that laws are needed to buttress what was instilled through youthful instruction. In his words:

> It is difficult to get from youth up a right training for virtue if one
> has not been brought up under right laws; for to live temperately and
> hardily is not pleasant to most people, especially when they are young.
> For this reason their nurture and occupations should be fixed by law;
> for they will not be painful when they have become customary. But it
> is surely not enough that when they are young they should get the right
> nurture and attention; since they must, even when they are grown up,
> practice and be habituated to them, we shall need laws for this as well,
> and generally speaking to cover the whole of life.[39]

Moreover, Aristotle claims that "most people obey necessity rather than argument, and punishments rather than the sense of what is noble."[40] There is a suggestion here that, no matter how much importance we attach to moral virtue and character, attention still needs to be given to the question of the appropriate degree of legal regulation. The point is further spelled out when Aristotle, alluding to Plato's *Laws*, continues with this assertion:

> This is why some think that legislators ought to stimulate men to virtue
> and urge them forward by the motive of the noble, on the assumption
> that those who have been well advanced by the formation of habits will
> attend to such influences; and that punishments and penalties should
> be imposed on those who disobey and are of inferior nature, while the
> incurably bad should be completely banished. A good man (they think),
> since he lives with his mind fixed on what is noble, will submit to

argument, while a bad man, whose desire is for pleasure, is corrected by pain like a beast of burden. This is, too, why they say the pains inflicted should be those that are most opposed to the pleasures such men love.[41]

Intellectual Virtues

The intellectual virtue of phronēsis, normally rendered as prudence or practical wisdom, concerns steering conduct through what we would today refer to as moral dilemmas. Just being aware that virtuous action is found as a mean between extremes leaves us with a certain vagueness. But prudence is what enables us to see what the right course of action is by taking all of the relevant specifics into consideration. A prudent person regularly renders correct judgments promoting all dimensions of the good life, from money and health to personal relationships and virtue.

> Now it is thought to be the mark of a man of practical wisdom to be able to deliberate well about what is good and expedient for himself, not in some particular respect, e.g. about what sorts of thing conduce to health or to strength, but about what sorts of thing conduce to the good life in general. This is shown by the fact that we credit men with practical wisdom in some particular respect when they have calculated well with a view to some good end which is one of those that are not the object of any art. It follows that in the general sense also the man who is capable of deliberating has practical wisdom.[42]

Aristotle observes that prudence will be exercised by a statesman and the head of a household (*oikos*) alike. As he expresses it, "We think Pericles and men like him have practical wisdom, viz. because they can see what is good for themselves and what is good for men in general; we consider that those can do this who are good at managing households or states."[43] The type of prudence exercised in these instances is especially praiseworthy to Aristotle, as compared to self-focused applications of this virtue. The reason is that overseeing both households and public associations impose stepped up demands and duties, that is, helping others and not just oneself. Today's stations of leadership within business enterprises provide a myriad of chances for exercising this type of prudence in connection with social and economic affairs.[44]

The other intellectual virtue is wisdom or *sophia*. Wisdom engages the part of reason equipped to apprehend necessary truths as opposed to the contingent ones that prudence grasps. Wisdom deals with theory rather than practice. A wise person has intuition along with scientific knowledge. Through intuition one discerns first principles upon which scientific results rest. Scientific knowledge enables one to make deductive inferences in reaching conclusions in theoretical science. "Therefore wisdom must plainly be the most finished of the forms of knowledge. It follows that the wise man must not only know what follows from the first principles, but must also possess truth about the first principles. Therefore wisdom must be intuitive reason combined with scientific knowledge—scientific knowledge of the highest objects which has received as it were its proper completion."[45] In contrast to narrowly technical or industrial ways of thinking, wisdom is not motivated, as, say, Thomas Edison and Henry Ford surely were, to bring new inventions and improved gadgets into existence.[46] Wisdom seeks knowledge for its own sake. It undertakes the search by adopting a contemplative stance. The philosopher, or lover of wisdom, embodies this quest. By "philosopher," Aristotle does not mean, as we do today, a person engaged in formal scholarship in the fields of logic, metaphysics, aesthetics, epistemology, and ethics. Aristotle's philosopher is the person in search of a complete reckoning of principles behind all reality—spanning human, natural, and divine spheres.

Contemporary Focus Point for Virtue: Executive Compensation

In the wake of the financial crisis, allegations of injustice stemming from apparently undeserved rewards for untalented performance have come to the forefront in discussion about executive compensation on national and international levels.[47]

Many would say top executives are siphoning off a disproportionate share of the fortunes generated (or worse, not generated) by the organizations under their watch. Studies document a meteoric rise in CEO compensation.[48] During 2008, which ushered in dwindling corporate earnings along with sinking share values, most CEOs got compensation hikes, not downgrades.[49] In the face of the economic downturn, average CEO compensation for 2008 was only slightly diminished.[50] The economic downturn did not inhibit financially distressed firms from granting supersized payouts to high-ranking corporate chiefs.

Who are these corporate leaders who, with the backing of boards of directors that set their pay, are rewarded with ostentatious rewards, so out of step with what everyone else struggles to eke out? What drives their acquisitiveness? Reflection on such questions is absent in all but a handful of studies on executive compensation. Let's drill down into the details of some of these individuals' remuneration arrangements.

At the summit of CEO earnings in the United States for 2008 was Sanjay Jha of Motorola. Despite the firm's precipitous 71 percent drop in shareholder price, he received US$104.4 million.[51] Robert Iger, Disney's CEO, was awarded US$51.1 million in 2008. That payment weighed in at almost twice the size of the US$27.7 million it had extended to him the year before.[52] The huge rise in pay appears especially openhanded having come about in the same year that Disney's profits experienced a 5 percent decline. At the helm of American Express, Kenneth Chenault, received a reduction of 14.6 percent—dropping from US$50.1 million for 2007 to a paltry US$42.8 million for 2008.[53] Yet the reduction did not quite mirror the 29 percent overall fall in profits his company had suffered.[54]

When AIG started channeling taxpayer bailout money it had received into its executives' paychecks, the public became outraged.[55] AIG's former CEO Martin Sullivan, who ran the company into the ground, was set to receive US$47 million in severance when he was fired, prompting New York State Attorney General Andrew Cuomo to place a stop on US$19 million of it.[56] In response to the granting of performance bonus awards for AIG top management, Charles Grassley, senior member of the Senate Finance Committee, proclaimed, "The first thing that would make me feel a little bit better towards them [is] if they'd follow the Japanese model and come before the American people and take that deep bow and say I'm sorry, and then do either one of two things—resign, or go commit suicide."[57] Elaborating on the comments, Grassley's spokesperson Jill Gerber clarified that "clearly he was speaking rhetorically—he meant there's no culture of shame and acceptance of responsibility for driving a company into the dirt in this country. If you asked him whether he really wants AIG executives to commit suicide, he'd say of course not. Point being, U.S. corporate executives are unapologetic about running their companies adrift, accepting billions of tax dollars to help, and then spending those tax dollars on travel, huge bonuses, etc."[58]

In directing the Treasury Department to pursue all available legal means of reclaiming the funds, President Obama described the bonuses as an "outrage."[59] Ohio Representative Dennis Kucinich called upon the SEC to launch an inquiry after the financially distressed Merrill Lynch doled out US$3.62 billion of the Troubled Asset Relief Program ("TARP") funds it had received as executive bonuses.[60] In Kucinich's words, the bonuses were "little more than a farewell gift from senior management to themselves."[61] Amounting to more than twenty-two times the size of AIG's bonuses, the Merrill Lynch executive disbursements constituted 36.2 percent of its TARP allotment.[62]

Adding to the dubious nature of any linkage between executive performance and financial reward, comes the extraordinary practice of companies lavishing enormous riches on CEOs even as they are firing them for failing on their jobs.[63] Upon incurring the biggest financial loss in corporate history, Merrill Lynch terminated its CEO, Stanley O'Neal. Yet that did not keep him from walking away with a sizable severance package totaling US$160 million.[64] Consider also the case of Home Depot's former leader Robert Nardelli. Even though he had been discharged as a result of his firm's lackluster share performance, Nardelli parachuted away with approximately US$210 million in severance.[65]

However, granted that some chief executives are overpaid, in light of simultaneously mismanaging their firms while getting handsome remuneration, not all of the complaints about CEO compensation stem just from these well-documented abuses. In addition, there is protracted debate centering around the sharp increase in average CEO pay that played out over several decades preceding the appearance of the financial crisis. Thus, the total real compensation for CEOs of large public companies rose 600 percent between 1980 and 2003,[66] while median full-time earnings over the same time span only approximately doubled.[67]

On average, the CEOs of the largest companies pull down nearly five hundred times what rank-and-file employees make. Stated differently, that means the typical daily earnings of CEOs of big enterprises surpass many of their individual employees' annual salaries. And the way stock options are distributed reveal big swings, depending on one's level in the corporate hierarchy. In the typical firm three-quarters of them are allocated to CEOs.

Conventional Arguments Given by Economists: The Pay-for-Performance Paradigm

In the eyes of some boards, executives, and investors, such disparities may appear palatable insofar as their judgments are based on the pay-for-performance paradigm and the various arguments that flow from it. According to the pay-for-performance rationale, the focus should be on the economic value generated for the firm by an individual leader. Pay for performance can be viewed, on the one hand, as a reward for performance, or on the other hand, as an incentive to encourage performance. Some debate has arisen in the literature about whether and to what extent these seemingly alternative justifications—pay for performance versus performance for pay—are distinct, or not.[68] At any rate, the underlying rationale for both is agency theory. The theory hold that agents, that is, managers and CEOs, should see it in their own interests to advance the interests of the principals, that is, the shareholders. Thus, if the agents are to be well compensated for superior performance the agents should be motivated to achieve that type of performance.

Competition

Competition for top management is a key pay-for-performance explanation. This position is advanced under several arguments. One argument asserts that, for publicly traded companies, a steady relationship exists in the market between total CEO compensation and the size of the firms they lead. The argument offers the so-called 30-percent rule as authority for this claim. For each 10 percent rise in the size of a company (calculated by sales, market value of assets, or other relevant indicia), CEO remuneration rises by approximately 3 percent. Since the correlation is alleged to have held constant since the 1930s, it is not thought to be the result of the steep escalation of stock options and other forms of compensation, which originated in the 1970s. And a seminal study found an average increase in CEO compensation of $3.25 for every $1,000 increase in shareholder wealth.[69] However, deeper questions arise: What do these correlations mean in a normative sense? Are the various pay-for-performance arrangements, alleged to be driven by competition, generous, or are they meager, and by what criteria might one decide? The standard discussions of this type of metric in the economics literature are characteristically devoid of moral reflection on such issues.

Talent

A second argument asserts that the biggest firms tend to draw the greatest management talent. Accordingly, the argument runs, larger companies need to compensate their CEOs more highly so as to provide a disincentive for them to abandon their firms and go lead smaller enterprises. What is notoriously absent from this line of argument, however, is any satisfactory notion of what "talent" actually means, beyond the bare threat of departure for greener pastures.

A closely related argument states that the rise in CEO pay is a product of the increase in market value of companies. The head of a more valuable enterprise is more productive because even if he ratchets up firm value by only a few percentage points, the increase in absolute value is greater the more valuable the company is. Assuming two managers with equivalent skill, one who directs a small hardware store and the other Xerox Corporation, the manager of Xerox is responsible for creating bigger value.[70]

It is worth pointing out that the disclosure of companies' executive compensation structures and levels requirements sometimes triggers invidious comparisons; boards and compensation committees, goaded by executives and remuneration consultants, approve escalating pay packages. After all, firms do not wish to be seen deficient compared to peers. Part of the ratcheting tends to be attributed to the aforementioned apprehension of a "flight of talent" to better paying firms, or migration to private equity, despite a dearth of empirical evidence of this. Yet one might ask: What exactly is meant by the "talent" of a corporate executive? Is there really a distinctive talent that can be moved so readily from firm to firm, as Toscanini was able to transport his stature as a maestro conductor from the New York Philharmonic over to the NBC Symphony?[71] And how deeply rooted, how sincere, are the commitments of a leader to the firm under his charge, given that he is so easily lured away, simply by the one-dimensional enticement of a bigger pay package?

Efficiency

Finally it is argued that considerations of social efficiency dictate that the best managers should lead the biggest firms. Their heightened skills, it is claimed, exert a greater influence, owing to the fact that they are managing a greater share of capital, labor, and other resources. In other words, an efficient coupling of superior management with bigger firms in a competitive market for top-flight executives implies a positive correlation between enterprise size and total compensation awards.

Counterarguments and More Questions

As others point out, such explanations about the allocation of CEO pay often have less to do with real talent, proven performance, and actual contribution than with brute power, cronyism, and outright manipulation. Moreover, the competition argument is attacked on the ground that if increases in CEO compensation really did attract greater talent, then the resultant heightened competition for CEO positions ought to have softened any steep rise in compensation. However, no significant overall dampening in CEO pay has transpired. Hence, it is claimed that a more plausible explanation is that the bigger a firm's market value, the more likely it is that the CEO's pay can be hidden away, along with the compensation of other high-ranking executives, such that the big disparities are not noticed. Thus, CEO compensation gets increased whether he or she has contributed to enhancing the value of the larger enterprise.

Further questions arise: What levels of executive remuneration are proper? How ought such levels to be established by a firm's board of directors? What standards should guide the establishment of compensation levels? Is this something that the government should keep out of? Is it best to leave everything to the market to decide?

One of the most heated topics broached at the Pittsburgh G-20 summit was executive compensation. Many believe that exorbitant remuneration is inappropriate in cases where financial institutions have enjoyed bailouts with public revenue.[72] Others contend that perverse incentive arrangements prompted financiers to assume inordinately high risks. From this they conclude that incentive structures ought to be reconfigured to reflect longer-term firm performance and broader social contributions. By contrast, some people would maintain on deontological grounds that over-the-top executive compensation is immoral per se, irrespective of the consequences they may or may not have brought about.

To sharpen our focus on this debate, let us bring Aristotle back into the discussion. By giving an account of the correct and fairest apportionment of labor, Aristotle connects reflections concerning the vertical array of human capabilities to the wider economic makeup of society, maintaining that those at the top of the natural pecking order ought to be occupied in undertakings so as to contribute the most to the economy and to society. From an Aristotelian standpoint, curtailing someone's chances to cultivate their skills in the name of equality contravenes justice. Even less justifiable is exalting those with little ability, making them leaders of society, or captains of enterprises, meanwhile keeping those of highest natural ability at the lowest strata. Aristotle's contention is that meritocracy provides the most just type of arrangement. All are better off from governance by the most proficient.

Firms need to make decisions about how they set compensation levels for all job functions. Assessing just what warrants merit is a matter of justice in distribution. However, as the following passage points out, those on contending sides of the issue are inclined to espouse positions in line with their personal interests. Within oligarchies, the governing elite pins merit to wealth. By contrast, in democracies the populace claims an equal entitlement to goods.

> Let us begin by considering the common definitions of oligarchy and democracy, and what is justice oligarchical and democratical. For all men cling to justice of some kind, but their concepts are imperfect and they do not express the whole idea. For example, justice is thought by them to be, and is, equality, not, however, for all, but only for equals. And inequality is thought to be, and is, justice; neither is this for all, but only for unequals. When the persons are omitted, then men judge erroneously. The reason is that they are passing judgment on themselves, and most people are bad judges in their own case. And whereas justice implies a relation to persons as well as to things, and a just distribution, as I have already said in the *Ethics*, implies the same ratio between the persons and between the things, they agree about the equality of the things, but dispute about the equality of the persons, chiefly for the reason which I have just given—because they are bad judges in their

own affairs; and secondly, because both the parties to the argument are speaking of a limited and partial justice, but imagine themselves to be speaking of absolute justice.[73]

Thus, to Aristotle each perspective carries a partial truth. Getting at the whole truth requires some philosophical reflection. Aristotle's conclusion is that merit is tied to traits that allow someone to perform a task in question. The problem of how to allocate instruments among flute players provides an illustration. Should we ask whether a flutist is rich or poor? Should we inquire whether the player is legally on par with the others? Aristotle's answer is no: what really counts is how well they can play the flute. The musicians that can play them well ought to get the best flutes. The players having less proficiency should get the inferior flutes.

> When a number of flute-players are equal in their art, there is no reason why those of them who are better born should have better flutes given to them; for they will not play any better on the flute, and the superior instrument should be reserved for him who is the superior artist. . . . For if there were a superior flute-player who was far inferior in birth and beauty, although either of these may be a greater good than the art of flute-playing, and may excel flute-playing in a greater ratio than he excels the others in his art, still he ought to have the best flutes given to him, unless the advantages of wealth and birth contribute to excellence in flute-playing, which they do not.[74]

To decide differently makes for a mismatch. Superior quality flutes are wasted on maladroit players. Interestingly, such a principle can be readily applied to the business world. A firm considering who'll get promoted to senior vice president, will query: Which of our candidates holds promise to be the most excellent for this role, adding maximum value to our enterprise? But notice that here the locution "maximum value," does not signify "maximum profit-maker." After all, profits are not the goal of life. Rather profit is merely a means to attaining happiness and the good life, which is constituted through virtuosity—that is, virtuous business conduct. We shall examine the connection between profit generation and virtue in greater detail in Chapter 3 ("The Art of Business").

Aristotle's take on this suggests that company heads ought to allocate benefits, bonuses, job advancements, raises, and the like, not simply along lines calculated to achieve maximization of profit, but as a way of rewarding and incentivizing virtuous behavior.

Aristotle's overarching regard is for the welfare of the whole community. Aristotle does not want to posit a natural human pecking order as a rationale for prizing the genetically endowed at the top. Nor is he seeking to lighten the load for the well-off. To the contrary: people having the greater abilities ought to be released from the more menial tasks in order to focus on things that maximize their capabilities and the social gains they may bring about. Those atop the ladder shoulder responsibility for assisting those on the lower rungs. By doing that, all are elevated from the presence of inequalities rooted in genuine abilities and aimed toward economic betterment.

To turn to a contemporary illustration, we might ask why Steve Jobs, founder, chairman, and CEO of Apple, ought to be the one rendering executive decisions at the company. The answer is not that he has some natural right to be in charge, or that he is "a productive narcissist."[75] Rather, it is to everyone's advantage, across the organization, that the best talent be placed at the summit. After all, who in their right mind would sign on at Apple if the firm's guiding mission was a commitment to uncompromising equality, mandating that those appointed to the firm's top-tier executive squad be mentally challenged workers selected from the cleaning crew, leaving Steve Jobs to be the elevator operator?

While taking an Aristotelian virtue perspective is not likely, by itself, to provide a comprehensive solution to the executive compensation imbroglio; doing so at least suggests some questions that virtuoso leaders would want to pose to themselves, questions that point in a much different direction than the one indicated by the sort of conventional economic analysis described earlier: Is my remuneration commensurate with my contribution to the firm? Is the current allocation of goods within our firm helping to foster the happiness of the community our firm makes up, or is it actually dampening morale and inhibiting other people from attaining happiness?

Moreover, an Aristotelian outlook implies that in assessing the conventional pay-for-performance paradigm, we ought to distinguish between, on the one hand, high financial rewards for "performance" in firms and, on the other hand, the value creation arising from the firms' activities. For instance, it has been argued that an aggressive quest for profits in banks and other financial institutions has been value destroying, not only for the institutions themselves, but ultimately for society and human welfare, as manifested in the financial crisis.

Indeed, it is arguable that the costs and externalities associated with a given profession's activities should be deducted in calculating that profession's Social Return on Investment (SROI) contribution, à la the New Economic Forum's approach.[76] Looking at broader indicia such as SROI prompts the question: Why on earth are executives working in certain sectors, such as banking and financial services, the privileged recipients of such extraordinary rewards?

On a wider account of wealth creation—particularly in light of the concerns voiced by Aristotle with regard to the proper and improper ends of money—such as his "money from money" critique cited earlier in this chapter,[77] it could be asserted within the spirit of this criticism that, even in the course of favorable economic periods, banks (to name but one financial institution), in the course of taking deposits, transmitting and clearing payments, and bringing investors and savers together with users of capital and borrowers, play merely a secondary role as facilitators for the primary economic participants who render more direct and pronounced contributions to society. So why are bankers the object of "hero worship," and why did the attitude emerge that treats bankers "as masters rather than servants of the economy"?[78] Arguably, it is in carrying out this secondary role that banks negligently overreached by overleveraging deposits in risky bids for ever greater profits, thereby destroying, rather than creating, value. Strangely, even in the midst of a massive credit crunch, created by their own calamities, banks were roundly refusing credit to what would have earlier been deemed viable business propositions.[79]

Turning to a question raised earlier concerning the personal motivation behind those in hot pursuit of attaining excessive executive compensation, lurking in the background is the specter of *homo economicus*, the lowest common denominator of human motivation. One writer, reflecting on the matter in the context of the banking industry, questions the wisdom of lavishing so much reward on the business activities of people who depend on "technology to present infinitesimal arbitrage opportunities around the world—which, when aggregated over very large leveraged balance sheets, create massive profits. . . . A growing undercurrent suggests that in fact these are not terribly useful economic activities. . . . This system also reinforces money—not values, strategy, culture, or the quality of the institution—as the only reason to work at a bank."[80]

Much of the current thinking about pay for performance is devoid of consideration of the sorts of values that emerge from adopting a virtue-regarding outlook. For example, there is little reflection on the character dimension of individuals who appear to be greedy beyond any limits or controls to accumulate as much money as possible.

It is in light of this void that Aristotle's thought affords a wider and deeper philosophical outlook. For instance, using an Aristotelian lens to look at the significant layouts of funds that typify the "reward me big-time" culture of many corporate executives, there is a peculiar sort of virtue to examine: magnificence. According to Aristotle, what makes you a magnificent person is having the good taste to divert big money appropriately and to advance a laudable end. In stark contrast to a vulgar kind of individual, you are magnificent if you are not being gaudy. That is, you are not showing off your affluence by spending more than circumstances warrant.

> The man who goes to excess and is vulgar exceeds . . . by spending beyond what is right. For on small objects of expenditure he spends much and displays a tasteless showiness; e.g. he gives a club dinner on the scale of a wedding banquet. . . . And all such things he will do not for honour's sake but to show off his wealth, and because he thinks he is admired for these things, and where he ought to spend much he spends little and where little, much.[81]

We can perhaps find no better illustration of what Aristotle is talking about by way of vulgarity through tasteless excess than to recall Dennis Kozlowski, the Tyco International CEO who fell from grace due to a string of malfeasances associated with his receipt of unauthorized bonuses and his misappropriation of corporate assets. In the course of his criminal trial we all learned about the details of the US$2 million, weeklong birthday bash (known as the "Tyco Roman Orgy") for his second wife on the island of Sardinia, complete with dancing nymphs, models dressed as gladiators and Roman servants, a performance by singer Jimmy Buffett and his group (flown in to the tune of US$250,000), a birthday cake in the shape of a woman's body with sparklers protruding from her breasts, and an ice sculpture imitation of Michelangelo's statue of David urinating Stolichnaya Vodka. Kozlowski also was noted for leading an extravagant lifestyle supported by the booming stock market of the latter 1990s and early 2000s. Purportedly, he had arranged to have Tyco shoulder the cost of his US$30 million Manhattan apartment on Fifth

Avenue, which included a US$6,000 shower curtain in the maid's room, a US$15,000 umbrella stand, and a US$17,000 traveling toilette box.

Ironically, Koslowski's defense insisted that he didn't "hide" anything; his self-serving appropriations of corporate resources were open for all to see. So, under his way of thinking, our categories of rational thought appear to have simply vanished: the normal distinction in both law and morality between "appropriation" and "misappropriation" has been repudiated, all in the service of the self-serving greed of the leader.

At the other end of the spectrum is the petty person that fusses over the smallest details of every financial layout. Listen to what Aristotle has to say about that: "The niggardly man . . . will fall short in everything, and after spending the greatest sums will spoil the beauty of the result for a trifle, and whatever he is doing he will hesitate and consider how he may spend least, and lament even that, and think he is doing everything on a bigger scale than he ought."[82] In the course of steering clear of the excesses of vulgarity and pettiness, you could be magnificent by allocating some of your wealth to the development of public goods, for instance by building a library, being a patron of the arts, or adding a new wing to a hospital. Consider the case of Bill Gates. His foundation contributed US$4.2 billion for ameliorating disease throughout the developing world.

It is interesting to note that, given the choice between, say, stretching beyond financial means to outfit one's residence with fancy, new-fangled gizmos and keeping to a budget with understated, more durable alternatives, a magnificent person goes for the second of these. "A magnificent man will . . . furnish his house suitably to his wealth . . . and will spend by preference on those works that are lasting (for these are the most beautiful), and on every class of things he will spend what is becoming."[83] A suitable modern contrast could be drawn between the homes and lifestyles of, one the one hand, Nicholas Gage (whose gaudy foreclosed Bel Aire mansion was described by a real estate agent as a "frat house bordello"),[84] and on the other, Warren Buffet (one of the world's richest persons, who still lives in the same modest home he bought for US$31,500 in 1958, yet gives thirty billion dollars to charity).[85] Yet Aristotle may not have been completely adverse to what is known today as consumerism as one might suppose, given his staunch opposition to the hedonistic life. For Aristotle the bottom line is that your consumption should be balanced, that is, under the guidance of what self-perfection requires.

Aristotle advances a universal vision of the good life, wherein human fulfillment is coextensive with moral and intellectual virtue. What is particularly noteworthy about Aristotle's treatment of the intellectual virtues from the standpoint of our inquiry into the broader intellectual and cultural implications for business life, is the insight that the highest deployment of the intellect is to be found in the leadership of others and in the philosophical search for truth. To propose such a vision for the life of business sets a higher bar than conventional thinking seems to allow. To adequately grasp some sense of this extended vision necessitates adopting an unconventional mind-set toward commercial life. For that end, it is vital to find a way of seeing business as essentially connected to basic goods of human nature. We shall extend discussion of this point further in subsequent chapters. For now, let us turn our attention to the connection between virtue and character.

Character

For Aristotle, a prime concern of ethics is human character. A virtuous person reveals the combined excellence of character and reason. As the following passage illustrates, the character of a person encompasses virtues and vices along with emotions and desires.

> Just and brave acts, and other virtuous acts, we do in relation to each other, observing our respective duties with regard to contracts and services and all manner of actions
>
> And with regard to passions; and all of these seem to be typically human. Some of them seem even to arise from the body, and virtue of character to be in many ways bound up with the passions. Practical wisdom, too, is linked to virtue of character, and this to practical wisdom, since the principles of practical wisdom are in accordance with the moral virtues and rightness in morals is in accordance with practical wisdom. Being connected with the passions also, the moral virtues must belong to our composite nature; and the virtues of our composite nature are human; so, therefore, are the life and the happiness which correspond to these.[86]

Thus, although having a virtue means being inclined to behave in a certain way, having a good character amounts to more than just checking off a list of worthy accomplishments. Having appropriate emotions counts too. In other words, a virtuous individual knows what doing the right thing is, and there is some emotional connection to it as well. In this way, character is fused to what a person enjoys.

> We must take as a sign of states of character the pleasure or pain that ensues on acts; for the man who abstains from bodily pleasures and delights in this very fact is temperate, while the man who is annoyed at it is self-indulgent, and he who stands his ground against things that are terrible and delights in this or at least is not pained is brave, while the man who is pained is a coward. For moral excellence is concerned with pleasures and pains; it is on account of the pleasure that we do bad things, and on account of the pain that we abstain from noble ones.[87]

A person having good character gets enjoyment from acting virtuously. That is, a virtuous person attains a kind of psychic harmony. Desires also come into play in the sense that a person who, for instance, has a generous character truly wants to be that way.

Aristotle states that the twin excellences of reason and character are closely linked. We cannot have one but not the other. "It is not possible to be good in the strict sense without practical wisdom, nor practically wise without moral virtue."[88] Since Aristotle does not explicate the precise way in which the two virtues are interdependent, scholars differ on this point. One view emphasizes practical wisdom (phronēsis), the intellectual virtue related to action, as the decisive disposition.[89] Another view lays stress on the inclination to have the right sort of feelings.[90]

Certainly Aristotle's doctrine of the mean is central to understanding the virtues of character.[91] A virtue of character is an action-directing disposition to strike a state of equilibrium, or mean, between two extreme emotions in particular situations. For example, when faced with danger, courage is a person's disposition to attain the mean between foolhardiness and cowardice. It is not that the extremes by themselves determine the mean. Rather, the mean is determined by extremes relative to demands presented by some given situation, which includes facts concerning the person facing that situation. Additionally, it is by way of the idea of the mean that we grasp the intellectual virtue of practical wisdom because it requires a reasoned outlook on a set of circumstances to attain the mean. The concept of the mean also supplies a basis for differentiating genuine virtues from natural dispositions or emotions.

The exercise of the intellectual virtues, including practical wisdom, is not merely something of instrumental value. As components of the fulfilled human life, the intellectual virtues as well as the virtues of character are each morally significant in their own right. Because they are part and parcel of the good life, there's no difference between selecting virtuous actions for their own intrinsic worth and selecting them as a pathway to happiness. Granted, both the nonrational and rational components of the soul are motivators of virtuous action. Yet just because the reason-holding portion of the virtuous person aims at virtuous conduct because it is good, constituting part of the good life, it does not follow that it is selecting such conduct simply as a route to happiness.

It is reasonable to take Aristotle as holding that the virtues of character make up a whole, meaning that, like buying tickets for a subscription concert series, you cannot have one of them unless you have them all. So displaying the virtue of generosity involves more than just giving the proper measure to the right person at the appropriate juncture for the right reason. It would also be necessary to have obtained what is being passed around in conformance to the other virtues, for instance, justice. Similarly, the courageous individual needs temperance so as to not overreach by being reckless. And the temperate person requires courage to resist the temptation of peer pressure. Hence the person of virtue needs to consolidate the various virtues into a unity, allowing each of the virtues to display their respective value. Prudence plays a role in each virtue and in turn depends on all of them to keep from being more than just a mean-driven excuse for risk avoidance. Armed with such a disposition, a person of prudence will reckon into a given circumstance the requirements of the various virtues in order to craft a well-arranged verdict about how to act.

Having merged the virtues of character into a concordant totality, could different virtues impose competing demands, pulling in different directions? For Aristotle, such dilemmas need not pose a threat to the excellent individual's virtue. When pressed to make a choice between distasteful alternatives, going with the least abhorrent one does not imperil your character, albeit you may experience a sense of remorsefulness for making the choice.

Raising Existential Thoughts

If you are consciously deciding that you wish to be a good person, are you thereby deciding the sorts of desires and emotions that you want to have? Based on the linkage of a good character to having the right kind of dispositions, it would seem that this would be the case. But on what basis should you decide what kinds of things you want to enjoy and desire in the first place? To be frank, if you take this route of inquiry, you are raising some deep existential questions for yourself. When I am getting to know my students at the beginning of a semester I ask them to write on a card what they want to do in their career, and what kind of lifestyle they want to have. "What are your objectives, both business and personal, and why," I inquire. "Are you interested in just making money? Or is there something beyond that you are after? Do you want a career-driven lifestyle where work is everything, or a more balanced lifestyle where work matters but is not necessarily the end-all-and-be-all? Is there anything that might lead you to prefer the one lifestyle to the other?" Then I probe further with a string of almost mind-numbing questions: "Can you tell me what, deep down, you desire your desires to be?" "What do you actually want your inner wants to be?" "What do you prefer your preferences to be?" "What are you interested in being interested in, and why?"

These questions matter. Sometimes people reflect back on their careers with a profound sense of regret of the sort depicted in Tolstoy's *The Death of Ivan Illich*. They question whether they have really lived a good life. It occurs to them that, given the chance to do it all over again, perhaps they could find a way to devote more of their time to family life, or to be less occupied with their own self and more concerned with others. A person who has attained great financial achievements yet has fallen short of living a genuinely good life may have gotten shortchanged by being devoted to the kinds of considerations parodied in Sinclair Lewis's *Babbit* [92]—materialism, conformity, and false values—instead of being guided by reflection and contemplation.

There is something exceedingly difficult about confronting such questions. Yet when you consider that the culture of the firm where you work sometimes exerts an enormous influence on your character, the task of selecting where you are going to work includes selecting the kinds of desires that you are likely to be fostering. This kind of choice is almost like selecting your character in advance. A choice about the character of the company you want to work at, and the line of occupation you will pursue, figures into a choice about the character of the person you wish to become. It is, in the end, an existential choice of the sort we will discuss further in Chapter 2 ("Authenticity and Freedom").

Opting to work at a particular company having a reputation for a virtuous culture might incline you to wish to become honorable and forthright as you imbibe that culture day in and day out. Making a decision in favor of some other firm, like the ruthless stock brokerage company portrayed in the movie *Boiler Room*, might lead you to prefer being cold-blooded and opulent. But how do you arrive at the knowledge beforehand of what sort of person you wish to become? Making a choice such as that is not what we would normally call a "rational" decision. (It is for this reason that we will look at the Sartrean account of character and the freedom of choice that lies at the heart of human existence in the next chapter.)

For Aristotle, being reared in a good community constitutes the chief means of becoming virtuous. What the community considers as important influences what is taken to be virtuous. From childhood, a person starts to understand what courage is all about by being shown that certain kinds of actions exemplify courage, while others exemplify cowardice. Then, over time, a person acquires a habit of behaving courageously.

Having a virtue requires using rationality and knowing what is important, being attuned to one's values. For instance, a person does not acquire the virtue of courage simply by going around mimicking courageous individuals. It is necessary for a courageous person to understand what she values. Only in this way can she be in a position to make a rational assessment of what degree of risk is called for to preserve what she deems important.

While ethics depends on rationality, it bears a greater resemblance to endeavors such as navigation[93] and the arts,[94] which are "less exactly worked out" than the sciences.[95] We will see in a moment how closely ethics is affiliated with the field of music and its study.

The way that Aristotle conceives of ethics and the good life are closely related to the idea of harmony. Instead of just involving a string of unrelated occurrences, the good life carries with it an underlying unity or totality. Well-being involves having rational desires. That means your desires are in harmony with each other and also in harmony with your values. It also means that your actions are in harmony with your desires. What all of this amounts to is that you are happy when you are living in a state of psychic harmony. Basically having a good character boils down to keeping your soul in such a state, where everything in your soul is functioning the way it is meant to. Naturally we want to avoid being troubled with conflicting desires. That only leads to a state of continual dissatisfaction with life, which Aristotle associates with wicked persons. Such people "shun themselves," because

> they remember many a grievous deed, and anticipate others like them, when they are by themselves, but when they are with others they forget. And having nothing lovable in them, they have no feeling of love to themselves. Therefore also such men do not rejoice or grieve with themselves; for their soul is rent by faction, and one element in it by reason of its wickedness grieves when it abstains from certain acts, while the other part is pleased, and one draws them this way and the other that, as if they were pulling them in pieces.[96]

To most of us this is self-evident. According to Aristotle's perspective, declaring the lack of any right or wrong in ethics—as many who buy into today's pervasive moral relativism are inclined to do—is tantamount to claiming that happiness and unhappiness are indistinguishable, that living a satisfying existence is identical to living a wretched one. But such an assertion flies in the face of common sense.

Music, Culture, and Character

Philosophers throughout the ages have been intrigued by the question of the broader significance of music for human existence. According to Jamie James, to retrace the paths taken not only by Western music but also Western intellectual history reveals a concerted quest for the supreme orderliness of the cosmos.[97] This idea of music manifesting a universal order is what Pythagoras claimed to be the music of the spheres: the apparent soundlessness across the firmament is eternally emitting a higher form of music that only the gods can hear. According to Liebniz, writing at the time of J. S. Bach, music represents a kind of unconscious calculation that produces, along with harmonic delight, an apprehension of the uppermost forms of truth. Schopenhauer believed music to herald an appearance of cosmic reality, which is suffused throughout our existence.

Yet music serves as more than a topic for meditation on its metaphysical features. The relationship between musical study and performance, on the one hand, and moral virtue and character, on the other, has been probed since the very origins of speculative thought.

As we saw in our discussion of Aristotle's concept of virtue, in classical teachings, the idea of "politics" is broad, and concerns not simply the activities of elected officials, but a wider range of activities that includes leadership of human associations. Accordingly, we turn to consider what insights that teaching offers for our understanding of virtuosity and the cultivation of excellence in business life and the broader culture of which it is a part.

Ancient thinkers, alluding to the elements of harmony, rhythm, and melody, deemed such features of music to carry moral and emotive force. Both Aristotle and Plato attach particular significance to rhythmic and harmonic phenomena due to the force they hold for impacting the attainment of the chief goal of the life of politics. To Aristotle that objective is to inculcate a particular sort of character in people, that is, to render them virtuous, able to accomplish noble acts. It is obvious, to Aristotle, that music contributes to virtue since we can see from numerous things that we take on a certain quality of character on account of its influence on us.

To the ancient mind, music is understood to be an "imitative" art in the sense that music portrays the range of emotions and forms of character that humans exhibit. In the words of Aristotle:

> Since . . . music is a pleasure, and virtue consists in rejoicing and loving and hating aright, there is clearly nothing which we are so much concerned to acquire and to cultivate as the power of forming right judgments, and of taking delight in good dispositions and noble actions. Rhythm and melody supply imitations of anger and gentleness, and also of courage and temperance, and of all the qualities contrary to these, and of the other qualities of character, which hardly fall short of the actual affections, as we know from our own experience, for in listening to such strains our souls undergo a change.[98]

Not only do musical representations appear to the soul (*psychê*), but they leave an imprint on it. Such an imprimatur tends to have substantial delibility for highly impressionable souls, as with youth. Such a character-shaping tendency exists with respect to one's exposure to works of art in general: sculpture, painting, and poetry. Accordingly, Socrates voices his position in the *Republic* regarding youth that, from immersion in beautiful works of art, youth will stand equipped for goodness, "likeness and friendship and harmony with the principle of beauty."

Yet for Socrates, of all the images of art, music remains the most influential. Thus he opines that "musical training is a more potent instrument than any other, because rhythm and harmony find their way into the inward places of the soul, on which they mightily fasten, imparting grace, and making the soul of him who is rightly educated graceful, or of him who is ill-educated ungraceful."[99]

Aristotle and Plato are especially intrigued by the notion that music can be conducive to one's capacity for self-restraint. Music can excite our passions, and it also has the power to calm them. Vladimir Horowitz believed that the virtuoso is able to contain inner passion, controlling its release during the performance.[100] The composed state of the passions cultivated through suitable upbringing in music is good preparation for virtuous activity. That is due to the tendency, Aristotle says, for undue passion to interfere with a person's aptitude for moral reasoning and choice. Aristotle contends that the virtuous life demands the exercise of prudence, understood as the dual capability to recognize moral virtues—first principles of conduct—and to ascertain how to actualize such virtues through specific behaviors.

Aristotle observes in *Politics* that receiving correct training in music empowers a person not simply to make appraisals of noble melodies, but also to appraise noble things as such.[101]

Turning our gaze higher, the early philosophers advise that suitable upbringing in music grooms the soul for philosophical inquiry and reflection. Aristotle and Plato alike teach that immoderate passion blocks not only moral efforts but philosophical pursuits as well. Therefore, by quelling passions that divert the soul away from its quest for truth, temperance-creating music clears a path for philosophy. Music kindles in one's soul a magnetism for the truth that philosophy pursues. The exquisiteness in music reveals to the soul the realm of the beautiful and the intelligible. With its charm and the natural delight attending it, music nurtures an enduring predilection for ordered beauty. And this is precisely what the philosopher is yearning for. As Socrates states in the *Republic*, the philosopher associates with the divine and orderly in the universe.

Closely connected with this notion, the Pythagoreans located harmonic, arithmetic, and geometric means underpinning the musical scale. In addition, they identified ratios associated with musical consonance, that is, intervals of the octave (1:2), perfect fourth (3:4), and perfect fifth (2:3). According to the Pythagoreans, the just and well-ordered society is analogous to a well-tuned lyre. Whereas the separate notes preserve their individuality, they are proportionally connected to the larger group that comprises the musical scale. As such the notes are in a state of interdependence.[102]

What does this all mean for the life of business? Can we somehow appraise the health of economic life today through an examination of our musical culture? In addressing this matter, it is instructive to consider the type of diagnosis of contemporary culture (especially music) and politics (in the broad sense discussed earlier, which encompasses business), along with their impact on the soul, that follows from the perspectives of Plato and Aristotle.

First of all, Aristotle and Plato argue that the type of character cultivated through musical study serves as the foundation of a civilization that is upright and free. Thus, in Plato's *Republic* music instruction will engender people who will be repulsed by vice and drawn to virtue. As a result, the city that is able to deliver high-quality music pedagogy will be freed from the burden of having to enact a massive amount of law. In today's parlance, we would say that good music education is a foundation for self-regulation or enlightened self-governance. This point is of vital importance concerning the issues of necessity for and appropriate degree of legal regulation of business.

Among the ideas explored in Aristotle's *Politics* and Plato's *Republic* is the claim that by and by the person in the grip of undue passions comes around to wielding unjust methods for fulfilling them. Consequently, when an entire people's character has been shaped from, on the one hand, inculcation in agitating music, or, on the other hand, from the absence of emotion-quelling music, they venture down the path toward widespread injustice, which in turn incites strife amongst a citizenry, which ultimately ushers in a proliferation of law—what we would today call overregulation—in a doomed essay to cure such maladies.

Secondly, the ancient's reflections on character development through music are related to the promotion of human excellence, therefore to human well-being as well. This is significant, since the kind of musical instruction that is endorsed mediates the passions but not with rigid restraints; rather, one's study of music is prompting yearnings for philosophical illumination and moral decency. These proclivities reside at the very heart of our human nature. For Aristotle our true self inheres in the intellect through which we are able to contemplate and also to undertake action with an eye toward what is noble and true. However, the true self requires the aid of music in order to actualize itself. Consequently ancient thought sees music as vital to one's realization as a complete human, to achieving full happiness.

It may be objected that there are people with no musical training and no interest or talent in music who nevertheless are capable of rendering sound moral decisions, sizing up other people according to their character, and acting virtuously. From the other side, there are certainly cases of gifted musicians who pass through life as evil psychopaths. Such considerations may prompt a skeptic to doubt the legitimacy of any connections we might claim between music and the cultivation of moral virtue.

By way of response, it is crucial to understand just what Aristotle and Plato are saying. They are not contending that music will, in any facile and direct manner, impel us to behave in some particular fashion. Instead, their view amounts to the twofold contention that (1) music influences human passions, and (2) such an influence will either make it harder or easier for reason to grasp and the will to select the right things in life.

These ideas acquire further illumination from the stress that ancient thought places on human flourishing as an attainment surpassing bare public stability. If you were to go around today asking what it means for human flourishing to take place, you would doubtless receive all sorts of answers, ranging from "spending more time with the kids" to "having enough money to play golf" to "getting in touch with my spiritual side." According to the ancient Greek mind, though, the utmost happiness arises out of the engagement of our intellect in leisure. Aristotle instructs that leisure is the objective of human life. Many people consider their work as simply a means to acquiring goods that they will be able to enjoy once they are away from work. By comparison, leisure is a state during which we are able to relish whatever we have chosen for its own intrinsic value. Leisure is what most of us prize and where we look to gain fulfillment.

A key issue for Aristotle and Plato, though is this: Is what we are enjoying in leisure genuinely the kind of thing deserving of a rational being, and is it fostering the kind of well-being that is fitting for that sort of being?

Another response, of a more general nature, is that we ought not to demand too much from music, as if it can supply something of a sinecure that even a modern legal order and religion are not equipped to do. What is more important to grasp from the enlightened ancient reflections is the idea that music imparts, even in the midst of our obvious moral crises and social failings, a glimpse of something in humanity that is higher, immutable, and most worthy. The ancient philosophers' insights into virtuosity help us to gain a greater awareness of our potential for fostering human excellence, whether in music, in the arts, or in business.

Assuming the vantage point of ancient philosophy, the importance that today's culture attaches to material wealth and hedonism, together with its acceptance of moral relativism and a general apathy regarding the pursuit of human excellence is utterly unsatisfactory. Early thinkers maintained that this sort of society attends to the lowest features of humanity. Consequently, the soul comes around to pine for sustenance that is absent in the culture at large. According to the classical account, the type of "society of pigs" rejected by Glaucon fosters irrational and disorderly passions that disfigure the soul while imperiling the foundations upon which society rests—an imperilment that is in fact mirrored in much of the turmoil and disorder transpiring within the global economic crisis.

My contention is that it is vital that people incline themselves toward the uppermost human ends singled out by ancient philosophers. Only out of the pursuit of human excellence—virtuosity—can a respectable social order and an ecology of the market materialize as a consequence. The early philosophers instruct as to why music stands indispensable to cultivating an adoration of the highest things, and thus to safeguarding civilization.

Raising Awareness

According to Aristotle, a person in possession of good character sees circumstances in the right way, discerning their relevant moral dimensions. Among other things, this explains, for instance, why we "punish those who are ignorant of anything in the laws that they ought to know and that is not difficult, and so too in the case of anything else that they are thought to be ignorant of through carelessness; we assume that it is in their power not to be ignorant, since they have the power of taking care."[103] It is by means of our imagination (*phantasia*), that we can comprehend the ethical features of our conduct, and our inability to grasp the morally significant aspects of a state of affairs is a mark of poor character. If we are a person of good character, we will see a given action, say, the racist comment of a client, as requiring us to exemplify courage in standing up to challenge the remark. In fact, being morally spineless, lacking the will to stand up for what is right, can be a symptom of incorrect moral awareness. "For [although] both the man who has knowledge but is not using it and he who is using it are said to know, it will make a difference whether, when a man does what he should not, he has the knowledge but is not exercising it, or is exercising it; for the latter seems strange, but not the former."[104]

Businesspeople enter judgment and chose how to behave based on the way they model complex phenomena—like the financial crisis. In Chapter 7 we shall consider how contemporary thinking about business has developed around different mental models. In particular we will discuss how various mental models have portrayed the global financial crisis differently, and we will suggest how those models need to be expanded.

Thus, for economists, issues surrounding the financial crisis are framed as technical problems, not moral issues. Typically the language used is descriptive, centering around raw sets of values fed into systems instead of normative analysis of obligations, rights, and fairness. Such an econometric language-game can be commanding and alluring, creating an illusion that considerations of morality, of the human side of things are somehow off-message for business culture. To the extent that a moral-cultural mental model can be brought to bear on business and economics, it will assist us in gaining fluency in the language of virtue, character, human dignity, and the common good. Such a way of thinking enhances our moral imagination and raises the likelihood that we will be able to provide a more comprehensive account of morally important states of affairs.

It is precisely to this end that I am endeavoring to weave into our tour of ethics in contemporary business a fair measure of allusions to artistic excellence. Here is why. Excellence in any human endeavor, be it in music, art, literature, science, or athletics, in the end points to our higher nature. Paradoxically, we may only be able to come to an adequate understanding of what is at stake in the world of business and economics today by looking beyond them. By casting our gaze away from the ever-present realities of commercial life, we may come to see new possibilities that have eluded our attention, to gain a vision of the transcendental, sacred side of our moral nature, to refresh our sense of one another as beings in pursuit of what is best in ourselves: our virtuosity. This is especially apt to be true during our collective experience of cynicism, anxiety, and moral disorientation occasioned by the financial crisis as well as the extended sequence of scandals that preceded it.

Returning to Aristotle, we are reminded that the way we portray a moral problem is a matter of our character. For Aristotle, the notion of character casts a wide net, extending beyond our values and principles to include as well our willingness to act on them. Our inclination to act is, in turn, often connected to the relative degree of intensity that an ethical issue has for us. The intensity of a moral matter flows from the significance we attach to it.[105] A significant number of managers at Enron attuned to the corporation's deployment of off-balance-sheet partnerships—which were eventually cited as a substantial reason for the company's implosion—perceived the complex scheme of partnerships as being legal and therefore ethically acceptable. Being disposed to accept legality as a sufficient standard of conduct, the Enron managers were not inclined to interpret them as raising any moral issues, so they did not take any action to oppose or question them. A similar situation appears to have existed at Lehman Brothers in advance of its collapse, through its use of "Repo 105" transactions to dress up the firm's financial results and hide debt.[106]

Our character also embraces our capability to discern how principles and values ought to be applied in concrete cases, no matter how complicated or knotty that might turn out to be. A middle manager may genuinely proclaim the value of courage, yet fail to put it into effect from a failure to appreciate that voicing an objection to an upper manager's order to overcharge a client is what courage demands now. Here, the middle manager may be earnest, yet lack courage.

Aristotle instructs that being ethical is mostly about being someone with good character. A good character comes from the right engagement of emotions, practical intelligence, values, and virtues. Moral values that we learn from our experience and from the wider culture constitute a starting point for gaining wisdom. Making headway in ethics means honing and fine-tuning our values, gaining greater expertise in bringing them to bear on decision making, and keeping them safe from threatening surroundings. By having self-knowledge, which is a key ingredient of a good character, we are guided to safeguard our paramount values by selecting an ethically hospitable habitat within which to carry on our business activities. Equally we will shield our highest values by steering clear of temptations to veer off-beam.

So how does the person having a good character render a decision when faced with morally complicated situations in the real world? To address this important question, we will benefit from having a look at a philosopher who hails not from the *peripatoi* of ancient Athens but from the Parisian cafés of post–World War II France, the existentialist Jean-Paul Sartre.

Chapter 2

Authenticity and Freedom

How could it be an exercise of true freedom to refuse to be open to the very reality which enables our self-realization?

—John Paul II, *Fides et Ratio*

Man is condemned to be free; because once thrown into the world, he is responsible for everything he does.

—Jean-Paul Sartre, *Being and Nothingness*

JAMES IS A branch manager for the Manhattan division of an international commercial bank. His boss tells him that the Manhattan offices are slated to close in a couple of months, soon after the first of the year, and the branch's functions will henceforth be handled in India, where labor costs are considerably cheaper. The executive asks James to keep the news to himself, since regulatory documents will need to be filed first. James promises to keep quiet. A few days later, James's colleague and trusted friend of many years asks him if a rumor floating around the office that the branch is shutting down is true. When James casts his eyes askance, the colleague gets irritated and says, "Hey c'mon, this is serious stuff. In this economic downturn there aren't a lot of jobs out there. Should I be cutting back on the holidays this year and sending out my résumé? Just let me know what's up, OK?" What should James do? As a corporate manager, James is bound to uphold confidentiality, and in fact he vowed to do so. However, he's one of only a privileged few who knows about the firm's future plans, and the employee questioning him is his trusted friend.[1]

According to the Aristotelian view presented in the previous chapter, practicing virtue—that is, finding the right blend of reasons and motives (including emotions) in the face of practical problems or moral dilemmas, such as the one facing James, the fictitious branch manager in the scenario sketched above—produces or leads to the greater perfection (or at least definition) of moral character, as if one's character is somehow a fixed attribute or objective feature of oneself.[2] On such a view, for instance, if James decides to help his friend by informing him of the plans for downsizing, such a choice is prompted by the nature of James's underlying character, which reveals the virtues of compassion and loyalty to friends. However, deciding to honor the obligation of confidentiality would be the result of a more dominant component of James's character winning out, a character revealed in the exercise of the virtues of promise keeping and loyalty to the firm. It is against this conventional conception of virtue ethics, which treats a person's character as a collection of objective facts about her, that we should view Sartre's view of human freedom, for Sartre provides a radically different perspective on the nature of character.

To anticipate Sartre's conclusion, the deployment of neither reason nor motives (including emotions) in the pursuit of moral virtue provides an ultimate ground for human action. Reason and motives are placed relative to something much more basic: the agent's freedom. According to a Sartrean point of view,[3] a businessperson like James confronting a moral choice, like the one set out above, is free to choose, and by making a free choice, he is creating his existence, much like a writer inventing the characters and plot of a novel. Values such as happiness, the good life, success, getting along with others, and economic security tend to fall by the wayside as justifying ends of action; rather, the authenticity with which we face our freedom seems to be the chief criterion for judging persons and their actions as good or bad. Thus, if moral character—that is, authenticity—has a treasured meaning in Sartre, it is to be found, not in narrow instrumental reason, but in being reflectively conscious of our human condition and standing well in relation to our essential freedom.

For the contemporary businessperson, the main obstacle to realizing an authentic character (as a realized vow and capacity to be reflectively conscious of our human condition) is the attitude of "bad faith" in its myriad forms. The questions to be explored in this chapter, on the basis of this forecast, are: (1) If we abandon the assumption that a person's character is made up of fixed, objective virtues, or "givens," by reference to what can we judge the actions of businesspeople, such as our hypothetical manager James, who confront hard moral choices in ambiguous or extreme situations? (2) What sense can be made of the notion of authentic character for people working in modern organizations? (3) In what guise does bad faith arise in business decision making and in the structure of the modern corporation? (4) How might a Sartrean approach direct us in fostering authenticity in business ethics education?

This chapter is divided into two main parts. In light of the widespread neglect of Sartre's thought in the business ethics literature, Part 1 provides an exposition of Sartre's point of view, centering on his treatment of human freedom and character.[4] Part 2 explores the implications of Sartre's perspective for business ethics. Specific attention is paid in the second part as to how a Sartrean vantage point might suggest changes in the way that business ethics is taught, changes in the way businesspeople deal with ethical issues, and changes in business organizations.

Part 1: Sartre's Account of Human Freedom and Character

Sartre begins his treatment of the role of reason and motive in *Being and Nothingness* by remarking on how they are related to action. To explicate the idea of action, Sartre uses an historical event: Constantine's act of founding Constantinople as a new home for emperors. To see the relevance of such an apparently archaic example for our reflections on contemporary business ethics, just imagine that we are analyzing the proposed action of a CEO reestablishing his multinational firm's corporate headquarters from the United States to the Far East, and we are inquiring into the leader's intentions or underlying motives for the reorganization, which might be complex and ambiguous, ranging from reducing the firm's worldwide tax obligations, to creating a new image, to leveraging the political environment in the new region for competitive advantage. "We should observe first that an action is on principle intentional,"[5] and Constantine intended to create a countervailing power to Rome.[6] Further, Sartre develops this example to show that intention is to be understood as "seeing a lack." As he writes, "Action necessarily implies as its condition the recognition of a 'desideratum'; that is, of an objective lack or again of a négatité [negation]."[7] Constantine acts in view of a desirable state of affairs not yet realized; in view of which, the current state of affairs is seen as lacking. Intentions are not constituted of the "simple consideration of the real state of things."[8] The statement that 60 percent of the projected tax revenues have been collected, implies in itself no judgment. But to claim that taxes are badly collected in Rome is to deem the situation as lacking. Seeing Rome's attributes as negatives compared to a desirable possibility provides the ground for Constantine's intention to establish a counterweight to Rome.

Sartre draws two conclusions: (1) No factual state of affairs, whatever it may be (the political and economic structure of society, a person's psychological "state," the forces of globalization and economic competition), is capable by itself of motivating any act whatsoever. An act is a projection of the for-itself toward what is not.[9] (2) No factual state of affairs can determine consciousness to apprehend it as a negation or a lack.[10] Action is intentional. Intentionality involves seeing situations as lacking. From these considerations, Sartre establishes two central points. First, consciousness has the power to break with, or distance itself from, its past and its surrounding conditions, and to confer a new meaning on them. Perceiving one's condition as intolerable, Sartre writes, "Implies for consciousness the permanent possibility of effecting a rupture with its own past, of wrenching itself away from its past so as to be able to consider it in the light of a non-being and so as to be able to confer on it the meaning which it has in terms of the project of a meaning which it does not have."[11] The second point is that the actor's freedom is a basic condition of action, and the elements—reasons and motives—of actions can be grasped only by reference to this freedom. Reasons and motives "have meaning only inside a projected ensemble which is precisely an ensemble of non-existents. And this ensemble is ultimately myself as transcendence; it is Me insofar as I have to be myself outside of myself."[12]

By positing the possibility of a nonexistent ideal state of affairs, the bad state of affairs in Rome provides a good reason for Constantine to make a new capital. (Again, to visualize a counterpart of Sartre's example to a contemporary business scenario, consider, say, a domestic firm's leaders weighing reasons for and against a decision whether to close a U.S. branch and set up outsourcing operations abroad.[13] Compared with the as yet "non-existent ideal state of affairs," that is, competitive advantage sought by reducing labor costs through outsourcing, the current "bad state of affairs," that is, high labor costs and competitive disadvantage, give the company's executives a reason to establish a foreign manufacturing base.) Unless a reason is experienced as such, it is not really a reason.

Likewise, motives can be understood only in relation to an end. The nonexistent ideal state of affairs which I posit gives to a present motive (qua desire) its meaning (object or end), and if it is impossible to find acts without motives or prior reasons, it is because motives and reasons are integral parts of actions. However, the act is not explained by these partial structures alone. Rather, "it is the act which decides its ends and its motives, and the act is the expression of freedom."[14]

It is significant to note that scholars who have employed virtue approaches to analyze business ethics have leaned on a traditional Aristotelian account of motives and reason.[15] Motives, emotions, and attitudes are taken as objective existents that basically determine the executive or manager in what she or he does: Jack Welch created a "lean and mean" culture at General Electric because he is an aggressive, driven person with a realistic orientation. He developed such a character from his childhood upbringing.[16] Such an interpretation of character traits can be found in virtually any business or leadership autobiography, from Donald Trump[17] to Rudolph Giuliani.[18] Reasons refer to the objective factors of a situation, which also have a determining role in what is actually done. So long as we see motives as determining and reasons as pointing to the objective facts, it is difficult to see how Sartre's point of view will provide us with an illuminating answer to the question: Which should have priority, motives or reasons?

On the objective or reasons side first, it is clear that Sartre acknowledges the standard meanings to a certain extent. Historians look to reasons or objective states of affairs to explain acts. Clovis's conversion to Catholicism is explained by reference to the power of the episcopate in Gaul, an objective fact. In this sense, Sartre writes, "the cause is characterized as an objective appreciation of the situation."[19] All the same, an "objective appreciation can be made only in light of a presupposed end and within the limits of a project of the for-itself toward this end."[20] The power of the episcopate is a reason for conversion for Clovis because he wants to conquer Gaul. Consequently, the meaning of reason is qualified as follows: "We shall therefore use the term cause for the objective apprehension of a determined situation as this situation is revealed in the light of a certain end as being able to serve as the means for attaining this end."[21] As compared to traditional meanings, it is not the objectivity of states of affairs that Sartre alters. After all, the Catholic Church of Clovis's time did or did not have power. The key point here is that constituting some state of affairs as a reason for acting depends on the ends we propose for ourselves. Think of a knife as an objective instrument; its instrumental implications depend on what we are about. Even though it is normally used for cutting, if I am hanging up a picture, I can use the knife handle as a hammer.[22] A reason, then, as objective evaluation of situations, does not determine an action; rather, it "appears only in and through the project of an action."[23]

We must have projected ourselves "in this or that way in order to discover the instrumental implications of instrumental-things."[24] An exposition of advertising strategies provides a somewhat more complex, yet highly apt example. Whereas we might think of the uses and appeal of automobiles as objective facts—there are sport utility vehicles (SUVs) for those with an interest in trendiness, spaciousness, luxury, and power, and there are small cars for those interested in economy and a competitive edge in tight parking conditions—a common practice in advertising takes advantage of the role of evaluation of given conditions by unique consciousnesses.

Thus, an advertising agency may write different advertising profiles for the same SUV for different audiences. One profile might develop the rugged, off-road capabilities of the vehicle; another, its practical appeal for parents (for example, so-called soccer moms); another, its greater safety and highway dominance relative to smaller cars; and a fourth, its sexiness. By projecting onto the SUV different sets of evaluative interests, the advertising agency has brought out (or created) varying use and appeal implications of the product. Such an advertising agency could well take these words of Sartre as a guiding precept: "The world gives counsel only if one questions it, and one can question it only for a well-determined end."[25] While reasons refer to objective calculations of a state of affairs in the light of given ends, motives refer to the subjective structures that Sartre sees as correlative with reasons. As he writes, "The consciousness which carves out the cause in the ensemble of the world has already its own structure; it has given its own ends to itself, it has projected itself toward its possibles, and it has its own manner of hanging on to its possibilities: this peculiar manner of holding to its possibles is here affectivity."[26]

In projecting toward some end, we constitute reasons of some objective state of affairs. Clovis, in Sartre's illustration, sees the power of the church as a reason for conversion. The motive is the consciousness of oneself as moved to some degree, as more or less keen, toward the end in the light of which the reason was constituted. "The motive," Sartre claims, "is nothing other than the apprehension of the cause insofar as this apprehension is self-consciousness."[27] Clovis's ambition is the subjective correlate of his constituting of the church's power as a reason for conversion; as a certain consumer's sense of adventure or another's intellectual snobbishness, in the advertisers' view, is the correlate of seeing in the projected feature a reason to buy the SUV. But such motives are not preexisting, impelling forces; rather, they are indistinguishable from the projects of which they are partial structures.

The cause, the motive, and the end are the three indissoluble terms of the thrust of a free and living consciousness, which projects itself toward its possibilities and makes itself defined by these possibilities.[28]

Sartre concludes that the idea of rational choice by cool, detached deliberation about objective factors alone is illusory. "How can I," he questions, "evaluate causes and motives on which I myself confer their value before all deliberation and by the very choice which I make of myself?"[29] Which car profile advertisement I find reasonable depends on the weight my project confers upon "the features profiled." "When I deliberate," writes Sartre, "the chips are down."[30] Summarizing the argument to this point: we understand reasons and motives only by locating them in the structure of action; action is necessarily intentional.

While reasons are objective evaluations of states of affairs, the constitution of reasons from states of affairs depends on the interest or projection of self of the evaluator. Motives are the subjective counterparts of reasons constituted by projecting the self in a certain way. But these basic projections are not to be confused with will. "Will" amounts to choosing some action. This could not happen without prior projection of the self-guiding deliberate choice. Our choices, in turn, make the projected self become real. If reasons and motives are constituted in the projection of being toward its possibilities, a number of questions arise about the nature of rational character in Sartre's philosophy. What are these more basic projects? How do we discern them in ourselves? Can we find any sense of reason or the reasonable in these? The particular reasons, motives, and ends of individual actions, and such actions themselves, are all to be seen as part of a more inclusive structure. By contrasting different reactions to a long hike, Sartre delineates what is involved in these basic projects of self. Sartre imagines himself, after hours of hiking, finally giving into his mounting fatigue, throwing down his backpack, and giving up.

Answering a critic's reproach that he could have kept going, that he could have done otherwise, he says that he is too tired. This interchange represents the positions of free-will advocates and determinists. In the spirit of what we have said of reasons and motives above, Sartre challenges the premises about who is right. Acknowledging that he could have done otherwise, the problem should be set forth: "Could I have done otherwise without perceptibly modifying the organic totality of the projects which I am? In other words: I could have done otherwise. Agreed. But at what price?"[31] It is not the fatigue per se that accounts for the decision to quit. His companions have walked just as far and they are in about the same physical shape. It is not a case of objectively reaching some threshold fatigue level, like watching the hand on a pressure gauge advance to the red shut-off zone. Instead, "I suffer my fatigue. That is, a reflective consciousness is directed upon my fatigue in order to live it and to confer on it a value and a practical relation to myself. It is only on this plane that the fatigue will appear to me as bearable or intolerable. It will never be anything in itself, but it is the reflective For-itself which rising up suffers the fatigue as intolerable."[32] This way of suffering fatigue is not a given. His companions respond differently; that difference throws into relief Sartre's way of regarding the suffering of fatigue as chosen. His companion is not overcome by fatigue; rather, the heat of the sun, the steepness of the slopes, and the effort of his legs are all felt as part of the enjoyable experience of a hike and of conquering the mountain. The "companion's fatigue," Sartre says, "is lived in a vaster project of a trusting abandon to nature, of a passion consented to in order that it may exist at full strength, and at the same time the project of sweet mastery and appropriation."[33] But this mode of living his fatigue that the companion exhibits is still unoriginal. It is not sufficient, since behind it rests "a particular relation of my companion to his body, on the one hand, and to things, on the other."[34] The original project of existing one's body in a certain way is a "certain choice which the For-itself makes of itself . . ."[35] In this choice, the body as given—and secondarily, the heat of the sun, our fatigue, and so forth—are "valorized" (given arbitrary value) in a certain way. Sartre depicts his own reaction to physical exhaustion as prompted by a much different way of "existing his body" compared with his companion's; he distrusts his body and doesn't like even having to take it into account. These examples show that the projects that give meaning to reasons and motives are basic choices that reflect who we are and that reveal the various ways we respond to the world. We witness the choices we have made about ourselves in the meanings we ascribe to the world. "The value of things, their instrumental role, their proximity and real distance . . . do nothing more than to outline my image—that is, my choice. My clothing . . . whether neglected or cared for, carefully chosen or ordinary, my furniture, the street on which I live, the city in which I reside, the books with which I surround myself, the recreation which I enjoy, every-thing which is mine . . . all this informs one of my choice—that is, my be-ing."[36] So we return to Sartre's question of what's involved in opting to press on with the hike rather than stopping. Giving up was not an arbitrary or gratuitous act; it was part of "a certain view of the world in which difficulties can appear 'not worth the trouble of being tolerated.'"[37] To have done other-wise would involve a fundamental alteration of his choice of self. But, asserts Sartre, "this modification is always possible." The feelings of anguish and responsibility mark our consciousness of our freedom to choose ourselves. We are (painfully) aware of our choices as "unjustifiable," that is, simply as free assertions of our selves. He writes, "We are perpetually engaged in our choice and perpetually conscious of the fact that we ourselves can abruptly invert this choice and 'reverse steam.' . . . By the sole fact that our choice is absolute, it is fragile."[38] Thus, the project, from which emerges a coordinate structure of reasons and motives, is a choice of self at a fundamental level. It is an absolute choice. Taking conditions as "givens" in the face of the conten-tion that freedom is absolute, the question of the status of various "givens" in human experience arises. At first glance, the company where we work, our employment history, our occupation, all of these seem to be irreducible "givens." Who can say we're free in relation to these objective conditions?

To clarify the question of limits to human freedom, and to show again Sartre's view of how reasons and motives emerge, I will review Sartre's dis-cussion of some of these givens. Sartre's principle is stated clearly at the be-ginning of his section on "givens"; he writes, "The given . . . could never be a cause for an action if it were not appreciated. In addition, the appreciation, if it is not to be gratuitous, must be effected in the light of something. And this something which serves to appreciate the given can be only the end. Thus the intention by a single unitary upsurge posits the end, chooses itself, and appreciates the given in terms of the end."[39] This is not to say that givens are chosen to exist. I cannot make the chair over there pop in and out of existence by mere choice. Instead, "by the choice which it makes of its end, freedom causes the datum be revealed in this or that way, in this or that light in connection with the revelation of the world itself."[40] Situations are constituted by the relation in which we stand to brute existents. To a hiker standing at the foot of a cliff, the cliff takes on the qualities of climbable/not-climbable. To a passing rubbernecking motorist, the cliff registers as beautiful/ugly. Moreover, whether the cliff will be difficult or easy to scale (its coefficient of adversity) is not simply an objective property. What's hard for one is easy for another. The body itself gets revealed as poorly trained or as well trained by the choice of ventures. So the coefficient of adversity in situations reveals as much about a person as it does about brute givens.

The Project

In a similar way, the past as a determinant of action depends on our freely constituted project in the now. I cannot literally change the past. No physical force in the world is powerful enough to do that. Still, the meaning of the past hinges on my present commitments. In Sartre's words:

> By projecting myself towards my ends, I preserve my ends, I preserve the past with me, and by action I decide its meaning. Who shall decide whether the period which I spent in prison after a theft was fruitful or deplorable? I—according to whether I give up stealing or become hardened. Who can decide the educational value of a trip, the sincerity of a profession of love, the purity of a past intention, etc.? It is I, always I, according to the ends by which I illuminate these past events.[41]

The common lament "if I had only" testifies to the relation of present to past. What, at the time, seemed "trivial" or "too difficult to be worth the effort," becomes illuminated as "what I should have done at all costs." Likewise, the urgency and weight of past engagements depends on present commitments. The gravity of a manger's professional and organizational commitments, the sanctity of her marriage, duties to her children, obligations to pay debts and carry the mortgage, and the like, may seem like unbreakable chains to the past. But, "suppose," asks Sartre, "that . . . I radically modify my fundamental project . . . my earlier engagements will lose all their urgency."[42] Consider "Moonie" religious converts. Bonds to family and old friends dissolve as their indoctrination crystallizes. Thrown out of relation to present commitments, the expected emotions are absent; we are not moved. In such cases, writes Sartre, "the past falls back as a disarmed and duped expectation; it is 'without force.'"[43]

What Is Character?

Character and temperament are often depicted in discussions of business as givens about a person. James Cramer, cohost of CNBC's *Kudlow & Cramer* show and cofounder of TheStreet.com portrays his high-octane disposition as if it is a kind of fixture of his being in his bestselling autobiography.[44] For Sartre, however, a fixity of character only means that the person persists in a certain projection of himself. He argues that "character is a vow. When a man says, 'I am not easy to please,' he is entering into a free engagement with his ill-temper, and by the same token his words are a free interpretation of certain ambiguous details in his past. In this sense there is no character; there is only a project of oneself."[45] The aim of Sartre's description of various "givens"— past, environment, character, and so forth—is to clarify the human situation, and his conclusions set the stage for an explicit return to the opening question in this chapter, whether reasons or attitude ought to be the priority in business ethics. While we live among various existents, it is we who give meaning and bearing to existents by the manner of our being. The situation—not the things themselves—comes into being only as we transcend the given toward some end. Yet the situation is neither merely subjective nor merely objective. It is neither my impression of the mountain I want to climb, nor the mountain itself. "The situation," writes Sartre, "Is a relation of being between a for-itself and the in-itself which the for-itself nihilates. The situation is the whole subject (he is nothing but his situation) and it is also the whole 'thing' (there is never anything more than things). The situation is the subject illuminating things by his very surpassing, if you like; it is things referring to the subject his own image."[46] It is the qualities of the mountain as to-be-climbed, and such hypothetical qualities as difficult, impossible-to-climb, and so on, which reflect the condition of my body. The "silly" choice of this mountain in spite of my condition indicates a certain state of determination to persist.

As the situations exist in the light of my projection of myself, as an individual, Sartre concludes that there is neither any privileged situation nor privileged point of view. To say there is a "privileged situation" is to say that the objective facts demand a certain countenance toward them. Yet, as Sartre argues, "the world gives counsel only if one questions it, and one can question it only for a well-determined end."[47] In respect to a projected end, the circumstances will indeed be more or less felicitous, but that is already to evaluate circumstances from some vantage point. Furthermore, the point of view a person assumes is, in the adopting, his own. And each situation, by virtue of the person being a certain way, amongst certain things, is to be thought of as eminently concrete.

Which Should Drive Moral Choice: Reason or Emotion (or Freedom)?

It is time now to summarize this discussion in terms of our question whether intellect or emotion should be business ethics' priority, and which is more likely to promote personal happiness and economic success. Those who argue for the priority of emotions stress the potency of emotions and attitudes in guiding what we do and what we believe. Similarly, those who argue for the priority of reason do so in terms of the importance of having good reasons as the grounds for our actions. Sartre transforms our way of responding to the question with the argument, which I have outlined above, that both reasons and emotions or motives are derivative from something more basic in human action, namely, our free projection of ourselves in our mode of being. If a priority for business ethics is concern for the ultimate ground of action, then, according to Sartre, our primary attention should somehow be with our freedom of choice. Thus, Sartre's view diminishes the status of rational character, if "rational" takes on the restricted sense of evaluating objective conditions as means to given ends. Evaluation may be objective, but it is necessarily done in the light of some end, argues Sartre, and such ends emerge with the free projection of oneself in this or that way. "It follows that my freedom is the unique foundation of values and that nothing, absolutely nothing, justifies me in adopting this or that particular value, this or that particular scale of values. As a being by whom values exist, I am unjustifiable. My freedom is anguished at being the foundation of values while itself without foundation."[48]

Authenticity: The Ultimate Ethical Value?

There is, however, a distinguished sense of being rational in Sartre, which is highlighted by a discussion of the status of happiness, security, and success—goals often stressed by those advocating virtue approaches to business ethics.[49] Bluntly put, happiness, as something like a utilitarian idea of surplus of pleasure over pain, security, and success, even the attainment of Aristotelian well-being or *eudaimonia*, all carry no special priority for Sartre. As one scholar puts it, "In its more common usage, the term 'happiness' finds no place in the authentic life prescribed by Sartre. The best that can be hoped for in terms of reward, end, or goal showing authentic existence is the satisfaction and dignity that arises from the individual's assertion of his freedom in the face of an absurd universe."[50] The aim of Sartre's analysis is not to liberate us from suffering, but rather to awaken us to authentic existence. If authenticity is the ultimate ethical value, and being rational means the conscious and deliberate acceptance of our human condition of freedom in our manner of being, then the chief barriers to being rational will be found in those ways of being that undercut such an acceptance. "Bad faith" stands for the ways we run away from acceptance of our freedom; discussing it will clarify what is involved in this sense of being rational.

This passage from *Nausea*, Sartre's well-known novel, expresses the spirit of bad faith: "For the most trivial event to become an adventure, you must (and this is enough) begin to recount it. This is what fools people: a man is always a teller of tales, he lives surrounded by his stories and the stories of others, he sees everything that happens to him through them; and he tries to live his life as if he were telling a story. But you have to choose: live or tell."[51] What such stories give us is a pattern to which to conform our lives. We say that the sense and direction of our lives is given in the story, while refusing to recognize that it is we who tell the stories. Insofar as we persist in living our life as a story, we make ourselves thing-like in denying our responsibility for our actions. We say that we are essentially the story we tell, but as Walter Kauffman explains Sartre's view:

> A man is not . . . a waiter, or a coward in the same way in which he is six feet tall or blond. . . . If I am six feet tall, that is that. It is a fact no less than that the table is, say, two feet high. Being a coward or a waiter, however, is different: it depends on ever-new decisions. I may say: I must leave now—or, I am that way—because I am a waiter, or a coward, as if being a waiter or a coward were a brute fact. Actually, this apparent statement of fact veils a decision.[52]

We are not what we are—a portfolio manager, sales clerk, or a CEO—in the same sense that a chair is a chair because of the possibility of choosing our manner of being. To impose a fixed role in a story upon oneself, as though that were the nature of things, is, in short, to reject our awareness of human responsibility and freedom. Bad faith rests upon the dual aspect of human nature: being at once (1) a facticity and (2) a transcendence. Judgments of ourselves in bad faith "aim at establishing that I am not what I am."[53] We affirm some aspect of our character, for example, to avoid the possibility of being different: the firm's budget administrator, explaining his explosive reaction to an erroneously completed expense report, quips, "Oh, I've always had this quick temper, it's too late to change now." Or, standing on the possibilities of transcending our past selves, we say that the past doesn't count, that we're really different from that. Whereas we should be able to coordinate these two aspects of human reality, in bad faith, instead of valid coordination, we stand on or in a view of one to avoid taking responsibility for the other. "The goal of bad faith," writes Sartre, "is to put oneself out of reach; it is an escape."[54] By way of summary about bad faith, Sartre's translator, Hazel Barnes, offers a concise account:

> It consists in not accepting one's responsibilities as a For-itself, in seeking to blame someone or something for what one has done freely oneself, in choosing to assert one's freedom only where it is expedient and on other occasions to seek refuge in a theory of psychological determinism. It is to pretend that one is born with a determined self instead of recognizing that one spends one's life pursuing and making oneself. It is the refusal to face the anguish which accompanies the recognition of our absolute freedom.[55]

Thus, rationality, as the conscious and deliberate acceptance of the human condition, requires that we avoid the ever-present plays of bad faith, which undermine the authentic acceptance of our freedom and responsibility.

Summary of Key Points

We can distill the preceding discussion down to a few central tenets, which will help in relating Sartre's ideas to relevant problems in business ethics in Part 2.

· Existence precedes essence. In other words, what we do, how we act, determines our apparent character traits (or virtues). It is not that someone tells the truth because he is honest. On the contrary, one defines oneself as honest by choosing to tell the truth again and again. A "courageous" person is basically just someone who usually acts bravely. Each act contributes to defining us as we are. But at any moment we are free to start acting differently. We can always start afresh, making different kinds of choices than we have in the past.

· People are subjects, not objects. Humans are not objects to be used by corporations or other organizations. Nor are people to be "motivated," "controlled," or "molded" into roles, to act as merely a waiter, or secretary, or programmer, or accountant. Treating people as objects is contrary to treating them as free subjects. Our freedom is what constitutes our humanity.

· Choices matter. We are our choices. We cannot avoid or escape choosing. Opting not to choose is still choosing. Even if stuck in inevitable conditions, we nonetheless still choose how we are in those circumstances, for instance, what attitude to adopt with regard to our working at a job that we hate.

· Universality of decisions: although we may be choosing what appears to be for ourselves only, we are, in a profound sense, choosing for all humankind.[56]

· Bad faith (self-deception) poses a persistent and pervasive threat to living authentically. We act in bad faith whenever we regard ourselves first and foremost as objects—for example, our professional roles within organizations—instead of as free persons.

Part 2: Implications for Business Ethics

In considering the ramifications of these Sartrean reflections for business ethics, a few cautionary notes should be made. First, I am inclined to believe that, in its normative aspect, business ethics does not, nor should it, purport to mandate or restrict itself to any one theoretical orientation. Rather, normative business ethics is most successful and illuminating when it perspicaciously deploys the strongest parts of moral theories, which may harbor significant defects standing on their own, for instance, utilitarianism,[57] rule utilitarianism,[58] deontological approaches,[59] rights perspectives,[60] justice conceptions,[61] contractuarian approaches,[62] stakeholder conceptions,[63] and virtue ethics,[64] as needed for understanding and resolving moral problems in the real world. It is in that spirit that I recommend including Sartre's ideas along with some of the more conventional philosophical concepts listed above. One chief benefit of taking a Sartrean point of view on business ethics is to foster one's awareness that the deepest moral dilemmas are not quite as amenable to being objectively "solved" as applications of traditional moral theory have suggested.

Second, for business ethics to draw on philosophical concepts in interesting and illuminating ways no particular process needs to be deployed. Indeed, with a notion like authenticity, it would be odd to specify, say, particular corporate initiatives or business school curricula to promote "training in authenticity." Any such regimen would no sooner be specified than it would become an insidious form of indoctrination, a front for imposters of authenticity. Thus, the points raised can only be sincerely transformed into practice by the art of inventive minds. Finally, as significant and potentially transformative as Sartre's concept of authenticity is, such a notion is certainly not the only one, and it is not necessarily the most important one for business ethics. It would pay to keep in mind a version of Dewey's phrase that it takes a good moral character to know when to raise the moral issue;[65] that is, perhaps it also takes an authentic character to know when to raise the question of authenticity. If character is interpreted from an "intellectual academic" standpoint, then the educational implications would run toward exercises in analytic and deductive skills, and so on. If character is interpreted from a socioemotional standpoint, then one might expect an emphasis on teaching approved or "rational" attitudes. If, by contrast, character is interpreted in light of Sartrean reflections, attention must be given in business ethics education to fostering the conscious and deliberate acceptance of the human condition of freedom in our manner of being, that is, authenticity. The short recapitulation of the main tenets of Sartre's view provided above suggests a number of points of attack for the present state of business ethics with regard to the task of fostering authenticity. The focal points to be considered are: (1) business ethics education, (2) managerial deliberation and decision making, and (3) corporate structures. In the following sections, fundamental changes in these areas that are prompted by a Sartrean point of view will be explored.

Changing Assumptions About Teaching Business Ethics

A Sartrean point of view suggests that, beyond learning processes of ethical reasoning, business students would be assisted by seeing that such reasoning processes are embedded in larger structures of action. In the delineation of reasons, the role of evaluator is critical. Reasons are constituted as one defines a situation, say, a Harvard Business School case study or an ethical dilemma. Situations are not simply the objective state of affairs or "the facts"; rather, situations come into being as one questions the facts from some point of view.[66] Thus, the coefficient of adversity in situations reveals as much about the manager or executive as about givens. The present custom in many business schools of taking the winner's view of history and of downplaying the extent to which economic decisions embody value positions and the moral dimension obscures the wider structures within which reasons are constituted. A treatment of "the facts" from conflicting points of view would begin to show (intellectually, at least) the import of choice of starting points in intellectual analysis. If point of view or attitude or, more generally speaking, created self has such a role in the constitution of reasons, it is not the original or generative element, for our choices actualize and specify what we are. Sartre shows how each of us has a fundamental project. Our free acts are always outlined for us against the backdrop of this project. We can see our choices in the selves we have created, and the projects that give meaning to reasons and motives are basic choices of ourselves in our modes of responding to the world. Surely business ethics educators in both the universities and the boardrooms can create many opportunities in the treatment of fiction and fact (contemporaneous and historical) to foster the intellectual apprehension of the role of attitude in the definition of situations; part of that apprehension involves seeing that there are alternative definitions and thus alternative attitudes.

Beyond the intellectual goal, businesspeople must be presented with opportunities to see that they could feel otherwise than they do. Others' characters provide an invaluable resource in this respect; the display of, say, gaiety, perseverance, or equanimity by others in circumstances where such is not a habitual response reveals more convincingly than moral maxims that one could be otherwise than one is. In response to these reflections, a critic might raise the following objection. People that enter business schools have already chosen their fundamental projects. Hence, they may well "freely" choose their motives, causes, and acts in terms of the ends that promote their project. But the project is usually to succeed, which means to gain power and make money. So what do they freely do? Upon entering the business world, graduates will act as the company tells them, so they and it can succeed, gain power, and make money. A reply to this objection would point out that, even granted that a business student's fundamental project arises within the conventional horizons of the business world, such a person must always choose how to act within the business world; her free acts may or may not reinforce the values of the business status quo. What is important is that a person be conscious of his or her freedom. Indeed, in today's emerging business world, rising expectations of corporate social responsibility, fueled by a scrutinizing public, media, and government are not allowing corporations to work exclusively on profit maximizing in the service of shareholders while ignoring impacts on other constituencies and on communities.[67] Thus, with the appearance of, on the one hand, massive scandals erupting in the business world,[68] and on the other hand, an increasing number of firms expressly devoted to social responsibility,[69] graduates of business schools are in a position to choose the kind of organization they want to work in, that is, one they perceive as having a fundamentally immoral, amoral, or moral management orientation.[70]

Enhanced Intercultural Understanding Prompted by the Universality of Human Choice

A greater willingness on the part of both business schools and corporations to identify with diverse representatives of a common humanity appears to be an important consequence of adopting a Sartrean stance toward business ethics. As Sartre writes:

> Every purpose, however individual it may be, is of universal value. . . . In every purpose there is universality, in this sense that every purpose is comprehensible to every man. Not that this or that purpose defines man for ever, but that it may be entertained again and again. . . . In this sense we may say that there is a human universality, but it is not something given; it is being perpetually made. I make this universality in choosing myself; I also make it by understanding the purpose of any other man, of whatever epoch.[71]

Accordingly, business organizations should show respect for humanity in its variant manifestations. In particular, this entails an appreciation that the capacity for suffering is universal; compassion cannot be hemmed in by the boundaries of a particular nation, religion, or skin color.[72] It is critical that this awareness is not confined to a mere dissemination of empirical facts about foreign cultures linked with the firm's operations—knowledge must be counterbalanced with a measure of emotional engagement. In efforts to foster intercultural understanding in business leaders, the importance of striking a balance between intellectual and emotional development is clear. As proponents of an "ethic of care" have shown,[73] the capacity to identify with the feelings and interests of others, and the ability to see what one's own and others' feelings are, is an important component of moral development.[74] Accordingly, insofar as moral development encompasses the attunement of attitudes and feelings, what one writer in the popular press has dubbed "emotional intelligence,"[75] corporate leaders should be prepared (which includes being properly trained) to deal with associates' feelings sensitively, especially when such feelings might range from guilt, shock, horror, outrage, to compassion.

An illustration will help clarify the force of this point. Layoffs are especially traumatic when managers ignore the way in which the message is delivered to employees. The manner in which people are terminated, including the kinds of words used to communicate the firing and the specific ways the day's events transpire, are of great significance in terms of perceptions of meanness and cruelty, on one hand, or kindness and compassion, on the other. The trauma impacts not only the person fired but also the colleagues left behind. Massive layoffs mean larger workloads for the people remaining. People missing the cut experience low morale. Productivity drops. They distrust management. Brutal downsizings, such as those conducted by CEO Albert "Chainsaw" Dunlap during his tenure at Sunbeam,[76] are an affront to the dignity of a firm's employees. Indeed, perceptions of a lack of goodwill in employee terminations often cause substantial harm to an organization in terms of sullied reputations and lawsuits.[77] From an existential point of view, such basic emotive concerns are, in the final analysis, all valid responses to much that business leaders may learn about the human condition upon adopting the basic attitude of authenticity in the Sartrean sense.

Confronting Ambiguity

Simone de Beauvoir, Sartre's lifelong companion, emphasizes the "ethics of ambiguity" in her reflections on the moral implications of Sartrean existentialism.[78] The ability of businesspeople to tolerate uncertainty is arguably an important characteristic to consider. There already exists an extensive literature on the centrality of the capacity for efficient thinking, problem solving, and general intellectual development for effective moral reasoning.[79]

Individuals who cannot tolerate uncertainty close too quickly on solutions, are less prepared to consider all aspects of a problem, adhere too rigidly to a first solution in the face of evidence of better alternatives, and are less capable of recognizing the frequent need for compromise and "best-fit" solutions. Moral maturity involves recognizing that there is much we cannot know, yet action must be taken. Most business organizations throughout the world are inclined to reward certainty and correctness, doing little to encourage tentativeness or creative thinking. The problems facing complex, culturally diverse societies do not lend themselves to simple, all-or-nothing solutions, and it is vitally important that those charged with decision making do not have limited vision.

Consider, for instance, the substantial ambiguity attending corporate decision making in the context of considerations of a firm's social responsibility, even when the firm's leaders attempt to utilize stakeholder theory for guidance in resolving problems. The essence of stakeholder theory, which has attained a prominent status in the fields of both business ethics and managerial strategy, is that maximizing profits for shareholders is not the sole purpose of a business; instead a corporation is to serve the larger society, including many other constituents: employees, customers, suppliers, and the communities in which the firm operates.[80] The stakeholder perspective asserts that the scope of corporate social responsibility is wider than meeting the bottom line for shareholders and assumes the existence of ethical and discretionary responsibilities that go beyond the purely economic and legal responsibilities of business firms.[81] But substantial situational ambiguities arise whenever a deliberator tries to apply the stakeholder theory to a problem in the real world. On its own, the theory provides no guidance as to how a firm's leaders should rank and balance the competing interests of various purported stakeholders, especially when such interests are conflicting and mutually exclusive.

The point being made in this consideration of the limits of stakeholder theory is that one of the illuminating aspects of a Sartrean conception is that it continually directs our attention back to the pervasive uncertainty that even the best theories cannot erase when it comes to making judgments on the moral plane. Inevitably, humans confront choices in the face of the ambiguity that comes from theory underdetermining the solutions.

Adopting the Authentic Attitude

Above all the Sartrean point of view suggests we aim at the sort of understanding and acceptance of the human condition of freedom so that we avoid projecting choices that are ours onto circumstances and onto others. If we conduct our professional careers as stories, laid down and fixed, we simply put up smoke screens to obscure our decisions. Sartre's thought aims to bring us to the point of confronting our decisions, choices, and characters head-on. I have tried to show that Sartre's position implies a rejection of the received view of moral character, which treats a person's traits as if they were purely objective, being-in-itself. A consequence of a Sartrean vantage point is that neither an intellectual academic orientation nor a social-emotional orientation should be the priority of business ethics. Sartre's stance on authenticity can be described as an attitude, since it is a way of orienting oneself to the world and to one's actions. Thus, Sartre's view is character-centered in that everything depends on the quality or degree of awareness of a person's acceptance of his freedom, and the responsibility that freedom entails, as he or she acts. For our purposes, this means that it is the state of, say, the manager conducting terminations in a firm's downsizing—as authentic, on one hand, or in bad faith, on the other—which is the proper focus of moral scrutiny, not—to draw one contrast—whether the action in carrying this out conforms to a rule. While business ethics educators ought not to neglect conformity of acts to rules or the consequences of acts in reflecting on education's priorities, we should remember that the Sartrean meaning of an act is to be discerned in the larger project of which it is a part and in the master passion or attitude with which the act is done, whether one of authenticity or of bad faith.

Making Decisions in Extreme Situations

At this point in the analysis it will be helpful to return to the illustrative moral dilemma with which this chapter opened. The counterpart of an executive or manager of today agonizing over a difficult choice of loyalties in their workplace appears in Sartre's well-known portrayal of an extreme moral conflict. Sartre urges us to consider the plight of young man in occupied France who finds himself at a critical turning point in his life: he is forced to choose between joining the Resistance and taking care of his aged mother.[82] Here, the conflict of duties, responsibilities, and moral intuitions is ultimately a conflict between two ways of life, and not merely a conflict between moral claims within a single way of life. A parallel dynamic underlies the hypothetical bank manager's dilemma. Thus, both Sartre's young man and our bank manager are forced to choose between two different moral practices, and two different moral environments, and the virtues and vices that will come to characterize their future actions are correspondingly divergent: on the one hand, courage, dedication, selflessness, and loyalty, as well as willingness to inflict pain, deceive, and betray; on the other hand, friendship, affection, and honesty. Conventional modes of ethical reasoning would lead one to focus on, say, the problem of resolving the conflict of role responsibilities at play (that is, role responsibility qua manager versus role responsibility qua personal friend),[83] or of identifying and adjudicating conflicting norms or precepts of common morality (that is, "always keep your promises" versus "never abandon a friend in need"). The force of Sartre's example is clear: what is fundamentally at stake here is a choice between different ways of life; this, in turn, is ultimately a choice between two possible types of person, for which there is no conceivable common decision criterion. The decision is a particularly torturous one because the young man's moral inquiry and reasoning about which of the two courses to follow inevitably comes to an unsatisfactory end. Sartre allows that he could guide his inquiry and eventual choice by relying on Christian doctrine, Kantian ethics, or utilitarian principles. But the abstractness of their principles in specific and highly complex historical situations unavoidably underdetermines his final choice and requires elements of interpretation, discernment, and decision on his own part. This sort of circumstance is depicted systematically in a business context by Joseph Badaracco in his book *Defining Moments*. In a chapter entitled "The Futility of Grand Principles," Badaracco points out how reference to general language in corporate credos and mission statements, general rules of law, and abstract principles from philosophical theory all lead to a dead end so far as resolving the various "right versus right" dilemmas of the business leaders featured in his book.[84] By way of personal example, I often have business students come by to visit me in my office seeking advice when they find themselves anguished about extreme choice-of-career situations. A student might be torn between, say, the allure of pursuing a lucrative, albeit potentially "high-burnout" life of a trader on Wall Street versus working for a nonprofit organization committed to alleviating world hunger or promoting sustainable development. For Sartre, a choice made on the basis of trusting one's feelings will itself rest on a prior choice about what counts as a morally significant feeling. Careful, rational, intellectual deliberation is equally unhelpful, for if one engages in deliberation, it is simply a part of one's original project to realize motives by means of deliberation rather than some other form of discovery (for example, by passion or action). As we earlier saw, when a person deliberates, Sartre claims, the "chips are down."[85]

In the final instance, when one is faced with a choice of whether to accept a way of life, moral argument, deliberation, and searching for rational justification come to an end. One finds oneself at the very end point of a whole way of seeing and doing things, and one must choose from a perspective characterized by ignorance, epistemic finitude, existential contingency, and moral uncertainty. Accompanying this is the stark realization that however sure and well made the choice may appear to be, it is neither self-justifying nor supported by an external foundation.

There is no possibility of putting one choice of a way of life on a secure and rational foundation. As Sartre puts it, "Who could help him choose? . . . Nobody. . . . I had only one answer to give: 'You're free, choose, that is, invent.' No general ethics can show you what is to be done; there are no omens in the world. The Catholics will reply, 'But there are.' Granted—but, in any case, I myself choose the meaning they have."[86] Asking what a Sartrean point of view would recommend so far as resolving such a dilemma would seem to be posing a somewhat misleading question. For many hard cases there simply may not be any single, best-justified answer other than a sober prompting to "be imaginative—create." This insight captures the importance of taking a Sartrean vantage point, especially since so many business ethicists would urge us to attempt to "solve" dilemmas by applying theory and utilizing deductive reasoning procedures. Confronting dilemmas authentically means that a deliberator squarely faces the openness and indeterminacy of the situation.

Reengineering Structures and Practices that Facilitate "Bad Faith" in Business Contexts

It would seem that many traditional organizational structures and conventions that make up the corporate world are veritable breeding grounds for bad faith. Recall, for instance, Robert Jackall's chilling depictions of the dehumanizing features of corporate bureaucracies, which he aptly termed "moral mazes."[87] By way of a partial, illustrative list, consider the following:

- roles and rigid ascriptions of role-responsibility that tend to make people identify primarily with an organizationally or professionally defined role, a psychological process known as deindividuation,[88] rather than with their essential human freedom;
- codes of conduct, mission statements, and credos that tend to commodify values by giving them a material form and that "package" values as a public relations ploy;[89]
- ethics programs that attempt to motivate compliance with the organization's standards by means of reward and incentive systems.[90] Essentially such systems are no different from command-and-control (sanction-based) approaches: however noble their ends may appear to be in a utilitarian sense, both are based on behavior control;
- ethics training regimens that champion "virtues" as cultivated, determinate properties of human character;[91]
- executives and managers that utter corporate-speak, double-talk; steering between not saying enough, saying too much, and saying the "wrong" thing, that is, the truth;[92] and
- mathematically driven economic theorizing that tends to reinforce the illusions that business and economics are value-free enterprises and that a distant, even contradictory, relationship exists between economics and ethics—the "separation thesis."[93]

My point here is not to "blame" or "condemn" such structures and practices. Rather, by simply drawing awareness to the pervasive sources of facticity within the conventional business world, at least people are accorded something of a greater "fighting chance" to change them, avoid them, or for that matter, accept and embrace them if they consciously choose to do so. The important thing is to reveal that these conventional structures (1) are not inevitable or "necessary," (2) are the product of choice, (3) pose a persistent threat to human freedom (in the radical Sartrean sense), and (4) if adopted unwittingly in the "spirit of seriousness" can be barriers to authentic living.[94] In the interest of cultivating authenticity, business students, employees, and corporate leaders should all be encouraged to launch their own inquiry into sources of bad faith in the organization, conventional business practices, and so forth, and to reflect on how they choose to live their professional lives in the midst of them. A Sartrean orientation would presumably advocate that corporate systems become more sensitive to individual decision-making processes in the context of corporate life. Some trends, outlined in Table

Table 2.1   Changes in Corporate Structure

Shift from:	To:
Stability, predictability	Continuous change
Hierarchical structure	Flat structure
Domestic business	Global organization
Homogeneity	Diversity
Reward for tenure, loyalty	Reward for performance, skills
Rigid structure	Flexible workforce
Product driven	Client/customer driven
Company management of career	Comanagement of career
Loyalty to organization	Loyalty to self
One-time learning	Lifetime learning
Dependent employees	Self-reliant employees

2.1, are already pointing to fundamental changes in corporate structures that are generally harmonious with this recommendation.[95]

Consider, finally, whether the following alternative structures and practices might foster a Sartrean-inspired approach to business ethics:

- not even attempting to write a code, but instead striving to live ethically (for example, Housing Development Finance Corporation of Mumbai, India, consciously eschews written codes of ethics, not out of a belief that ethics is to be disregarded, but instead to avoid the "deadening effect" that codification often brings about);[96]
- encouraging questioning and creative attitudes toward moral choices that associates face in the workplace;
- cultivating sensitivity to the "situational" nature of moral issues;
- allowing for the exercise of individual autonomy within organizations; and
- promoting "democratic" elements of a workplace (for example, Internet, ESOPs, flextime).

In both capitalism and democracy, freedom is a prized and honored value.[97] Arguably, freedom is the central, driving force for efficiency and success in modern economic institutions.[98] This chapter has offered an explication of Sartre's notions about human freedom in an effort to show how such ideas might complement and improve, on the one hand, the standard virtue approach, and on the other hand, the conventional rule-based ethical approaches offered in mainstream business ethics scholarship. As well, the hope is that reflection on Sartre's ideas may serve to enhance ethical life in the business world. A Sartrean perspective on business ethics is most valuable not for providing technical or secure guidance in "solving" moral dilemmas, but rather for exposing otherwise hidden assumptions and beliefs about the nature of human character and freedom so that such assumptions and beliefs may be questioned and intuited in radically different ways.

Freedom and Its Relationship to Morality

In effect, Sartre's position is that we have, to borrow a phrase from Ronald Dworkin, "discretion in the strong sense," in making moral choices. But, the dual theses of the virtuosity-invisible law approach seem to be opposed to such a radical conception of freedom. Because, on the one hand, there is an objective human nature (in-built to pursue virtue and happiness) and because, on the other hand, there is an objective moral order (whose precepts consist of invisible law), our discretion—at least regarding moral choice—is not completely free and open-ended in the manner Sartre's view suggests. Granted we are free to decide, to choose whether to act in accord with the moral law. No one is positioned to compel us in this way; indeed our human dignity requires that we remain free to choose. Yet it does not follow from the fact that we are free, from according freedom a supreme existential status, that all choices are the same from a moral point of view. It is thus necessary to distinguish existential freedom from moral freedom. It does not follow from our existential freedom (even a radical freedom) that we have absolute moral freedom. Even in the face of "hard cases" or right-versus-right dilemmas, where the uncertainly of how the moral law might apply to the particular problem at hand, the intellectual virtue of phronēsis is there to assist us in decision making.

Placing the view of the ancients, that humans seek happiness according to their nature, alongside the existentialist view that humans are "condemned to be free," invites the further question: Can humans, of their own free will, choose not to want happiness? Although such a persistent philosophical issue as this cannot be definitively resolved to everyone's satisfaction and requires considerably more discussion than can be given for purposes of this book, I will direct a couple of reflections toward it here.

First, the natural inclination toward happiness flows from the heart of our being just as surely as the inclination toward freedom does. Indeed, the disposition for pursuing happiness stems from our free will in the sense that our will is not subject to any outside force or coercion. Second, I would refer to the interpretation given by Aquinas when he states:

> The natural necessity under which the will is said to will a thing of necessity—happiness, for instance—is not incompatible with free-will: but free-will is opposed to violence or compulsion. Now there is no violence or compulsion when a thing is moved in accordance with the order of its nature, but there is if its natural movement be hindered, as when a heavy body is prevented from moving down towards the centre. Hence the will naturally desires happiness, although it desires it necessarily.[99]

Aquinas's idea is that by desiring happiness, you are subject to a gravitational attraction of sorts. The center of the gravitational field is located within your own heart. However, there is no separate self having the power to control your disposition for happiness. Rather, the disposition itself forms an integral part of who you are in your authentic self. It is for this reason that it has been recognized as far back as Plato that no one can give an explanation for why they want to be happy. Consider this exchange between Diotima and Socrates in the *Symposium*:

D: If he who loves, loves the good, what is it then that he loves?
S: The possession of the good.
D: And what does he gain who possesses the good?
S: Happiness; there is less difficulty in answering that question.
D: Yes, the happy are made happy by the acquisition of good things. Nor is there any need to ask why a man desires happiness; the answer is already final.
S: You are right.
D: And is this wish and this desire common to all? And do all men always desire their own good, or only some mean? What do you say?
S: All men; the desire is common to all.[100]

I grant that the notion of having an inherent impulse of happiness, hard-wired into our human composition, appears difficult to reconcile with the existentialist idea that we are always free to choose otherwise. Yet I would reply to this existentialist claim that no matter how alluring the idea of absolute free choice may seem, we are not completely free to make ourselves happy, even when we appear to be choosing to be that way. That is, we cannot attain happiness simply by directly pursuing it. That accounts for why one of the features that accompanies happiness is the sense that somehow we ought to be grateful for it when we obtain such a state. Yet we do not sense that we should be grateful to ourselves; our awareness of being prompted by a sense of gratitude calls for acknowledging that we are recipients of a gift, just as we are aware that ultimately life itself is a gift. Much as we may like to think so, we did not create this world. The world did not begin with us. It was here long before we arrived, and it will remain long after we have left it. In this vein, we find a concurrence with Sartre's observation that human existence is gratuitous.

The artist's state of contemplation before her created work is connected to our contemplation as we stand before the world and comprehend it as something created. There is a reciprocal dynamic in play, since such an awareness itself becomes a source of artistic inspiration.

> Out of this kind of contemplation of the created world arise in never-ending wealth all true poetry and all real art, for it is the nature of poetry and art to be paean and praise heard above the wails of lamentation. No one who is not capable of such contemplation can grasp poetry in a poetic fashion, that is to say, in the only meaningful fashion. The indispensability, the vital function of the arts in man's life, consists above all in this: that through them contemplation of the created world is kept active and alive.[101]

Chapter 3

The Art of Business

My work in music helped my business and work in business helped my music.
—Charles Ives

IN BUSINESS, AS in music, virtuosity matters. To illustrate why it does matter, I ask you to consider two apparently dissimilar occurrences, reflecting on the ways they show an underlying similarity. To be clear, I offer the artistic metaphor of virtuosic business, not to denigrate musicians but to inspire businesspeople, encouraging them to meditate on what their vocation might look like were it conducted with the exacting self-imposed standards of excellence that guide musical artistry. The challenge is to craft a narrative for business and economic life that issues from a higher, more noble vantage point.

On the one hand, consider the dynamic at play when a virtuoso artist fails to deliver the outstanding performance his audience has come to expect. Normally, a sub-par performance leads the artist to suffer a momentary loss of honor and reputation, though in some circumstances it may be the deathblow to a career. This occurred when tenor Robert Alagna delivered a performance of *Aida* at La Scala that was met with hisses and jeers from an audience that deemed his singing of the opening aria in his role as Radames to fall short of their notoriously high standards of excellence.[1]

Consider, by contrast, the situation involved when a business leader or firm falls short of an anticipated level of virtuosic performance. In the wake of his handling of executive compensation practices, in light of questions raised about whether his firm properly disclosed information to both sides of trades on complex financial instruments (CDOs) that bundled mortgages, and in regard to suspicion about having assisted Greece in masking the extent of its debts,[2] Lloyd Blankfein, chairman and CEO of Goldman Sachs, was branded one of the "Most Outrageous CEOs" by *Forbes* magazine, and shortly thereafter his venerable firm was excoriated by the U.S. Financial Crisis Inquiry Commission.

Of course, making this comparison of music and business trades on two distinct senses of "virtuous" performance.[3] Critics will be quick to point out the many differences between inspired musical performance and enlightened business performance. For instance, the moral dimension, which I am seeking to showcase in my conception of the virtuous businessperson and firm, does not figure directly or prominently into one's assessment of a musician's virtuoso status.[4] Furthermore, there are differences between the respective purposes of music and business, different types of harm resulting from failure in each, not to mention the different ontological makeup of individual artists and business entities. At any rate, the differences are not, I maintain, as significant as may first appear, and we can learn a good deal by *looking past them* to fix our gaze on the intriguing ways in which the two cases are analogous. For instance, in both music and business there is a vital dependence on self-regulation and self-imposed standards of excellence. In both, mere "compliance" with rules is but the barest of minimal conditions. Alagna was not being faulted for any mere *technical* lapse in execution of "Celeste Aida." Nor were Blankfein and Goldman Sachs being cited, in regard to the moral dimension, for technical noncompliance with crisp legal directives. The moral critique of their performance delved deeper into matters of probity and character not readily captured in any bill of do's and don't's.[5] This chapter seeks to highlight such similarities in an effort to point to a higher path for business. That path is formed by the standards and state of the soul of the virtuoso.

Virtuosity in musical performance is about artistry. Although the cultivation of artistry demands consistent practice and fastidious attention to detail, artistry is not simply a matter of technical mastery of an instrument and execution of the right notes (though these are obviously important). Similarly, the virtuoso businessperson or company does not attain that status through any mechanical or technical achievement alone.

Conceptual Framework for Interfacing Music and Business

Remaining mindful of the obvious differences between music and business, let us now turn to a set of concepts to help draw out salient features the two callings share. The aim is to arrive at a fresh understanding of significant yet otherwise unnoticed moral characteristics of business through an examination of fundamental aspects of music. As will be seen, many of these aspects figure prominently into other creative human endeavors too, such as sculpture, architecture, painting, and other fine arts.

Praxis, Artis, Reinforcing Institutions, Goods, and Virtue

I propose that the concept of *praxis*, together with associated notions of *artes* (virtue-rich practices), reinforcing institutions, internal and external goods, and the vitalizing role that virtue performs within them, will assist in establishing a plausible congruence between musical virtuosity and its counterparts in the life of business, and so it is to an examination of these intertwined concepts that we now turn.

By *praxis* I mean the customary, creative, cooperative process through which an *artis*—that is, some theory, art, lesson, or skill—becomes enacted, embodied, or realized. Within this process, various goods (which may be tangible or intangible) that are internal to the particular kind of practice at hand are brought to fruition as a result of efforts to attain levels of excellence both tied to and partly constitutive of such an endeavor.

In this account of praxis I will highlight a cluster of five elements: (1) praxis involves social and cooperative human activities; (2) the creative human process is engaged; (3) the outcome of engagement in praxis is the achievement of internal goods appropriate to the particular artis, understood as goods identified with both the excellence of the products that result from the praxis (such as the excellence of a musical composition and the excellence of the musicians' performance of it), as well as the perfection of participants in the process of their production; (4) the relevant standards of excellence for the artis have been established historically by some community of practitioners; and (5) activities undertaken through praxis get transmitted and reshaped through traditions comprising successive rounds of internal debate about, among other things, their own standards of excellence.

Our participation in praxis can be quite complex. It may be simultaneously determinate yet indeterminate in the way that, say, Beethoven's Opus 13 ("Pathétique") piano sonata is: the composition is fixed by notes and markings in the score, yet amenable to being rendered in innumerable ways by its performers' variant interpretations of it. Likewise, a franchise business may embody a high level of determinacy (McDonald's restaurants are uniformly prescribed to have the French-fry cookers in the same location); even so, countless features are open to the discretion of the franchisee running an individual outfit. Moreover, involvement in praxis may be self-interested but at the same time community situated. It is not simply an object for detached investigation, nor is it merely a set of institutions. For both music and business, their lifeblood involves relationships based on the human practice of exchange, even though the substance of what is exchanged is much different in these respective endeavors. Nevertheless, both music and business involve an ongoing process of meaning and value creation. The wealth-promoting exchanges of business and the enrichment-giving exchanges of music are sustainable only to the extent that they activate the dynamic process of creativity and are embedded within multivalued communities.

Furthermore, praxis involves fundamental tensions between efficiency and creativity, which require a degree of artistry to balance successfully. Thus, on one side, efficiency is rooted in habit, convention, and continuity. Efficiency is reactive and based on the status quo; it involves a determinate process of calculation identifiable within a relatively static and closed environment. By contrast, creativity flows out of an environment of potentiality, discontinuity, and indeterminacy. Creativity involves a dynamic process of discovery and invention. It is proactive and continually evolving.

The phenomenon of praxis in the sense we are considering is all-pervading. Indeed we spend much of our lives in praxis-based activities, since they range from involvement in the arts and sciences to participation in sports and games, from the practice of politics in the broad Aristotelian sense to the maintenance and enjoyment of family life. Virtue plays a vital role across all of these undertakings since the deployment of virtue is the sine qua non for the achievement of the goods internal to such artes or virtue-laden creative practices.

Goods internal to praxis, however, are not the only kind of goods. We may contrast them with goods external to particular practices such as survival, power, profit, reputation, and success. External goods are often the objects of competition in which there are both winners and losers. With internal goods, however, although there is competition in one sense, this is competition to excel. As such, this kind of competition serves to benefit not just the "winners" but all the members of the community engaged in the practice, as is seen in the way that participation in music competitions improves the performance ability of all the contestants.[6]

In order for internal goods to be realized, the traditions and practices out of which they arise need to flourish. Usually, to accomplish this, reinforcing institutions involved with external goods play a crucial role. As Alasdair MacIntyre has noted, such supporting institutions typically deal with the acquisition of money and a range of material goods. Reinforcing institutions are configured by means of norms that establish authority and also by prestige, and such institutions allocate wealth, power, and status as recompense.[7] As well, such sustaining institutions play a key role as social transmitters of praxis-based activities.

Numerous examples of reinforcing institutions contributing to musical flourishing can be cited: orchestras, bands, and ensembles; teaching studios, music schools, and conservatories; churches and other houses of worship; agents, managers, and producers for concerts, recitals, gigs, and recordings; competitions, festivals; publishing houses, and other media for visual and audio dissemination; instrument manufacturers and craftspeople, and so on.

To be sure, this account of reinforcing institutions and their relationship with praxis can be applied to many diverse contexts, including not only music but productive arts, broadly construed, as well. Along these lines, one may regard the business organization as a peculiar sort of hybrid made up of, on the one hand, praxis and, on the other hand, a form of reinforcing institution affiliated with the praxis. A given artis might be blacksmithing, computer programming, soybean production, or graphic design, or it might involve producing pharmaceuticals, delivering on-line retailing, or providing financial services. What these artes have in common is that such practices fall within the scope of the aforementioned idea of praxis, and that in order to be sustained, the artes are typically institutionalized, to a greater or lesser extent.

Following this line of thought, we can turn our attention to business in an effort to identify various features of a virtuous organization, inquiring as what kinds of leadership responsibilities might ensure that these features exist and are fostered. The first requirement of a virtuous organization, in accordance with the Aristotelian orientation developed in Chapter 1, would be that there is a good purpose for the particular artis-institution fusion that it represents. Second, the institution would be aware that it is founded on and has as its most important function the sustenance of the particular practice that it houses, and following from this, the organization would encourage the pursuit of excellence in that endeavor whatever that may mean for the particular practice in question. Third, the institution would focus on external goods (such as survival, power, profit, reputation, or success) as both a necessary and worthwhile function of the organization, but only to the extent necessary to the sustenance and development of the practice. Finding the right balance between internal and external goods stands as an essential challenge for business organizations.

The Challenge of Integrity

There are two significant factors influencing the ability of a practice to cultivate and maintain its internal integrity. The first factor is what I will refer to as *lex artis* (law of the art or skill), meaning respect for the spirit and letter of rules and principles that help to guide the practice qua professional activity. The second factor concerns what is throughout this book termed *virtuosity*—the way in which virtue can be and is exercised in sustaining the institutional forms, which are the social transmitters of the artis. Accordingly, on the one hand, the integrity of an artis flows from an appropriate regard for *lex artis*, the relevant norms that make it hang together, along with the exercise of virtue by at least some of the participants who embody it in their activities. On the other hand, the corruption of institutions—as witnessed in corporate scandals and across the financial crisis—is typically attributable at least in part to violations of norms along with the proliferation of vice.

As such an analysis would lead one to expect, a failure to possess and exercise virtue along with a disregard for *lex artis*, ultimately leads to the inability of practices, whatever variety they may be, to retain their integrity, and hence to the demise of associated institutions that cease to foster the practice upon which they are based. Although an extended account of how this integrity-collapsing dynamic has played out in connection with the financial crisis will be provided later in Chapter 7, suffice it to say here that the crisis cannot plausibly be attributed solely to any lack of technical knowledge, but rather from inattention to, among other things, moral standards, themselves in a state of disarray from myriad social and philosophical dysfunctions within the wider culture.

We can build further on the music analogy. Horowitz's great artistic achievement came not simply from technical prowess, though his was enormous, but from the overall integrity he championed: his matchless taste and inclination for making correct judgment, his great reservoirs of passion and creative vision. On those rare occasions when he delivered a wrong note from the concert stage, it was understood by all but pianistic dullards or pedantic critics that such a technical blunder was a mere trifle, the unavoidable consequence of Horowitz pushing the envelope in the quest for the highest possible interpretation he was inspired to concoct.

Whether people are seated around the table of a corporate boardroom making decisions that carry moral import, or whether they are seated as players in a chamber orchestra, the center of gravity of their shared endeavor is excellence, the pursuit of the very best they can be as individuals and as a group, seeking a state of happiness, for themselves, and for those whose lives are touched by their art, in the deep sense expressed by ancient minds. Doing something well is profoundly more important than simply doing something.

During the past decade, the moral volatility of business has become manifest in striking ways. The global financial crisis has shown that virtuosity cannot be underrated regardless of how intricate the financial formulas may become. It would not be fair to say that the prior collapses of the dot.com firms, Enron, Adelphia, Parmalat, Tyco International, Arthur Andersen, and WorldCom were occasioned entirely by ruthless and evil individuals, but rather by financially savvy and technically adroit people who lost track of moral values in their pursuit of narrow economic objectives. Devoid of any robust appreciation for the moral and cultural significance of what they are *accomplishing* in their enterprises, there is a persistent danger that businesspeople may misapprehend the impact that their pursuits have on the broader culture. In due course they become detached from their own souls and the souls of their companies.

The Role of Virtue in the Market

A recent study shows that there is widespread distrust of the U.S. financial services industry, and that many people characterize that industry with terms such as "greedy," "opportunistic," "distant," and "impersonal."[8] But if we are going to count virtues as business assets, are there not situations where greater profitability comes from making a pretense of virtue rather than the authentic cultivation and exercise of it? As Groucho Marx famously quipped, "The secret of life is honesty and plain-dealing; if you can fake that, you've got it made." In fact, the inclination of market participants to imitate moral virtues such as honesty and generosity bespeaks the presumed competitive advantage that flows from acting virtuously. In the words of La Rochefoucauld, "Hypocrisy is the homage that vice pays to virtue."[9]

There is a moral disconnectedness both within business and within the wider culture. This decoupling arises from a self-understanding of business that has unwittingly abandoned the moral virtues in relation to economic life, together with their broader cultural underpinnings. Consequently, not only are people alienated from each other and from the deeper reality of economic life, but also they are divided even within their own selves.

For this reason, it is urgent to enter into a philosophically rigorous conversation regarding what being "good" and "successful" means in business and to clarify the virtues required for being a good businessperson. By entering into such a conversation, we start to discern specific illustrations of the good businessperson and the good business enterprise. At the same time, we begin to acquire a deeper and more comprehensive and accurate knowledge of what it means to generate wealth than what is provided in mainstream economic literature.

The conversation is aided by reflection on the profound significance of cultural capital, conceived of as an intangible moral resource necessary to develop the virtues for achieving excellence in business, whatever one's station. The virtuoso businessperson is not only a self-project of individual motivation and effort, but also the cultivation of her virtuosity ultimately depends on the culture—its institutions of family, education, and the arts—to provide the formation that fosters excellence.

In my advocacy for taking a broader moral-cultural approach in this chapter I am rejecting several extreme positions that still hold some currency among economists, academics, practicing businesspeople, and the general public. One extreme viewpoint is the proprietor-focused or shareholder-centered approach, which takes businesses to be amoral profit-machines whose primary function is to maximize profits for the owners of the enterprise. A second extreme view, which often teams up with the first, proceeds from a strong hypothesis about the free market, which maintains that ownership of property is exclusively a private, individual right and that the economy operates optimally when left to its own direction. (Against this position I endorse a weaker hypothesis: that the economy operates best when virtuous persons are running the enterprises, constrained by the objective moral order such that they respect human dignity and act in pursuit of the common good.) The third extreme view is the interventionist approach (an extreme version of the stakeholder model), which countenances forced redistributions of profits through excessive governmental intervention. All of these extremes are antithetical to the enlightened vision of business countenanced by the virtuosity ideal. We shall consider each of them in turn.

The Place of Profitability

In order to grasp how restrictive the first extreme view—the profit-maximization ideal—is, we will benefit from assuming an unconventional stance and looking at business as essentially a human enterprise. To aid in our reflections on what business is from the perspective of people, rather than from that of traditional economic models, we might pose the question, what's in it for us, the human community?

If you consider business in this way, you will find that deep down, the reason you work is that you are searching for a better, fulfilled life not only for yourself and your loved ones, but also for the community in which you live. And you will acknowledge that for this kind of betterment to come about, it is vital that you and anyone else working in a free-market economy have opportunities to willingly invest whatever talent, vigor, and know-how you each possess.

I believe that it is through precisely this dynamic of freely investing themselves, that a free people is guided, in Adam Smith's imagery, by an invisible hand toward prosperity and well-being. In this way, under conditions fostering human freedom, we expect that wealth will be created, not just in the short term but in a sustainable fashion. In this regard, Adam Smith's allusion to the invisible hand need not be taken to convey any mysterious process. To the contrary, it expresses the common-sense notion that by letting people pursue their self-interest, unintended yet favorable social outcomes will naturally ensue. In the course of seeking profit, people unwittingly contribute beneficial effects: increasing the overall wealth of society, facilitating technological innovation, fostering peace and civility, enabling workers to obtain more and improved jobs, and bringing inhabitants of different lands together to know and respect one another.

However, there is a fundamental malaise, recognized by thinkers such as Hayek, Röpke, Adam Smith, and many others, that comes from turning instinctively to governmental regulation over spontaneous approaches springing from our moral and cultural impulses as free people with a nature that inclines us to pursue excellence. A postulate repeated throughout this book is that the free market is healthiest when it operates within a culture that encourages and rewards people for making a wise, balanced exercise of their talents, their virtuosity. Such a market enables an assignment of values to occur without the interference of freedom-dampening government regulation. Ordinarily, wages operate as an adequate index for the value of various human abilities. Similarly, price functions as a suitable index for the scarcity and desirability of goods and services. Finally, profit serves as a dependable signal that some product or service carries social utility. So in a free market, people are able to arrange to put their capabilities to optimal effect and to earn and spend money so as to fetch the greatest net benefit. What this means is that people have an incentive to pursue what is worthwhile for themselves and beneficial for others with whom they are enmeshed in a complex web that involves relationships—some immediate and some remote—of both competition and reinforcement.

None of this is to say, as the first extreme view does, that all motivations underpinning markets are purely self-interested and that the invisible hand operates as a completely reliable check on individual rapacity. Adam Smith understood the dynamic according to which commercial life sprouts up from people being led by moral sentiments, by following the dictates of duty, responsibility, and justice.

Today's free-market economy represents one component of what may be termed the commercial society. The additional elements are private property, free exchange, democracy, and the rule of law. Taken together, these components provide a state of affairs within which individual initiative is fueled, engaging the creative capacities across the population so as to give those potentials the best chance to become ignited, express themselves, and lead to contentment and well-being.

Yet the profit motive is increasingly seen in the wider culture as the end-all-and-be-all of business, and the relentless pursuit of profit is often held up as a source of praise. As the saying goes, "The honor is in the dollar." But the concept of the "profit motive" has been distorted by exceedingly narrow economic models of the firm. The mind-set that sees markets as fueled entirely by self-interest, and that takes self-interest as the single-minded hunt for profit, is rooted in a fundamental misunderstanding about both "self-interest" and "profit maximization." We shall consider each of these concepts in turn and offer a more coherent account of them.

Self-interest

As Tocqueville observed in America, the same character and moral attentiveness that inspired patriotism contributed to the prominent place given to commerce. What he saw was an attitude of rational self-interest properly understood. According to this way of thinking, each person identifies their own self-interest with that of all in the society. When rightly understood, self-interest places people on a level above their narrow selfish preoccupations. As Tocqueville put it, "Every American has the sense to sacrifice some of his private interests to save the rest."[10] Although self-interest properly understood might not instantaneously manufacture virtue, it wields a discipline that "shapes a lot of orderly, temperate, moderate, careful, and self-controlled citizens."[11] Thus, from Tocqueville's vantage point, a person's rational concern for self gets joined to a broader sense of esteem for the various cultural, moral, and legal establishments that enable the wider population to follow their freely selected ambitions, principally through business enterprise. Tocqueville thought that America's peculiar mix of moral norms, cultural traditions, economic institutions, and jurisprudential arrangements could enable most people to enjoy prosperity. Any disturbances that might be caused by people's exercise of freedom tended to be offset by a framework of public order and stability.

Profit-maximization

A virtuoso company is a far cry from the stereotypical "profit machine." Even though it seeks to generate profit, the virtuoso company looks at profit along the lines that we view the air we breathe: of course everyone knows that we need it, but it's not the end-all-and-be-all of life. Writing about visionary companies, Collins and Porras state, "Profitability is a necessary condition for existence and a means to more important ends, but it is not the end in itself for many of the visionary companies. Profit is like oxygen, food, water, and blood for the body; they are not the *point* of life, but without them, there is no life."[12] Such companies embrace a "core ideology," or "vital shaping force," which might stem from their origins, as in the case of Sony; or, as with Merck, from a successive generation; or even remain quiescent to be revivified at some subsequent point, as occurred with Ford.[13] A virtuoso firm might have as its principal motivations professionalism, civic responsibility, and customer service, like the Housing Development Finance Corporation.[14] Its driving force could be "bedrock values" of personal accountability, respect for the individual, truth, and fair dealing, like the Sealed Air Corporation.[15] Or it may be spurred on by a commitment to integrity, fairness, fun, and social responsibility, as the AES Corporation is.[16]

There is an important connection between the existentialist idea of individual human authenticity that was explored earlier in Chapter 2 and what may be termed a *corporate existentialist* idea related to a firm's commitment to a core moral or social project. As with a human being, the organization must have an authentic commitment to its objectives, in a way that is true to its own character and internal nature as a moral agent that is free to choose. It cannot simply mimic the values of other firms, conform to external diktats, or smartly calculate which roster of values will likely prove to be the most lucrative, trendy, or well liked.[17]

No matter how a company articulates its mission, profit maximization normally is not listed as its objective. Instead, profit is a predictable and reliable side effect that arises in an indirect fashion from the company seeking other aspirations. To situate this thought within the real world of business, we can turn to the results of Collins and Porras's extensive study of companies noted for attaining exceptional long-term performance. Among their findings, the authors note a shattering of the myth that the companies achieving the highest degree of success owe their existence principally to the quest for profit maximization:

> Contrary to business school doctrine, "maximizing shareholder wealth" or "profit maximization" has not been the dominant driving force or primary objective through the history of the visionary companies. Visionary companies pursue a cluster of objectives, of which making money is only one—and not necessarily the primary one. Yes, they seek profits, but they're equally guided by a core ideology—core values and sense of purpose beyond just making money. Yet, paradoxically, the visionary companies make more money than the more purely profit-driven comparison companies.[18]

The idea here is clear-headed and insightful: narrowing in on profit alone makes an enterprise lose sight of its authentic mission.[19] Conversely, if a firm remains guided by its true objective, then profit is naturally produced in due course. An analogy to music will underscore and clarify the point. For a pianist who practices a difficult passage of a piece slowly and carefully, velocity will eventually come as an organic outcome of the performer's diligence, a natural result of the fingers having gained confidence in their movement from note to note. Attempting to play the passage too soon at top speed will prove counterproductive. In the same way, for the firm that narrowly pursues profit directly, in too hastily a fashion without regard for care in gaining the assurance of customers and other constituents that it is accomplishing its purpose, the effort is bound to backfire.

Collins and Porras demonstrate in their work how companies that elevate profit to the apex of their business plan, considering everything else as subordinate to it and deeming this to be the principal means by which to beat the competition, quickly forfeit whatever competitive advantage they may have been pursuing. Rather than "beating the competition," visionary companies,

> focus primarily on beating themselves. Success and beating competitors comes to the visionary companies not so much as the end goal, but as a residual *result* of relentlessly asking the question "How can we improve ourselves to do better tomorrow than we did today?" And they have asked this question day in and day out—as a disciplined way of life—in some cases for over 150 years. No matter how much they achieve—no matter how far in front of their competitors they pull—they never think they've done "good enough."

This countercompetitive dynamic triggered by a misplaced emphasis on attaining results rather than on cultivating excellence can also be seen in the case of institutions of higher learning. Consider, on the one hand, the university that is hell-bent on boosting its rankings directly, undermining its ultimate educational purpose in the process, as compared to the school that works hard at being an excellent institution for higher learning, knowing that if it achieves this objective, it will eventually attain recognition in the rankings.

The upshot of this discussion is that we see how the invisible hand celebrated by Adam Smith is more flexible, having a wider range of motion than is normally thought. The invisible hand can guide in not just one but two directions: social good gets generated as an unwitting consequence of businesses' quest for profit; as well, businesses' quest for social good generates profit as an unintended result. Economic and moral values are not at odds with one another but are instead complementary, in the sense that "yin" and "yang" are harmonizing forces in Eastern philosophy.

Essentially, these observations about loosening the grip on profit-maximization squares with the dynamic of detachment espoused by spiritual traditions from antiquity. As Deepak Chopra expresses it, "The Law of Detachment says that in order to acquire anything in the physical universe, you have to relinquish your attachment to it. This doesn't mean you give up the intention to create your desire. You don't give up the intention, and you don't give up the desire. You give up your attachment to the result."[20] These reflections help to illuminate the moral foundations of the free market, as well as the kind of resources on which it depends. Yet they draw our attention to an important intangible asset that is largely neglected by mainstream economics: cultural capital.

Cultural Capital

The concept of cultural capital refers to the reservoir of lively interrelations among people, along with mutual concern, shared understandings, common moral values, and trust. This intangible social asset solidifies affiliates of human communities and associations. It enables cooperative pursuits to materialize. Cultural capital lifts organizations and business communities higher, making them more than just a haphazard group of people each bent on advancing their respective private projects. The idea signifies the wherewithal required in running everyday dealings in public life. Those resources comprise *moeurs*, beliefs, customs, habits, and morals, that is, the multifarious traditions we learn from our parents that render us suitable participants in the social and economic order.

A number of questions arise. Are we equipping our children with what they need to cultivate their virtue and moral character? Are the moral messages we send them getting drowned out by signals they receive from mass media, the state, the advertising industry? Part of what makes for a good nation hinges on what gets handed down from generation to generation. As a matter of course material things (real property, financial assets, belongings) along with information and know-how get transferred to the next generation. However, such things taken alone are not sufficient to build virtuosity, to make one moral. It is essential to educate and mold our children in virtue. We must nurture the intellectual, emotional, philosophical, and social facets of our entire selves. It is imperative that we understand that even though we might be able to attain significant accomplishments in our careers, engineering IT platforms, designing business plans, recruiting clients, and amassing substantial fortunes, we might yet be falling down on one of the crucial challenges for our culture: bequeathing a moral tradition that inculcates virtue and good character in our children and adds to the stock of moral and cultural capital of our civilization.

The way we interpret the mutual influences that are exerted among our common culture, the regulatory authority of government, and the businesses that operate in the economy shapes the way we comprehend the virtuous businessperson and the virtuous company.

Let us now consider what I earlier referred to as the second extreme view, what we can call the *strong free-market premise*. It is founded on the belief that private property ownership is a basic individual right. Under this view the economy operates best when left to its own. Governmental intervention is seen to inhibit economic development in the long run. Legal regulation is seen to constrict growth and impose needless costs. Excessive regulation restricts the liberty of property owners to maximize their individual wealth. Accordingly, the government should limit its activities to the margin of the market to ensure fair and open competition. The goodness of business enterprises is ultimately indicated by the uptick in GDP.

However, granted that businesses may have the ability to generate wealth, the question remains: For what purpose? Considering, in light of financial engineering advancements, the momentous technical progress that can be achieved in constructing wealth, what remains unanswered is whether we are left any better than before. Of course, empirical data culled from balance sheets and revenue statements can indicate that a firm has generated greater wealth than the previous quarter. And technological innovation might raise its levels of productivity. But KPIs (key performance indicators) will not provide any indication of whether our character is improved, or whether we are in a state of overall well-being. The intricate issue regarding to what extent our creative drive guides us toward authentic human betterment cannot be completely comprehended from the perspective of a market devoid of moral-cultural capital. On its own, such a market gives no signals as to whether we are approaching greater alignment with our human nature. Considered apart from cultural capital, the economic system itself does not provide criteria for making judgments distinguishing between higher modes of human satisfaction, based on authentic needs, and lower modes that chase after fake needs and cripple our opportunities for genuine human fulfillment.

Beginning in approximately the 1970s, a paradigm shift began to take place involving a transition to what might be termed the government intervention model for the economy. The point of departure of this approach (and the transnational occurrence of it, which will be explored later in Chapter 8 in connection with the rise of CSR in global governance) is the alleged incapacity of corporations to police their negative externalities. Even though the interventionist approach (earlier designated the third extreme view) concedes the weight of private property rights, it views government as the key supervisory organ for the deployment of capital. Capital is basically a public good, and the firm is a quasi-public institution from the interventionist standpoint. Private ownership of business enterprises and of the capital deployed in commercial activities is seen as a privilege. The government's job is to devise regulations that take responsibility for numerous business activities out of the hands of business and away from the operation of market forces and to put them in the realm of policy. Social and economic policy is set forth by means of regulations covering banking, consumer protection, employment, the environment, land use, and so on. Under the interventionist mind-set, although market forces are seen as significant, the market must be guided and restricted, taking a back seat to governmental controls. This outlook assumes that powerful and pervasive corporations must be reined in with powerful correctives to provide for a fairer and more just economic order. According to such a standpoint, good business is an outcome of legal compliance, the contours of which are established by governmental authorities.

I believe that each extreme—the profit-maximization shareholder-centric view, the strong free-market premise, and the strong interventionist regime—must be rejected. In reaching some plausible appropriately nuanced alternative to them, it is vital not to downplay the influence culture carries in guiding the moral conduct of people in business.

Forming the core of my approach is a devotion to moral virtues developed within a culture, which have the ability to ripen the excellence of the whole person. Considered alone, neither the market nor the government can accomplish this. The virtuosity approach acknowledges that technical business competence and informed government policies, while imperative, cannot in and of themselves assemble a good company or a good business-person. The virtuosity approach, comprehended within a broader philosophical tradition that recognizes what I call *invisible law*—an objective moral order—understands that the wellsprings of goodness mainly flow out of culture and the institutions it inspires, not from markets or governments. Absent a morally fortified culture, the state inclines toward totalitarianism, while the market leans toward rampant careerism and crass consumerism. These points hearken back to the ancient wisdom that counsels, "Without vision, the people perish."[21]

The free market is the engine of economic advancement. To be sure, government is required to lay down rudimentary rules of the road. However, at the end of the day it is culture that formulates the point, the mission, and the final destination of the voyage.

Given the importance of culture, it would be a good idea to clarify what is meant by the term. As its root suggests, culture serves to inculcate a way of viewing the world, to perceive what is real, to bring sense to reality. Culture generates a feeling for what matters, what is deserving of sacrifice. Culture illuminates what we hold as sacred, guiding us to apprehend the deepest meaning extending back to our beginnings and ahead to the future. With the help of culture we can sift through data, opinions, and choices to arrive at what matters.

Human society is built on a foundation of cultural institutions. Family and education are two of the foremost institutions vital for economic society.[22] The central importance of family can be appreciated when we acknowledge that it comprises the primary component of human culture; family is the basic unit of society.[23] As for education, it cultivates an awareness of and sensitivity toward the world, inspiring a sense of wonder (for Aristotle, education is the origin of all knowledge), firing the imagination, and granting the moral vision necessary to enlighten scientific, technical, and commercial undertakings.

Philosophy, understood in its wider sapiential sense, along with religion, the arts, music, literature, and other humanities are at the center of culture. These endeavors are concerned with what is most precious and noble in our lives. These wellsprings of higher culture prompt us to engage the deeper significance of our world by pointing beyond the drab concerns of everyday things to what is more enduring, by directing us toward ultimate questions concerning our nature, our purpose, and our destiny. To be sure, there are also influences from mass culture such as television, the Internet, sports, and games. Yet compared to philosophical, religious, and artistic sources of inspiration, mass culture does not provide a rich enough soil for human flourishing to occur.

The reason for this stems from a dynamic that has been understood from antiquity: by drawing us back to our purpose, to our authentic nature, to our destiny, the higher forms of culture equip us to perceive the whole, not simply the fragments. Culture equips us to assimilate the totality of the cosmos and guides us to comprehend how we fit into it. We grasp the wholeness by being united with elemental cycles of our existence such as living, growing, dying, loving, and working so as to relate them in an organic unity instead of in a subdivided way. Hidden at the center of all cultures deserving of the name is a yearning to reunite what is detached.

In concrete terms, culture establishes a shared way of life that is informed by moral norms and values. Having its roots in tradition, it is infused in education, family, the arts, and humanities, providing a way for us to grasp reality as a meaningful whole. These cultural institutions help to implant in us a love of virtue and to point us toward the purpose for which we were made, the good life.

When considering the influence that cultural institutions wield on business, it is critical to be specific and concrete as opposed to exclusively universal and abstract. The reason is that cultural institutions derive their vitality from particular features of the communities out of which they grow. Instead of confronting head-on the skirmishes between cultural differences, many people are inclined to retreat up into the high country of highly abstract values that are sanitized of any specific cultural or religious reference. Such an approach typifies many theoretical approaches to business ethics, which attempt to lend moral guidance by assuming a "view from nowhere." Certainly, it is important to accommodate some measure of cultural relativity. Nevertheless it is equally crucial to bear in mind a fundamental insight. You become the best you can be when you are animated from the core of your being rather than from the margins of your being. To the extent that you veer away from the core in your daily life, you will be compromising your potential for excellence.

When we consider the landscape of cultural pluralism across the globe, it is tempting to think that the preferred way, or perhaps even the only way to conduct public discourse is to proceed from the standpoint of the least sophisticated level, that is, on the basis of that which is accepted by the widest mass of people rather than what is most rational. Certainly it is necessary to listen to a variety of viewpoints. Yet this mode of discourse seldom lets people get in touch with their innermost convictions and develop the virtues that are required to realize those convictions. The gulf that separates work and virtuosity engenders a kind of nihilism throughout much of today's business world, crossing all peoples and cultures. People toil away for the bulk of their lives in soulless organizations that drive on as if respect for persons does not matter, as if nothing in the tasks they undertake pertains to the pursuit of the good life and to timeless human values.

What is needed is a way of connecting one's vocation in business to an ethical outlook on commercial life. This would involve relinking:

· business life to a community of virtue;
· generation of goods and services to the end of human flourishing;
· allocation of wealth to the merits and needs of contributing stakeholders;
· private profit, private ownership, private risk, private initiative to the common good; and
· employment to the cultivation of excellence and pursuit of well-being in employees.

At its zenith, culture engenders a commercial order that civilizes the business world so as to promote the growth of virtuous enterprises, which in turn advances the common good.

We must not turn away from the promise of building authentic cultural capital in business in the name of the postmodern retreat from objective values and out of some absolute worship for diversity, pluralism, and tolerance. Placing an emphasis on virtue and the objective moral order supplies the mind-set and the vocabulary with which to approach this challenge. Straightforward conversation about the ways that cultural capital inspires and develops virtuous businesspeople can stimulate meaningful discourse across cultures. This, in turn, may engender harmony among them. Such a heightened degree of rapprochement between morality and business may promote more profound interactions among cultures around the world that will equip them to negotiate whatever thorny ideological divergences exist. Yet it is not plausible to believe that we impart moral wisdom to one another if we simply follow government laws and regulations or mimic technical financial methodologies. In truth, the profit-driven mind-set, collective laws and conventional practices, and the econometric worldview are all too constraining for the art of business to flourish.

The stock of cultural capital is too expansive and deeply entrenched to be reinvented generation by generation. It is a reservoir that has been steadily built up and refined over the long term. Through an extended evolutionary development involving both competition and cooperation, a corpus of customs, rules, and traditions emerges as a kind of spontaneous spin-off from the invisible hand. Out of the same freedom that animates the free market blossoms the cultural capital necessary to sustain the vibrancy of that market. As with financial capital, a business can build up reserves of cultural capital. It can accumulate this asset by helping to establish relationships of accountability, commitment, fair dealing, goodwill, mutual respect, and trust, and in the process, by helping people to direct their respective talents toward a shared venture.

The notion of cultural capital provides a means of explanation for why the so-called profit motive is best interpreted as something broader than a relentless quest for profit maximization. Most of what is needed to create profit is attainable only through the cultivation and deployment of cultural capital. And although this type of intangible capital is not amenable to being reduced to a specific item on the balance sheet, it nevertheless contains value as a path to enhancing the bottom line. Therefore, the idea of cultural capital should be brought within the orbit of economic thinking. A business can invest in cultural capital in much the same way that it can invest in reputational capital, human capital, or other types of capital. Likewise, a business can draw upon cultural capital just as it can draw upon these other forms. Yet accomplishing this involves adopting a nontraditional style of management, one which is as vital in business as in day-to-day living, even though it has tended to elude economic understanding: the sapiential management of intrinsically valuable human goods, in particular faith and trust.

Faith and Trust

A well-known irony accompanies the way virtues operate. If I place my trust in another person without thinking about any long-range benefit it may produce, I may thereby be producing a long-range benefit, that is, a lasting and trustworthy friendship. You might be generous because you feel touched by seeing someone suffering a hardship. You want to help them. But suppose you begin to calculate how your assistance might burnish your reputation. You start thinking about how indebted they are going to be to you now. Suddenly, your motives have switched. It's not generosity anymore.

A similar oddity comes about in connection with religious faith. Why should you believe in God? Is it to gain eternal life? If your faith in God is based on your expectation of salvation, of gaining some reward for that faith, then it seems like something short of real faith. But why have faith if there is no assurance of some benefit coming of it? Kierkegaard thought that we ought to have faith in God, to make a "leap of faith," even if that appears absurd from the standpoint of our reason. Stated otherwise, reason occupies no place in faith, for God is beyond reason.

I do not extend my trust to you looking to gain something in return. And yet I receive something. By giving my trust, I am hopeful that I will enjoy more and better opportunities than I could ever hope to secure by withholding my trust from you. It is only by trusting you that I can become your friend, and our friendship is in danger of vanishing the moment you perceive that I have been calculating, that I have extended my trust only to secure some advantage from you. Ironically, we extend our trust because it is simply right that we do so. But at the same time, we are most apt to obtain what is in our own interest from giving trust and getting trust in return. In its most authentic form, trust is a kind of faith, and it is mainly aimed at establishing upright relationships, whether they are relationships with others, or with the world at large. But as an expression of faith, trust in this sense requires a relinquishment of self-advantage both in the short-term and in the long run. If trust and faith are motivated mainly by personal advantage, sooner or later both are doomed to fail.

While these meditations matter for their own sake, they also matter so far as market interactions and the economy goes. The commercial advantages obtained from the artful deployment of faith and trust in building relationships with people are objectively real and are of paramount importance to any enterprise. However, their benefits come about through the operation of an invisible hand—as a product of conduct undertaken with an utterly separate target in mind. Through the exercise of virtue, trust and faith can be established; out of this dynamic, businesspeople and the companies they work in build an invisible asset: moral capital. They accomplish this, however, not by seeking to secure the financial benefits of this intangible asset directly, but rather by pursuing other aims, albeit while maintaining an eye on their own financial success.

As our earlier reflections about how extensions of faith and trust figure into the cultivation of authentic relationships suggest, keeping in mind a good result that might flow from pursuing your aim, while not making that the goal itself is something of an art. To analogize, the concert pianist who has attained great success in her career—sold-out concerts wherever she tours—has done so not by devoting her attention directly and exclusively to that goal, but rather by focusing her intentions on other goals: playing her instrument well, building a solid repertoire, maintaining disciplined practice, being the best she can be with the talent she was given. When all of those things are in place, her recognition and the success that accompanies it follow as natural by-products.

We see this dynamic at work in the motivation for virtuous conduct as well. The virtue of courage can help bring about good results. When you have courage, you are poised to go after what you want. However, as a courageous person, getting what you want is not your main motivation. After all, a cowardly person is also motivated to get what he wants. What sets you, the courageous person, apart from the coward is that you view your behavior as an external observer would survey it. Adam Smith refers to this as the point of view of the impartial spectator. You carry a sense of pride by acting courageously. You believe that your sense of responsibility and a due regard for your reputation and honor warrant assuming a risk. As a result of viewing your behavior in this way, as seeing that it is the morally correct action to take, independent of the concern for simply getting what you want, you gain recompense.

The inability, or persistent unwillingness, to apprehend this dynamic leads to profound misunderstanding and confusion concerning the profit motive. The assumption underlying mainstream economics is that a business seeks to turn a profit; within the market system, the profit-seeking efforts of many enterprises synchronize their behavior to attain a balance. However, in declining to scrutinize real motivations of human beings making up the businesses, the neoclassical synthesis fails to supply any adequate account of the manner in which the profit motive actually arises within people. Accordingly, for some, it appears as if the entire economic order is based on the pursuit of cold-blooded selfishness.

Yet Adam Smith delivers a much different interpretation in *The Theory of Moral Sentiments*. Competition within a free market is accompanied by a multitude of moral concerns, among them benevolence, sympathy, and the stance of the impartial spectator (the counterpart of which may be found throughout the legal tradition as the "reasonable person"). All these characteristics flow directly from the wellsprings of human nature. Thus moral considerations temper the otherwise ruthless pursuit of profit. What appears from one standpoint to be a savage quest for self-gain might be, from an alternative interpretive standpoint, a manifestation of benevolence.[24] Human motivations are typically multidimensional and highly nuanced. Sometimes the best means of attaining an objective is by disregarding it, rather than attempting to go straight to it. (That is what Bertrand Russell said about the pursuit of happiness in life.) You may find that in business, your greatest profit results when you set aside financial yield in order to follow the dictates of respect, kindheartedness, or benevolence. This view was seen in the conduct of Merck & Company, which gained widespread recognition for its commitment to social responsibility during the 1980s. The company made its drug for "river blindness"—a parasitic infection common in tropical regions and afflicting eighteen million individuals—available at no charge. In 1987, Merck shared its findings regarding treatment of human immunodeficiency virus (HIV) with its business competitors. The business justification for such efforts can be traced back to the philosophy of its founder, George W. Merck, who expressed his vision for the company as follows: "I want to . . . express the principles which we in our company have endeavored to live up to. . . . Here is how it sums up: We try to remember that medicine is for the patient. We try never to forget that medicine is for the people. It is not for the profits. The profits follow, and if we have remembered that, they have never failed to appear. The better we have remembered it, the larger they have been."[25] Reflecting on these sorts of concerns provides a strong impetus for rejecting the extreme view about the place of profit-maximization in the free market. The fruits of the free-market economy come about only within a framework of cultural norms and moral values, and when a steady eye on profitability is maintained, yet practically never held out as the primary motivation for doing business.

Aristotle held that happiness arises out of virtue. However, if you are a virtuous person you are not aiming directly at happiness. Instead, your motivation for everything you do is to attain something else: honor, rectitude, nobility. As we saw in our earlier discussion in Chapter 1, for Aristotle, happiness does not arise from ephemeral feelings of pleasure experienced alike by self-centered and altruistic persons. Happiness is tied to an established state of satisfaction with who you are, your plight, and your relationship with others and the world. Human well-being is not situated in any

Table 3.1   The Moral and Economic Value of Virtue

Virtue	Moral Value	Economic Value
Civility	Treating others with respect, courtesy, and politeness; due regard for respecting cultural differences	Success in business typically requires treating people with courtesy and respect. After all, customers and clients are free to take their business someplace else. Also civility increases the efficacy of communication.
Sympathy	Capacity to understand the emotions and feelings of other people	Success requires understanding the needs of customers as well as employees
Justice	Inclination to act equitably	Treating small matters fairly will engender heightened degree of trust in business relations over the long run
Gratitude	Inclination to show appreciation for assistance, benefits, and gifts received from others	Shows that people are not capable of attaining success only through their own efforts, but require the assistance of others
Trustworthiness	Disposition to be consistently dependable	Removes necessity for excessive oversight of contractual compliance, reducing agency costs
Honesty	Inclination to tell the truth	Reduces occurrence of fraud and deception, leading to greater degree of trust
Temperance	Self-discipline; tendency to avoid immediate gratification for long-range achievement	Engenders sustainable growth and long-term stability
Courage	Disposition to assume appropriate level of risk, avoiding rashness on the one hand, and timidity on the other; elevation of concern for common good over narrow regard for self-preservation	Inspires confidence and trust among others in leadership ability
Humility	Tendency to be humble; not seeking recognition or credit; willingness to admit mistakes and assume blame	Prevents expectations from becoming over elevated; inhibits being placed under the spotlight so that when mistakes are made, even trivial ones, one becomes vulnerable to attack, thus threatening reputational assets

Table 3.1   The Moral and Economic Value of Virtue (continued)

Virtue	Moral Value	Economic Value
Friendliness	Treating people equally with the thought of good in mind; passing along one's own happiness to others	Creates incentives for others to make initial approaches, opening the door for entry into transactions and establishes a willingness to cooperate
Generosity	Reaching the right balance between the extremes of miserliness and prodigality	The giving, philanthropically minded businessperson or firm is seen as a genuine leader, which inclines business partners to extend their trust

particular set of experiences you are having. Rather it inheres in the state within which you are flourishing in line with your nature, the way that a sunflower blossoms in the sun and a dolphin thrives in the open sea. In order to ensure that a child will be capable of exercising control over his or her life, to be assured in his or her choices, and to earn respect from others, we give him or her guidance in developing wisdom, temperance, courage, and a sense of justice. Such is the route toward human well-being. It is the same route as that toward enduring success in business.

Table 3.1 illustrates some of the ways various virtues bring advantages in the business context.

An important point needs to be stressed. As should be clear from the analysis given in this chapter, by indicating that there is a connection between virtuous conduct and market benefits, I am not in any way suggesting that virtue be taken to be something of instrumental value only. Virtue must first of all be valued for its own sake to maintain authenticity.

Exemplars of Virtuosity

In both music and business there is a reciprocal input-output relationship between cultural assets and the creative fruits that emerge from them. That is, cultural resources are initially drawn on and then reproduced in return. On the one hand, it takes cultural backing, knowledge, institutions, and traditions to give rise to composers who can write beautiful music, performers who can give life to it, and teachers who can pass on our collective musical heritage. By contrast, by

Table 3.2   Exemplars of Virtuosity in Music and Business

Virtuosity in Music	Virtuosity in Business	Characteristics
Compositional: J. S. Bach engages invisible laws of harmony within a particular historical and doctrinal context (Baroque-era system of tonality).	Entrepreneurial: envisioning a new business model; a blueprint. Bill Gates, Steve Jobs, Mohammed Yunus (social entrepreneurship)	Creativity, vision, confidence, trend-setting
Improvisational: J. S. Bach, as a master improvisator, is able to extemporaneously create complex contrapuntal renditions.	Strategic: Mark McNeilly's *Sun Tzu and the Art of Business*	Resourcefulness, courage, flexibility, adaptability, preparedness
Performative: J. S. Bach is one of the greatest organists of his time. (Clementi vs. Mozart; Liszt vs. others; Tchaikovsky and Chopin piano competitions).	Administrative skill: excellence in putting a plan into action; being detail-oriented and efficient; delivering results; evidenced in the concept of "performance-based" bonuses	Competitive instinct; "practice, practice, practice"; ability to learn from mistakes; greatly exceeding technical mastery; not simply mechanical but artistic
Directive: J. S. Bach is director of the Collegium Musicum.[27]	Executive talent: According to Alan Keith of Genentech, "Leadership is ultimately about creating a way for people to contribute to making something extraordinary happen"	Helping others to be the best they can be

creating and performing beautiful music, our common cultural resources are in turn replenished. When operating at its best, the same dynamic occurs in business. For instance, the existence of a talented, well-educated workforce assists companies in providing quality goods and services and in being innovative.

It is instructive to consider commonalities between virtuosity-in-music and virtuosity-in-business. The comparison should not be too surprising. After all, music in many respects owes its existence to business (we speak of "the music business") and like music, business (at least considered in its most positive aspects)[26] is sometimes capable of providing enrichment, bringing a sense of purpose and meaning, and importing beauty in people's lives.

Accordingly, Table 3.2 above highlights common threads of human excellence in music and business. In distinguishing the various exemplars of virtuosity, I do not mean to suggest that these exemplars are isolated from one another in practice. To the contrary, these forms reinforce one another. And virtuoso businesspeople as well as virtuoso musicians often embody more than one or even all of them.

Interlude: Meditations on Time and Virtuosity

Virtuosity is performance in time.

*   *   *

In both music and business, achieving excellence is linked to the temporal dimension. Music is architecture in time. And in business, as the saying goes, time is money.

*   *   *

Time is not everything, but it matters.

*   *   *

Much unethical conduct stems from short-term outlooks and pressure to produce quick results. At the same time, due to its competitive nature, business rewards first movers and fast-paced decisions and quick results.

*   *   *

In music as well virtuoso performance is often linked to velocity. Speed matters (especially for pieces marked "presto"), yet as with everything in music it is a question of balance.

*   *   *

Philosophical or artistic contemplation invokes a sense of timelessness. We do not suppose there is any special benefit from rapid contemplation (which just sounds wrong-headed), although we do treasure precious flashes of insight, where all at once we gain insight or understanding.

*   *   *

Of special interest is to consider how rapidly some composers created timeless masterworks. J. S. Bach composed the cantata *Preise dein Glück, gesegnetes Sachsen* (BWV 215) in no more than three days. Here are Bach scholar Stephen Crist's reflections on it:

> Although we have known for nearly forty years that Bach wrote the majority of his cantatas at the rate of one per week, his amazing facility as a composer has not yet fully penetrated our picture of his genius. Perhaps the consistently high quality of his music has misled us into thinking that it could not have been composed quickly. But an examination of the evidence surrounding the composition of Cantata 215 has demonstrated that Bach was able to create an enduring work of art almost as quickly as he could move his pen.[28]

*   *   *

Many employees are paid by the hour. Bach was given fifty thalers as an honorarium for composing Cantata 215.[29]

*   *   *

There is something about witnessing a phenomenal display of speed in executing a musical piece that seems almost otherworldly, as if the super-speed invokes an entirely separate dimension beyond our familiar existence in ordinary time and space—pointing us perhaps to the eternal.

*   *   *

Music creates its own imaginary space that the mind comprehends through sound being sculpted in time. And in analogous fashion, business innovation creates its own "space," as when a business model envisions the design of temporal and spatial enterprises that will be called into existence, propagating itself as a physical reality according to the design of its entrepreneurial "creators." In this sense, Henry Ford, Bill Gates, and Steve Jobs are "composers" working in a medium, no less than the one their musical counterparts use, which depends on virtuoso performers to realize their imaginative masterpieces.

Personifications of Virtuosity

We need not strain too hard in linking virtuosity in music and business. History provides instances of individuals embodying twin gifts of musical genius and exemplary business acumen. Such cases abound, stretching from Haydn contemporary Johann Tost (an accomplished Hungarian violinist as well as respected wholesale cloth merchant),[30] up to jazz artist Kenny G of the present (who studied accounting at the University of Washington while performing his saxophone by night).[31] I shall showcase here two especially intriguing music-business masterminds: Muzio Clementi and Charles Ives.

Muzio Clementi

Apart from his prominence as a composer and virtuoso pianist, Muzio Clementi was also a highly successful entrepreneur, a fact that may come as a surprise to many unfamiliar with the extent of his extramusical exploits. Born in 1752, four years before Mozart, Clementi began his musical career as a child prodigy, playing both harpsichord and the organ with great virtuosity. As a teenager, he practiced and experimented relentlessly, developing a bold and brilliant technique, with an impressive legato style. He played rapid octaves and often composed passages in his signature style of thirds and sixths. Ignatz Moscheles, a conductor, composer, and himself one of the greatest piano players in history, wrote, "Clementi's pianoforte playing, when he was young, was famed for the exquisite legato, pearliness of touch in rapid passages, and unerring certainty of execution. Even now the remains of these qualities were recognized and admired, but what chiefly delighted his audience was the charm and freshness of his modulations in improvisation."[32] Clementi countered Mozart in a pianistic duel on December 24, 1781, in front of Viennese Emperor Joseph II and his guests. Clementi opened with an extemporaneous prelude, followed by his own *Sonata in B-Flat Major* (Op. 24, No. 2) and then a toccata showcasing his trademark double-notes. His contender Mozart followed with an improvised prelude and a sequence of variations. Music critic Harold Schonberg dramatically recounts what transpired next:

> The Grand Duchess produced some sonatas of Paisiello ("wretchedly written out in his own hand," later complained Mozart), and both pianists read them off at sight, Mozart playing the allegros, Clementi the adagios and rondos. Both were asked to select a theme from one of these sonatas, developing it on two pianos. Presumably Mozart would have taken a theme and played it, Clementi noting the harmonies. Then Clementi would have accompanied Mozart on the second piano while Mozart developed his material. And vice versa. It probably ended with a grand two-piano splash, in which all the melodic fragments were woven together.[33]

Clementi's technical skill turned out to be equal if not superior to that of his rival, who nevertheless infinitely surpassed him by the passionate beauty of his interpretation. The emperor called the match a draw.[34]

After the event, Mozart intimated his impressions of Clementi's playing in a letter to his father: "He has great facility with his right hand. His star passages are thirds. Apart from that, he has not a farthing's worth of feeling; he is a mere *mechanicus*."[35] Clementi's impressions of Mozart, by contrast, were enthusiastic and filled with praise for Mozart's fine taste and singing touch.[36] Later on, Clementi's student Ludwig Berger recalled, "Until then I had never heard anyone play with such spirit and grace. I was particularly overwhelmed by an adagio and by several of his extempore variations for which the Emperor had chosen the theme."[37]

The main theme of Clementi's *Sonata in B-Flat Major* captured Mozart's imagination. Ten years later, in 1791, Mozart incorporated it in the overture to his opera *Die Zauberflöte* (*The Magic Flute*). This so embittered Clementi that every time this sonata was published, he made certain that it included a note explaining that it had been written ten years before Mozart began writing *Zauberflöte*. Clementi's admiration for Mozart, obviously not reciprocated, was reflected in a large number of transcriptions he made of Mozart's music, among which is a piano solo version of the "Zauberflöte" overture.

The business side of Clementi's life began to take root in England, where he entered the business of crafting pianofortes. First, he acquired shares in the pianoforte business of a firm that had gone bankrupt in 1800. He then established a pianoforte and music business of his own, under the name Clementi & Company. In the course of running this firm he dramatically improved the art of piano building. Clementi was a music publisher as well, and he brought to the public a stream of new publications, including much of his own music. As a piano teacher, Clementi produced important pianists, including John Field, composer of the famous *Nocturnes*, as well as Johann Baptist Cramer, a friend of Beethoven's who also became a successful music publisher and instrument manufacturer.

Clementi helped to establish respect for the musician and also for music teaching, a profession that at the time was considered neither respectable nor gentlemanly. Franz Joseph Haydn and other master musicians, for instance, were accorded a status not much higher than that of servants. Clementi's enlarged view of piano technique was codified in his 1817 magnum opus, *Gradus ad Parnassum,* a set of one hundred pieces including etudes, slow movements, fugues, and canons. Clementi's pianism was still of the Classical period, but his work in many ways presaged what the piano would eventually be required to perform.

Beethoven was deeply indebted to the Clementi sonatas and is said to have kept his volume of them always at hand. Brahms, too, admired Clementi's adventurousness and freedom of form. From the pianist view, Clementi's etudes formed the foundation for the future of etude writing, culminating in the Chopin etudes. It is worth noting that Chopin's pupils were not permitted to even come close to their teacher's own etudes unless they already had gained a solid grasp of Clementi's.

Clementi maintained extensive contacts with European publishers and instrument sellers, including Artaria, Breitkopf & Härtel, Erard, Naderman, Nägeli, Pleyel, Ricordi, and Streicher. Clementi was held in great esteem among musicians all over Europe, including Haydn, Dussek, Beethoven,

Bomtempo, Himmel, Righini, and Nezot. He was adroit at making use of his reputation as a musician to strengthen his business dealings.

In summary, Clementi was an intelligent and cultured person. Not only was he an energetic musician at the heart of the development of European musical institutions, but also he prospered as an extremely astute and well-respected businessman.

Charles Ives

With a reputation as one of America's most significant composers, of particular interest is the way Ives's music is far ahead of his time. Although conceived back at the start of the twentieth century, his pieces already embody elements emerging decades later: polytonality, free atonality, preserialism, spatial music, music with microintervals, chance and collage effects, polyrhythm, polymeters, and polytempi. One of his most forward-looking works, the *Universe Symphony*, heralds "sound mass" composition, employed by György Ligeti and Krzysztof Penderecki in the 1950s and 1960s. In other ways, the symphony anticipates spectralist composition (which seeks a deep structure of sound embodied in its harmonic spectrum) of Tristan Murail and Edgard Varèse, which emerged in the 1960s and 1970s.

By studying the various biographical portraits that have been rendered of Ives,[38] one can discern an underlying philosophy connecting Ives's musical vision and his career in business. This philosophy is based on a quest for authenticity and integrity. It also flows from the pursuit of community and the values that sustain and enrich it.

Also strangely ahead of its time in the sense that it almost foreshadows some aspects of the financial scandals of recent vintage was a wave of malfeasances in the insurance industry within which Ives was building his business career. Insurance profits were being channeled into various kinds of clandestine speculation, while the "big three" insurance firms (Mutual, Equitable, and New York Life) controlled many of their own banks and trusts. Consequently investors were led to unknowingly assume risks flowing from the insurance business. In response to the rash of corruption and widespread abuses in the insurance industry, a committee established by New York's state legislator and chaired by Senator William Armstrong targeted the nature and amount of compensation for insurance agents and agencies. In the wake of the investigation, New York State ended up adopting the strongest regulations in the United States.

There is no evidence implicating Ives himself in any illegal or unethical business conduct. However, since his work inside the insurance industry under scrutiny made him close enough to feel the heat, during the time surrounding the investigation Ives changed both artistically and personally. He suffered health complications. His business career nearly collapsed, yet he steered it in innovative directions that enabled it to flourish in new and unanticipated ways. Meanwhile his compositional style changed radically.

After a compositional hiatus in 1905, perhaps occasioned by anxieties arising from the Armstrong investigation, Ives devoted himself to writing exceptionally original and experimental works. Many of his pieces raise fundamental questions concerning the nature of music, while at the same time testing its stylistic and structural limits. His philosophical questioning pervades many of these compositions. For instance, Ives's *The Unanswered Question* probes a philosophical point similar to one raised by Rilke when the poet stressed the existential importance of learning to "love the questions."[39] In the background a whispering string chorale evokes, in Ives's terms, "the silence of the Druids." Piercing this muted backdrop a trumpet repeatedly states, in Ives's words, "the perennial question of existence." Responding to each question, a quartet of winds that Ives dubbed the "fighting answerers" scrambles to put together a reply. Yet the ensemble turns increasingly agitated to the point of blurting out a seething and incoherent rant. At the end, the trumpet raises the question once more, answered by a hushed fade-out into silence.

While in the midst of the Congressional investigation Ives may have tried to escape into his inner world of musical creation, but he was not able to avoid the business world he was immersed in, nor could he ignore the moral questions that accompanied it. He needed to come to grips with the insurance world from both philosophical and financial standpoints. As the Armstrong investigation unfolded, Ives could find an answer to at least the moral questions being raised. Thus, according to testimony given by Richard McCurdy, president of Mutual Life, although life insurance as practiced by mutual companies was actually a philanthropic and eleemosynary undertaking that served to benefit humanity at large, it was misunderstood as a crass and narrow moneymaking pursuit: "Every person ought to understand that when he takes a policy of life insurance that he is not doing it solely for his own benefit, but he is participating in a great movement for the benefit of humanity at large and for every other person who comes in and takes a policy in that company, and in that way joins the great brotherhood."[40] According to Michael Broyles, that statement "is an almost exact statement of the beliefs that would guide Ives's work in the insurance industry and by extension become part of his overall philosophy."[41]

In his personal life Ives was a religious believer, and he also kept faith in the redemptive capacity of art. He was ultimately seeking, he wrote, a "vision higher and deeper than art itself."[42] Ives believed that, according to an invisible law the human spirit evolves along with the rest of nature, toward perfection.[43] This idea is prevalent both in his writing about his music and in business literature he produced as a practical guide to selling insurance. For instance, in a how-to sales publication *The Amount to Carry—Measuring the Prospect*, Ives writes, "There is an innate quality in human nature which gives man the power to sense the deeper causes, or at least to be conscious that there are organic and primal laws (or whatever you care to call the fundamental values of existence) underlying all progress. Especially this is so in the social, economic, and other essential relations between men."[44]

Much of Ives's vision remains prescient and vital. Especially in a time when many seem to resist the idea that music, not to mention business, ought to have depth and substance, it's worth recalling how much Ives believed in the moral and spiritual importance of both endeavors. As Ives scholar Jan Swafford notes, "It is no accident that his phrase 'human life values' means at once the cash value of a person's life and labor, and the humanistic and spiritual values people live by."[45]

A founding partner of Ives and Myrick, the preeminent insurance agency of its time, he was not a conventional boss. His employees recalled Ives as an unforgettable figure who, in a shy and retiring way, was able to galvanize them with his ideals. "When [Ives] talked with someone," recollected one employee, "he elevated them. . . . It's very hard to describe, but he made everyone feel important." He taught his employees that "there was not a service that I could render to my fellow man that was more important than the business of life insurance, because it instilled in the soul and mind of my fellow man the responsibility of meeting his obligations."[46]

To Ives, community originates with family and expands outward to towns, countries, the insured, the globe, the universe. Business was the fount of many of his artistic and spiritual ideals. As he studied actuarial science, which entails calculating risks and generating premium schedules that predict mortality probabilities over the long run, he was prompted to view human life in large terms, from the vantage point of masses of people progressing from birth to death.[47]

He left the Mutual Insurance Company in 1906 to form his own insurance firm, Ives and Company, which three years later became Ives and Myrick. The company prospered, growing into one of the largest agencies of its kind. As senior partner, Ives was proud of his business success, feeling that experience contributed something important to the music he was composing, and vice versa. Here is how Ives expressed it, in terms that vividly encapsulate a number of insights explored in the present chapter and throughout this book:

> My business experience revealed life to me in many aspects that I might otherwise have missed. In it one sees tragedy, nobility, meanness, high aims, low aims, brave hopes, faint hopes, great ideals, no ideals, and one is able to watch these work inevitable destiny. And it has seemed to me that the finer sides of these traits were not only in the majority but in the ascendancy. I have seen men fight honorably and to a finish, solely for a matter of conviction or a principle—and where expediency, probable loss of business, prestige, or position had no part and threats no effect. It is my impression that there is more open-mindedness and willingness to examine carefully the premises underlying a new or unfamiliar thing, in the world of business than in the world of music.
>
> It is not even uncommon in business intercourse to sense a reflection of a philosophy . . . akin to a strong sense of beauty in art. To assume that business is a material process, and only that, is to undervalue the average mind and heart. To an insurance man there *is* an "average man" and he is humanity.
>
> I have experienced a great fullness of life in business. The fabric of existence weaves itself whole. You cannot set an art off in the corner and hope for it to have vitality, reality and substance. There can be nothing *exclusive* about a substantial art. It comes directly out of the heart of experience of life and thinking about life and living life. My work in music helped my business and work in business helped my music.[48]

Finale

If one is seeking to draw a lesson from this chapter perhaps it is this: the best way to prepare for achievement in business is by cultivating virtues, by exercising discipline in yourself. The virtuoso businessperson, no less than the virtuoso artist, is one who loves excellence and pursues it passionately. She will seek to become properly trained, not just technically but in accord with deeper intellectual and professional promptings. Such an individual will make up her own mind, in authentic freedom, concerning the kind of moral environment in which she and her firm will move.

Virtues are dispositions that assist you in assuming risks, in making judgments, in taking ownership of your conduct, and in recognizing and appreciating sage counsel. The moral virtues constitute a vital portion of our ethical capital. However, drawing on this stock of moral-cultural resources is not something you can accomplish entirely from your own effort and initiative, since it is rooted in our shared cultural legacy. Since we are social animals, we can achieve virtue and its attendant well-being only by playing our social roles well.

That is the true art of business.

Chapter 4

Trust, Personhood, and the Soul of an Enterprise

Can a building have moral opinions? Can a building have social responsibility? If a building can't have responsibility what does it mean to say that a corporation can? A corporation is simply an artificial legal structure.
—Milton Friedman

WE NOW TURN our attention to two interwoven relationships. The first concerns the way moral virtue and character of individual businesspersons—flesh-and-blood human beings—relate to virtue and character of business enterprises, assuming such enterprises are even capable of displaying such moral features. Addressing this relationship raises several difficult questions: Are corporations moral persons in some sense? Can they, like humans, display virtues and vices? Do corporations have a distinctive and authentic character? Are they, as artificial legal entities, the kind of things that are worthy of receiving our trust?

The second relationship concerns how moral virtue, with its mainly inward focus on the character traits of the individual businessperson, relates to justice, which reaches outward to the social order, particularly as seen in the case of contemporary trends toward corporate social responsibility (CSR). Can virtue, trust, and justice all work together somehow in a moral design for modern business activity, where moral ideals often seem to be so squarely at odds with the pursuit of profit?

If you are virtuous, possessed of prudence, temperance, and courage, such character attributes will often benefit you personally. You'll be able to with-stand and cope with troubles facing you in both personal life and career. Forti-fied with courage, you might even be able to march into your boss's office and demand the raise you deserve. Justice, however, is a different sort of virtue in that it is not just about you; rather, justice looks outward in the sense that it pertains to the way you regard other people, and how you ought to treat them. Thus, in contrast to Plato's conception of justice as concerned "not with exter-nal actions" but rather with the "inward self,"[1] Aristotle regarded the virtue of justice as an inclination to accord others what they are due.[2] You exhibit the virtue of justice when you view other people as equals, naturally heeding their legitimate claims. But why should you bother to be just in your dealings with others? After all, what's in it for you? Even more to the point, why should a for-profit corporation, struggling to survive in a fiercely competitive environ-ment, conduct itself justly? A recognition of the complexities tied up in such questions has roots in ancient thought, where extended contemplation on the many faces of justice was showcased in Plato's *Republic* and also in sundry Greek tragedies.[3] We will confront these questions anew, relating our medita-tions to the contemporary commercial world.

Aristotle deems justice and other virtues to be both individual and so-cial. Justice and courage and honesty are all states of the individual soul and constitute the bases of eudaimonia. At the same time, since we are social animals, we can achieve virtue and its attendant well-being only by per-forming our social roles well. As rational beings, Aristotle reasoned, we all require justice because we depend on the cooperation of others and hence also the trust upon which that support hinges. Accordingly, there is a basic question that comes into play that is as vital today, or rather more so, in our postindustrial free-market economy, as it was in the ancient world: On what grounds will you or I be able to confidently place our trust in the vast array of people and companies with whom we seek to do business?

Ancient Roots of the Corporate Form

The precursors of what we today know as multinational enterprises emerged in the second millennium B.C.. The businesses were run by ancient Assyrian colonists headquartered in the religious capital of Ashur, and they operated across the continents of Asia, Europe, and Africa.[4] It is, of course, odd to use the term *multinational enterprise* to designate something predating the modern nation-state. Nevertheless, such enterprises operated across territorial borders and had structures similar to modern multinational companies. Indeed, the magnitude of their commerce was immense and likely was conducted with established customer contacts in remote locations.[5]

Centuries later, in ancient Greece, it is surprising to note that business and personal conduct had no crisp separation. Although, as mentioned, corporate organizations had already been well under way by the fifth century B.C., in the Greek city-state, businesses emerged as an outgrowth of the household (*oikos*), and the sort of trust necessary for business transactions evolved as an accompaniment of personal integrity, reputation, and honor.

Today, by contrast, the market leans on promises regarding future behavior that are prone to being breached as soon as conditions no longer are favorable to honoring agreements; hence, these assurances carry significant risk. When a contract is tied to the kind of conduct that is frequently repeated, between parties familiar with one another, a self-interest in not going back on one's word is present. In such a context, it makes sense to say "my word is my bond." However, proximate self-interest is absent in one-shot deals, particularly if the business associate is geographically remote. This brings about a multiplicity of temptations for cheating and other forms of misconduct.

It bears mentioning that Aristotle, for similar reasons, was dubious about the prospects of successfully conducting trade at a distance. To his way of thinking, carrying on business deals far and wide ushers in too many opportunities for immoral behavior that might sour the transactions. This skeptical attitude gained strength during the Enlightenment, when a tradition of thinking laid stress on the benefits of sticking with local commerce over taking on more extended trade arrangements. For such a mind-set, commerce conducted close to home is superior since it serves to bring people into habitual contact with one another, providing opportunities for mutual education not present in sporadic commercial associations with more remote peoples.

Yet through modern economic advances, long-established methods that had relied so much on the building up of personal honor and trustworthiness came to be replaced by an alternative viewpoint that provided a new-fangled source of constancy for the nexus of agreements that make up commercial life. Regulating business practices through laws issuing from nation-states that, following the American and French revolutions, enjoyed a newfound variety of legitimacy predicated on popular sovereignty, moved the world away from the European sovereign authorities of an earlier era. What emerged alongside this stepped-up governmental regulation of business was the modern idea of a business firm that has a legal structure providing limited liability, that internalizes its ethical decision making (in CID structures, which will be explained in a moment) and thus has the ability to take on an appearance of a rational moral agent (by means of its corporate image), and that provides for a diffusion of individual responsibility.

Limited Liability

The importance of limited liability was singled out in 1911 when Columbia University's president, Nicholas Butler, observed that "the limited liability corporation is the single greatest discovery of modern times. . . . Even steam and electricity are far less important . . . and . . . would be reduced to comparative impotence without it."[6]

There was a lengthy process of evolution behind this idea of corporations enjoying limited liability. The corporate form emerged out of the early Middle Ages. Townships, universities, and religious orders made up the earliest corporations. These entities were chartered by sovereign authority, with their activities narrowly constrained according to public edicts. Because they were corporate associations, they enjoyed a separate existence from the individuals who comprised their membership. The limited liability doctrine had been formulated by the English judiciary by the fifteenth century. But in medieval times, the law did not extend corporate recognition to exclusively profit-seeking associations. Back then, what bound members of a corporation together was a common trade, shared religious beliefs, or mutual political commitments, not a collective pursuit of economic self-interest.

In Elizabethan times, the situation was altered with the advent of business enterprise incorporation. Entrepreneurs hailing from Europe had set out to arrange trade expeditions to the Orient and to the New World. The East India Company exemplifies trading firms during this era. Elizabeth I extended to an association of merchants the privilege to form themselves as a "body corporate," conferring a trading monopoly to the East Indies. Like many of the large merchant enterprises of this era, the British East India Company even boasted its own army. Subsequently, many other incorporated enterprises obtained colonial charters and trading monopolies. A good deal of the settlements on the North American continent received financial backing as business ventures.

While the state normally granted the first corporations special trade privileges, owners did not pool capital. Instead, they would finance separate expeditions under the corporate name, individually assuming the risk of loss should their ship sink or pirates besiege it. However as the size and cost of ships increased, individual buyers became incapable of buying and out-fitting them. The financial risk from a lost ship turned out to be too much for individuals to bear. The notions of pooling capital and sharing liability provided a way around this obstacle. These ideas formed the archetype of the modern corporation.

In 1813 the earliest corporate organization of a U.S. manufacturing firm took place. The big drive toward corporate business organization began to acquire momentum following the Civil War, as a lessening of strictures on corporate chartering methods came about. Prior to the war, candidate corporations would need to petition for their charters. In the United States they would apply to the states, and in England they would apply to the Crown. Such corporate charters were custom-made in the sense that each represented a specific act of legislation. Typically, in reference to advancing public good, charters spelled out specific limitations and were restricted to designated business objectives. A corporation's charter designated some exclusive objective, such as a conurbational movement of cargo. Or a charter could specify the origination and terminus points of a corporation's projected rail lines. Opponents of the incorporation regimen averred that it engendered corruption and cronyism, while also instituting inequitable monopolies. Eventually, the former incorporation scheme gave way to the familiar modern arrangement whereby corporate status is conferred upon business associations completing the appropriate forms and paying the necessary fees.

Underlying this evolution were changes in thinking. The erstwhile arrangement had been predicated upon the mercantilist notion that corporate pursuits ought to further well-defined public aims. However both Adam Smith and subsequently Alexander Hamilton, as United States treasury secretary, questioned the wisdom of maintaining too close of a linkage between commercial enterprise and public policy. In their opinion, people ought to be prompted to delve into their own commercial interests. The "invisible hand" of the market does a better job than public authorities in guiding commercial pursuits down socially beneficial paths. In addition, when nineteenth-century advocates pressed for reforms in incorporation practices, they spoke not simply against governmental bias and in favor of the laissez-faire outlook. They also argued in support of the right of a corporation to exist. Virtually all organs satisfying rudimentary requirements and filing a petition are deserving of a corporate charter. In contradistinction, earlier

sovereign-chartered enterprises owed their existence to a special dispensa-
tion granted by the sovereign as it deemed appropriate. Nevertheless, the
contention of the reformers was that, rather than being a gift of the state,
incorporation was an extension of a right of association of the people.

While the right of association endorses an easing of the incorporation
process, government continues to oversee that process and ensures that corporations maintain legal status. So that they may enjoy their privileges and
rights, corporations need to be accorded recognition as distinct agents by
law. Thus, to a significant degree, the corporation lives as, in the words of
Chief Justice John Marshall, "an artificial being, invisible, intangible, and
existing only in the contemplation of the law."[7]

Internalization of Ethical Decision Making

It is evident that corporations are empowered to act as legal agents. Corporations are able to enter into contracts with people, as well as with other corporations and various legal entities, such as governments and nonprofit organizations. They exercise ownership over property. And they are authorized
both to bring legal actions and to be the objects of civil lawsuits and criminal
prosecutions. Yet the deeper philosophical question is whether corporations
are actually moral agents that can be trusted and depended upon. Do we
sometimes have good grounds not to trust them in the way that we naturally
extend our trust to fellow human beings?

Corporations are associations having an existence apart from the individuals constituting them at any point in time. They are accorded legal
recognition as artificial persons. By contrast, the reality is that corporations
are not authentic human beings. As Edward Thurlow, Lord Chancellor of
Great Britain, intoned, "Corporations have neither bodies to be punished,
nor souls to be condemned; they therefore do as they like."[8] Can corporations shoulder moral obligations in the same way as humans? Should we
consider corporations to be morally responsible, and not merely liable at
law, for their behavior? Answering these queries revolves around a further
issue: Is it coherent to view corporations as authentic moral agents—beings
with a capacity for moral deliberation and judgment? If it makes sense to
see them in this way, then we can properly judge corporations as morally
responsible for their conduct. The corporate entities themselves, as opposed
to the separate human beings that populate them, can be viewed as carrying

moral obligations, as being culpable when they fall short of satisfying such obligations. As such, they are worthy of attracting praise or blame or even punishment for decisions they render and for the policies they pursue.

In moving through such issues it is important to bear in mind the distinction between a moral person and a moral actor. Thus, even if one does not wish to concede that corporations are moral persons, whether literally or figuratively, one may still have sound reasons for thinking that virtue ethics, as well as legal and moral responsibility, applies to corporations in their capacity as moral actors to which notions of collective responsibility attach.

Out of a rich literature dealing with such matters,[9] one particularly insightful approach that emerged developed the concept of the corporate internal decision configuration, or CID for short.[10] The CID may be simple or quite complex. An example of a simple CID used in a small-scale organization like a club, would be decision by majority vote. A more intricate CID can be found in organizations such as BP or ExxonMobil, which normally contain their own systems of checks and balances. Indeed, the structure may be so complex that the resulting diffusion of responsibility means that no identifiable individual or set of persons appears to be morally responsible. At the very least, it becomes difficult to assign personal responsibility for certain corporate outcomes. This problem can be seen in connection with the attempts to assign blame for BP's response to the massive oil spill from its drilling operations in the Gulf of Mexico.

The idea is that with the organization's CID matrix, all information passes through a kind of filtration process made up of various corporate goals and procedures. The resultant distillate makes up the corporate decision. To be sure, real people are on board in making the decisions. Yet along with those individual persons, there stands another key element of corporate decision making. This other part is the structure within which policies are formulated, plans laid out, and activities executed.

A CID arrangement spells out lines of authority and specifies the circumstances under which the deeds of individual humans are deemed to be official corporate undertakings. In this way the corporation might be compared to a machine or computer program. The corporation itself supplies sometimes quite intricate formal mechanisms for breaking up, rebundling, and redistributing human intentions, decisions, and actions as corporate ones.

This leads to a split of interpretation concerning whether corporations, as opposed to the individuals toiling within it, can be seen as morally responsible, and whether we can suppose a corporation to be capable of, at a minimum, exhibiting moral characteristics, much less cultivating and exercising virtues such as generosity, courage, and wisdom. On one side—the "collectivist" account—is the view that the CID structure effectively soaks up the motives and deeds of separate human beings into a corporate decision or judgment. Even though no single corporate authority (manager or executive) may have intended the particular decision branch mapped out by the CID matrix, the argument runs, the corporation itself intended it. The presence of such a formal corporate decision procedure suffices to render corporate conduct genuinely "intentional" and hence to render corporations morally responsible.[11]

This position is further supported with the claim that a CID matrix operates, as a human does, to amass information about the consequences of its behavior. By means of its formal structures a corporation tracks efficiency ratios, productivity formulas, impacts, and so on. Consequently, the collectivist argues that it makes good sense to say that corporations can display rationality and can show respect for human beings, just as flesh-and-blood people do. Speaking about corporate moral responsibility is as coherent as talking about personal moral responsibility.[12] Moreover, it makes sense to think of a corporation as a moral agent if moral reasons hold some sway over its decision making, and also if the firm's decision-making methods govern its conduct and play a role in its adoption of policies and norms.[13]

The other side—the "individualist" account—objects that an action can only be deemed to be intentional if the being creating an intention makes steps toward realizing the act with some expenditure of physical effort. It is only human beings working in the corporation and on behalf of it who execute acts that can be imputed to the firm. Consequently, it is argued that we should consider only human affiliates of the corporation, and not the corporation as such to be morally responsible actors.[14]

The collectivist, then, says that both individual human beings and business organizations count as morally responsible agents, whereas the individualist says that human beings, but not business organizations, count as morally responsible agents. As we have seen, the collectivist argues that a company's CID matrix supplies policies and procedures according to which people in the firm arrive at collective decisions and consequently also take collective action that is attributable to the business enterprise itself (as opposed to the people in it). However, a difficulty with this account is that there seems to be a disconnect between a corporate intention, understood figuratively or metaphorically, and our familiar human intentions, understood literally. It is not clear how a firm's internal decision methodologies establish collective mental states or collective minds, at least in the literal way of speaking. The collectivist position seems to require some demonstration of how, simply by following decision procedures, groups create actual intentions that were previously nonexistent.

It may be, however, that collective intentions can be metaphorically ascribed to business entities. We typically employ the language of intentionality in a literal way.[15] You might say that you intend to take a walk, and you mean this in a literal sense. It is literal because you possess a mind that produces conscious thoughts, intentions, and beliefs, and such mental states literally exist in your mind. You might also use an intentional manner of speaking nonliterally, or metaphorically. You might say that your computer "wants" to reboot itself. Yet you don't literally mean that your computer has an intention. You are drawing an analogy with the familiar sort of way that people act in order to describe what is happening with your computer.

How does this apply to the case of attributions of intent to business organizations? If we impute some intention to a group of people that we are not able to attribute to the individuals in that group, normally we do this recognizing that the conduct of the group shows some characteristic we deem similar enough to the conduct of human beings to warrant describing the group's conduct that way. You might say that your company "wants" to move to a new location, meaning that there is some plan in place to relocate the firm. You do not mean that your company literally has a mind that is generating a desire or intention.

Another kind of figurative situation occurs in regard to talking about a collective organization. You might attribute an intent to a whole group when in reality the intent is only of some, or maybe none of its members. Here, you are not applying the figurative language in a descriptive way but rather in a normative way. Normative attributions of figurative intention occur frequently in law. According to well-settled principles of contract law, for instance, there is an implied warranty of merchantability that arises in sales of goods. The law does not say that sellers have literally uttered any promises, only that the law treats the commercial transaction in a figurative way, as if the seller had actually given a promise to the buyer.

This is what happens when a firm's leaders gather a committee to prepare a mission statement for their code of conduct, setting out the values and mission of the company. Here, the attribution of moral beliefs, values, and a vision to the organization is metaphorical (as your description of the computer "wanting" to reboot was), but it is normative as well, not simply descriptive. In circumstances where the members of a company use its CID matrix to undertake some action on behalf of the firm, the attribution of responsibility for that action to the firm is normative rather than merely descriptive.

The upshot is that we can understand our imputations of intent to business organizations without advancing the bolder metaphysical claim that the intentions we attribute to organizations are literal intentions of the kind we predicate of human beings.

Let us consider what is bound up in attempting to show that the kind of intentionality we ascribe to a firm is of the same order as the natural, organic intentionality that human beings possess. Our desires, intentions, and beliefs are the product of our conscious minds. Our consciousness enables us to be aware of our desires, intentions, and beliefs. But if we attribute desires, intentions, and beliefs to a firm, are we prepared to say as well that the organization has a conscious mind, enabling it to be aware of what its desires, beliefs, and intentions are? What would it mean to say that an organization itself has a unitary consciousness? A more common sense way of looking at it would be to say that an organization is made up of a host of isolated consciousnesses, namely, those of its individual human members.

Yet if corporations do not bear moral responsibility for their conduct, who carries responsibility if, say, someone is injured by a firm's defective product? It frequently happens that an organization's actions are the product of a sequence of actions of many people. No single person may be aware of the collective result of the entire series of separate actions.

It may be that one person has designed the product, a different person selected materials for it, another employs the design to make the product from the chosen materials, then a different person arranges for the product to be marketed, and yet another sells it. Possibly no one of these people is aware that the product is unsafe. In such a situation, it makes sense to say that, in the absence of negligence on behalf of any particular person, no one person is morally responsible. In a case such as this, we might conclude that the firm should bear the cost of compensating those harmed by the product, and the rationale may be unconnected to moral responsibility. The doctrine of strict liability (liability without fault) is based on that sort of justification. Some of the reasons supporting the imposition of strict liability on corporations are that (1) due to their comparatively deeper pockets, corporations are better positioned to shoulder compensation costs than other parties; (2) since corporations receive benefits flowing from conducting activities connected with such costs, they are in a position to carry the costs tied to these cumulative benefits; and (3) corporations are in a position to internalize external costs, to research and test products, to make price adjustments for activities generating external costs, and so on.[16] Imposing legal liability on the corporation to pay for these costs does not necessarily mean that the organization bears moral responsibility for injuries. Rather, it means that if no party is morally responsible for some injury, then the law seeks to provide an equitable method for allocating costs. Sometimes the most equitable approach dictates assigning liability costs to the corporation's coffers.

That said, the reality is that the public expects corporations to be morally responsible, considers them to the blameworthy and praiseworthy, and as such does attribute a special kind of moral status to them. Indeed, through their branding techniques, corporations have done much to encourage the public to see them in this way.

To this we might add that, even if solid reasons exist for attributing moral responsibility to corporations, there remains a "virtue gap" between human beings and corporations. We will elaborate on this in a few moments.

Diffusion of Responsibility

Whether or not we regard business firms as ersatz persons upon which moral responsibility can be predicated, the way today's enterprises are designed permits virtually all who participate in them to bear some measure of accountability for their actions. But this diffusion of responsibility can lead to situations in which no one in particular is held morally responsible. Regarding the recent revelations of defective automobiles and the associated recall by Toyota, where does responsibility for the injuries and deaths occasioned by the malfunctioning cars rest: on dealership personnel who were last to handle automobiles, workers who built them, assembly-line foremen, plant superintendents, quality control teams who ran inspections, engineers who created the cars' blueprints, regional managers who introduced the models into the market, or the firm's CEO, whose office is outside of the country (and who was summoned to testify before Congress about the problem)? To be sure, all of these people might have followed standard operating protocols and adhered to official guidelines. Within a large, extended organization it can prove hard, perhaps futile, to trace responsibility for some result back to any particular person. Legions of various individuals, all engaged in a particular CID matrix, may have played a part.

The blurring of moral accountability need not appear completely shocking. As witnessed in the Nuremburg trials, laying blame in circumstances not primarily involving corporations can also prove troublesome. However, this calls up a disturbing query: Due to the sheer enormity and convoluted decision mazes in many of today's corporations, is the whole mess so engulfing the human element that it is becoming futile to search for individual moral agency, much less to expect virtuous behavior? We are left with a nightmare of acts performed by nonexistent actors. Ghosts are peddling defective products, breaking your agreements, slipping through legal loopholes, with no individuals owning up to these malfeasances.

Is there a way out of this predicament? We might consider assigning moral agency to corporations in the same way we assign it to people. However, we can acknowledge the pervasive tendency of people today to dodge moral responsibility. We often hear grumblings like "it's not my fault," "my boss told me to," "that's not my problem," "our other department handles that," all muttered in an attempt to shuffle some obligation further down the CID deck. Maybe what is needed is a reconfiguring of CID matrices to accommodate more of the human element and to absorb the virtuosity of the people at all levels of the organization where they are working.

It is evident that throughout our wider culture, corporations are more and more seen as having in many respects a stature equivalent to real persons, with images and reputations to match. In an amusing segment of the popular movie *The Corporation*, various people on the street offer their free-association verbal portraits of famous companies: "General Electric is a kind old man with lots of stories"; "Disney: goofy . . . young, energetic"; "The Body Shop: deceptive . . . very beautiful"; "Monsanto: immaculately dressed."[17] (We shall revisit this tendency, specifically in connection with its international implications, later in Chapter 8.)

Conoco articulated this way of thinking as follows:

Although it may be true that Conoco remains an inanimate being for legalistic purposes, the company has a very real personal existence for its shareholders, employees, officers, and directors. The success or failure of Conoco affects most of them during their working lives, and may affect them during their retirement. And to the employees, officers, and directors, Conoco's reputation concerns their reputations as well.

No one can deny that in the public's mind a corporation can break the law and be guilty of unethical and amoral conduct. Events . . . such as corporate violation of federal laws and failure of full disclosure [confirm] that both our government and our citizenry expect *corporations* to act lawfully, ethically, and responsibly.

Perhaps it is then appropriate in today's context to think of Conoco as a *living corporation*; a sentient being. . . . [18]

The notion that corporations are moral agents that possess authentically moral, and not merely legal, responsibilities is prevalent in today's culture.

The point is brought out poignantly in the movie *A Civil Action* when the mother of a child (Mrs. Anderson) who has died as a result of corporate dumping of pollutants into the ground water complains to her attorney (Mr. Schlictmann) suing the firm that they are not primarily seeking money, but rather an apology:

> *Mrs. Anderson (client):* What we want is to know what happened. And we want an apology.
> *Mr. Schlictmann (attorney):* From whom?
> *Mrs. Anderson:* From whoever did this. I want somebody to come to my house, knock on the door and say, "We're responsible. We did this. We didn't mean it, but we did it and we're sorry."
> *Mr. Schlictmann:* But who is that?
> *Mrs. Anderson:* Well, we don't know.

But is a corporation really capable of apologizing? After all, the term *apologize* carries a sense of humility and shame.[19]

Moral Status of Humans Versus Corporations

The self makes up the nucleus of human freedom. For Kant, what is peculiar to the human species is the ability of a person to reference herself—as a self—by using the word "I."[20] As we discussed earlier in Chapter 2, our self-awareness is the starting point of our freedom and our responsibility. Adopting the pronoun "I" you are in effect proclaiming your existential core. You are putting your body to one side and pointing to your free, invisible self. In this way you hold out for other people an additional point of reference for their engagement with you. They do not need to limit themselves to dealing with just your physical aspect, but can also take into account your mind and your thinking. Other people can converse freely with the being you call "I." They comprehend it as situated in a sphere of freedom that is simultaneously within the material world yet moving along its rim.

This sort of dynamic between the invisible moral self and others is lurking beneath our normal business relations. Recall the scenario at the beginning of Chapter 2. Imagine that you are the colleague and trusted friend of James, the bank's branch manager who fails to share with you the information he harbors about an impending confidential closure that will get you fired. It is not as if you regard him as, say, some lifeless computer system, in which data was stored but which you could not access from lack of a security code. The question is not the technical one of why pertinent data could not be retrieved from inside his brain. After having been let go without him giving you any advance warning, you solicit an explanation, some accounting of his behavior. You address James person-to-person. "You knew all along," you complain. Your message transmits to the very core of his moral existence, the place where his authentic self abides. You are not laying blame on him to trigger a bodily response from him. You are eliciting an answer from the hidden hub of his freedom. The core of his human freedom dwells not in any bodily matter but in the invisible space that he, you, and all self-reflective persons occupy as authentic moral agents. Your eyes turn to him for an apology. You hope he will assume personal responsibility so you can trust him once again. You expect him to make it up to you, to extend some gesture of humility or shame that can get your relationship back on track and help you forgive.

But what happens when we change the cast of characters? What about when, instead of another person betraying your trust, it is a corporation. Suppose we are looking at the plight of an Ecuadoran harmed by oil-drilling pits abandoned by Texaco and its corporate successor Chevron? If this person seeks to gain a moral accounting from another person, it will be in vain. Although Chevron is a party to a US$27 billion lawsuit, it denies any responsibility for damages and points to the government of Ecuador as shouldering responsibility. The government, in turn, claims it is Chevron's responsibility to carry the cost for cleanup and to compensate those injured.

There are some metaphysical points that have important moral consequences here. The first point is that we human beings—unlike corporations—possess dignity. Bound up with that dignity is our identification of ourselves and of other people as moral agents that are utterly inimitable, incomparable, one of a kind. The same cannot be said of corporations, as witnessed in the way that a legal corporate form such Chevron can (and in fact did) replace that of Texaco. Immanuel Kant expresses this idea of human dignity in his account of a moral person as having worth, not merely as means to an end but rather as an end in himself. Because of this distinctive characteristic—dignity—that we have as moral agents, we stand apart from the corporation on an altogether different footing. Consider how the relationship between a corporation and a human person differs fundamentally from the relation between two humans. A corporation might hire you for a position, in complete recognition that somebody else can do the job for it as well as you. As an organization it literally cannot but treat you other than as a means to its own ends. Having no consciousness itself, the corporation cannot be aware of your dignity. However when we confront one another human-to-human, in whatever business context it might be, we cannot, if we are acting as authentic moral agents, treat each other simply as a means. Even if we are operating within the context of a functional commercial relationship, whether as supervisor-subordinate, as seller-buyer, or as competitors, we confront one another as free human beings: one moral self to another.

A second point is that human persons, unlike corporations, have a conscience and a soul in the deepest, original, and literal sense. Any attribution of these to a business corporation will remain merely metaphorical and derivative from the human case. (Admittedly, it is still meaningful to make the metaphorical attribution.)

So, as a practical matter, we may wonder whether people should indeed "act like corporations" when it comes to their business conduct. Recently the question has arisen whether, when a person's home is "underwater," is it moral for a person to walk away from their mortgage, acting strategically with the stock "it's nothing personal, it's just business" rationale, just as a company might do?[21]

Legal Developments and Image Creation

A central impetus for an enlivened sense of assurance and trust in business transactions arose out of a sequence of developments in the legal environment. For instance, throughout the eighteenth and nineteenth centuries, contracts tended to be upheld by the judiciary rather than, as in former times, repudiated on the grounds that they contravened a nebulous sense of natural justice.[22] The resultant widespread sense of confidence in commercial dealings in general, and trust in protection of property rights in particular, gave rise to an explosion in economic growth.[23] Yet it was owing more to the growth of modern law, as opposed to any heightened achievement of moral sensibility, that a stepped-up sense of confidence on the part of businesspeople in protection of commercial dealings took place.

Further, by equipping corporations to assume a legal personality, the evolution of business law has in turn provided a means by which corporations can be made accountable. When a corporation commits malfeasance, that entity—instead of the people making the mistake—bears responsibility for the consequences. As a result, the notion of a corporation as akin to a natural person has spread out to various quarters. Novel branding methods now serve to convey the perception that corporate personalities, corporate cultures, and corporate social roles all exist. Correspondingly, corporations increasingly see the need for putting together their own narratives, or sometimes mythologies, telling how their image and structure forged the personalities of their associates. Moreover, corporate culture is viewed as pivotal in inspiring and stimulating customers and workforce.

Thus, today corporate image is key in creating and perpetuating consumer culture. Big firms dealing with a large customer base must engineer an image that is expressive of the personal, say, by naming the enterprise after a flesh-and-blood or even an imaginary human being. So, on the one hand, Martha Stewart (former CEO of Martha Stewart Omnimedia) is an actual human being (having her own all-too-real regulatory difficulties); Ann Taylor, on the other hand, is purely fictitious. (See Table 4.1.)

As a result of these developments, the celebrity CEO turns out to provide a quick road to corporate identity. This trend began with Lee Iacocca using his magnetic persona to makeover Chrysler's stolid image. Chief executive superstars like GE's Jack Welch or HP's Carly Fiorina turn into standard fixtures of business.

All of the developments we have been rehearsing (shift from personal to corporate transactions, limitation of liability, internalization of ethical decision making, rational moral agency, diffusion of responsibility, legal developments, image creation) have been pointing toward new ways of approaching trust that do not hinge on the existence of personal truthfulness

Table 4.1   Familiar Persons: Real and Fictitious

CEO	Metaphysical status
Thomas Pink	Fictitious
Martha Stewart	Real
Ann Taylor	Fictitious
Mary Kay	Real
Uncle Ben	Fictitious
Betty Crocker	Fictitious
Aunt Jemima	Fictitious
Eddie Bauer	Real
Prince Matchabelli	Real
Thornberg & Forester (NYC design and communications group)	Fictitious

or dependability grounded in character. A rise in institutional innovation and the substitution of adeptness in public relations for the expression of virtue in personal behavior have in effect enabled many modern business relations to be founded on a sort of faux confidence that is established at a distance.

As a consequence, one wonders whether corporate behavior has become so far removed, in both the geographical and qualitative senses, from personal behavior that it is judged by an altogether different set of criteria. Worse, there is the prospect that, under the rising influence of the ersatz "corporate self," the authentic moral selves of those who place themselves in its service will become objectified "with the same kind of calculating functional rationality that one brings to the packaging of any commodity."[24] Some of the potential debilitating effects of corporate bureaucracy on individual moral consciousness are chillingly depicted in the following passage from Robert Jackall's *Moral Mazes*:

> Instead of the satisfaction of believing that one is acquiring old-time moral virtues, one becomes a master at manipulating personae. . . . One is subject to pencil-snapping fits of alternating anxiety, depression, rage, and self-disgust for willingly submitting oneself to . . . the constant containment of anger, to the keeping quiet, to the knuckling

under that are all inevitable in bureaucratic life. One experiences great tensions at home because one's spouse is unable to grasp or unable to tolerate the endless review of the social world of the workplace, the rehearsals of upcoming conversations, or the agonizing over real or imagined social slights or perceptions of shifts in power alignments. One wishes that one had spent more time with one's children when they were small so that one could grasp the meanings of their adolescent traumas. Or one withdraws emotionally from one's family and, with alternating fascination and regret, plunges ever deeper into the dense and intimate relationships of organizational circles where emotional aridity signals a kind of fraternity of expediency.[25]

To recapitulate, due to legal and regulatory issues of corporate responsibility, and as an outgrowth of motivational and marketing tools, our traditional analysis of conduct and character has gradually gotten transferred from the individual level to the corporate level.

But if a corporation is capable of assuming a quasi personality, one that has been assembled by artful PR specialists, then is the signal being sent out that the people working in the firm do not have to act like real or ethical persons any longer? By contrast, going back to our observations in Chapter 2 (Table 2.1, "Changes in Corporate Structure"), we can see that with a flattened business structure, in which corporations are not subject to hierarchical control, the individual personality counts more.

The conception of the human person that emerges from our analysis of the individual who cultivates virtue, builds character, and exercises freedom reveals that such an individual is an integrated person—consisting of a unity of body and spirit—whose life and behavior cannot readily be walled off into business and private spheres. Therefore, finding dependable and forthright individuals, and channeling their conduct to be forthright and constructive, especially in today's technological era, poses the following challenges, to list but a few:

· Within industries where rapid technological innovation and globalization render governmental regulation ineffectual, distinctions between value systems and cultural norms turn visible and are more pronounced.
· Throughout societies around the world, many people are losing the

notion of a common culture, a common morality, and the common good.

· The magnitude of the need for fostering an awareness of the moral life as something deeper and more firmly grounded than a set of rules appears to overtax both governments and business firms, which are erroneously expected to supply it.

Returning our attention to justice, we are able to discern that, accompanying the shift from individual to corporate accountability, the idea of justice that originated in ancient Greek thought has been supplanted today by a different notion according to which justice is understood to be a characteristic of the social order instead of a trait of individual conduct.

In the tradition of Catholic social thought, social justice refers to establishing the right conditions under which people will attain just interaction while living in the various communities they inhabit. Social justice dictates preserving distinct hubs of social relations, to ensure each is guided by its respective spontaneous mode of organization and governance. Human associations, whether they are families, business and industry, schools and universities, hospitals, the arts, and so on, are left to freely follow their peculiar self-ordering dynamics. Social justice is not primarily about governmental control of society. Rather, it involves the government remaining out of the way of self-regulating realms that do not need it. According to the doctrine of subsidiarity, social institutions are free to regulate their own affairs. Wilhelm Röpke used this notion to demonstrate that the free-market economy may be harmonized with social justice through the buttressing of organs of public life. In this way, people become better equipped to assist one another and to allay the pressures imposed by a competitive market.[26]

In looking at justice and respect for dignity and human rights as a virtue of both people and of business enterprises, we may help revivify our culture's recognition of the necessity of these ethical elements for a hale and hearty market. However, there is a trend that has accompanied the rise of the corporate role in business, which threatens the potential for such a reintegration of ethics and economics. This is the trend toward what I will call *inauthentic CSR*. It is a way of thinking that replaces authentic commitments to ethical conduct with inauthentic mutations of corporate social responsibility (driven by window-dressing objectives).

Authentic Versus Inauthentic CSR

Corporations sometimes pretend to commit to corporate social responsibility, not out of concern for justice but either (1) in pursuit of greater profits, or (2) as a response to stakeholder threats. Rather than turning completely cynical, however, the crucial points to bear in mind are, first, that exercising virtue is not the same as carrying on window dressing. And secondly, CSR that is grounded in a legitimate promotion of the common good and respect for human rights should not be crassly denigrated as an interference with "capitalist acts between consenting adults."

It is crucial not to confuse virtuous business with the sort of marketing gimmicks and PR ploys that so many corporations throw satchels of money at. Both Enron and Bernard Madoff were adroit in dishing out faux CSR. The year before Enron collapsed, its annual corporate responsibility report boasted of its contributions to diversity, sustainability, and charitable concerns.[27] An online brochure of Madoff's firm boasted, "In an era of faceless organizations, Bernard Madoff has a personal interest in maintaining an unblemished record of value, fair-dealing and high ethical standards." The promotion also touted his family's leadership positions in industry organizations. Such roles exemplified "the respect the firm and its management have achieved in the financial community."[28] However, engaging in vigorous public relations campaigns and pricey marketing displays is not authentic CSR any more than brute displays of power against corporations by irresponsible activists are.[29] At their worst, such practices amount to what Elaine Sternberg, in her condemnation of "conventional business ethics"[30] calls "running a protection racket."[31] In truth it often amounts to clever pretension. Consider commercials for BP (renamed from "British Petroleum" to "Beyond Petroleum"), which portray the company as thoroughly engrossed in sustainability initiatives and the promotion of alternative energy sources, yet which avoid any reference to either the environmental risks associated with offshore drilling operations or to the firm's perpetuation of carbon emissions and attendant contribution to global warming.

None of this is to assert that petroleum firms should abandon environmentally friendly initiatives. On the contrary, it is to stress that the virtuoso business enterprise will conduct itself autonomously, that is, through self-regulation, as an honest and forthright citizen. The firm that is bereft of virtue, by contrast, will cling to whatever veneer of public relations happens to be in vogue, until circumstances conspire to make the pretense fall away, revealing the firm's true colors, as happened recently in connection with BP's failed performance in response to the Gulf of Mexico oil-spill fiasco.[32]

Business ethics must be squarely addressed to the interior realm of moral character, which in turn points directly to reputation and honor, in other words, the hearts and souls of businesspersons and the organizations in which they work. A virtuoso enterprise does not require elaborate legal directives commanding it how to respect the dignity of its employees, how to treat its customers fairly and honestly, or how to protect the environment, any more than a virtuoso conductor needs a regulatory agency to spell out how to bring forth a masterful rendition of a Brahms symphony. Nor can the law ever realistically hope to successfully bring any of these moral objectives into being.

However, although ideally speaking, virtuous organizations may need no regulations compelling them to be virtuous, in the absence of regulation their competitors may be so vicious as to drive the virtuous out of business. So the virtuosity approach should not be taken to belittle the importance of regulations per se, but rather it should be seen as a way of understanding regulation in a wider context. That is, while some regulations might not be needed for those individual and organizational market participants that are or strive to be "virtuous," they may still be needed for those that are not so inclined. Accordingly, a proposal for a merely minimal or libertarian set of regulations, even if it respects "the invisible law," does not constitute an adequate answer to this problem.[33]

That being said, the widespread fascination of business ethics with technical devices invoked to confer strategic advantage in the marketplace ought not to detract from our recognition of the authentic makeup of a commercial enterprise, which illuminates its basic nature and character. A business firm is a human endeavor. It is an alliance of human beings conjoined by a cluster of freely pooled elements: talent, effort, risk, ingenuity, inspiration. The members of this alliance, whether they are rank-and-file employees, managers, executives, or investors, expect and deserve to be remunerated for their collectively earned profits. This voluntary pooling of contributions engages human moral relationships of responsibility, what Ronald Dworkin, in his book *Law's Empire*, terms "associational obligations." Such obligations, which may at times prove more demanding than any legal relationships established by the business alliance, are in a significant sense more fundamental than rules of law in that our dispositions toward the force of their obligatoriness and the benefits they aim to provide is a moral and not simply a legal matter. It is the shared moral ties that imbue the business enterprise with its characteristic soul. And the persistent failure of an enterprise to honor those associational bonds, either within the firm or between the firm and the wider society, often will cause that soul to whither away if not completely vanish.

Business enterprises exist not simply as artifacts of law and mirages of marketing but as unique moral creations. Although many of them trudge along as sterile bureaucratic moral vacuums, just as many others have genuine souls infused with the cultural capital invested in them; such firms are sustained in the marketplace by the reputational capital that they build through virtuosity.

Critics may be averse to using the sacred term "soul" in connection with corporations. After all, corporations surely do not have a soul in the same sense that a human being does. Yet just as was discussed in the case of attribution of intentionality to corporations, my attribution of a soul to corporations is meant to be figurative, not literal. So when we speak of the soul of a corporation we are employing metaphor. This is not as strange as it seems. After all, there are many times when we depend on metaphors to accurately express our thoughts: "I'm weighing my options," "I see what you mean." That is the case when we refer to a company's soul. People working in a business organization quickly become mindful of its peculiar culture, values, habitual ways of doing things, and overall sense of how business gets transacted. We might be prompted to use the metaphor of a company's soul as a means of articulating its organizational *ethos:* a common spirit of zest and dedication to a cause among the members of the firm. Therefore, under the right conditions, we can reasonably expect a business enterprise to cultivate and display virtuosity, just as we can expect this of people; however, in the case of companies, we are speaking metaphorically, while in the case of people we are speaking literally.

The company of virtue enters the marketplace not as an engine of greed, but, in the words of *The Economist,* as "an intelligent actor, of upright character, that brings explicit moral judgments to bear on its dealings with its own employees and with the wider world."[34] A company's reputation for virtuosity is its most valuable asset.

Among the various approaches to ethics and business, it is astounding to see that the most vital component of the free market is repeatedly left behind: the element of human freedom. That is not to say that our freedom demands running after some orgy of unbridled and irrational choices. As we learned from Chapter 2, freedom is an existential condition within which humans and business enterprises alike go about their affairs. Bringing rational choice to center stage in business will help in guiding our human freedom along the pathway to fulfillment. It requires channeling business activity toward the pursuit of the virtue of justice through proactive compliance with human rights, conceived as basic, intrinsically valuable human goods. Within a free market, linking business conduct to virtue, to respect for human rights and human dignity, and to the common good constitutes the most dependable path to inviting profitability.

From Virtue to Justice

There is a growing need, particularly in the global marketplace, for virtuosity to be joined with CSR. The reason for this has to do with mounting questions concerning the authenticity of CSR, and the motives of firms seeking to integrate CSR into their operations. Firms that are seen to be forthright corporate citizens gain an obvious trading advantage. However, they will not be able to obtain such an advantage from simply following the barest of legal requirements or by launching elaborate window-dressing campaigns. A firm's CSR commitments must be guided by an authentic ethos of care and service to others. This kind of sincerity can be seen in HDFC's[35] and AES Corporation's[36] initiatives in India, Haier Group's commitments in China,[37] and GTB's efforts in Nigeria.[38] If such socially minded corporate undertakings have helped their companies gain eminence in communities where they conduct their business it is due to an appreciation that their projects are undertaken, not as superficial flirtations with pseudo-CSR, but as true gestures of concern for people, for respecting human dignity and proactively advancing justice, responsible citizenship, and human rights.

We shall explore these themes further in Chapter 8.

Chapter 5

Discerning a Higher Law

Music is a moral law. It gives soul to the universe, wings to the mind, flight to the imagination, and charm and gaiety to life and to everything.
—Plato

One moon shows in every pool; in every pool, the one moon.
—Zen proverb

THE MORAL ORDER pertaining to economic life in the free market provides a normative backdrop for business conduct, which includes not only principles and norms but also human goods and virtue.

Proponents of human rights and other ethical pronouncements for business often neglect consideration of an important point. Someone might agree that human rights exist, yet wonder why we cannot simply speak of an institution violating, or honoring, them. What does reference to moral law add? The answer is that what needs to be shown is not simply that business enterprises and the people in them should respect human rights and other institutionally sponsored global imperatives but that they stand under a more fundamental law, what Kant and others term "the moral law," and what I have termed *invisible law*. As rational, free, creative moral actors, businesses and businesspeople are bound not only by written moral precepts but by an objective law from which such precepts derive.

We can understand invisible law in two ways: substantive and procedural.

The idea of *substantive* invisible law means that we discover an aspect of the world, its moral dimension. So substantive invisible law is made up of the knowledge we possess of the normative features of our world. *Procedural* invisible law provides a means for giving answers to moral questions. Stated otherwise, procedural invisible law encompasses correct procedures for answering moral questions; substantive invisible law encompasses moral facts and truths that exist separate from procedures that are pursued by the procedures.

This amounts to something like the process Aristotle calls "dialectic."[1] One begins with settled views, intending to find principles harmonious with most of them. Then one moves on to give some explanation for the opinions or to correct them should they prove deficient. Throughout the dialectical process, one will set forth value assertions that express views about what the good life is.

Those who, in effect, deny the existence of procedural invisible law claim that there can be no pathway guiding us toward genuine moral truth. Under such a view, it doesn't matter what we do or fail to do. This is nihilism: the astonishing claim that words like "ought," "must," and "should" express deep conceptual error. We shall test the cogency of this position toward the end of this chapter. For now, let us turn our attention to the idea of a higher law and how it is infused into the moral realist conception of virtuosity for business ethics.

Seeking an Order of Things

It has been known from antiquity that there exists a law higher than written human decrees. In Sophocles' tragedy, Antigone points to a higher law that compels her to bury her rebel brother Polyneices, killed in a civil war, in contravention of Creon's edict forbidding any burial of rebels as a sign of their disgrace. Concerning such unwritten laws, Antigone says, "Not now, nor yesterday's, they always live, and no one knows their origin in time."[2]

Insofar as the ancient Greek notion of music carried a wider meaning than it has for us, we find in it a conception of a higher law–like harmony. As an adjectival designation for the Muses—the goddesses reigning over arts and sciences—the notion of music pertained to human activities aimed at beauty and truth. Later on, this broadened conception can be seen in the thought of Boethius, who classified music into *instrumentalis*, *humana*, and *mundana*, according to which harmony is found within the spheres of the human body, the human soul, and the physical world, respectively. Music is an ordering principle that keeps these three systems connected in a unified way.[3]

Stoic philosophy, originating in ancient Greece and expanding into the Roman Empire, contributed a concern for universal human dignity at the heart of the moral law. Subsequently the rich heritage of Roman jurisprudence emerged, especially as expounded by Marcus Tullius Cicero, who wrote in the *Republic* that "there will not be different laws at Rome and at Athens, or different laws now and in the future, but one eternal and unchangeable law will be valid for all nations and all times."[4]

As well, the idea of an unseen higher law is at the foundation of the modern concept of rights. John Locke maintained that even in the state of nature there is a law, recognized by all people and implanted in human reason. Such a law of nature engenders natural rights discernible by all rational beings. The notion of natural rights is proclaimed in the United States Declaration of Independence: "We hold these truths to be self evident: that all men are created equal; that they are endowed, by their Creator, with certain unalienable rights; that among these are life, liberty, and the pursuit of happiness." Such a conception designates rights that are taken to be independent of, and prior to rights established by particular political arrangements.

Even in the realm of international law, the notion of an unwritten invisible law has been vital. For instance, during the Nazi war-crimes trials at Nuremberg, jurisdictional limitations precluded prosecuting the crimes pursuant to the laws of the various participating nation-states. Accordingly, the indictments referenced "crimes against humanity."

Recourse to the idea of invisible higher law has been central to many civil-rights cases throughout United States history. Martin Luther King Jr.'s famous "Letter from Birmingham Jail" decried the persistence of racial prejudice from extant law. As King writes, "A just law is a man-made code that squares with the moral law or the law of God. . . . An unjust law is a code that is out of harmony with the moral law." To put it in the terms of Thomas Aquinas: "An unjust law is a human law that is not rooted in eternal law and natural law."[5] For Aquinas, natural law is that part of the eternal law of the Creator that is presented to human reason. We are guided by a rational apprehension of the eternal law, which is imprinted as precepts, rules of behavior, or broad principles of natural law. Because humans are autonomous beings, they must choose to observe the law of nature through their own acts of free will. Natural law is a product of unaided reason. Human laws are positive laws that are, or should be, derived from natural law.

Running along similar lines, my argument is that it is the correlation between invisible law and written norms for business enterprises that establishes the moral legitimacy of those norms. We can, by the way, also see in Aquinas's thought a concern for something we are confronting in this book again and again: the complex interplay between law and virtue.

Aquinas built on and further developed Aristotle's virtue ethics. Both maintained that human well-being is related closely with a person's purpose or end. However, Aquinas added the notion of a supernatural end to Aristotle's naturalistic conception according to which one attains virtue and *eudaimonia* through the fulfillment of one's natural capacities. For Aquinas, human nature does not embody its own standards for achievement. Accordingly, discerning that Aristotelian ethics was incomplete, Aquinas was concerned with both a person's natural end and his supernatural end. He concluded that human perfection is the work of two societies—one concerned with immanent good and the other with transcendent good.

Recognizing the limits of positive law in producing virtuous people, Aquinas taught that law should not directly dictate the exercise of all the virtues nor directly forbid the exercise of every vice. True virtue consists in using one's reason and free will in making the right choices. For Aquinas, the primary practical problem of an individual's moral life is to decide what to do in the inimitable circumstances in which each unique person finds himself.

Moral Precepts, Human Well-being, and Corporate Governance

The normative principles of invisible law that are connected to fundamental aspects of human well-being guide our practical reason; they inform our moral deliberation about how we should act. Logically speaking, such foundational principles of practical reflection entail norms that lead us to pursue some options, while requiring that we abandon others. How does this approach apply in the context of rendering business decisions?

In its broader sense, "corporate governance" concerns decisions made by a firm's executives, along with the impact that those decisions have on an array of stakeholders.[6] Accordingly, considering the contemporary context of global corporate governance in the wider sense, among such principles are to be counted those that direct economic decision making toward human well-being and those that demand respect for rights people have simply by virtue of their humanity: human rights.[7] Let us specify a set of these highly general principles for corporate governance:

- Companies should choose and act in ways compatible with a will toward integral human fulfillment.
- Companies should respect rights people have by virtue of their humanity: human rights.
- Having been created *imago Dei*, human beings are sacred with rights originating in their very nature.
- The economic system exists to serve humanity, not vice versa; meeting the needs and wants of the human body and spirit is the ultimate purpose of an economic system.
- There are constraints on economic affairs that exist due to the very nature of human beings as materialized spirits.[8]
- The authentic human person replaces *homo economicus*.
- Business ethics takes economics to be a value-laden discipline, and the moral perspective it adopts on economics seeks to impose principle in sorting out uncertainty and conflicts in economic affairs.
- Justice, virtue, and human rights are necessary to check abuses that derive from excessive gain-seeking behavior and other unbalanced business tendencies.

Drawing on a conception of a higher moral law provides a means of calling attention to objective principles of right action for business. The above list of principles begins with what is, from a logical standpoint, the initial as well as the most abstract moral precept. This precept asserts that one ought to choose and act in harmony with a will aimed at overall human fulfillment. This is followed by a principle concerning respect for human rights, which counts businesses as shouldering obligations correlative to those rights alongside of individuals, governments, and any other organizations that can be counted as moral actors in the sense discussed earlier in Chapter 4.[9]

Some would argue that using human rights language to account for broad moral principles of corporate governance is unnecessary. But while it may not be absolutely necessary to employ the vocabulary of rights, it seems altogether reasonable and indeed efficacious to do so. We properly speak of an employee's right not to be discriminated against by her company on the basis of her gender. We can accurately describe a garment subcontractor's trafficking in human slavery as a violation of human rights. Such rights are significant moral rights that people possess. All individuals, from whatever communities they are drawn, are bound to respect them, not because of their membership in any particular "visible" domestic or even international legal order (albeit the latter is comparatively less enforceable and less clearly articulated), but rather by virtue of our shared humanity. What is of particular importance in regard to this shared human status is a feature explicated earlier in Chapter 1: our nature as rational beings. As Aristotle and other thinkers have endeavored to show, the nature of human beings is a rational nature. Therefore, it is with regard to our distinctive human nature that we are endowed with a profound, robust, and inherent dignity.

So in a fundamental way, basic moral rights are rights predicated of humans. As well, there exist along with negative duties and their correlative rights, various positive duties for business enterprises, individuals, governments, NGOs, and so forth. Such corresponding moral duties may also be specified and assigned with a vocabulary of rights. However, in this regard it is necessary to pay special heed, as George Brenkert,[10] Thomas Donaldson and Thomas Dunfee,[11] Henry Shue,[12] James Nickel,[13] Wesley Cragg,[14] John Ruggie,[15] and many others have, to questions concerning precisely by whom and exactly how any given human right is to be honored.

The conception of human rights being advanced here follows from a view about human dignity. According to this view, our natural capacities for reason and, as was shown in Chapter 2, the radical existential freedom that we possess, are fundamental with respect to our dignity as human beings. Human rights serve to safeguard and to further advance that dignity. The basic goods of our human nature are the goods that a rational creature enjoys. Frankly, the human capacities of rationality, freedom, and creativity that were explored in the first three chapters of this book are virtually deific, although in an imperfect way. This triad of human capacities represents an embodiment of divine attributes in us, as expressed in the idea that humans have been created imago Dei, in the image of God.[16]

Of course there are those of a secularist mind-set unwilling to sign on to any assertions of a religious basis for such a conception. However, regardless of one's particular religious commitments or beliefs, or lack thereof, it may be granted that humans have a gift of the sort that was traditionally assigned, if not to the Master of the Universe, at least to the Demiurge—the artisan-like cosmic figure equipped to craft and sustain the universe. The counterpart of this is the astonishing creative power of humans, expressed in its most concentrated form in the artistic effort that underpins the notion of virtuosity: imagining a possible state of affairs (a painting, symphony, ballet, poem, recital) discerning the worth of calling it into existence, choosing to actualize it, and finding the means for doing so. As was seen in Chapter 3 through the concept of praxis, the intended states of affairs need not be something as exalted as works of fine art; they might be crafts, or products, or services. They may be tangible or intangible. The cultural or moral import of such human creations might be of any magnitude, whether miniscule or monumental.

It remains debatable by reasonable minds whether beings endowed with these sorts of characteristics and capabilities could even exist absent some supernatural point of origination or divine ontological basis. However, it seems implausible to claim that a being whose very nature is to cultivate and engage such a capability—to realize, in a word, their human virtuosity—are devoid of dignity and rights such that they can be treated merely as instruments, objects, or property.

We might question whether human beings are really as rational as this account supposes them to be. Are there intelligible reasons for human choices and actions? We all can see that some ends or purposes are intelligible in the sense that they afford a means to other ends. In working to earn money, our conduct is rational. After all, money is a valuable means to numerous important ends. No one doubts its instrumental value. So even moral skeptics do not deny that there are instrumental goods. But the question becomes whether some ends or purposes are intelligible as supplying more than just instrumental justifications for acting. Are there intrinsic, as well as instrumental, goods? Moral skeptics deny that there are intelligible ends or purposes that make possible rationally motivated behavior. Their opponents assert that aesthetic appreciation, friendship, knowledge, virtue, along with other purposes or ends carry intrinsic value; they are ends-in-themselves.[17] We cannot reduce them to and we cannot account for their worth solely in terms of nonrational motivational elements like desire and emotions. As basic human goods they are part-and-parcel of the well-being and fulfillment of both individuals and human communities. Consequently they serve as a basis for moral judgment, including our normative interpretations concerning justice and human rights.

Underlying this way of thinking is a realist epistemology. We acquire genuine knowledge of the essence of humankind. Even given obvious variations manifested in different cultures, in different historical contexts, and in different traits, enough similarity exists among humans to reveal an enduring and universal human nature. However, it must be granted that some subscribe to worldviews that give a different account of the human capacities I am alleging to form a ground for human dignity. Such philosophies give an instrumental and noncognitivist account of practical reason and maintain that our experiences of deliberation, judgment, and choice are illusory. David Hume's contention that reason is subservient to the passions (which I shall elaborate on in a moment) and Thomas Hobbes's portrayal of our thoughts as "scouts and spies" of our desires are the *loci classici*.[18] If the advocates of these noncognitivist and subjectivist views of human action are correct, then any project of business ethics would be doomed, and the notion of human dignity would be tenuous.

However, I would argue that ethical noncognitivism and moral subjectivism actually depend on the very standards of rationality that they seek to attack in constructing their arguments that humans are incapable of having more than just instrumental rationality and in their denial of authentic freedom of choice. In saying this, I do not mean to deny that emotion figures into human action. Certainly it does hold sway, and as was discussed in Chapter 2, sometimes it or other nonrational elements are key motivators (as advertising industry participants are well aware). Nevertheless, people can and do properly appeal to reasons for action. These reasons relate to ends that are taken to be aimed at human fulfillment. Moreover, our pursuits of such ends are desired as just that. Stated otherwise, our rational ends have an essential role to play in our motivations.

But if all of this is true, how do we account for widespread neglect of human rights and other moral principles? One reason is that while we are rational creatures, our rationality is far from perfect. We remain vulnerable to error in moral judgment. Another reason, as Kenneth Goodpaster has shown, is that many people in business are prone to "teleopathy," a character habit that "values certain limited objectives as supremely action-guiding, to the relative exclusion not only of larger ends, but also of moral considerations about means, obligations and duties."[19] To Goodpaster, teleopathy is an unbalanced pursuit of purpose, either directly in decision making or indirectly in loyalty to some function or role. This fixation on purpose, Goodpaster argues, in turn leads to rationalization, which in turn leads to detachment (for instance, in the form of careerism). The result can be unethical conduct, which would certainly include neglect for human rights.

So, if there is a set of moral norms, including norms of justice and human rights, that can be known by rational inquiry, understanding, and judgment even apart from divine revelation, then these norms of invisible law can provide a backdrop for the human rights paradigm of global corporate governance, the details of which are further set forth in Chapter 8. As a matter of justice, governments, persons, and corporations alike are bound to respect and, to the extent possible (affordable), be proactive in protecting and advancing such principles.

Modes of Derivation and Discernment

Following the tradition of Aquinas, natural law theorists hold that just positive law is "derived" from natural law in the way that was explained earlier. But there are two distinct kinds of derivation. In certain cases, law directly forbids or requires what morality forbids or requires. The positive law derives from the natural law in a way analogous to the deduction of conclusions from premises in the natural sciences or mathematics. For other types of positive law, however, such a "deductive" approach is not possible. Instead, they invoke an activity of the practical intellect that Aquinas called *determinatio.*

Aquinas illustrates this by analogy with the activity of an architect. There is no uniquely correct way to design a house. A variety of alternative designs are reasonable. Certain design features will be dictated by the needs of the people living in the home, others are matters of style and taste, and others still of optional compromises between expense and risk. So, in most cases, the architect exercises significant creative freedom within a broad set of boundaries. Consider ceiling height. While some possibilities are excluded on pragmatic grounds—ceilings only four feet high would make a dwelling uninhabitable for most people, and ceilings fifty feet high would probably break the budget—no principle of architecture fixes ceiling heights at any particular height. The architect tries to select a ceiling height that harmonizes with other features of her design, including features (such as doorway heights) that are themselves the fruit of determinations.[20]

Like the architect, a corporate governance body guided by invisible law exercises creative freedom in working from a grasp of basic practical principles directing actions toward the advancement and protection of human rights and away from their privations to concrete schemes of regulation aimed at coordinating conduct for the sake of the all-round well-being of various economic communities impacted by the firm's activities. Among the key considerations for assigning corporate responsibility for human rights is the fairness of the distribution of burdens and benefits attending any scheme of regulation.[21] Yet because on the invisible law account all persons have a profound, inherent, and equal dignity, the interests—more precisely, the well-being—of each and every person or stakeholder must be taken into account, and no one's interests may be unfairly or otherwise unreasonably favored or disfavored. The common good, however, is not the utilitarian stakeholder theorist's "greatest good of the greatest number"; rather, it is the shared good of all.

The belief in a higher invisible law for human societies has not been restricted to Western civilization. Not only is it the case that such a concept is found in ancient China; it was of greater significance than the comparatively weak Chinese counterparts to Western positive law. Arguments in support of the existence of such a law, which encompasses a broad scope of human conduct, appearing in canonical philosophical writings from China extending back to the fifth century B.C. Confucian thought, (ca. 551–479) held that economic, social, and political order was attainable only if people conformed themselves to the ways of Heaven. This invisible order could be known by introspection, meditation, and the investigation of things. One of Confucius's disciples, Mencius (ca. 372–279), articulated various kinds of protocols that would enable an economy to flourish "on its own" in the manner of self-actualization, which is accomplished not by positive means but instead by way of inaction, known as *wuwei*.[22]

What we are concerned with, then, along with Aristotelians and numerous thinkers from Confucius to Aquinas and Adam Smith, is the thesis that an objective moral order—an invisible law—exists, and we are equipped to discern it with human reason. As well, we contend, along with existentialist philosophers such as Jean-Paul Sartre, that it is an inescapable feature of the human condition that we are "condemned to be free," that is, we have a free will. Accepting these two primary theses means, in the final analysis, that it is our free choice to either follow objective morality or to run away from it. At the same time, however, using an insight from Plato to elucidate the concept of virtuosity, we can say that in the well-ordered soul, reason will have the upper hand over emotion.

The Ought-Is Conundrum

This viewpoint puts us at odds with a tradition of thinkers from Hume up to contemporary positivist economists. According to this line of thought, although the universe contains facts, it does not contain values. It is not possible, according to what has been called the "naturalistic fallacy," to formulate moral norms by looking at the world, that is, deriving "ought" from "is." If we are unable to formulate moral standards from fact, then morality is simply a manifestation of emotion and desire. Since we cannot get past desires and emotional impulses to any genuinely rational motivation, in Hume's eyes, reason remains subservient to desire and emotion. Because only desires motivate us, reason just plays an instrumental role.

Further, we cannot point to any objective and preestablished ground for selecting one end over others. The noble altruistic objectives embraced by Blessed Mother Teresa's ministry to the poor, compared to the grotesquely selfish aims underpinning Bernard Madoff's and R. Allen Stanford's con artistry are on equal par. Reason is the instrument for whatever desire floats my boat. Recall Hume's quote: "Reason is and ought only to be the slave of the passions."[23] If we lack rational grounds for choosing one pursuit over another, then we lack authentic freedom of choice. Moral virtue becomes an illusion. We are stuck with preordained passions, the product of one's genetic makeup, one's environment, anything that might lead one to want to care for the less fortunate on this planet, on the one hand, or perpetrate wide-scale financial scams, on the other. So we come to a fork in the road. Along one path is authentic free choice and reason; the other path leads to determinism and amorality.

Rather than attempting to deduce a moral "ought" from a descriptive "is" through theoretical reasoning aimed at a philosophy of human nature, perhaps we do better by focusing on practical reasoning. Taking that approach shows how moral argumentation requires giving reasons for actions that get laid out in the course of discerning potential ends or valuable objectives.

There are, accordingly, two challenges. One is giving a satisfactory account of human freedom. How is a person at the same time both free and morally bound? If the nature of things is what produces our moral obligations, then is the moral world as determinate as the physical world? A second challenge is overcoming consequentialist reasoning to the effect that no moral absolutes exist. A utilitarian will claim that ultimately all values are commensurable; they can be measured, balanced, and traded off with one another. That means any adverse moral judgment is always subject to being offset by amassing enough countervailing beneficial consequences.

Incommensurable Goods

Both challenges are met by showing that some basic, incommensurable goods exist. The incommensurability of goods means we cannot rationally measure one against another. None of them should be completely disregarded. Their importance and choice-worthiness are self-evident. Among these basic goods, three are substantive (existing prior to action), and four are reflexive (depending on our choices). The substantive goods are human life (health and procreation); knowledge and aesthetic appreciation (beauty); and skilled performance. The reflexive goods are self-integration; authenticity/practical reasonableness; justice and friendship; and religion/holiness.[24] (See Table 5.1 below.) The basic goods also provide reasons for us to act. Yet when you behave ethically, you need reasons according to which you may deem other choices to be unethical because they are somehow less than completely reasonable, even though those choices might still be backed by reasons of some sort. In treating basic goods as incommensurable, we accomplish two things. First, although humans are free to choose, some moral absolutes remain. While you possess freedom as a human being, that freedom is not absolute (although, of course, you are always free in the deepest existential sense to reject morality). You may not purposely assail a basic good like health or friendship. Second, we eliminate right away utilitarian calculations of values that might license one to "do evil that good may come of it."

It should be noted that there is a degree of resemblance between this conception of basic incommensurable goods and ISCT's "hypernorms." (See Table 5.2 below.) In this regard, although contractualist in its basic structure, as offering an account about how we reach agreement concerning "authentic" norms of business ethics, ISCT can be understood as drawing on invisible law at least for one of its cornerstone concepts regarding the basis for making judgments about which authentic norms are legitimate or illegitimate, that is, passing or flunking the hypernorms test, respectively. In other words, ISCT presupposes that there are certain correct hypernorms that we ought to follow in judging whether local norms are finally morally right.

Table 5.1   **Basic Incommensurable Human Goods**

Substantive	Life
	Knowledge and aesthetic appreciation
	Skilled performance
Reflexive	Self-integration
	Authenticity/practical reasonableness
	Justice and friendship
	Religion/holiness

Understanding Our Understanding

The question of how we know invisible law is exceedingly challenging. What complicates matters is that (like natural law) invisible law "is known by way of inclination before it is known by way of cognition."[25] According to Aquinas, our inclinations comprise the "seeds" (*seminalia*) not only of our shared legal norms but also of our virtues.[26] In other words, the order of human inclination gives birth to the order of precepts as well as the order of virtue. It is through our inclinations that we initially grasp what our actions aim at, such as friendship, as well as, in an elementary way, actions that are concordant with such aims. Hence, goods-qua-ends and goods-qua-actions are embryonic in our understanding *per inclinationem*. Nevertheless inclinations alone do not suffice either for generating a system of norms or for supporting wholly practical reckonings about action. They must be specified initially as judgments directed at particular situations and later arranged into an intelligible array of norms. Regardless of whether serving to advance the ends of a normative system or helping to promote personal and intersubjective aspects of practical reasoning, a good deal of interpretation is needed to reach a satisfactory degree of awareness and consensus about what invisible law dictates. Among the things required are guiding of inclinations by culture, acquiring lasting patterns of behavior, and cultivating attitudes and beliefs toward volitional rectitude.

Accordingly, invisible law carries two separate albeit interlinking senses likely to be confounded owing to an initial oneness concerning that which is initially apprehended via inclination: (1) invisible law refers to the grounds for our conduct (including the conduct of organizations), expressible in the form of precepts or lawlike norms; and (2) invisible law refers to dispositional

Table 5.2   Hypernorms

Structural	Duty to develop and fulfill obligations in connection with social structures that are efficient in achieving necessary social goods
Procedural	Rights of voice and exit essential to support microsocial consent
Substantive	Promise keeping, respect for human dignity

components dictating rectitude of human conduct, which rest primarily in our inner states: beliefs, short-term desires, framing capacities, emotions, higher-order desires and values, and enduring patterns of behavior, that is, our virtues. Invisible law encompasses both the dimension of moral law and the dimension of virtue (or "virtuosity").

Since an inchoate understanding of norms, on the one hand, and virtue, on the other, is initially embedded within our inclinations, a thorny matter concerns how to differentiate and correctly accentuate one or the other of these subjects. By analogy, some approaches to natural law tend to stress its legal and rationally determinable dimension, while other approaches highlight the affective aspect.[27] At any rate, my stance on the function of inclinations prevents me from identifying invisible law with pure practical reason (as Kant does), in the hopes of providing some completely rationalized basis for legal or moral consensus concerning human action.

Relativist Challenges and Objections

Relativist approaches (positions shown in Table 5.3 situated left-of-center) claim that intractable uncertainty—rooted in worldwide cultural, ethical, and institutional diversity—defeats attempts to take any purported moral guidelines for business seriously. The threat this poses for a moral realist approach to business ethics is that the modern firm is seen to be basically "footloose,"[28] free to conform to whatever practices prevail in its areas of operation. Bribery, slavery, child labor, repression of free speech, and torture all become fair game. The "mixed" and nonrelativist approaches (positions indicated in Table 5.3 situated right-of-center) claim that, although interpretations of international rights can be touchy in multicountry settings, firms are everywhere bound to respect some base-line standards, period.[29] (See Table 5.3.)

Table 5.3 Spectrum of Moral Truth

	Relativism		Moral Principalism		Nonrelativism	
	Descriptive moral relativism	Cultural relativism	Moral pluralism	Moral objectivism	Moral absolutism	Ideological intolerance
Extreme moral relativism — Contradictory moral judgments can be equally correct. There are no fixed absolutes; at least if there are, they cannot be known by human beings. Meta-ethical relativism: moral truth shows itself equally in contradictory viewpoints.	Conflicting moral judgments exist as a matter of fact.	Ethical perspective of any given culture is as valid as the perspective of any other culture.	A variety of moral viewpoints exists and a plurality of beliefs and values is justified. But limits to differences exist, as when vital human needs are violated.	An objective moral order exists, and moral truth can be discerned by reason and/or faith.	A unitary set of moral standards governs all ethical issues, excluding any possibility for reasoned disagreement and debate.	Refusal to tolerate any moral standards or practices other than one's own, for example: radical Islamic fundamentalism.

Extreme ethical relativism warps back toward moral absolutism and ideological intolerance, at the opposite end of the spectrum, at least in the sense that it asserts—as its own brand of absolutism—that all moral truth is relative, and also in the sense that it accords an absolute status to moral meaning, that is, that moral utterances are all merely emotive expressions.

Conversely, rumblings of extreme and descriptive ethical relativism can be detected even in the heart of their polar opposites—moral absolutism and ideological intolerance—in the sense that, since the absolute status they attribute to moral standards is so extremely wrought, it is in fact not universally recognized, but rather espoused by various fragmented extremist groups. Furthermore, such purportedly unquestionable moral standards are frequently met with counterarguments advanced and defended by reasonable people of good will.

Table 5.3 identifies extreme moral relativism and ideological intolerance as opposing endpoints. For moral relativism (in all forms: extreme, descriptive, and cultural), since moral viewpoints are relative and since any response to a moral question is just as good as any other, there is an excessively high degree of tolerance for the views of others. Thus, in holding that one should be thoroughly tolerant, relativism actually advances its own particular moral position and in fact assumes an absolutist stance of its own: that it is intolerant of viewpoints, which are themselves intolerant of certain kinds of conduct. But that is precisely what its posture toward tolerance ought to rule out. Hence relativism winds up undermining itself, showing its ultimate implausibility.

For moral absolutism and ideological intolerance, all moral positions are fixed. The difficulty is that both of these viewpoints inhibit any process of inquiry or discussion from taking place. At the center, away from these extremities, is the space where moral conversation can be the most fruitful. This is the region of moral principalism, which mediates relativist and nonrelativist approaches. Moral principalism stresses the necessity of conducting moral conversation due to the complex nature of issues at stake, the impact of decision making on the wider community to which we are accountable, and the fact that in making moral choices we are simultaneously expressing and shaping our values, calling us to use thoughtfulness and care.[30] As Table 5.3 shows, the relativist side of moral principalism encompasses moral pluralism, within which one is tolerant and accepting of alternative views, thereby incorporating the tolerance feature of cultural relativism. As well, the nonrelativist side of principalism encompasses moral objectivism within which one understands the world in terms of right and wrong, thus adopting the moral clarity feature of moral absolutism. Within the region of principalism the need for ongoing moral debate, reasoned discussion, reflection, and respect for others in confronting moral questions is confirmed.

Confronting Skeptical Arguments

Critics allege that any effort to ground morality in objective normative truth must be unsuccessful.[31] Skeptics may concede that there may indeed be such a thing as objective normative truth. They may admit that many people sincerely believe they know the truth. Nevertheless, the skeptics assert that there is no reliable means available for validating this truth to others. Various methods that have been advanced for discerning objective moral truth, whether through intuition, revelation, or reason, put forth divergent and conflicting theories about right and wrong. In light of such variance and conflicts, skeptics claim no credible scheme can be turned to for ascertaining and exhibiting objective normative truth.[32] Absent any such scheme, all moral accounts premised on the notion of objective moral truth remain suspicious.

One point worth noting is that for skeptics, reason, understood as rational or logical argument, does no better than intuition or revelation as a way of revealing objective moral truth. In part due to the subjective character of intuition and revelation, their strength as a source for apprehending objective moral truth has waned in modern, technologically advanced societies, where scientific methodology is often held out as a paragon of knowledge. By way of contrast, rational analysis continues to carry credibility owing to its usefulness in evaluating theories by exposing initial assumptions, ambiguous or vague concepts, inner contradictions or inconsistencies, and defective arguments. Therefore, reason seems to provide a means for undertaking a public, objective methodology for detecting and exhibiting objective moral truth. For skeptics, though, even reason remains too narrow to accomplish such a task since reasoned argument can be put to work only after initial postulates have been accepted. Reason can employ logic to maneuver assumptions and stage-manage theories founded on the initial premises. But should the assumptions themselves be doubted, logical analysis by itself lends no assurance.

This constraint on rationality is significant for one's understanding of business ethics. That is because the particular premises selected can profoundly influence one's conclusions about, for instance, the shareholder versus stakeholder models of private enterprises, or government intervention versus free-market approaches. Thus, if we assume that the product of your talent and work effort belongs solely to you, and that forced transfers of private wealth by the state are wrong, then we can enlist reason in demonstrating that an economic system permitting robust ownership private property and allowing minimal government are just.[33] Alternatively, if we assume the fruits of your labor and talent may be susceptible to some scheme of redistribution pursuant to fair procedures, then reason can step in to establish that a socialist-oriented or welfare-based economic arrangement will be just.[34] However, for skeptics, neither one of these foundational assumptions regarding your talents and expenditure of labor can ultimately be shown to be objectively correct.

For the moral skeptic, because no provable objective moral truth exists, a person's choice of fundamental postulates must stem from her subjective opinion that these chosen assumptions are right, or at a minimum, the best of available alternatives. Here, the supposed constraint on one's personal choice is the point of departure for postmodern views that seek to confront by "deconstructing" every moral theory. In each instance the enterprise of advancing a moral theory is taken to ultimately fall prey to various conceptual booby-traps. One of them is purporting to select whatever root assumptions the theory requires according to a criterion of objective moral truth, whereas the selection is actually driven by subjective viewpoints or personal preferences. Another trap comes about from bypassing any demand for opting among opposing values by deploying a conceptual model that remains ambiguous or vague, or is plagued with internal inconsistencies. Finally, there is the peril of adverting to initial normative assumptions while erroneously holding that, since no assumptions are being made, the theory being proposed remains morally neutral. This is the way that economists sometimes reason, claiming that they are offering descriptive explanations that are value-free. (We shall consider the perils of taking such an approach in connection with mainstream economic accounts of the financial crisis in Chapter 7.)

According to the skeptic, an individual's preferred outlook might be exposited with all of the appearances of a theory buttressed by reasoned argument. Yet the skeptic insists that no argument can claim a privileged status since logical argument resting on subjectively favored premises is not sufficient to establish objective moral truth. Rather, all theoretical arguments represent furtive efforts to pass off a person's preferred point of view dressed up as "the truth."

But we need not jump on the skeptics' bandwagon and agree that moral judgments amount to no more than expressions of personal preference. The most important point is that the skeptic is offering a critique that is presumably purporting to be objectively true. Otherwise, why should anyone, other skeptics included, be inclined to accept it? Yet the skeptic denies that there is any objective normative truth on the more general ground that objective truth as such is possible. But if there is no objective truth, then what the skeptic asserts cannot be shown to be true along with all the other theories that it wants to repudiate. Therefore, the argument of the skeptic is logically incoherent from the start.

There is another way of responding to the skeptic, and it has to do with what we have identified as the process of dialectic at work in procedural invisible law. Contrary to what the skeptic seeks to attack, it is not necessary to cling to absolutely certain propositions that operate as a platform for the whole of moral knowledge. Instead, there is an ongoing process—what John Rawls called "reflective equilibrium"—whereby we compare our principles with our deliberative judgments concerning particular cases. When they do not make up a coherent whole, we make adjustments. We fine-tune the principles, or we fine-tune the judgments, in order to arrive at an internally consistent set of principles that will cohere with nearly all of our judgments about moral matters. So neither the principles nor the judgments carry priority. Each is susceptible to being adjusted by the other. Along the way we supply relevant scientific knowledge, established views about human nature, and applicable facts. When we operate at the ethically optimal level, we bring to bear in our considered judgments a core of intuitions, beliefs, and principles, which hang together coherently, along with apposite emotions.

Chapter 6

Polycentered Phronēsis

Plotinus was preaching the dangers of multiplicity of the world back in the third century. ... The problem is ... to have interests and duties, raying out in all directions from the central ... core, like spokes from the hub of a wheel. The pattern of our lives is essentially circular. We must be open to all points of the compass ... stretched out, exposed, sensitive like a spider's web to each breeze that blows. ... How difficult for us, then, to achieve a balance in the midst of these contradictory tensions, and yet how necessary.
— Anne Morrow Lindbergh, *Gift from the Sea*

BUSINESS MOVES WITHIN an intricate web of norms. The corpus of norms along with the practices they prescribe, which we characterized in Chapter 3 as *lex artis,* arise from sundry institutional sources: corporate codes and national, regional, and international legal systems; norms also originate from diverse nongovernmental elements, together with multicultural influences. So although the ethical businessperson may display essentially the same sort of morally virtuous characteristics that Aristotle so penetratingly analyzed, to exercise virtue today means contending with a context that is densely populated with normative entities and institutions whose existence would have been unimaginable in ancient times. Our challenge is to find a way of fitting the timeless features of virtuosity into a contemporary ethical mosaic assembled with the likes of hypernorms, soft law, microsocial contracts, multilateral agreements, and multistakeholder partnerships. Accordingly this chapter fashions a conceptual interface for relating character and virtue to a range of other theoretical models of business ethics that are geared to the modern business milieu.

Confronting Polycentric Situations

A key feature of the contemporary environment of business ethics is that it demands virtuous moral deliberation of a special kind that I will call *polycentric*. The chief characteristics of polycentricity are as follows: multiple conflicts arise among the interests and rights of affected parties; relevant norms are generated by a multiplicity of exemplars of normative ordering; and multiple exemplars of ordering are triggered in interpreting and applying relevant norms. Here, "exemplar" refers to a form or pattern. So legislation is a distinctive exemplar in which norms are decreed in a written form; adjudication is an exemplar in which norms are interpreted and applied to particular cases; contract is an exemplar in which norms are put in place by agreement, and so on.

With regard to the idea that polycentric problems involve conflicts of rights and interests between parties, consider the following scenarios:

Enslavement of Children

In the rural heart of Tamil Nadu, fourteen-year-old Vinothini is well acquainted with the thriving Indian trade in child labor. She rises at 4 am and toils until 7 pm making rope by the side of the road in the brutal south Indian sun. Her parents owe 35,000 India rupees (US$760), a debt extending back to before Vinothini was born and for which she has been offered as collateral. "We will never have 35,000 rupees," says Vinothini. "We are poor and nobody cares, and because of that I am a slave." Monisha, another child worker, age eleven, was sold by her father for about US$240 to a factory owner when she was seven. Pursuant to that business transaction, she became one of the approximately fifteen million child slaves in India.[1]

Sweatshop Labor

A significant quantity of athletic attire is made by sweatshop workers toiling long hours in hazardous conditions without the benefit of trade-union rights. Low pay and long hours are common in outsourced workshops. Instead of pulling down a "living wage," as human rights advocates urge, workers are paid the local legal minimum wage, which often translates to barely half the amount required to bear the cost of food, shelter, education, and healthcare for a small family. Some manufacturers use bonded or prison labor, prohibit collective bargaining, threaten and harass workers, and coerce women to undergo pregnancy testing. Actual working conditions tend to be much worse than publicly revealed since many factories falsify wage and time records in order to pass audits.[2]

The Interest-Rights Distinction

Do these scenarios center on competing interests or competing rights of the affected parties? Table 6.1 illustrates the difference between interest-centered disputes and rights-centered disputes. Notice that, according to this characterization of the interests-rights distinction, the problems in the above scenarios involve a mixture of interest-based and rights-based disputes.

However, the interests-rights distinction is based on the logically prior question of whether some norm exists to settle the matter. This is a "hermeneutic circle." We do not know whether to characterize a problem as involving interests or rights (or a mixture of these) without a normative theory, such as the one given in Chapter 5 establishing how moral obligations of business people and multinational corporations flow from international human rights according to a conception of objective moral law, that will provide the grounds for such a categorization.

Theoretical Backdrop for Business Ethics: The Normative Matrix

Let us designate the fount of normative theory for business ethics with the concept of the *normative matrix*.[3] The normative matrix is a conceptual background constituted by well-established theories of business ethics. The matrix is made up of root assumptions and understandings, which lets consensus

Table 6.1   Interests-centered and Rights-centered Disputes Distinguished

Center of Dispute	Characteristics	Examples
Interests	No standard or principle (norm) exists to resolve the dispute. The dispute is about power and politics.	Workers' interest in higher wages and better working conditions conflicting with employer's interest in cheaper labor.
Rights	There exists some standard or principle (norm) according to which the dispute can be resolved. The dispute is about what is right and wrong, just and unjust, what the parties are legitimately entitled to.	Contractual dispute between parties; violations of human rights standards (e.g., prohibitions on child labor exploitation, unjust employment conditions, violations of human dignity).

develop. A normative matrix enables some convergence in professional opinions to exist on ethical issues in core areas. It upholds a general endorsement of key disciplinary models such as stakeholder theory, integrative social contract theory, and ad hoc philosophical theories, which collectively define much of the field of normative business ethics. The following elements make up the normative matrix:

- Assumptions about what is being interpreted in issues of business ethics. Basic understanding of what a business ethics norm is.
- Consensus on the sources of business ethics norms.
- Regular use of certain methodological rules and principles. (Such as those used in stakeholder, social contract, and ad hoc theories.)
- General agreement that values and evaluations—not empirical data alone—are needed to interpret business ethics norms. Value concepts are essential tools for the theory and practice of business ethics.

One may think of a harmonic system in music as expressible by a set of "laws" patterned after conventional expectations of composers, performers, and listeners. Such laws, which are specified by music theory, accord a peculiar hierarchy of significance among notes making up a scale.[4] Thus, tonic and dominant notes are among the most stable, in contrast to others, especially the leading tone. Accordingly, the internal law of the scale dictates the way we experience a pattern of sequential tensions and releases. Equally, chord progressions are governed by a kind of law that assigns significance to their order of sequence. One discerns that certain sequences of chords, such as tonic-subdominant-dominant-tonic, conform to invisible rules. We naturally sense that there is something "legal" about a tonal composition that conforms to established norms of chord progression like the familiar twelve-bar blues archetype in the jazz tradition. Twentieth-century composer Paul Hindemith believed that the force of tonality in music is as inexorable as the law of gravity in physics. Accordingly, Hindemith theorized that the alternative combinations of intervals available from the twelve tones of a musical scale reflect naturally ordered relations to one another and, further, that these natural relationships ought to be respected in musical compositions.[5]

Likewise, one may think of a legal system as the set of legal norms for a community whose members are related to one another by a shared set of assumptions and understandings of legal professionals. Along these same lines one may conceptualize the normative matrix of business ethics as systems of business ethics norms for communities, interlinked by shared institutions and underlying assumptions and understanding of business communities. (See Table 6.2.)

Exemplars of Normative Ordering

The familiar models of legal ordering may be assimilated to exemplars of normative ordering in music and business ethics in order to highlight intuitive connections between them. For instance, to grasp how a legal model of ordering bears likeness to, yet also contrasts with, a normative exemplar of ordering, consider how the legal model would operate devoid of centralized enforcement mechanisms. Or, to visualize how a legal system shares features with a musical system, consider how rules and principles governing music theory resemble legal and moral norms. For instance, traditional rules of counterpoint forbid doubling the leading tone, exposing the tritone interval between voices,[6] and using parallel fifths.

These postulates pertain to the exemplars of ordering within which business ethics norms are created and interpreted (as various musical forms are also created and interpreted):

· Normative exemplars of ordering reflect *responses to moral situations*

Table 6.2   Core Features of Music Theory and Legal Theory Correlated with Business Ethics

Music Theory	Legal Theory	Business Ethics
Harmonic system (tonal, atonal, microtonal)	Legal system (legal order)	Normative matrix
Sources of music (written scores, improvisation, folk traditions) and their respective interpretation and performance traditions	Sources of law and their respective interpretation standards	Exemplars of normative ordering · Norm-generating exemplars · Norm-interpreting exemplars
Musical communities (audiences, orchestras and ensembles, conservatories)	Legal communities (law profession, legislative bodies, court systems, citizenry)	Normative business communities (companies, trade associations, corporate stakeholders)

common to all communities. Thus, communities throughout the world and extending far back into history that have looked for a way to exchange of goods and services under conditions of equal bargaining and informed consent have recognized the essential normative form of contract.

· Each exemplar has a core magnetism or *internal integrity.* The exemplars are constituted by abstract moral principles (such as human dignity, due process, fairness, freedom, justice, and reciprocity). These principles are distinct from the more concrete objectives pursued by the exemplars.

· The exemplars embody moral virtues and *moral aspirations.*

· The exemplars *shape moral relationships* in business. The justification of a norm in a business context centers on a satisfaction of moral conditions tied to a particular normative process. Deciding what moral conditions an exemplar requires in a particular case poses no larger casuistic obstacle than appears in legal reasoning.[7]

· Each exemplar possesses a *distinctive competence* for certain types of ethical problems. For instance, formal norm promulgation is well suited for "legislating" ethical standards for members of FINRA doing business in the United States. If that habitat is changed, the force of well-established forms is diminished,[8] as when securities are traded in other countries that have their own written norms governing such transactions. In such cases, the exemplars must be supplanted by others that offer a new ground for determining what is ethical in the new situation. Transnational arbitration may be needed to resolve differences between written norms in each country.

· Implicit business ethics norms are triggered in interpretations of *made norms*. Obligations arising from an express contract are grounded in the idea of an implicit reciprocity, which renders it possible to interpret provisions of the agreement. As an illustration, in the day-to-day unfolding of a complicated agreement among friendly parties, an explicit written contract provides merely a generalized framework for ongoing interaction.

The contract is almost never an exhaustive definition of the norms governing the business relationship. Conversely, implicit norms are often infused with aspects of made norms. Customary business practices are not merely the result of arbitrary, mindless ordering. Rather, they are better understood as the product of conscious, rational decision making of individual people and communities seeking their respective ends.[9] (See Table 6.3.)

Generating Norms

The following tenets concern the process of *norm generation*:

1. Norms of business ethics may be created (or modified) within a single exemplar of ordering, or within hybrid exemplars.
2. Norm creation or modification in (1) above may occur within exemplars of ordering (or hybrids thereof) on any level (local, national, regional, international, global). Norm modification need not be hierarchical, but may be *heterarchical*, that is, sensitive to both horizontal and vertical review from other exemplars as follows:

    Horizontal checks and balances: Norms created in one exemplar (or hybrid) may be checked and balanced with norms from another exemplar (or hybrid) on the same level.

    Example: Arbitration of issue within securities industry that denies due process rights to an employee is "checked" by judicial review of the arbitration.

Table 6.3 Capabilities and Limits of Various Exemplars of Normative Ordering

Normative Exemplar	Sphere of competence	Sphere of incompetence	Function of normative process manager	Mode of party involvement	Result of normative process	Normative conditions (internal integrity)
Formal norm promulgation	Aligning behavior with rules	Moral decisions targeting specific individuals	Providing moral guidance according to rules	Following moral rules	Explicit norm creation as impersonal directives of conduct	Rules must be general, impersonal, clear, consistent
Contract, agreement	Exchanging goods and services	Informal, personal, or unlimited obligations	Facilitating a "meeting of the minds"	Bargaining and consent	Norm creation by explicit consent; promoting reciprocity and economic self-determination	Equality of bargaining, informed consent, no coercion, no monopoly of resources
Norm adjudication	Interpreting and resolving conflicts of norms; resolving matters of rights; determining fault	Polycentric disputes; coordinating collective goals	Declaring rights; evaluating competing arguments	Offering reasoned argument	Norm interpretation and application via fair and impartial decision based on relevant facts and preexisting norms	Justice, fairness, due process
Mediation	Conflicts arising between strongly interdependent relationships	Lack of interdependent relationships; triadic or more complex relationships	Facilitating harmonious interaction of parties	Negotiation, compromise, and concession	Norm interpretation and application leading to settlement	Impartial mediation
Reasoned dialogue	Controversial moral issues	Authoritative resolution of problems	Facilitating an exploration of reasonable alternative views	Rational persuasion	Debate over norm interpretation leading to sensitivity of alternative viewpoints	No coercion, avoidance of personal motivations, factual accuracy

Table 6.3   Capabilities and Limits of Various Exemplars of Normative Ordering (continued)

Normative Exemplar	Sphere of competence	Sphere of incompetence	Function of normative process manager	Mode of party involvement	Result of normative process	Normative conditions (internal integrity)
Managerial direction	Efficient resolution of moral problems	Situations where individual autonomy is at stake	Giving orders and directives	Obedience to orders and directives	Norm creation and application to coordinate communal action toward shared ends	Existence of a coordinating hierarchy
Elections	Reaching decisions by majority, proportional representation, or single transferable voting	Regulation of highly personal relationships	Ensuring that votes are accurately counted; prevention of intimidation and "stuffing" of ballot boxes	Voting	Formal expression of collective public decision-making and organization	Informed and intelligent electorate; active interest by electorate in the issues
Custom	Complex, interdependent relationships incapable of organization through formal rules of entitlement and duty	Situations where repetition of human interaction is absent	Forecasting shifts of opinion and behavior	Interactional expectancies which guide conduct	Tacit norm creation leading to an ordering of interactions	Regular (recurrent) business practices involving reciprocity of expectations of behavior
Virtue- and character-driven approaches	Situations where legal regulation is ineffective, or establishes too low of a standard; character-based judgments	Situations requiring precise delineation of rights and responsibilities	Exercise of wisdom; sapiential judgment	Human interactions	Happiness, well-being, fulfillment, dignity	Self-knowledge

Vertical checks and balances: Norms at one level may be checked and balanced with norms from another level. For example, OECD guidelines promulgating formal norms that prohibit bribery "check" a local customary norm in Spain allowing bribery.

3. Norms may be created (or modified) in exemplars external or internal to a firm. Since norms are an essential element constituting a significant portion of international business ethics,[10] it is necessary to account for the specific institutional structures in which norms live and represent the processes by which norms are created, interpreted, and justified in concrete situations. The following sections focus on the exemplars of contract/agreement, formal norm promulgation, and custom insofar as they serve as sources of norm generation.

Creating Norms Through Contractual Agreement

Contracts arising in international business contexts are increasingly establishing their own noncontractual bases with self-regulating forms.[11] The depiction of the various normative exemplars of ordering helps to conceptualize this trend from a business ethics standpoint. The distinctive internal integrity of the normative model of contractual agreement mandates that conditions of equal bargaining must obtain.

Therefore, agreements must not involve coercion or a monopoly of resources, and informed consent must exist. Both contract and agreement involve respect for the principle of private autonomy: the parties establish, within bounds, the norms governing their relationship. A "checkerboard" scenario (Solomonic compromise) is not necessarily a problem within contract/agreement. Members of a community and business associates could agree to disagree. They can agree to accept internal compromises on contested matters. Notice that in arbitration, the parties agree to be bound by whatever decision the arbitrator produces.[12]

The limits of more formalized species of agreement (written contracts) are situations and relationships in which impersonal, limited noncontinuous obligations to others are inappropriate, for instance, parent-child relationships, and business relationships with "regular" (frequent and loyal) customers and clients. Contract occupies a midpoint position between custom and legislation. It resembles custom in that norms are not wielded by an external authority. Instead, they are instituted by the contracting parties themselves. It resembles legislation in the sense that it utilizes an explicit articulation of rules that direct and regulate the relationship between the parties. It is significant to note that very few of what pass as "contracts" in business have the defining underlying elements of contract. Many are in truth just "boilerplate" documents drawn up to protect the interests of the party that prepares it. The documents are handed over to the other party under a "take it or leave it" arrangement.

Specifying Norms with Formal Norm Promulgation

This exemplar of normative ordering in international business ethics is the counterpart to a legal system's use of legislation as a vehicle for norm specification.[13] Norm specification can bring an international manager's normative commitments into greater relief and link general precepts to concrete cases.[14] There is a great deal of similarity to be found between specifying norms in a corporation's ethics code and specifying laws through legislative sources such as statutes and ordinances.[15] Through its code a company sets out the rules and principles that it expects members of the organization to follow. As is detailed in Chapter 8 below, many corporations have adopted codes addressing human rights issues. Similarly, on their own some companies address child labor issues.

Several works on international business ethics are strongly flavored by formal norm promulgation.[16] For instance, among the legislation-like norms Richard De George recommends for multinational enterprises is a kind of "moral strict liability" rule holding that such enterprises "are responsible for making due compensation for any harm they do, directly or indirectly, intentionally or unintentionally."[17] Perhaps a firm such as H.B. Fuller following this norm would have acted much differently than it did in the face of demands that it accept accountability for misuse of its glue by homeless children in Central America who became addicted to it after sniffing it as an intoxicant. H.B. Fuller denied for many years that it was morally accountable for this situation.[18] However, over time they became legally accountable when legal actions were filed against it.[19]

Since legislation-like guidelines are offered as principles for managers to use while competing in global markets, managerial direction plays an important role. A code also embodies managerial direction in that it is formulated by corporate leaders, not by democratic representatives. Corporate codes contain an aspect of contract in the sense that the code becomes a part of an associate's employment agreement with the firm.

An important factor in effectively addressing the child labor problems that exist in the global marketplace is cooperation among governments, multinational corporations, and employees' organizations in enforcing norms that have been formally promulgated. No one country or corporation should attempt to bear the brunt of this immense task. Where child labor is widespread in a region, multinational corporations should work for industrywide, regionwide, and nationwide agreement on the fundamental standards and conditions. One decisive recommendation for a set of improvements is the following:

> Multinational enterprises could start with the immediate removal of children from any processes or premises where they might be physically or morally at risk. They could ensure the welfare of children engaged in nonhazardous work by providing child care, raising awareness of parents of the importance of schooling, and establishing minimum-wage and maximum-hour protection for young workers. Business firms could also stipulate that no additional children would be employed in their plants and subsidiaries.[20]

Custom as a Norm Generator

Custom constitutes as much a source of norm creation in business ethics as formal methods.[21] A key problem in the interpretation of norms of custom is knowing when to read into a series of repeated actions an obligation tantamount to one that might be explicitly given as a promise. The interactive practices of innumerable individuals that occur beyond formal and official conduct lend force and give shape to formal and official conduct.

Custom facilitates norm identification in Integrative Social Contracts Theory (ISCT). ISCT's model of what it is for an "authentic norm" of business ethics to exist is a consensus model of customary business practices. The existence of a norm N requiring certain behavior is established by the following empirical conditions: "Most members of community C approve of compliance with N in recurrent situation S, most members of C disapprove of deviance from N in S, a substantial percentage (well over 50%) of members of C comply with

N when facing S."[22] Thus, ISCT's consensus model holds that a norm exists in an economic community whenever there is a uniform, or almost uniform, actual agreement regarding what comprises a deviation and hence a good reason for criticism. ISCT's model reduces the issue of whether a norm exists to an empirical question about whether virtually all members of the economic community *agree* that such-and-such behavior is required. Indeed, ISCT is parasitic on other forms of normative ordering that extend well beyond the province of contract such as adjudication (priority rules are laid out as rules of thumb for resolving conflicts between norms), and formal norm promulgation (some economic communities use codes to specify their norms).

Interpreting Norms

The following tenets concern the process of *norm interpretation*:

1. A deliberator should understand norms of business ethics from an *internal point of view* (*verstehen*).
2. A deliberator should take a constructive interpretive perspective toward the norms. This entails: (i) interpreting norms as expressing a coherent embodiment of abstract concepts such as justice, fairness, liberty, autonomy, dignity, and due process; and (ii) interpreting norms as expressing a consistency and fidelity to principles that are basic to the institutional forms they inhabit.
3. Norms interpreted in association with regular (recurrent) business practices should respect reciprocity of expectations of conduct that relate to an understanding of the norms as shared behavioral standards.

The following sections discuss the exemplars of adjudication, mediation, managerial direction, and reasoned ethical dialogue with regard to their role in interpreting norms.

Adjudicating Norms

What moral tasks are handled by *adjudication*? The mode of participation by the affected parties in moral adjudication is presentation of proofs and reasoned argumentation before an impartial referee. The parties are at odds with one another.

Moral adjudication is a good forum for competing claims of rights to be entertained. An institutional example of this can be found in the fact that some corporations are instituting internal corporate tribunals—a "jury system" within a company—to process employee complaints in nonunion contexts.[23] An analogue of judicial decision making is found in the effort to identify relevantly similar situations in business ethics. Interpreting such "precedents" requires gathering information about a relevant community's beliefs, attitudes, behaviors, and practices. The case of human rights violations in Myanmar provides an instructive example on the forms and limits of adjudication as an exemplar of normative ordering for international business ethics. Unocal's position on Myanmar was that its investments benefited the country more than economic sanctions. John Rafuse, a Unocal executive based in Washington, said that Myanmar's struggling economy and its move toward democracy would benefit from more, not less, U.S. investment.[24] Additionally, Unocal executives argued that U.S. investments in Burma were so small that the impact of sanctions on Myanmar was minimal at best. Officials of the company derided suggestions that a prohibition on U.S. business dealings would help the cause of human rights there. They pointed out that the United States accounted for only 3 percent of Burma's trade and 8 percent of its foreign investments.[25] Unocal had the benefit of a base of public shareholders that were pleased with the company's strong operating performance and its plans to expand overseas, especially in Asia and specifically in Myanmar. In June of 1997 the company's stockholders rejected a request for a report on the actual and potential economic and public relations costs to Unocal of its investments in Myanmar. The company's stockholders overwhelmingly voted to ignore public pressure from the United States to divest its interest in Myanmar by a margin of 94 percent. Also at this meeting, stockholders rejected by more than 95 percent a proposal requesting an investigation into the internal financial operations of a state-owned energy company involved in the Yadana natural gas development project.[26]

It should be noted that in this regard, another form of normative ordering internal to a corporation—elections (of shareholders)—influences the effectiveness of the adjudicative form of ordering. Thus, by rejecting this investigation, the company's stockholders were basically thumbing their noses at the court decision that held that Unocal could be held responsible for the actions of its business partner, the Myanmar Oil and Gas Enterprise (MOGE), in connection with the construction of the Yadana pipeline. A lawsuit brought by the Burmese government-in-exile indicted Unocal, Total, and the Burmese junta, the State Law and Restoration Council (SLORC), for alleged violations of human rights.[27] Lawyers for the plaintiffs, the National Coalition Government of the Union of Burma (NCGUB), based their case on the Alien Tort Claims Act. As initially established in the case of *Filartiga v. Pena-Irala* and successor cases,[28] such as those mounted against Shell,[29] the Alien Tort Claims Act allows foreign citizens to sue U.S. companies for violations of international human rights law, conferring on them the right not to be a victim of wrongful acts "against all of humankind" (*hostis humani generis*).[30] The plaintiffs charged that the SLORC forced tens of thousands of Burmese into slave labor and leveled entire villages that lay in the path of the US$1.2 billion pipeline. Given the company's interest in the construction of the pipeline and its payments to the government to help in its construction, Unocal was indicted for its involvement. Unocal's motion for dismissal was rejected. A U.S. District Court ruled that Unocal could be held liable for alleged abuses that Myanmar waged against its citizens. The ruling was a landmark in that it vastly expanded the jurisdiction of U.S. courts.[31] On appeal, the claims against the SLORC were dismissed on the grounds of the sovereign immunity doctrine. However, the claims against Unocal and Total were not dismissed. The management of Unocal then attempted to de-Americanize Unocal in response to this litigation. On April 21, 1997, Unocal opened what it termed a "twin corporate headquarters" in Malaysia.[32] The new Malaysia headquarters came after Unocal had sold off much of its U.S. operations and issued statements indicating that it no longer considered itself a U.S. company, but rather a "global energy company."[33] Thus, the company abandoned its status as a U.S. company (though in 2005, the firm merged with Chevron to become a wholly owned subsidiary) and in doing so was able to avoid compliance with the sanctions against Myanmar.

An analogue of statutory and constitutional interpretation in business ethics decision making is found in the quest to interpret codes of ethics and human rights standards that have been penned with open-textured or underinclusive terminology.[34] A norm's meaning eludes any superficial "plain fact" identification.[35] A significant corpus of corporate guidelines, international declarations, treaties, and conventions set forth human rights norms.[36] Judgment is needed to decide which, and to what extent, human rights norms establish obligations for multinational firms. Accordingly, the task of rendering interpretations of human rights norms in international business contexts raises problems akin to those connected with delivering judicial interpretations.

Mediation: Forum of Interdependent Relationships

Mediation is a good environment for handling situations in which a significant degree of interdependence among parties exists. Such a situation is present with closely held corporations or condominium dwellers that share a common building. In these kinds of business relationships, stabilizing ongoing interactions may be a more weighty concern than a formal declaration of rights and obligations through adjudication. Mediation stands apart from the adjudication exemplar of dispute resolution. The key task of the mediator is to assist the parties in discovering a way to promote their respective fundamental interests. Unlike the process of adjudication, mediation is not primarily focused on expositions of argumentation and proof that depend on the existence of established norms and standards for settling a party's disagreement.

Arbitration: "Adjudication" by Agreement

Arbitration is a normative exemplar that stands in between contract and adjudication. Constructive interpretation figures into normative interpretation in arbitration contexts at the critical point at which the intent of the parties, as contained in the agreement to arbitrate,[37] is determined by a deliberator. In arbitration, the contour of the normative process is largely dictated by the agreement. Within wide parameters, parties set up private tribunals to resolve disputes about norms. The moral authority of this process flows from the concept of private autonomy as the ground of the law of contract.[38] Many industries have instituted arbitral forums by means of chambers of commerce, exchanges, and trade associations. Self-regulatory organizations such as the New York Stock Exchange and the Financial Industry Regulatory Authority (formerly the National Association of Securities Dealers) arbitrate disputes in the securities brokerage business, including matters such as employment discrimination that sometimes deal with issues of human rights.[39] Many brokerage houses mandate that customers execute account agreements that contain arbitration clauses.[40] Thus, disputes between the brokerage firms and customers typically are handled by such self-regulatory organizations.

Formal norm promulgation also influences arbitration. The Uniform Code of Arbitration was instituted by the Securities Industry Council on Arbitration, an organization made up of representatives from self-regulatory organizations, the Securities Industry Association, and the public.[41] The rules from this code govern procedural aspects of arbitration conducted by self-regulatory organizations.

Managerial Direction

Managerial direction takes center stage in stakeholder theories of business ethics.[42] According to stakeholder theories, managers balance the various interests of stakeholders—any individual or group that affects or is affected by a business decision. One limitation of stakeholder theory is its exclusive focus on managerial direction to the neglect of other important exemplars of normative ordering. Another weakness of stakeholder theory is that it declines to insist on consistency of principle in successive resolutions of conflicts among stakeholders. Stakeholder theory takes the values, aims, and interests of the stakeholders in a situation at face value. No interpretation standards emerge to distinguish which are more or less worthy of being recognized. The theory provides no grounds for a reasoned judgment about how a deliberator ought to interpret rights at issue in hard cases. While it is true that stakeholder theory provides a valuable first step in orienting the deliberator as to which parties affect and are affected in the situation, the theory gives no help in charting alternative interpretation paths concerning the scope and applicability of the rights. Stakeholder theory fails to hold out any account of relevant sources of norms that would assist a deliberator, much less an account of what the dispositive norm might be for such rights-centered problems. A deliberator using only stakeholder theory has discretion in a strong sense.[43]

Reasoned Ethical Dialogue

Reasoned ethical dialogue is appropriate for open-ended issues and may be conducted without the expectation of consensus emerging from the process.[44] This aspect contrasts with bargaining, which seeks consensus manifested in

the agreement that the parties intend to reach. Key benefits of reasoned ethical dialogue are that participants may come to see that a contrary position
to their own may be rationally defended, and their moral sensitivity may be
enhanced in part by the realization that their moral argument is not universally accepted. This encourages moral reflection and may lead to a reformula-
tion of a party's position. The Table 6.4 summarizes principles applicable to
key exemplars of normative ordering normally present in polycentric ethical
problems.

Polycentric Situations

Polycentric situations are not well suited for adjudication in a "pure" form.[45]
Instead, dealing with them requires a deliberator (or group of deliberators) to
use some combination of normative exemplars of ordering, guided by constructive normative interpretation. The hallmarks of a polycentric situation
are as follows. First, there is no clear, single issue to which an affected stakeholder can direct proofs and arguments. Although the setting of wages in
less-developed countries involves the issue of respecting the basic right of
subsistence,[46] there are a host of other issues that intermingle with the human
rights issue. Second, it involves a situation with interacting points of influence, so that any decision in favor of a given stakeholder will result in a complex set of repercussions affecting other stakeholders. Thus a decision to raise
wages of garment industry workers in Honduras will have repercussions on
wages in other industries in the country that may in turn have to be adjusted
and will impact on garment workers in other countries as well. The situation
here is analogous to a spider web: pulling on one strand distributes tensions
throughout the whole web in a complex pattern. Doubling the first pull will
not simply double each resultant tension. Instead, it will produce a new complex pattern of tensions. The web is polycentered because each intersection
of strands is a separate and distinct center of tension distribution. Suppose a
deliberator attempted to resolve the fair-wages issue in developing countries
the way it is customarily done in employment adjudication, applying a principle such as equal pay for equal work. A decision in favor of workers on this
principle could result in workers in developing countries earning a tremendous amount more in a few weeks, or possibly even days, than most of their
fellow citizens could amass in a year. Such a decision could wreak economic
chaos in a country. Third, polycentricity is a matter of degree. What makes a

Table 6.4   Components of Discursive Justifications for Business Ethics Norms

Type of Component	Content of Component	Illustration
Theoretical component	Theoretical concepts	National sovereignty, due process, dignity, fairness, justice, liberty
Interpretive component	Norm standpoints: specifying the "gravity" of a norm relative to other norms and other considerations, making judgments about exceptions to norms, delimiting the scope of norms	Sale of commodities to or investment in country C in situation S [satisfies/violates] norm N
Normative component	Norm specifications	Refusal-to-do-business-with-rights-violating-country norm
Formal (institutional) component	Forms of normative ordering	Human rights standards (formal norm promulgation), expectations of international community (custom), treaties & trade agreements (contract/agreement)
Empirical component	Concrete business situation handled by norms	Termination of contract to sell product P to country C in situation S

task unsuitable for adjudication is a high degree of polycentricity. Fourth, a large number of stakeholders is not the dispositive element of polycentricity (for example, some class-action lawsuits that have a large number of affected parties are appropriate for adjudication so long as common issues affecting all of the plaintiffs can be grouped together). Finally, polycentric elements are present in almost all matters treated in adjudication. Thus, declaring the rights and obligations of the two parties may set a precedent, which in turn gives rise to unexpected repercussions for other parties, other areas of the law, and so forth.

Polycentered Interpretation

In the actual world of business, managerial direction is a central mechanism in which ethical decision making occurs. Managerial direction constitutes one of the array of modes of normative ordering. Corporate codes of conduct, customary business practices, contracts, administrative regulations, and canons of professional responsibility are all potential sources of business ethics norms. But often such precepts do not, on their own, provide enough guidance as to their scope, weighting, and applicability in specific contexts. The active interpretation of a deliberator in a specific problem is called for in the real world. Statutes, regulations, and rules from codes of conduct frequently are open-textured. It is not possible to formulate precisely norms restraining innumerable possible self-serving transactions and conduct favoring various stakeholders in every situation. As a result, participants must be guided by commonly accepted norms and norms grounded in social expectations of ethical conduct. Some interpretations of norms may be rendered by centralized authoritative bodies, such as the International Labor Organization. Other interpretations may be given by a small-business proprietor.

However, on the abstract, ideal plane of normative philosophical theory business ethics decision making may be represented within a number of different normative processes. For instance, integrative social contracts theory represents business decision making at a high point of philosophical abstraction in a contractual domain. However, modifications of Kantian ethics for use in business ethics textbooks cast the moral reasoning of managers into a legislative mold.[47]

Most likely, there is no single form of normative ordering that provides an optimal habitat for the enterprise of business ethics decision making at this level of philosophical abstraction. Each has its own strengths and weaknesses. Nevertheless, adjudication is arguably a well-suited mode for representing normative *interpretation*, since adjudication is an appropriate forum for applying principles to hard cases (an essential feature of ethical decision making). Here, it may be helpful to visualize an idealized virtuosic jurist offering a sagacious interpretation of norms to a universal audience.[48]

Ethical interpretation in business contexts is, in a sense, strongly analogous to legal interpretation. However, unlike legal interpretation, business ethics interpretation is often tied to a more *fluid* set of institutional and conceptual material, of which legal material is but one of several elements. That is why virtue ethics is so vital to it, and why in an equally important sense, ethical interpretation in business is akin to musical interpretation. A conception of business ethics should not presume to settle questions that need to remain open-ended. It should be receptive to the wide range of cultural manifestations of normative ordering in a variety of economic institutions. Business ethics is as much an interpretive art as it is a practical tool for effective management. A philosophical understanding of business ethics is an internal demand of its integrity. In addition, an adequate conception of business ethics must capture the sense in which business ethics is an endeavor that must be undertaken and carried forward. It is an *aspirational enterprise*.

Example: Interpreting the Norm of Corporate Philanthropy

Suppose a deliberator must decide, as executives at Merck & Co. in fact did, whether to use corporate funds to initiate research for a new drug that will cure river-blindness, a debilitating disease that plagues millions of people in underdeveloped countries.[49] The virtuous deliberator must first reflect on the empirical sources of norms applicable to the situation. He knows that the firm's code of conduct states that the company has a history of helping people first and that profit-making will follow from pursuing that goal. He also knows that there are norms mandating fiduciary duties to shareholders, as well as norms imposing responsibilities to employees. In addition, he knows that there is a customary norm prescribing corporate philanthropy. A constructive stance can be taken toward these empirically based norms. The norms are not reducible to plain fact. Interpreting what the practice of philanthropy means and requires involves making the norm the best it can be in light of all relevant considerations. Reasonable deliberators will differ in the accounts they give and in their interpretations of what specific obligations philanthropy imposes.

The virtuoso deliberator may start by setting out contenders for the best interpretation of philanthropy: (1) corporations should only contribute in ways that will realize tax benefits for themselves; (2) corporations should not give in situations that "invade" the province of public institutions; and (3) corporations have great discretion in choosing how much, to whom, and whether to give (Kantian imperfect duty). Option (1) will be rejected after further reflection. It does not express an altruistic conception of the norm that due regard for the company's code requires. Assessing option (2) requires abstract reflection on the proper roles of private corporations versus public institutions charged with promoting public welfare.[50] Option (3) does not, by itself, help in reaching a decision one way or another, but supports the general interpretation that the custom of corporate philanthropy is not simply a conventional business practice, but instead a morally obligatory norm.

The deliberator's task is complicated since the situation involves interpreting the practice of philanthropy in an *international*, not a domestic context. So an interpretation based on a local understanding of philanthropy may not be the best. Considerations about the availability of public institutions, and the magnitude of the need for assistance that may exist in domestic settings may not be applicable. The deliberator must ask which conception of international philanthropy is the best. This may require modifying the list of candidates: (4) corporations should contribute in ways and to the extent that will realize some international competitive advantage for themselves; (5) corporations should not give in situations in which other entities (international relief agencies, foreign governments, wealthy benefactors) would be better equipped to render assistance;[51] (6) corporations have obligations to render aid in situations in which they can afford to do so.[52] In constructing the best interpretation of these empirical sources, the virtuoso deliberator is, like a jurist in a hard case at law, and also like a performing musical artist, involved in a mixture of discovery and creation.[53] The sage deliberator must justify the interpretation so as to make it consistent with broader principles that are engaged, such as the appropriate role, if any, of multinational corporations in global distributive justice.[54] Rendering a decision may also establish a "case precedent," which will exert an influence on how other similarly situated firms, as well as the international community at large, will interpret philanthropy.

Norm Justification and the Interpretive Standpoint

The following tenets are advanced with regard to *norm justification*. In hard cases (where empirical sources of norms are indeterminate, underinclusive) interpretations of norms should be patterned as follows. (1) An idealized deliberator appropriate to the form or hybrid involved,[55] presents a discursive justification. (2) The discursive justification makes the norm interpretation the best it can be within the context of all relevant forms of ordering. (3) The idealized deliberator presents the discursive justification to an ideal (universal) audience—the relevant normative community—for counterfactual acceptance.[56] (4) The audience (normative community) determines the rational acceptability of the justification constructed by the interpreter. Such an audience may be thought of either as an empirically real, concrete one relevant to the assessment of the justification in question or as some idealized version thereof, constituted with characteristics such as rationality and reflective capability.

An interpretive standpoint is tied to hard-case business ethics scenarios. The deliberator faces at least two alternatives from which to choose. This may involve a choice between which of the alternative norms apply to a given situation, or a choice between alternative meanings to be given to the same norm in a given context. The goal of the (actual and idealized) deliberator may be expressed as follows: *Taking into account all relevant sources of business ethics norms S, interpretation I of norm N is the best justified.* But what provides a deliberator with a justified interpretive standpoint? Assume that a hard-case scenario presents two competing interpretations I_1 and I_2. Suppose an international company's code of conduct forbids employment of children below age fifteen, even in countries where local law permits such a practice. I_1 interprets the child labor norm broadly to forbid even part-time employment of fourteen year olds where the company provides educational assistance. Deliberator D offers a standpoint regarding interpretive content I_1. An array of statements, A, is comprised of statements S concerning the sources of business ethics norms (for example, "the child labor policy is provided in the company code of conduct, as well as international labor organization standards"),[57] and of judgments J connected to a value system V (for example, concern for lost educational opportunities for children working fulltime, or avoidance of physical and emotional harm to children working in factories).[58] The origins of such value systems, in turn, are traceable to cultural traditions from around the world and may also be linked directly or indirectly to a variety of religious and wisdom traditions, such as Buddhism, Christianity, Confucianism, Hinduism, Islam, Judaism, Sikhism, and so on. The statements are arrayed in a plausible fashion P, which specifies the content of the norms (for example, "full-time employment of children under fifteen is expressly prohibited"; "even part-time employment with educational benefits is encompassed by the spirit, though not the letter, of the policy") so as to constitute an interpretive alternative I_1. This conception may be expressed as follows:

$$I_1 : A_i P_i (S_1 \ldots S_n) \, \& \, V_i (J_1 \ldots J_n)$$

I_2, by contrast, maintains that such modified circumstances would constitute a permissible exception that extends outside the scope of the code's prohibition on child labor. This alternative interpretation may be represented in this way:

$$I_2: A_j P_j(S_1 \ldots S_n) \ \& \ V_j(J_1 \ldots J_n)$$

An interpretive standpoint deploys relevant sources of business ethics norms S in some satisfactory way. The interpretation standards associated with the form of normative ordering (or hybrid) that generates relevant norms must not be violated. So far as their norm-generating function is concerned, the forms of ordering (and hybrids) are analogous to the sources of law in a legal system. If norms have been specified by agreement, then the conditions for that form (no coercion, informed consent) have been satisfied.

Since interpretations of norms are often controversial, it is a good idea to look for some reasoned basis for ranking one interpretation over another. Discursive justifications, which require the exercise of a deliberator's phronēsis and do not involve any merely mechanical or algorithmic procedure, generate the best possible moral justifications for interpretations and applications of business ethics norms. Discursive justifications ground normative interpretations. They establish the way that specific norms are entailed by more abstract considerations. Some specific norms may be derived from abstract considerations that are taken as weighty relative to institutional capabilities such as corporate financial resources.

Playing to the Universal Audience

How do we know when a deliberator's interpretive standpoint has reached the status of "best justified"? The point at which a chain of arguments may be terminated depends on the conditions of acceptability of a given interpretation. This is linked to the audience receiving the interpretation. The end point of justification is established by the interpretation community. Justifying interpretive standpoints involves a dialogic process. A justification flows out of a line of questions and responses in terms of which competing arguments unfold. A deliberator constructs arguments that will serve to justify an interpretation so as to link it to a higher moral law. The logical relationship between the interpretive standpoint and the justifying material will normally consist of a plausible, albeit nondeductive nexus.[59] The audience can be said to rationally accept some proposed interpretation when the justification has issued forth a coherent array of statements.

Sometimes more than one right answer may emerge from ethical reasoning in business since differences in value judgments can dictate which interpretation is taken to be the best. Axiological validity gets established in terms of norms that would be accepted in a community on the basis of its prevailing system of values if the matter is assessed rationally. Counterfactual acceptability is a yardstick of an interpretation's legitimacy. It serves as an ideal with which to evaluate and to criticize norms that are formally and factually valid. The following principle is set forth to summarize: *Normative business ethics pursues interpretations of norms that would be endorsed by most members of a rationally reasoning interpretive community.*

The collectivity that receives an interpretation is not just an economic or legal community, but rather an *ideal particular* audience.[60] Pursuant to this conception, constituents of the audience embrace common values. Rational acceptability should not be thought of as merely an abstraction. On the contrary, it is a valid and effective principle active in day-to-day life. It aids the virtuous business decision-maker in reaching the best interpretation possible when solving polycentric problems.

Chapter 7

Moral-Cultural Undertones of the Financial Crisis

> Art also has its morality, and many of the rules of this morality are the same as, or at least analogous to, the rules of ordinary ethics. Remorse, for example, is as undesirable in relation to our bad art as it is in relation to our bad behavior. The badness should be hunted out, acknowledged and, if possible, avoided in the future.
> —Aldous Huxley

> We have met the enemy, and he is us.
> —Walt Kelly

WHEN DIAGNOSING THE financial crisis one should take care in framing the terms of discourse. Ever since the signs of economic collapse began appearing, it has been commonplace for pundits as well as the general public to call the fiscal meltdown a "crisis," a term that conveniently carries no ascription of moral disapprobation. Yet, after one has reckoned the extensive list of both personal and corporate malfeasances that have played a significant role in precipitating the financial turmoil and paid heed to the underlying cultural-moral factors accompanying the wrongdoing, a more apt description would be "scandal," a term that implies some degree of cultural-moral failure.

This is not idle quibbling over terminology. Most people would agree that it is of critical importance whether an economic downturn is branded a "recession" or a "depression." There are significant political consequences of using one term or the other. Similarly, it matters whether we characterize the global financial imbroglio in amoral (scientific) or moral (human-oriented) terms. It matters whether we approach the crisis with the attitude that we can understand it simply by looking at economists' equations and statistical analyses, annexed to business managers' technocratic jargon, or, instead, decide that looking beyond these mental models to the broader realm of moral and intellectual culture can achieve a more satisfactory understanding.

Looking at the financial scandal from a moral-cultural frame of reference reveals a moral-cultural malaise, and it matters how we respond to this condition. Do we acquiesce to legislators' attempts to promulgate new laws and regulations? This response is common, but it ultimately cedes responsibility for solving the dysfunctions behind the crisis to legal authorities. Such an approach is inadequate. We would do better to act as if the crumbling of the current economic edifice is a massive chastening, with a call for deepened moral reflection and reform. We ultimately have no one but ourselves to blame for this economic collapse, and there is no one else to whom we can look to chart a new course to prosperity.[1]

The widespread tendency to stress the amoral sense of the word "crisis" when speaking of the meltdown likely flows from an ingrained habit of viewing the world of business in general, and financial markets in particular, as if they operated according to the same kind of mechanistic, determined, and repeatable behavior, as the chemical reactions that scientists study in the laboratory. Those disposed to explain market phenomena with a positivist mind-set, who see the business of business as business, in some cases reduce both the symptoms of and the cure for today's credit malaise to mathematical equations.[2] Sometimes they diagnose the problem in squarely scientific, even medical terms,[3] as evidenced by the quick US$700 billion and US$2.3 trillion prescriptions of government leaders in the United States and Europe respectively.[4] In line with such viewpoints, we have heard many talk of how the economic meltdown was precipitated by a falling real estate market, the product of recurring bubbles that appear every ten or twenty years.[5] According to this account, fundamental dynamics in housing and property markets lead to speculative bubbles that inevitably bring financial systems down with them because financial systems are heavily involved in mortgage lending. Even those systems that do not have substantial securitization and are not dominated by private banks, it is averred, are susceptible to those trends.[6] But using the reductive mathematical and scientific explanations of some economists and business theorists to account for the present financial crisis may turn out to be as serious a delusion as the false belief peddled by the current administration that government bailouts, coupled with the geyser of regulations that has been gushing from congressional committees, can fix it.

Although it is necessary to ground any meaningful discussion of the financial crisis in the received views of economists, business managers, and legal experts, gaining a deeper understanding of the current financial predicament requires that one advance beyond the mental models upon which such viewpoints are based and adopt the perspective of a moral-cultural mental model as well. Indeed, such a vantage point is essential for discerning the lessons for enlightened business leadership going forward. From a moral-cultural point of view, several causes of the present economic crisis, particularly financial innovation and complexity, excessive executive compensation, and neglect of moral hazard, are seen to be rooted in deep-seated moral-cultural tendencies. Most notable among these are technocratic and dehumanized economic thinking, egoistic individualism, greed, short-termism, rejection of objective moral values, and a highly speculative culture.

Granted, a reasonable amount of law and regulation did indeed serve to provide an answer to the question, "What do we do right now?" However, solving moral and cultural problems cannot be done on an emergency basis. These underlying moral-cultural trends cannot be resisted or reversed simply by increased law and regulation. Instead, they must be addressed by more nuanced ethical thinking and collective activity grounded in virtue, regard for the common good, and respect for the long-term preservation of market ecology, as well as by paying greater attention to the cultivation of intangible capital assets such as reputational and social capital. Our thinking needs to be more sensitive to the complexity of the relationship between ethics and economics and more attuned to the importance of trust, truth, and transparency. We must also establish localized and spontaneous social structures that are better equipped to foster such elements in business conduct than stepped-up regulation ever could.

Received View of the Financial Crisis

Looking at the economic crisis prompts some important questions: What happened? Why did it happen? What sorts of regulatory responses are called for? I will provide a brief sketch of widely recognized responses to these questions and will proceed in the terms of the conventional discourse of economists and legal experts.

We live in a world of mental models.[7] To oversimplify for the sake of illustration, we could say that the mental model of the economist inclines him to look for mathematical formulas. Similarly, the mental model of the business management theorist leads him to seek causal scientific explanations. The mental model of the legal expert inclines him to suggest new laws and policies to "fix" the problem at hand. We have heard a lot of discussion about the financial crisis from each of these respective models. I will briefly summarize the distinctive ways in which these mental models have framed the financial crisis.[8]

What Happened and Why?

Leading economists and business writers have asserted that the recent financial blowout represents the most severe economic downturn since the Great Depression.[9] The crisis has had global consequences: collapses of major businesses, sizeable reductions in personal wealth, extensive financial commitments taken on by governments, and a substantial downturn in economic activity. Economists and business experts have offered an array of explanations concerning the origins of the crisis.

For many economists, the proximate trigger of the financial turmoil was when the U.S. housing bubble popped after reaching its apex in 2005 and 2006. Soon after the bubble burst, the default rates on subprime and adjustable rate mortgages began to mount. Enlargements of loan incentives, particularly favorable initial terms, and a long history of rising housing prices had prompted borrowers to take on burdensome mortgages with the hope that they could readily refinance at more affordable rates. Yet when interest rates started rising and housing prices began dropping across the United States during 2006 and 2007, refinancing proved harder. Defaults, followed by foreclosure actions, increased appreciably as comfortable initial terms ended, house values did not increase as expected, and rates on adjustable rate mortgages were recalibrated at higher rates.[10]

Before the crisis, substantial sums of money had been pouring into the United States from rapidly growing foreign economies. The heavy influx of funds, coupled with low rates of interest in the United States from 2002 to 2004, tended to ease credit conditions. The easing of credit, in turn, led to the inflation of housing bubbles and credit bubbles alike. Because of the ease with which a variety of loans could be obtained, especially those for automobiles, mortgages, and credit cards, consumers built up an unparalleled debt burden.[11] The magnitude of mortgage-backed securities, which acquire their value from mortgage payments and home prices, also intensified. These forms of financial innovation permitted investors and institutions across the globe to invest in the U.S. housing market. Coupled with the immersion of credit-rating agencies in conflicts of interests, serious flaws in methodologies used by such agencies led to underestimation of the credit-default risks of instruments collateralized by subprime mortgages. Credit-rating agencies lowered the perception of credit risk by extending AAA ratings to the senior tranches of structured finance products such as collateralized debt obligations (CDOs), the same rating they accorded to government and corporate bonds that yielded systematically lower returns.

When housing prices fell, large global financial institutions that had borrowed and invested heavily in subprime mortgage-backed securities started reporting major losses.[12] In addition, declining prices caused houses to become valued below the amount of their mortgage loans. Owners then had a financial incentive to abandon the houses, leading to foreclosures. The rash of foreclosures that began in the United States at the end of 2006 depleted consumer wealth and abraded the power of financial institutions. In addition, defaults and losses on other types of loans escalated as the upheaval spread from the housing market to other sectors of the economy.[13] As the credit and housing bubbles grew, a dynamic took hold whereby the financial system was expanding while simultaneously becoming more and more fragile. In the main, policymakers did not perceive the significant role of the financial institutions that made up the so-called shadow banking system, especially hedge funds and investment banks.[14] In the eyes of some experts, such institutions became as significant as retail depository banks in supplying credit for the United States economy.[15] Not only were such institutions exempt from the regulations that applied to depository banks, but, together with some regulated banks, they had taken on substantial debt loads while making loans. Yet they lacked financial cushions adequate to withstand large loan defaults or mortgage-backed securities losses. Such losses dampened the capacity of financial bodies to extend loans, which consequently tended to slow economic activity.[16] Doubts surrounding the solidity of key financial organizations led central banks to extend funds to stimulate lending and shore up confidence in commercial paper markets, which are vital to supporting business operations. The government intervened to bail out major financial establishments and rolled out economic stimulus initiatives, taking on enormous financial obligations ranging from asset purchases, guarantees, and loans to direct spending.[17]

What Regulatory Responses Are Called For?

Beyond the government bailouts, and in line with the picture of the crisis presented by leading economists, influential legal experts have proposed a wide array of market-based and regulatory solutions, a number of which have either been put into action or are still being contemplated. What follows is a short, nonexhaustive summary of the regulatory proposals.

Generally, the regulatory proposals have been aimed at reducing the impact of the current crisis and preventing recurrences. The proposals have targeted a host of issues, including executive pay, financial cushions, consumer protection, the regulation of derivatives and the so-called shadow banking system, and the power of the Federal Reserve to wind down systemically significant financial institutions. In particular, some of the more prominent regulatory proposals have included allowing debt-for-equity swaps to reduce mortgage balances for struggling homeowners,[18] requiring minimum down payments together with income verification to inhibit the proliferation of "liar loans,"[19] nationalizing major banks,[20] establishing rules to insulate investors and financial institutions from systemic risk,[21] imposing constraints on executive compensation so as to reward long-term performance rather than excessive risk-taking,[22] regulating institutions that "act like banks" in ways similar to how banks are regulated,[23] breaking up financial institutions that are "too big to fail" to mitigate systemic risk,[24] returning to the separation of retail depository banking and investment banking established by the Glass-Steagall Act of 1933,[25] establishing resolution or wind-down procedures to sort out liabilities of failed investment banks and hedge funds,[26] requiring banks to maintain a stronger capital cushion with graduated regulatory capital requirements,[27] and requiring that standardized derivative contracts are traded on regulated exchanges.[28]

Taking Another Perspective and Posing a Further Question

A vital question remains. It is one that economists, management theorists, and legal experts are not well suited to tackle: What are the implications of the crisis for business leadership? For reasons laid out later in this chapter, addressing this question requires us to probe deeper than the received views of economists and legal authorities by adopting a moral-cultural mental model. First, however, I will offer a critical account of prevailing mental models of economists, management theorists, and legal experts.[29]

Critical Exegesis of Mental Models

Mental models provide the conceptual lenses through which we see the world.[30] Accordingly, depending on how they are put to use, such lenses serve either to clarify or to distort our view. The mental models of economics, business management, and law have equipped us with knowledge to comprehend and to manage, albeit in an imperfect and limited way, complex financial systems and institutions. But are they adequate? Have they warped our vision in some important way?

Mental Model of the Economist

Although economists have the most to say about the causes of the financial crisis, they have been squarely faulted for the inability of their econometric models to predict the crisis.[31] The economics profession has also been criticized on the ground that the financial modeling it has used since the mid-1990s may have led a substantial number of banks and financial institutions to commit improprieties.[32]

Whatever the merits of such accusations, the key explanatory limitation of the economist's mental model is this: economics is becoming so excessively mathematical that its human element is being eclipsed.[33] Yet the human dimension is precisely where we must look to achieve moral and cultural reform. In the wake of the financial crisis, the mental model of the economist, when directed toward the world of business, is deficient to the extent that it overlooks the fundamental complexity of human nature that is at the core of economics and business, properly understood.[34]

In a trend that originated during the time of John Maynard Keynes, ordinary economic theorizing has gradually become oriented toward mathematics and quantification.[35] The evidence supporting this claim is readily available from a random walk through the stacks of any library to inspect leading journals of economics. Even a cursory examination reveals the superfluity of quantitative formulas, statistical analyses, and algebraic equations that typify the thought processes of conventional economics.[36] The profusion of quantitative detritus seems to issue forth whether its instigators are neo-Keynesian disciples or adherents of the efficient markets hypothesis.[37] Yet a major deficiency of this intellectual trend is that it effectively conflates the study of economics with but one instrument of economic examination. As Albert Einstein is supposed to have put it, "Not everything that can be counted counts, and not everything that counts can be counted."

As symbolic language that originally developed as a method for examining natural science, mathematics is well suited to the study of the natural world. It is also an effective means of representing comparatively steady and straightforward economic patterns. But mathematics is not as suitable for examining a broad range of phenomena—such as institutions, values, culture, and traditions—that clearly have an enormous bearing on economic life. In other words, it is highly dubious that the mental model of quantitatively oriented economics is an adequate intellectual framework for understanding the entire range of economic life, given all of its instabilities, complexities, and unpredictabilities.

Granted, economics can achieve sound results by deploying mathematics when explaining relationships that have distinctively quantitative features. But as economics continues to examine the world in almost purely quantitative terms, it tends to neglect the human side of things, which is to say, the part that is nonmathematical and that does not behave according to fixed laws. In the words of Wilhelm Röpke, "Economics is no natural science; it is a moral science and as such has to do with man as a spiritual and moral being."[38] Röpke's insights point directly to a fundamental limitation of the mental model of the contemporary economist. In its quest for formulas, the "new economics," especially as it is enshrined in "financial engineering," is gradually eroding our comprehension of economics as a "moral science."[39]

Business Management Mental Model

The rise of a narrow positivism or scientism in theories of business management has accompanied the mathematization of economics. Like the economists, business researchers have typically misdirected scientific methods by incorrectly assuming that the subject of their investigations—the world of business—closely resembles the physical sciences. They thus wrongly believe that business unveils itself as an objective phenomenon governed by repeatable and predictable processes. Associated with this positivistic outlook is the further assumption that the only legitimate objective of business is maximization of shareholder value.[40] How did such a restrictive narrative about business come about in the first place?

In answering this question, it is helpful to consider some points that emerged from a recent, penetrating study of business education by Rakesh Khurana.[41] He maintains that the need to "professionalize" business schools was connected, as in the disciplines of engineering and medicine, with a need to convey knowledge that would function as a wall around the profession and thus keep amateurs out of the picture.[42] Yet unlike fields such as engineering or medicine, the exact content of that specialized knowledge remained obscure until 1959, when the Rockefeller, Carnegie, and Ford Foundations began to devote extensive resources to the development of technical subjects at business schools such as linear programming and statistical quality control.[43] Underpinning this project was the assumption that introducing mathematics-infused social science into the curriculum would accord an aura of academic respectability to business schools. Thus, for instance, business faculty would be recruited, hired, and tenured according to their production of scientific publications. Khurana points out the irony that, from the 1970s on, this scientific turn led innovative business schools to embrace the agency theory that was itself an outgrowth of neoclassical economics. The widespread acceptance of agency theory's seductive language, which was seen as useful for understanding a world in which business organizations, ownership, markets, and technologies are constantly in flux, served to dissolve traditional ideas of responsibility. According to this academic paradigm, managers are agents whose interests are not necessarily aligned with those of the principals, meaning the owners of a firm, the shareholders. The company is seen as a mere legal fiction, a "nexus of contracts."[44] Within the nexus-of-contracts theory, however, there is no place for a corporate ethos or corporate responsibility. Managers pursue their own advantage rather than the good of the company, much less the community's welfare.[45] For instance, managers have incentives to magnify their compensation by increasing the size of the enterprise and expanding the reach of their responsibility, even when there is no profit to be gained from this kind of arrangement.[46]

Agency theory emphasized monitoring management performance and providing incentives for managers to improve business performance. Various financial innovations that emerged in the 1970s and 1980s, such as the deployment of leveraging and debt in restructuring business organizations, accordingly enjoyed a compelling justification in terms of heightened efficiency.

As a legacy of this approach, the dominant focus of business management today is on the model of large, publicly traded corporations that present a complex agency problem in which managers occupy the role of shareholders's agents. Within the field of business management, theories of social science take center stage, while many business people act as if corporations and agency problems are virtually immune from any consideration other than shareholder value. According to Sumantra Ghoshal, "In courses on corporate governance grounded in agency theory, we have taught our students that managers cannot be trusted to do their jobs—which, of course, is to maximize shareholder value . . . . In courses on organization design, grounded in transaction-cost economics, we have preached the need for tight monitoring and control of people to prevent 'opportunistic behavior.'"[47] Thus, underpinning a great deal of the management discussion is a positivistic and deterministic outlook on business. This way of thinking is persuasive in consulting, securities trading, and investment banking, which hire a substantial number of graduates from the premier schools of business.[48] For investors and consultants alike, their tasks involve diagnostics and analysis. So there is a tendency in both of these lines of work for practitioners to adopt a reductionist mindset, regarding the businesses under observation purely as independent, determined phenomena. In the ordinary curriculum of a business school, the primary components of analysis are products and services, cash flows, processes, brands, and other stylized ideas that have taken on their own metaphysical stature. The narrow, functionalist thinking that produced the orthodoxy surrounding the notion of agency, the restrictive view that value can only mean economic value to shareholders, and the myopic perspective that regards the purpose of the firm as shareholder-centered, all constitute the dominant narrative in business education.

George Anders explains Khurana's assessment of the situation as follows: "M.B.A. training has deteriorated into a race to steer students into high-paying finance and consulting jobs without caring about the graduates' broader roles in society." According to Khurana, the "logic of stewardship has disappeared from business education." "Panoramic, long-term thinking," Anders contends, "has given way to an almost grotesque obsession with maximizing shareholder value over increasingly brief spans."[49]

According to this received view of business management, what counts above all is "winning the war" against competitors and maximizing the bottom line. From this viewpoint, the idea of applying moral principles to business conduct is inconceivable, or as the cliché goes, business ethics is an oxymoron. Such a mental model rejects the notion that economic value is in any way related to moral conduct in business. Economics and morality are viewed as wholly dissimilar forms of discourse for managerial decision making and business practices. According to this view, the expectation that corporations exercise moral behavior beyond the requirements of law betrays a fundamental misconception about the nature of a free economy, unnecessarily imposes restraints on corporate activity, and squanders corporate value on social initiatives of unsubstantiated value.[50] The only plausible case for obeying legal and ethical standards, under this position, is to avoid the monetary cost of noncompliance.

Not only has business management theory been misdirected by positivist and scientist assumptions, but also it has failed to provide any satisfactory understanding of what business actually is. For all of the technocratic blatherskite it generates, business theory gives little attention to the basic human interactions that make business a profoundly human enterprise.[51] Yet business, in its most essential form, is a way that we create value for each other by cooperating and specializing our labor. Business is fundamentally about human relationships addressed to the proximate objectives of creating wealth and fostering trade, and to the broader objective of human fulfillment. In reality, business is utterly incapable of even occurring, much less flourishing, outside of interpersonal moral-social matrices. It is astounding that most theories of business—for instance, those premised on shareholder theory—divorce business decisions from this human sphere. The point is this: not only have the mental models of economics and business management likely played a significant role in bringing about the financial crisis, but to the extent they neglect the moral and human dimensions of business, they are ill-equipped to provide any meaningful guidance for business leadership in the future. Providing such guidance will require a fundamental reframing of management practices to be more concordant with human nature and enduring moral values.

What is not ordinarily acknowledged is that classical economic theorists such as Adam Smith espoused principles that are in line with a robust pursuit of the common good in business. Barely one hundred years have passed since economic theory changed tracks and began developing an individualistic frame of mind grounded in the notion of scarcity and the view that people participate in the market purely as self-regarding profit-maximizers.[52]

Notwithstanding this relatively recent transition in economic thought, three key ideas upon which a human focus and classical economic theory come into agreement are the concepts of virtue, human dignity, and public happiness or the common good. The term *public* underscores the reciprocal character of happiness, as opposed to affluence. That is, one can be affluent alone, but to be happy requires others.[53] Public happiness is diagnosed in a stream of economics literature stressing the concept that commodities and profits engender prosperity only when situated within a broader context of meaningful interpersonal relationships within which human dignity is accorded proper respect. Moreover, in the eyes of many classical economists, the market did not contravene civil society but was in fact the embodiment of it. Proper functioning of the market depended on contracts, cooperation, institutions, and trust. These in turn promoted reciprocity. Economic activity thus provided a setting where humans manifest their social being and reveal their desire for camaraderie in relationships of equality and civility.[54]

Given contemporary technocratic understandings of the market, such characterizations no doubt appear strange, perhaps almost incomprehensible. Nevertheless, the crucial insight is this: the market reveals itself as a manifestation of social life when we can discern its strong dependence on the exercise of virtue, respect for dignity, and a shared sense of the common good. Logically, these moral elements must exist before effective bargaining can take place. By building good and just institutions, and by forming agreements grounded in authentic trust rather than on the basis of deceptive and disingenuous transactions, market interactions can take on a wider and more virtuous role. This deeply human-centered conception of business is supported by a long tradition of thought common to ancient cultures.[55] That intellectual tradition emphasized the dependence of commercial life on human characteristics taken to be ennobling and immutable.

Mental Model of Lawmakers and Legal Authorities

A key limitation of this model inheres in the reality that law ordinarily intervenes to supply enforceable norms where trust is lacking. Legal regulation, however, is no substitute for trust in business. The impotence of law to replace trust poses an especially acute problem since a retreat from trust was one of the principal reasons for the near collapse of the world's financial markets. Credit, which constitutes the lifeblood of the world economy, virtually dried up. Even large banking establishments were adverse to lending to one another; they simply did not trust that they were going to obtain repayment. Granted, legal structures assist in the enforcement of contracts, and contracts in turn facilitate the creation and enforcement of deals, agreements, and other business transactions. Nevertheless, one is not likely to sign a contract if there is no basis for trusting one's counterparty. The existence of trust is vital for any business to forge solid relationships with key constituencies such as customers, employees, suppliers, and the wider social orders within which the business carries on its activities. Furthermore, trust impels the basic dynamic of taking risks, which serves to foster progress and innovation.

Not surprisingly, consistent with their disposition to approach all problems with increased regulation, many government agencies started contemplating new laws and regulations in response to the subprime housing and credit crisis as early as 2007. Thus, U.S. federal regulators started proposing new rules requiring mortgage lenders to peg loan decisions on borrowers' capability to repay adjustable rate mortgages at the full interest rate rather than on borrowers' ability to pay lower introductory rates.[56] Moreover, industry trade journals began sending out smoke signals to their constituents announcing that new regulations would be a virtually certain consequence of the crisis.[57]

Nevertheless, it is clear that such efforts at legal and regulatory intervention did not stop the crisis from unfolding. What the mind-set of lawmakers and legal experts typically ignores is that a great deal of business activity cannot be effectively regulated, partly because it is normally too difficult or costly to do so and partly because legal regulation typically triggers ever more elaborate loophole-hunting avoidance schemes. Plus, excessive regulation threatens to dilute, if not completely annihilate, entrepreneurial initiative.[58]

One might turn to music as an analogy. The idea of perpetrating some mode of malfeasance on par with fraud while delivering a live violin performance is inconceivable. Without authentic technical and artistic mastery of the instrument there can be neither genuine musicianship nor decent music. For purposes of fostering musical artistry there are not, nor could there be, government regulatory agencies charged with such a mission. Imagine the absurdity of a law specifying how properly to deliver a trill, complete with a list of penalties for violations. Music is, in its essence, a self-regulating enterprise. A technical execution of all of the notes of a piece of music—call it "minimal compliance"—is understood by all reputable musicians to be merely the barest of requirements. Outstanding musicianship is all about the artistry that is added to the "minimal" accurate rendering of the notes. Just as integrity in music cannot be externally imposed, neither can integrity in business be legislated. In both music and business, the exercise of virtue is fundamental, unavoidable, and part of the very lifeblood of the endeavor.

Moral-Cultural Mental Model

Beneath the all-too-real empirical crisis revealed by the mental models of economics, business, and law, there is a moral malaise that calls for a fresh mind-set that can penetrate deeper and reach wider than these disciplines. To bring the distinctly moral dimension of the crisis into focus, consider the extent to which the subprime business market has been intimately bound up with a host of moral malfeasances. Moral failures leading to the financial crisis include:

- lenders enticing homebuyers into unsuitable mortgage arrangements;[59]
- approximately 70 percent of homebuyers falsifying data on their mortgage applications;[60]
- financiers creating nontransparent financial products (securitized mortgages) with risks obscured in vague or utterly indecipherable legal terminology, if disclosed at all;[61]
- rating agencies immersed in massive conflicts of interest issuing biased valuations of companies' financial postures;[62]
- hedge funds intentionally circulating false information to "short" the shares of companies' stock ("predatory short selling");[63]
- corporations instituting compensation plans ("golden parachutes") that rewarded executives for poor performance and for making decisions that contributed to the financial crisis by fueling excessive risk taking;[64] and
- hedge funds misleading investors by faking high performance.[65]

We are, it seems, barking up the wrong tree by looking to mathematized economics and positivist business management theory for enlightened understanding, and to stepped-up legal regulation for solutions. Given the moral dimensions of the crisis, where might we turn in the quest for a solution?

One answer might be to require business ethics courses in MBA programs. Regrettably, however, it is doubtful that the conventional business school ethics curriculum is capable of giving present and future business leaders the proficiencies they will need to navigate the dangerous currents flowing out of the current economic tumult.[66] Several serious defects in business education cripple the ability of a large number of business schools to come to terms with business's moral sphere. One defect is their tacit encouragement of the attitude that if something is not illegal then it must be acceptable.[67] Another defect is their retreat from any rigorous engagement in matters of right and wrong. Their reason for shirking from such matters is the threat that a careful study of right and wrong poses to the strong moral relativism that pervades so many cultures and societies around the world today.[68] Consequently, business education frequently mistakes the idea of morality to be coextensive with, on the one hand, a program of ethics "window dressing" and, on the other hand, a program of "political correctness" pretending to be corporate social responsibility.

Under the "window-dressing" approach, efforts to inculcate authentic moral sensitivity in future business leaders get sidetracked into image-conscious marketing strategies.[69] Armed with such strategies, MBA graduates, once absorbed into the corporate culture for which their business education has prepared them, perfect the art of crafting pious declarations of rectitude and peppering them throughout the annual reports, codes of conduct, and mission statements of business organizations. In the aftermath of the financial crisis, we have learned that many of these same institutions have been culpable for unprecedented levels of fraud and other forms of misconduct.[70]

Under the "political correctness" approach, the province of "business ethics" gets denigrated to harum-scarum stratagems formulated as reactions to alarms sounded by "stakeholders" that are in turn dictated by galleries of activists purporting to be their appointed representatives. This variety of business ethics is mainly bent on promoting fashionable politically correct agendas detached from the sincere objectives of CSR.[71] Moreover, these agendas are placed under strict accountability, compliance, and enforcement demands in utter disregard of the type and character of the business at hand and the conditions under which it might prosper. This mind-set concerning the nature of business ethics engenders the technocratic mental model of the lawmaker and legal expert discussed earlier. Those who espouse this mind-set instinctively turn to government to concoct increasingly detailed regulations and to impanel officious bureaucrats (who are typically clueless about—if not downright antagonistic toward—the world of business) to go about putting such regulations into effect.[72]

It is reasonable to look to business education to provide professional guidance and intellectual leadership for a postcrisis moral-cultural mental model. Rather than relying on the run-of-the-mill "business ethics" approach, however, moving out of the crisis calls for a reckoning with enlightened philosophical concepts. Our thinking must be guided with timeless ideas like trust, honor, dignity, virtue, and the common good, wrought from ancient heritage. Yet it is equally important to see clearly the demands that moral wisdom anchored in the past imposes on us today.

At this point the moral relativist is likely to object, questioning the fundamental premise of the moral-cultural model, namely, that the concepts of right and wrong are objective realities. Granted, there is no universally persuasive argument for the objectivity of moral standards. Nevertheless, the absence of a knockdown argument does not imply that the notion of an objective moral order is just a matter of parochial social construction, as the postmodernists, deconstructionists, and ethical relativists claim. If, however, enough people in our society and around the world are unable to identify something objectively wrong with the culture of business scandal that is beneath the financial collapse, the result will be to encourage behaving as if there are no moral standards in business at all.

It is now appropriate to discuss three pillars of ethical thought that provide a foundation for new moral vision in today's business environment: virtue, human dignity, and the common good. These ethical concepts invoke the language of the natural law tradition. That venerable tradition offers an alternative to the reigning outlook on economic life, which has brought many institutions and investors to ruin.

Moral Virtue

In the *Nicomachean Ethics,*[73] Aristotle grounds his moral philosophy in a number of basic propositions. As was explained earlier in Chapter 1, Aristotle holds that possessing the capability for reason constitutes the essence of what it means to be human, with abstraction and moral reasoning comprising the uppermost modes of thinking.[74] This capacity includes the ability to decide among ethical and unethical means of living one's life and of arranging human enterprises. Accordingly, individual moral virtue arises from cultivating one's faculty of reason. In other words, we complete our humanity through cultivating our naturally given aptitude for rationality. All human beings thus possess the capability to learn and develop. The good life consists of being engaged in a process of fulfilling one's capacities—not in the attainment of complete fulfillment, which is impossible. Although improving on a person's natural capabilities constitutes the *summum bonum*, it does not comprise the "complete good." One does not develop oneself for narrow self-centered purposes, but rather to add to the good of the community to which one belongs.

Again, as was seen in Chapter 1, human happiness, for Aristotle, arises from having chosen virtuous actions.[75] A virtuous action falls within the "golden mean," which rests midway between two vices that make up the extreme endpoints of any character trait: deficiency and excess.[76] For example, Aristotle states that people should be generous, meaning that they should be neither too wasteful nor parsimonious.[77] They ought to be temperate. As such they will prevent having their lives dictated by irrational appetites like envy and lustfulness. Happiness demands that they remain even-tempered. Of course, they may exhibit some measure of anger when the occasion warrants, yet they will eschew irascibility or wrath. They should take appropriate pride in their attainments without being boastful. Aristotle thinks the golden mean can be struck for other character traits as well.[78]

Some contend that certain types of executive compensation arrangements have contributed to the financial collapse. The arrangements are supposed to have offered inducements to cheat, perpetrate fraud, and cook the books to fabricate levels of reported corporate performance so as to elicit exorbitant payoffs. That is, they would reward businesspeople for immoral practices.[79] Accordingly, such executive compensation plans are squarely counter-Aristotelian and contrary to virtue ethics. Executive compensation plans that motivate managers to manipulate performance levels rather than to build genuine value for their firms fail to promote virtue; instead they encourage and reward vice, namely, the character deficiency of "acquisitive ungenerosity," which for Aristotle amounts to the dishonorable worship of profit.[80]

Human Dignity

The idea of human dignity encompasses the intrinsic worth inherent in all human beings. From the natural law perspective, and in the eyes of Catholic social thought, the source of human dignity is the concept of imago Dei, which conceives of the human person as having been created in the image and likeness of God.[81] Human dignity surpasses any particular social order as the foundation for moral rights and can neither be bestowed nor legitimately infringed by society. As such, human dignity forms the conceptual core of human rights. Within the tradition of Catholic moral thinking, insofar as there is a communal or social aspect to human dignity, persons ought not to be regarded in excessively individualistic terms. Rather, persons should be considered as essentially connected to the rest of society.

Immanuel Kant states that it is morally impermissible to treat people merely as a means rather than as an end.[82] That is to say, it is wrong to treat a human being simply as if he or she were an instrument, tool, or object. This aspect of Kant's philosophy encourages us to reflect on our reaction to treatment received in situations of indignity where we may have exclaimed, "Hey, you've been *using* me!" Kant's thinking also helps us to envision what it means to treat people in morally permissible ways—that is, as ends in themselves, dignified beings worthy of respect.

Many of the kinds of unethical business conduct that have rendered the financial crisis a serious moral scandal fail to respect human dignity, in the sense that such behavior infringes the moral rights of others. For example, consider the practice of predatory lending, which involves entering into unsound secured loans for inappropriate purposes. Countrywide Financial Corporation used a bait-and-switch technique, advertising low interest rates for home refinancing.[83] Loans were written into extensively detailed contracts and then swapped for more expensive loan products at closing. An advertisement might show that 1 percent or 1.5 percent interest would be charged. Then, a consumer is placed into an adjustable rate mortgage (ARM), allowing homeowners to make interest-only payments, yet the interest charged is more than the amount of interest paid. This mismatch creates negative amortization, which the homeowner might not notice until long after the loan transaction has been consummated. It is clear that business practices such as predatory lending treat people merely as means to an end. Businesspeople flout principles of human dignity whenever they deceive, manipulate, or otherwise treat individuals as if they were not worthy of moral respect.

Rabbi David Novak stresses, in his reflections on the threat to human dignity that sundry improprieties associated with the financial crisis represent, the need for cultivating a greater awareness of moral conscience in business culture. According to Novak:

> What is new is not what these [corporate] thieves have done, or even how they have done it. What is new is the political culture that has deprived them of the capacity for any real agony before they steal, or the capacity for any real remorse after they have stolen, even after they have been caught. What is new is the political culture that has deprived too many of us, who are not thieves, of the capacity to demand any real regret from those who are thieves, because we have lost the capacity to judge thievery with any real opprobrium. . . . The key . . . is to distinguish a political culture that cogently encourages one to be ashamed of wrongdoing, and a political culture that only pragmatically judges the good or bad consequences resulting from the exercise of one's self-interest or actually approves of what one has done. That kind of culture only pities the criminal for his or her bad luck in getting caught, and especially for having to "do hard time" in prison.[84]

The Common Good

How should we understand the concept of the common good? Certainly, we can associate a variety of meanings with the term.[85] For purposes of the present discussion, the common good is more than the competing interests of selfish individuals and more than the composite interests of special groups. It is the good we have in common—the communal conditions necessary for the virtuous pursuit of human fulfillment, flourishing, and perfection by all in society.[86] Ultimately, the common good is the aggregation of collaborative initiatives and shared restraints by which society helps everyone achieve what in the end only each individual can accomplish for himself: shaping a good will and constituting an authentically human self by freely choosing to actualize the good every time one is given the chance and responsibility to do so.[87] In addition to its tendency to reward unscrupulous conduct, the executive compensation schemes connected to the financial crisis are inimical to the common good in that they provide powerful incentives to people to maximize their selfish interests at the expense of the well-being of persons throughout society.

The moral degradation leading to the financial crisis reminds us of our interdependence and summons us to mutual responsibilities. Catholic thought provides a rich resource for embarking on just such a path. Consider John Paul II's encyclical *Centesimus Annus*:

> We see how [Rerum Novarum] points essentially to the socioeconomic consequences of an error which has even greater implications. As has been mentioned, this error consists in an understanding of human freedom which detaches it from obedience to the truth, and consequently from the duty to respect the rights of others. The essence of freedom then becomes self-love carried to the point of contempt for God and neighbor, a self-love which leads to an unbridled affirmation of self-interest and which refuses to be limited by any demand of justice.[88]

For a reframing of our mental model to occur in the aftermath of the financial scandal, we must return to the ethics of virtue, human dignity, and the philosophy of the common good. Here is where human freedom and individual interest reach their proper proportion.[89]

Moral-Cultural Dysfunctions Indicated by the Crisis that Are Not Treatable by Legal Regulation

Postmodernism

What are the moral-cultural roots of the economic crisis? Could it be that, as historian Harold James has suggested, under the influence of postmodernism within the broader culture, what has emerged is a greater eagerness to take irrational risks and to supplant reason with subjective feeling and intuition? Has such a trend in turn fostered a willingness, for instance, to provide and accept valuations of complex and basically incomprehensible securities?[90]

To posit the existence of linkages between postmodern culture and financial decrepitude may not be as implausible as it first appears. Recall the movie *Wall Street*.[91] Oliver Stone's masterful portrayal of a postmodern abandonment of reality through the character of Gordon Gekko depicts a financial world that has become as ephemeral as streaming real-time stock quotes.

Thus, in one of Gekko's memorable lines, he intones that "money itself isn't lost or made, it's simply transferred from one perception to another." In a scene (immediately following his purchase of obscenely overpriced abstract expressionist artwork in an auction) with his ex-lover, Darien, Gekko announces, "We are smart enough not to buy in to the oldest myth running: love. A fiction created by people to keep them from jumping out of windows." In a soliloquy to his protégé, Bud Fox, Gekko cynically proclaims:

> The richest one percent of this country owns half the country's wealth: 5 trillion dollars. One third of that comes from hard work, two thirds of it comes from inheritance, interest on interest accumulation to widows and idiot sons and what I do—stock and real estate speculation. It's bullshit. Ninety percent of the American people have little or no net worth. I create nothing: I own. We make the rules, buddy, the news, war, peace, famine, upheaval; the cost of a paper clip. We pull the rabbit out of the hat while everybody else sits around their whole life wondering how we did it.

Looking back at the various forms of financial innovation and complexity that precipitated the economic crisis, one can see that the financial experts who appeared to be selling wealth-producing innovative ideas did so with the encouragement of a cultural climate that is enamored of excessive experimentation, prone to disrespect for discipline, authority, and hierarchy and opposed to traditional values. The shocking result is that any kind of value—whether moral, aesthetic, or financial—is in danger of becoming regarded as arbitrary and fundamentally absurd.

It is important to point out that, in earlier times, mainstream education stressed these virtues. For instance, the study of musical harmony, undertaken within a framework of tonality, emphasized order and hierarchy. Similarly, in the study of syllogisms of logic, students were made aware of external authority and the demands of order and stability.[92] Contrast this tradition with today's violent rap music and trends in education, such as the "self-esteem" movement, which essentially serve to cultivate indiscipline.[93] Is it any wonder that signs of disorder and systemic crisis eventually appeared in the sphere of finance and business?

Rise in Speculative Culture

In finance, the concept of a speculative bubble can be explained roughly as follows. First, a quick yet normally short-lived run-up in prices comes about, not as a result of basic underlying market fundamentals, but rather from irrational exuberance. Then, while the speculative bubble grows, increasing numbers of investors are prone to buy, until it starts to look as if "everyone" thinks that prices are going to move yet higher. Finally, when the bubble eventually bursts, prices drop even more quickly than they ascended, with everybody clamoring to sell at once. Such panic selling in turn triggers widespread and acute losses.

To think about how the speculative bubbles underlying the recent financial crisis are connected to the rise of "speculative culture," it is helpful to go back to the work of Thorstein Veblen. Writing at the beginning of the twentieth century, Veblen offered a nuanced distinction between entrepreneurs and speculators: the entrepreneur is a businessman with a project who calculates the success of his business according to its realization of that project. To the entrepreneur, however, profit represents only one gauge of the goodness of the activity, not the end-all-and-be-all.[94] A speculator, however, pursues a particular project with the sole objective of making money. Whatever the material object of the activity happens to be is inconsequential. Indeed, a speculator will switch ventures or change to a different economic sector the moment he finds a more profitable pathway to generate money.[95]

An illustration of the peculiar fascination with—indeed, the outright glorification of—speculative pursuits in our culture can be seen in bestselling books such as Victor Niederhoffer's *The Education of a Speculator*, in which representations of stock charts are absurdly juxtaposed with the musical manuscripts of such timeless masters as Ludwig van Beethoven and Alexander Scriabin.[96] It is interesting to note that, on its back cover, the book's promotional blurb proudly recites the paradox that its author is "a contrarian trader" who attained "staggering wins and stellar performance" yet "was forced to close his fund due to heavy losses."[97]

Turning to the economic crisis, examples abound of unsound business practices fueled by a speculative economic culture. For instance, consider "flipping."[98] In the case of house flipping, a speculator might buy a house for US$300,000 in February. The speculator's intention is not to live in the house or even to rent it out for others to live in, but rather to turn around and sell it for US$400,000 as early as July and pocket the profits. Flipping became so popular in the United States that some do-it-yourself television programs, such as A&E's *Flip This House*, portray the method in detail.

Another example of speculative culture is the prevalence of so-called NINJA loans, a variety of subprime loans issued to borrowers with "No Income, No Job and No Assets."[99] They were especially prominent during the subprime mortgage crisis, serving as an example of poor lending practices. The term grew in usage as the subprime mortgage crisis came to be blamed on such loans.

Egoistic Individualism

It is a symptom of our disorder that a sizable segment of today's culture is inclined toward the glorification of the self, a trend that is based on the philosophy of egoistic individualism. This philosophy embraces the belief

> that the individual exists solely for her own happiness and thus that rational self-interest is the only objective basis for moral action. There are no moral constraints on the selfish pursuit of personal happiness, except force and fraud. And there is no moral duty to sacrifice individual advantage for any greater good because there simply is no greater good than personal happiness. . . .[100]

Such an outlook goes hand-in-hand with two of the chief tendencies toward which contemporary business education is inclined: subjective moral relativism (emotivism), and the assumption that if something is not illegal, it must be okay.

According to the storyline of this philosophy in the context of business, "corporate executives . . . seek what [is] best for the institution and its investors— and . . . self-interest . . . align[s] private profit with institutional good."[101] Market participants pursue their respective individual "advantage[s] regardless of others, because individual happiness is the ultimate good."[102] Consider how this ideal works in the context of executive compensation. In many instances, as was detailed earlier in Chapter 1, the compensation packages of high-ranking executives provide lavish remuneration irrespective of the firm's stock performance. As in the collapse of Washington Mutual, Lehman Brothers, Bear Stearns, and others, top executives were able to escape with "golden parachutes" such as cash bonuses, severance pay, stock options, and other benefits.

The egoist ethos amplifies this divergence between private interest and common good throughout many sectors of the financial market. Consider the mortgage market. For the mortgage lender, issuing risky loans that are unlikely to be repaid is a good investment, so long as the secondary mortgage market allows him to pass the risk of default to others by selling mortgage-backed "securities." Even if the borrower later goes into default, the mortgage lender has gained in the market so long as he is able to remove the loan from his books and reap his commission.

Furthermore, for the investment banker, purchasing bonds backed by risky loans is also a good investment, so long as a derivatives market allows him to "swap" the risk with a leveraged investor or an insurance company. Even if the loans go into default, the investment banker has still maintained his market position, so long as his credit-default swaps pay out and he covers his losses.

In short, so long as there is a market for betting on loan defaults and so long as there are investors willing to take the bets, financial risks that promise individual profit with potential cost to the common good make rational sense. Of course, this game of risk is sustainable only so long as the bets continue to pay off—which means in the case of the financial crisis, only so long as housing prices continued rising. With the burst of the bubble in the housing market, resulting in a flood of mortgage defaults, bond sellers and default insurers alike were left unable to make good on their promises, leaving bondholders to absorb the losses they had gambled others would pay. Although the risk-takers have reaped their reward, stockholders and taxpayers have borne the real cost.

The proposals of those using the mental model of legal experts to expand regulation of capital markets and executive compensation to rein in self-interest do not get to the heart of the matter. The deeper philosophical issue is that the egoist ethic as such is an insufficient foundation for economic life. What the financial crisis teaches is that excessive self-interest is economically destructive. Unrestrained selfishness is a vice, undermining not only the general welfare but also self-interest.

The pursuit of rational selfishness untempered by moral constraint erodes the trust between financial institutions necessary to sustain the flow of credit upon which a market-capitalist economy depends. Insofar as buying into the market carries risk, it also necessitates trust. Trust in the market, however, can neither be purchased nor legislated into existence. Trust arises out of the trustworthiness of market participants, whether they are buyers or sellers, borrowers or lenders. Without mutual trustworthiness, opportunities for commercial interaction are constricted. In this sense, whether in the public square or the marketplace, moral virtue is at the heart of human liberty. What Benjamin Franklin wisely said about political liberty is therefore true of economic liberty as well: "Only a virtuous people are capable of freedom."[103]

Safeguarding Market Ecology

Since Aquinas, the natural law tradition has sought to use human reason to derive moral principles that promote human well-being.[104] The moral urgency engendered by the present economic crisis ought to prompt a return to reason so as to discern moral principles that impose civic moral obligations on market participants from corporate leaders to behind-the-scenes "gatekeepers," such as accounting and law firms, to avoid the infliction of systemic abuse on—indeed, the outright sabotage of—the overall market system. Such duties of avoidance are important to achieve all market participants' shared goal of overall economic welfare as a necessary, albeit not sufficient, condition for achieving human well-being. We might think of this as the "ecology" of market efficiency.

Moral Coordination

Maintaining market ecology demands moral coordination. The challenge of preserving the ecology of market efficiency is particularly relevant to the present problem of subprime business scandals because it requires that market participants not, among other things, distort information that ought to be available to other market participants—that is, information on which market efficiency itself depends. Turning to the ideas of Adam Smith and Friedrich Hayek will prove particularly instructive with respect to the concept of market ecology.

Adam Smith

For Adam Smith, individual choice and personal freedom drive free commerce and enlightened commercial society in general. They inspire an attitude of industry that brings about enhanced opportunities, leading vast portions of humanity to enjoy a more appealing and remarkable existence. Across any free capitalist economy individuals—seeking betterment for themselves, their loved ones, and their communities—willingly contribute vigor, aptitude, and expertise. In the process—by the operation of an "invisible hand"—they are simultaneously improving the economy as a whole.[105] The strength of their initiative, and consequently the fruit of their productive efforts, will diminish if they sustain it only by force. Moral behavior is a prerequisite for the invisible hand to operate. Business activity is not possible without basic regard for ethical standards that respect property rights, honor promises, and ensure mutual commitments.

It does not follow, however, that the impulses responsible for enlivening the market are purely self-interested. Nor is the invisible hand simply a disinterested curative for greed and selfishness. Adam Smith argued that humans have a basic regard for others, or a sentiment of beneficence, in the absence of which the market would not function properly.[106] Economic activity thus flourishes among people only in the presence of moral sentiments, including norms of duty, integrity, and fairness.

Smith's portrayal of free-market competition is best interpreted in association with his views on human motivation, as laid out in *The Theory of Moral Sentiments*.[107] Sympathy, benevolence, and the stance of the "impartial spectator"—part and parcel of our moral nature—continuously modulate the brute pursuit of profit. According to Smith, what appears from one perspective as self-gain is seen from another viewpoint as benevolence.[108] Indeed, the most profitable business strategy often involves sublimating short-term financial yield to long-term investments in honor, kindheartedness, or benefaction.

Friedrich Hayek

According to Hayek, social institutions such as money, credit structures, markets, and property represent "spontaneous orders."[109] Hayek asserts that spontaneous orders are complex and abstract, and depend on general rules. In his words, "The insight that general rules must prevail for spontaneity to flourish, as reaped by Hume and Kant, has never been refuted, merely neglected or forgotten."[110] Although spontaneous orders are governed by general rules of conduct (which in turn are under the influence of human choice in various times and places), they depend mainly on self-generating characteristics resting at the center of market activity. Individual freedom and personal choice make up the heart of the market economy. For Hayek, a well-working market economy cannot be a constructed order because the market is much too complicated to be designed by humans. Instead, the market is the by-product of countless human interactions over time.[111]

For Hayek, "we are able to bring about an ordering of the unknown *only by causing it to order itself.*"[112] Failure to recognize the difference between constructed orders and spontaneous orders amounts to the "fatal conceit," which breeds social engineering that restricts individual freedom and erodes market economies. The result of treating spontaneous orders such as the market as if they were merely constructed orders formed by human design is to advance on a path toward totalitarian serfdom.[113] Conducting business freely belongs to the realm of spontaneous ordering that draws upon self-generating features. Stressing the fundamental difference between spontaneous ordering and artificial ordering is fundamental in Hayek's thought. His writings continually stress the supremacy of the former over the latter, claiming that it is next to impossible to make spontaneous order better by supplanting it with artificial varieties. Indeed, trying to "fix" apparent problems in spontaneous orders just ends up making things worse:

> Most defects and inefficiencies of such spontaneous orders result from attempting to interfere with or to prevent their mechanisms from operating, or to improve the details of their results. Such attempts to intervene in spontaneous order rarely result in anything closely corresponding to men's wishes, since these orders are determined by more particular facts than any such intervening agency can know. Yet, while deliberate intervention to, say, flatten out inequalities in the interest of a random member of the order risks damaging the working of the whole, the self-ordering process will secure for any random member of such a group a better chance over a wider range of opportunities available to all than any rival system could offer.[114]

The natural law tradition supplies a theoretical basis for Hayek's preference for the classical liberal ideal of limited government and strong confidence in competitive markets for the production and distribution of goods and services. Hayek deemed the free-enterprise economy to be a spontaneous order, and any substitute for it, like socialism, to be artificial. As such, the ascendancy of the free market over planned economies follows a fortiori from the preeminence of spontaneous order over artificial alternatives to it.

Applying Hayek's insights to the ecology of the modern market, it is evident that today's financial institutions are not isolated entities. Instead, they are thoroughly enmeshed in a web of property rights and innumerable day-by-day dealings, conventions, and traditions, including reputation and trust.

Pulling together the conceptual threads that have been spun, private property, private initiative, private risk, and private profit are all essential attributes of the capitalist system. These things, however, are economically effective only against a background of norms and values in which profit may certainly be kept in view, but seldom is the only goal at which business activity aims.

Francis Fukuyama has shown that populations possessing a culture of integrity and trust will succeed in generating material wealth and prosperity despite being situated under unfavorable conditions.[115] In this regard, a society that has succeeded in amassing pools of social capital, such as that of the United States, not just through law and regulation, but also through the development of a broader culture, social networks, and a wide array of private institutions, is going to be ahead of the curve in its ability to emerge from economic devastation. Furthermore, it is reasonable to suppose that human nature leads us to build up, in addition to reputational and social capital, more tangible assets such as health care, food, housing, income, and so on. We regard an increase in such resources as good even before considering how the increase will be passed around to everyone.

Other things being equal, achieving more efficiency means having greater aggregate resources, in both tangible and intangible forms. Yet because regulatory regimes are unable to legislate and enforce all of the moral conduct necessary for optimal efficiency, market participants, in their pursuit of profit, have basic civic responsibilities to support cooperative business practices that enhance the overall efficiency of the market. What does this duty mean in the specific context of the current financial debacle? Market participants ought to:

- promote transparency of relevant information (for example, disclose the value of mortgage-related securities and other investments);
- refrain from abusing business-government relationships (for example, creating a dependency on, and expectation of, government bailouts);
- honor contracts, promises, and other commitments;

- resist crony capitalism;
- avoid fraud;
- shun insider trading; and
- develop compensation programs that are fair and reasonable and reward executives for forthright conduct, not for indulging in vice.

Business leaders must develop virtues of cooperative action that will foster market efficiency, not burn it down. Based on views such as those of Smith and Hayek, it is clear that the task of cultivating such economic virtues penetrates far deeper than legal regulation. Moral coordination, as a response to the rash of scandals, promises to circumvent the drawbacks of overt regulation and will be a step in the direction of building trust from Wall Street to Main Street.

No Bailout for Loss of Reputational and Social Capital

The preservation of overall market efficiency requires much more than market freedom and government regulation—it requires trust, transparency, and truth. In principle, governments possess the authority to enforce business agreements. Yet official efforts to provide legal insulation from all contractual breaches would be utterly futile were it not for a thick blanket of shared moral standards of promise keeping and honor. Moral standards are essential for facilitating efficient economic activity. In a free market, these moral standards are properly "enforced" against individuals and firms alike, not primarily or exclusively with government regulation, but rather with reputational standards established by members of a free society.[116] Recent studies show that a majority of people believe businesses ought to be held to the same or even higher moral and ethical standards as individuals.[117] Moreover, a sizable percentage think we ought to hold companies to even more stringent standards than those to which we hold people because businesses' size, resources, knowledge, and impact greatly exceed those of individuals.[118]

One important lesson from the crisis is that a deep connection exists between economic value and moral virtue. The physical and financial assets that market participants work so hard to establish on their books are fundamentally linked to the way they deploy—or destroy—intangible reputational assets such as credibility and transparency. Such intangible assets, which represent the most powerful force behind a firm's long-term performance, are vanishing from our financial system virtually unnoticed. Thus, all of the effort to tally up the staggering financial losses from the collapse of Lehman and other financial institutions ignored a much greater and more significant loss of wealth from the raft of financial scandals: the catastrophic exodus of reputational and social capital from financial institutions and from corporate and political leaders. Indeed, even the reputation of capitalism itself has been sullied as a consequence of financial malfeasance.

Both reputational capital[119] and social capital[120] constitute valuable forms of intangible wealth. Any business typically is involved in either creating or depleting them in their day-to-day activities. When tallying up the assets of a business enterprise one should include trust, good will, respect, fellowship, and sympathy among its stakeholders, as well as social networks that will serve to implant the enterprise within the field of moral sentiments of its constituencies. Among the valuable contributions of emerging theories of social capital and reputational capital are their explanation for why running a successful business does not necessarily require the kind of relentless pursuit of profit that is emblematic of the shareholder-centric theories of business.[121] What it takes to build the reputational capital of a business—perhaps its most valuable capital asset—comes about from working toward things that are not readily captured explicitly on the balance sheet, even if part of their valuation concerns their contribution to the bottom line.[122]

People are apt to flourish in surroundings in which overall social progress and cultural advancement are taking place. Growth comes about as a cooperative—not simply an individual—enterprise. The ability of sizeable groups to operate in conjunction with one another generates social trust, one of the essential components of market activity. Fukuyama states that "trust is the expectation that arises within a community of regular, honest, and cooperative behavior, based on commonly shared norms."[123] "These norms," he notes, "can be about deep 'value' questions like the nature of God or justice, but they also encompass secular norms like professional standards and codes of behavior."[124]

The notions of reputational capital and social capital should both be brought squarely into the province of economic study. Both of these concepts capture intangible assets that businesses must cultivate. Although their origins are nonmonetary, the resultant value of such assets can be reckoned in monetary terms. Established econometric theory is capable of making allowance for forms of intangible capital assets, such as social and reputational capital, just as it has for other varieties of capital—financial capital, organizational capital, human capital, and knowledge capital.[125]

Lessons to Be Learned

Contrary to the amoral forms of discourse in which it has customarily been framed, the financial crisis is freighted with moral and cultural significance. Attempts to understand the crisis purely in functionalist, mathematical, and legal terms inevitably lead to a distorted view that will not help in mustering the enlightened leadership required to advance beyond the crisis toward a preferable situation of a sustainable market ecology. In this regard, the current economic scandal provides a special opportunity to recalibrate moral standards for market participants.

Two vital components of market ecology—reputational capital and social capital—are in part created and deployed by market participants themselves. In this sense, we might refer to them as microintangible assets. Moreover, such intangible capital assets are created and deployed by the broader culture in which businesses operate. In this sense, we could speak of them as macro intangible assets. Whether we are talking about their micro- or macroforms, reputational and social capital are fostered by cultivating moral virtue, according respect for human dignity, and advancing the common good, rather than aiming at profit maximization directly.

The ecology of the market, because of its deep dependence on spontaneous ordering and its imperilment in the face of constructed ordering, will be sustained more by increasing the stock of reputational and social capital (at both micro- and macrolevels) than by legal and regulatory intervention. The big lessons for leadership are therefore to be found in seeking moral reform rather than just passing new laws.

Thus, there are two crucial points to bear in mind. First, there are grave perils in conceiving of the market as detached from the rest of society. Market failure points to a more general failure of responsibility, not only in business institutions but in the wider culture as well. By looking beyond the mindsets of the increasingly dehumanized fields of business management and economics and into a moral paradigm that sees the essential challenges as abiding in the hidden chambers of the human heart, we might approach the interconnected challenges of moral reconstruction and economic recovery.

Second, although some legal regulation is necessary to reduce the costs of responsible business behavior, we need to look to moral reform. Regulation is no substitute for virtue. Stepping up government regulation in an attempt to enforce moral conduct in business will provide neither a satisfactory nor a lasting solution. What is lacking in the received narratives of the financial crisis is a robust conception of moral virtue, human dignity, and the common good. Adopting a wider moral-cultural mental model to examine the crisis has revealed that ultimately the economy and its current malaise rest not simply on observable and repeatable dynamics played out in housing and credit markets, but within a moral and cultural framework. If suffering the costly experience of our financial turmoil has not been enough, perhaps the foreshadowing of a much bigger collapse—that of our moral and cultural framework, which stands imperiled by the insidious and profound financial scandals beneath the crisis—will serve to summon us to a higher calling.

Chapter 8

Symphony of Soft Law

The brands that will be big in the future will be those that tap into the social changes that are taking place.
—Sir Michael Perry

CSR Has Made Firms' Reputations Accountable to Moral Standards

Global civil society primarily demands that businesses abide norms of social responsibility in their pursuit of profit. This emphasis on the "character" of transnational business conduct is a departure from the entrenched metaphor that sees corporations as amoral profit machines, devoid of moral character, virtue, or probity.[1] The fact that transnational firms adopt civil regulations voluntarily to build credibility in the eyes of global civil society—that is, the fact that firms proactively comply with the new global social contract—presupposes that international businesses and the people that run them are able to exercise virtue in distinguishing moral choices and then making them.

Unlike traditional legal regimes whose norms are enforced through centralized systems of sanctions, the emergent "soft-law" norms of global economic governance rely on decentralized enforcement mechanisms.[2] These emergent norms are not the product of parochial regulation or local cultural mores.[3] Rather, they represent expectations of economic communities around the world that together comprise global civil society.[4] The promulgation of voluntary civil regulations by firms reveals an acceptance of global social contracts borne of growing global societal consensus as to the proper performance, responsiveness, and responsibility of transnational corporations.[5]

Consequently, transnational business enterprises are further committing to rule making and rule implementation in the spheres of social and environmental responsibility, as well as financial integrity.[6] They engage in interfirm cooperation and collaborate with nongovernmental organizations.[7] Over the past decade, CSR has gained prominence in both developed and developing countries at local, national, regional, and international levels.[8] International businesses are therefore under increasing pressure from civil society organizations and corporate accountability networks that monitor business conduct.[9]

Although the conventional views of corporate governance—"shareholder theory" and "stakeholder theory"—reach divergent conclusions about the proper nature and scope of CSR, both evolved at a time when firms were constrained, at least in principle, by the rule of law and legal sanctions. Yet, unlike traditional hard-law enforcement regimes, today's emerging "civil regulations" are grounded in the "rule of reputation," which ties accountability to reputation capital, or lack thereof. Operating internationally and faced with pressure to self-regulate, a company's reputation has become one of its most valuable assets.[10] Of course, one of the problems with so much stress being placed on reputation is that sometimes a reputation can be damaged—or enhanced—undeservedly. Regardless, it is clear that today's companies must reconcile economic and moral value with traditional notions of corporate governance.[11]

Attention to the ethics of international business has been mounting since the late 1960s.[12] It began as an activist movement aimed at U.S.-based multinational companies in France and later spread to other parts of the world.[13] Less-developed countries were especially worried about outside infiltration into their economies and the resulting dilution of national control. Yet, as a means of economic development, they were interested in attracting foreign investment that would lead to a rise in employment. The expansion of direct foreign investment around the world prompted attempts to create codes of business conduct at the intrafirm and international levels.[14] One notable example of this dynamic could be seen as early as the 1940s with the promulgation in the United Nations of the Universal Declaration of Human Rights. Another later example is the attempted development of a Voluntary Code of

Conduct for Transnational Corporations at the United Nations Conference on Trade and Development ("UNCTAD") beginning in the 1970s. Similarly, national legislatures, backed by enforcement regimes, adjusted their laws to reach transnational firms doing business overseas. International treaties and national legislation, however, did not succeed everywhere in combating misconduct. Rather, in a significant number of cases, business reforms were precipitated by public outrage at corporate malfeasance.[15]

In the 1980s, a number of ecological and social calamities began impacting the reputations of individual firms and the corporate world in general.[16] The ensuing reputation crises vividly illustrated the consequences of embracing a self-regulating, profit-maximizing, shareholder-focused brand of corporate governance, notwithstanding its substantial reputational risks.[17] Hitherto, the traditional governance paradigm of multinational corporations rigidly stressed shareholder profit maximization.[18] Essentially, in an effort to reach narrowly defined goals in the form of financial targets, many transnational firms failed to consider how backlash from public perceptions of raw corporate greed could affect business.[19] Instead, leading and aspiring multinational corporations traversed the globe seeking locations that offered low labor costs and lax environmental and socioeconomic regulations.[20]

With the advent of the 1990s came a succession of ecological crises stemming from morally questionable business practices. This propelled multinational corporations further into the spotlight. The Exxon Valdes disaster in Prince William Sound and the Royal Dutch Shell controversy over the disposal of the Brent Spar in the North Sea were two well-publicized incidents that caused considerable damage to the reputations of the firms involved. Royal Dutch Shell also suffered reputational damage over its apparent complicity with the execution of Ogoni indigenous leaders in Nigeria, and Nike suffered backlash, especially between 1992 and 1997, when reports regarding the company's operations in Southeast Asia spawned public concern over child labor and poor working conditions in "sweatshops."

As a result of these public controversies, corporations began guarding their reputations while global civil society began questioning the unregulated market dominance of transnational firms.[21] Such unbridled control was exacerbating social inequalities and human rights violations while endangering the earth's ecological systems and depleting natural resources.

Seeking institutional authority to voice its position, global civil society condemned multinational corporations collectively for failure to provide proper employment conditions and decent wages, and for failure to foster human rights as mandated by the United Nations Declarations and International Labor Organization Conventions and Recommendations. With respect to ecology, civil society began to insist that firms comply with United Nations' agreements and conventions on development and the environment. Furthermore, pressured by civil society, firms began to recognize state-sanctioned environmental regulations promulgated by regional organizations, such as the European Commission.

Consequently, in the latter part of the 1990s, many firms began advocating the notion that responsible corporate conduct produces mid- to long-term financial rewards.[22] This idea stood in opposition to the long-held notion that corporate wealth is solely grounded in maximization of profits for stockholders. Firms that were clinging to the conventional viewpoint were equally opposed to the advent of CSR because they believed it entailed significant financial costs. To this day, the international business community remains at odds over these divergent perspectives. Nevertheless, several features of CSR have gained prominence, including:

- adoption of voluntary initiatives aimed at elevating the ethical level of operations above that which is required by law;
- internalization of externalities;
- consideration of a range of stakeholder interests;
- integration of the firm's social and economic mandates;
- contributions to nonprofit, charitable, and other civic organizations and causes; and
- provision of employee benefits and improvement of quality of life in the workplace.[23]

Corporate Social Responsibility and Global Governance

The emergence of CSR poses a challenge to a corporate governance framework centered on shareholder value creation.[24] The rise of CSR has engendered a debate about the ultimate purpose and essential nature of a business corporation.[25] The competing visions expose conflicting political and moral preferences regarding the corporation's nature.[26] In the same vein, scholars sympathetic to CSR argue that both the contractual model of the firm, where the corporation is seen as a "nexus of contracts,"[27] and the legal person model, where a corporation has a distinct legal personality,[28] do not establish a basis for conferring superior property rights to shareholders over employees.[29] It is argued instead that employees contributing labor to the firm are entitled to legal recognition of their residual interest in the assets of the enterprise.[30]

In addition, CSR advocates challenge narrow economics-based justifications for the stockholder-centered view, asserting that the ideal of corporate efficiency carries a broader meaning than elevated stock prices.[31] Accordingly, CSR-oriented theorists have generally repudiated the type of cost-benefit analysis that ignores and segregates distributive considerations from conventional notions of profit-maximizing efficiency.[32] Because a corporation's existence depends on sophisticated financial transactions, contracts, managers, employees, and other relationships among investors, it functions as a semi-public enterprise.[33] However, this view is not universally shared among corporate governance scholars.[34]

Consequently, CSR's main tenets have highlighted corporate stakeholders' interests. They have recognized that firms' constituencies play similarly active roles in corporate conduct and strategy. Moreover, scholarly literature illustrates that conventional approaches to corporate governance are changing due to concerns facing management of multinational firms.[35] These changes have led to economic analysis of managerial incentives for undertaking corporate social responsibility,[36] fiduciary duties,[37] stakeholder-oriented management strategies,[38] and pro-CSR activism by corporate boards and their shareholders.[39] The inquiry also highlights quantitative metrics of ratings, reporting practices, and indexes that relate to corporate responsibility governance.[40] In addition, new methods have been suggested for allowing enhanced participation on the part of boards of directors.[41] Greater inclusion on a board will foster a stronger connection between corporate accountability and governance.[42]

Responsibility, Responsiveness, and Performance Differentiated

Scholars have crafted a distinction between CSR, which stresses obligations and accountability, and "corporate social responsiveness," which emphasizes action and activity.[43] But beyond these distinctions, there is a third, results-oriented concept known as *corporate social performance.*

Corporate Social Responsibility

Some say it is futile to attempt an operational definition of CSR because there are too many conceivable applications of CSR.[44] But, broadly stated, CSR merely implies that businesses share responsibility for societal conditions. Archie Carroll separates business obligations into four classes: economic, legal, ethical, and discretionary.[45] A firm has an economic responsibility to provide goods and services, offer employment at a living wage, and generate profits to survive.[46] Through these obligations, firms enhance societal well-being. Similarly, corporations shoulder legal responsibilities imposed by courts, legislatures, and administrative agencies.[47] These responsibilities can assume many forms and may extend to consumers, employees, stockholders, suppliers, and other stakeholders.[48]

In addition, CSR signifies conformity to society's expectations of appropriate business behavior such as honoring unwritten ethical standards.[49] For example, while corporations are not legally bound to contribute to charities, many citizens expect profitable enterprises to do so.[50] Moreover, as law sometimes lags behind social norms, some of society's normative expectations may eventually evolve into law.[51] Lastly, some of society's expectations are not clearly defined for corporations.[52] For instance, although society might expect corporations to invest in efforts to resolve significant social problems, society does not have a clear idea of what shape or form those solutions might take.[53]

Corporate Social Responsiveness

Robert Ackerman and Raymond Bauer claim that the term "social responsiveness" is a label more apt for a process-focused social outlook.[54] Ackerman and Bauer have argued that emphasizing companies' obligations places too much importance on motivation rather than on performance.[55] In their words, "Responding to social demands is much more than deciding what to do. There remains the management task of doing what one has decided to do, and this task is far from trivial."[56] Focus on responsiveness allows companies to fulfill social responsibilities without being distracted by issues of accountability that arise when organizations attempt, prior to acting, to determine their precise responsibilities.[57] Social responsiveness addresses a firm's ability to be alert to social pressures.[58] Thus, rather than simply reacting to a crisis, the socially responsive firm would have preempted the crisis by implementing a process that enabled it to foresee predicaments and be proactive in a productive and humanitarian manner.[59]

Corporate Social Performance ("CSP")

Under the "performance" viewpoint, it is firms' capabilities that are paramount. In other words, once a firm accepts that it has a "social responsibility" and adopts a responsiveness mentality, the *results* achieved thereafter are critical. Constructing a CSP framework requires more than a determination of the nature of the responsibility. It also involves articulating certain philosophies, patterns, modes, or strategies of responsiveness. Carroll has designed a CSP model around three key facets: (1) social responsibility categories—economic, legal, ethical, and discretionary; (2) philosophies (or modes) of social responsiveness—reaction, defense, accommodation, and pro-action; and (3) social (or stakeholder) issues involved—consumer issues, environmental issues, and employee issues.[60] This configuration illustrates that corporate social responsibility is not separate from financial performance. Moreover, it places ethical and philanthropic expectations into a rational, economic, and legal structure.

Alternative Governance Models

From the standpoint of global corporate governance, the discussion regarding corporate social responsibility (including its extension to corporate social responsiveness, and corporate social performance) boils down to a debate about what may be termed a monophonic versus a polyphonic view of corporate objectives. I use these terms by way of analogy to music. In musical composition, polyphony (derived from the Greek words for "many" and "voice") refers to a texture made up of two or more independent melodic voices. By contrast, monophony refers to music composed with only a single voice.[61] Accordingly, a monophonic orientation in global corporate governance is characterized by its concern for the single voice of shareholders, while a polyphonic orientation seeks to orchestrate a plurality of stakeholder voices.

For years, assuming various labels, the debate between the monophonic and polyphonic camps has encompassed business ethics, management, corporate law, and corporate governance theories.[62] The debate has focused predominately on the behavior of domestic, rather than multinational, business enterprises.[63] It has thus centered on interpretations of domestic corporate law (for example, U.S. corporate law).[64] As the following discussion demonstrates, the monophonic-polyphonic controversy—either in a local or global context—aims to explain what form of governance would fulfill the obligations of corporate social responsibility while moving beyond the narrow goal of shareholder wealth maximization.[65]

Monophonic Portrait

Over the years, the debate over the nature and purpose of the corporate enterprise has lingered and has sought to apportion priority between shareholder and nonshareholder interests.[66] In the United States, the debate extends back to the landmark case of *Dodge v. Ford Motor Company*,[67] where the court held that a business corporation is organized primarily for the profit of its stockholders, rather than for its employees or the community.[68] The debate then poured into academia. Whereas Adolf Berle advocated the stockholder-centric view, E. Merrick Dodd urged increased consideration for nonstockholders.[69]

For a considerable time, the prevailing corporate governance paradigm was dominated by the monophonic perspective, which emphasizes the stockholder-centric approach to corporate governance. Consequently, corporate governance was focused mainly on the board's structure, its functions, and its relations with other corporate organs, and the emphasis was on profit maximization. This governance model was heavily influenced by both Berle's and Means's analyses of principal-agent problems arising from separating stockholders' ownership rights from corporate managerial duties.[70] The business community relies on corporate law to influence management so as to reduce such agency-cost problems.[71] This enables shareholders to trust managers with their investments. With an emphasis on resolving agency conflicts, the monophonic corporate governance paradigm embraced a view of economic efficiency,[72] which favored cost-benefit analysis and value-maximization objectives in business decision making.[73] But it typically ignored adverse social and environmental externalities, downplayed the stakeholders' interests,[74] and disregarded firms' obligations to nonshareholders.[75] Milton Friedman advocated an extreme version of the monophonic view for promoting a free-market economy: "In such an economy, there is one and only one social responsibility of business—to use its resources and engage in activities designed to increase its profits so long as it stays within the rules of the game, which is to say, engages in open and free competition, without deception or fraud."[76] This view emphasizes competition to maximize the bottom line. This approach, called the "separation thesis" is antithetical to the view that economic value may flow from a firm's commitment to social responsibility.[77] Business managers view economics and ethics as two mutually exclusive spheres. From the monophonic standpoint, "social responsibility" possesses three key defects. First, it expresses a misunderstanding of the essence of a free market.[78] Second, it mistakenly allows the interests of groups other than shareholders to constrain, rather than expand, corporate activities.[79] Third, it does not acknowledge evidence of the economic benefits from investing in social initiatives.[80] This position suggests a single argument for legal and ethical compliance, namely, to sidestep the monetary costs of noncompliance. Accordingly, the monophonic view of corporate governance leads to reactive compliance with environmental and human rights standards but only insofar as these norms are grounded in the "hard" rule of law. That is, under the monophonic view, corporations comply only when noncompliance threatens sanctions pursuant to the "hard" rule of law. The monophonic view is hardwired to legal accountability (legal norms backed by hard sanctions) and fiscal accountability to stockholders, insofar as this is mandated by corporate law.

Polyphonic Portrait

Whereas the monophonic model is addressed to matters of agency, the polyphonic archetype focuses on ethics and accountability to parties outside the firm. Under the polyphonic approach, maximizing profits for shareholders is not the sole purpose of a business. Polyphonic corporate governance seeks to link relationships among various parties together with a broadly defined corporate mission.[81] This model sees businesses as fulfilling various functions within a society. Here, businesses serve an array of other constituents.[82] Thus, the scope of social responsibility extends beyond merely meeting the bottom line, and business firms' ethical and discretionary responsibilities go beyond their purely economic and legal objectives. Nevertheless, the polyphonic view retains the basic assumption that corporations are fundamentally profit-making enterprises. Corporations strive to meet the bottom line as it is necessary to preserve their economic viability. They are not social welfare agencies. Stated differently, managers have an institutional and moral duty to broader constituencies to keep the firm profitable. Norman Bowie writes, "Not only does Wall Street expect a business rationale for corporate good deeds; Wall Street has a moral right to those expectations."[83] Bowie continues, "This strategy grounds the motive to seek profits in ethics itself."[84] The polyphonic view, however, correctly assumes that, even in pursuit of profit, corporations must deploy financial, political, and social capital in a socially responsible way. Corporate governance must seek to confer not only financial benefits to shareholders but also social benefits to all of the firm's stakeholders.

Turning back to the monophonic perspective, one sees that it fails to account for the reality that, in today's information age, corporations are under meticulous observation.[85] It neglects to consider that a watchful public, media, and government will hold multinational corporations accountable for dishonorable conduct; it ignores firms' broader social responsibilities; and it ignores the potential for firms to incur "ethical blowback" from broader constituencies.[86] Robert Solomon once attacked the monophonic exemplar for its "pathetic understanding of stockholder personality as *homo economicus*."[87] Whereas Amartya Sen challenges the mind-set according to which "business principles are taken to be very *rudimentary* . . . essentially restricted . . . to profit maximization, but with a very wide reach [to] . . . all economic transactions."[88]

Before turning to the question of whether a polyphonic approach to corporate governance provides a satisfactory theoretical anchoring for the emerging regime of civil regulations that increasingly characterizes global governance, it will be useful to examine an additional approach, the "integrative social contracts theory."

Integrative Social Contracts Theory (ISCT)

Both corporate social responsiveness and the stakeholder view alike are criticized on the grounds that they do not provide management with precise standards of conduct.[89] By itself, the concept of corporate social responsiveness falls short of offering normative guidelines for managers to pursue in response to social expectations and demands.[90] Likewise, stakeholder theory has been faulted for its failure to reconcile the competing interests of various stakeholders.[91]

In response to these challenges, Thomas Donaldson and Thomas Dunfee developed a social contract theory of business.[92] The ISCT develops two key concepts: hypernorms and moral free space.[93] These concepts are illustrated by a reference to a series of concentric rings that represent core norms accepted by corporations, industries, or economic cultures.[94] Hypernorms, which rest at the center, are norms embodying transcultural values fundamental to human existence, such as prescriptions shared by main religions around the world and most basic human rights.[95] Such higher-order norms impose minimal necessary constraints on the capacity of communities to formulate their own rules.[96] Advancing away from the center of the rings, one finds norms that have greater cultural specificity than those at the center.[97] These rules are molded by the social norms of sundry economic communities, such as corporations, subunits within firms, industries, professional associations, trade groups, governmental bodies, and so on.[98]

The next ring represents moral free space, where one finds norms that are inconsistent with at least some other norms embraced by other economic communities.[99] Within moral free space, members are free to establish their own norms for economic conduct.[100] However, such norms must have the status of being both "authentic" and "legitimate."[101] A norm is "authentic" if community members have given their informed consent to the norm's existence while still retaining a right to exit the community should they come to disapprove of the norm.[102] The existence of specific authentic norms is established by empirical conditions expressing customary acceptance by the relevant economic community.[103]

A norm is "legitimate" if it does not run afoul of a hypernorm.[104] At the outermost ring are illegitimate norms, which are incompatible with hypernorms. Donaldson and Dunfee assert that integrative social contracts theory provides a normative core for stakeholder theory.[105] Following this line of thought entails consulting relevant community norms to decide, first, who counts as a stakeholder, and, second, what obligations extend from the firm to the stakeholders.[106] Conflicts between norms are resolved by determining the dominant legitimate norms, which are accorded priority.[107]

The preceding discussion shows the need for corporations to adapt to societal expectations and adopt societal norms. While both CSR and stakeholder theory advance the general notion that corporations should be attuned to a variety of stakeholders' demands, social contract theory makes a significant contribution beyond those accounts. Social contract theory accords deeper meaning and substance to the notion of CSR by fastening it to communal norms.[108] The social contract perspective on corporate governance provides an explanation for corporations' acceptance of global civil regulations.[109] These regulations, as understood in ISCT's terminology, are "extant social contracts"—the product of economic communities voluntarily adopting norms within moral free space.[110] ISCT highlights the normative content of the standards necessary for adopting moral principles. Without definite content—that is, without a definite mission for corporate governance—stakeholders would engage in power-wars over their respective interests.[111] CSR scholars and ethicists, for instance, consider the human rights and environmental norms that are voluntary established by multinational firms to incorporate genuine moral obligations that are recognized by worldwide consensus.[112] Accordingly, ISCT's notion of hypernorms accounts substantially for the emergence of global civil regulations in the form of "soft" and "hard" law.

Reputation Capital: A Key Ingredient in the Governance Recipe

Given its emphasis on the wider society, the rise of civil regulation should lead corporate governance to embrace the polyphonic view. Paradoxically, however, its rise has not diminished the importance global companies attach to the monophonic portrayal.[113] Nevertheless, as many global companies have discovered, there is evidence that commitment to responsible global corporate citizenship comes with financial advantages.[114] The rise of civil regulations, therefore, begs the question whether corporate governance can effectively synchronize the monophonic and polyphonic viewpoints. When corporate governance, in an effort to stockpile reputation capital, begins to maximize shareholder wealth by properly accommodating various stakeholders' interests, synchronization may be attained.[115] In other words, reputation capital provides a missing ingredient in global governance. The notion of reputation capital recognizes that the volume and breadth of social expectations are increasing. The ISCT provides the theoretical foundation. When microsocial contracts are breached, the breaches cause direct reputational harm and diminish corporate "reputation assets."[116] When the "contracts" are "performed," the firm's reputation capital grows.[117]

The concept of reputation capital emerged in tandem with the ideal of free-market capitalism, which has been modified with the advent of civil society's focus on CSR.[118] Reputation capital may prove to be indispensable for modern corporate managers. It illuminates how managers should commit to CSR to preserve and build a firm's intangible reputational assets.[119] Managers' commitment to CSR is further buttressed by the emerging corpus of global civil regulations.[120] Simply put, the "sanction" for noncompliance with civil standards translates into reputational loss. The "reward" for honoring the standards is reputational gain. Accordingly, the emerging "accountability regimes" sanction corporations for breaches of their CSR.

For the past several decades, globalization has transformed the landscape of international civil and business regulations.[121] The polyphonic view has finally caught up with corporate governance.[122] That, together with the advent of CSR, reveals the private sector's intensifying influence on public policy and regulation.[123] Scholars have noted that the regulatory power of the state is undergoing extensive decentralization under the influence of globalization.[124] Accordingly, blends of state and market, public and private, and traditional and self-regulatory institutional structures, characterized by alliances built among nation-states, NGOs, and business enterprises, are replacing the traditional mode of top-to-bottom hierarchical regulation.[125]

Public policy once created and enforced through official regulatory organs, such as environmental boards and employment nondiscrimination panels, is being handled by means of dialogue, negotiation, and cooperation between the public and private sectors.[126] Consequently, global business regulatory instruments are undergoing transformation.[127] Global business regulation is no longer restricted to administrative and legislative activity.[128] It encompasses market-oriented agents that impose business disclosure, monitoring, reporting, and transparency requirements, backed with reputational sanctions to address business misconduct.[129]

The Governance Triangle

Civil regulation is comprised of market-based, nonstate, and private regulatory structures.[130] These components govern the behavior of transnational enterprises along with their global supply networks.[131] One of the chief characteristics of civil regulation is that its enforcement, governance, and legitimacy do not rest on traditional institutions of public authority.[132] Whereas, traditionally, corporate governance was shaped by substantive law promulgated by governmental authority, today's transnational businesses function within a new slate of authorities.[133] Areas of authority traditionally reserved for government are now shared with non-state authorities.[134]

Civil regulations ordinarily function alongside nation-states, not from within.[135] Thus, as opposed to hard law, civil regulations are the product of "soft law," or private law, rather than of nation-states' legally enforceable norms.[136] In that sense, companies subject to a multitude of civil regulations face reputational rather than legal penalties.[137] The advent of soft-law's regulatory influence outside nations' regulatory schemes has empowered transnational nonstate actors.[138] The result is that the private sector has a much more prominent public role, and private authorities have a growing role in transnational economic regulation.[139] Corporations increasingly form a part of an emerging global public domain.

Civil regulations, however, do not supplant nation-states. Instead, they institute governance systems within wider global structures of "social capacity and agency" where none existed before.[140] The advent of civil regulation spells the emergence of what some scholars term a global "governance triangle," wherein nation-states constitute only a part of global regulatory authority.[141] The notion of governance without government made its debut in the scholarly literature during the 1990s.[142] Its debut, precipitated by economic globalization, highlighted the changes that globalization caused in the governance structure of international society. The term *governance* came to be used to refer to self-organizing systems that stand alongside the hierarchies and markets that comprise government structures.[143] Global governance, in turn, refers to the expansion of the sphere of influence of governing structures to entities beyond nation-states that do not possess sovereign authority.[144] Governance and government are, in fact, two logically distinct notions. Governance connotes a process founded on absence of centralized international governmental authority. Ideally, "global governance" undertakes the role within the international realm that governments assume within the nation-state.[145]

Global Governance Mechanisms

The growth of corporate social responsibility reveals the emergence of novel global governance mechanisms and business civil regulations. Global companies are deploying a variety of devices to propagate principles for responsible business conduct. These may be categorized as follows: (1)

self-regulation—voluntary mechanisms taken on individually in the market; (2) interfirm cooperation—voluntary tools established cooperatively between firms and business associations; and (3) coregulation and multistakeholder partnerships—voluntary mechanisms developed collaboratively with other entities, such as public-private and hybrid partnerships (governments, international organizations, NGOs, trade unions, and governments).[146]

Voluntary Self-regulation

Numerous large, global companies institute their own codes of conduct that aim to regulate their operations worldwide.[147] One example of voluntary self-regulation is the Leon Sullivan Foundation's promulgation of the Global Sullivan Principles of Social Responsibility (the "Principles") in 1999.[148] The Principles encompass a breadth of CSR concerns, such as employee freedom of association, health and environmental standards, and sustainable development.[149] Fortune 500 companies are now motivated to adjust their internal practices to comply with the standards found within the Principles.[150]

In 2005, the Global Business Standards ("GBS") Codex was published by a group of scholars.[151] Intended "as a benchmark for [firms] wishing to create their own world-class code," the GBS Codex set forth eight principles shared by five well-known codes that are embraced by the world's largest companies.[152] Incorporated in the principles were standards in the following categories: citizenship, dignity, fairness, fiduciary, property, reliability, responsiveness, and transparency.[153] Individual corporate codes of conduct usually contain an amalgamation of prudential, technical, and moral norms, declared as general principles.[154] Critics point to the various codes' failures to include enforcement sanctions and failures to emphasize profit maximization.[155] Yet corporations increasingly specify criteria such as "profitability" and "shareholder interests" in their mission statements.[156] Nevertheless, they also affirm that corporate responsibility for "stakeholder interests" means considering both community interests and sustainability.

Interfirm and Cross-industry Cooperation

As key agents in the global economy, transnational firms wield enormous clout to influence economic activities. Firms utilize various instruments to influence global civil society. Among the more significant mechanisms are interfirm and cross-industry cooperative instruments. These instruments are developed through CSR business associations, which formulate strategies for concerted action in the form of self-regulating proposals within the private sector.[157] These nongovernmental associations of businesses promote the dissemination of best business practices.[158] They seek to establish universal, uniform standards to combat a wide range of practices including apartheid, conflicts of interest, deception, discrimination, embezzlement, executive compensation, fraud, forgery, genocide, insider trading, the misuse of pension funds, slavery, theft, and corruption.[159]

Business associations serve as forums for corporate leaders to discuss and agree on a CSR plan. This entails creation of consolidated private rules, standards, and management instruments, all in the absence of legally enforceable "hard" sanctions. The associations often serve as a means for collective exertion of pressure, in order, for instance, to defend the corporations' positions before national governments and international organizations, such as the European Union and the United Nations.[160] As such, business associations serve as an interface between public and private authorities.[161]

Joining cooperative regulations is a wise business tactic for companies whose social or environmental practices have been targeted by activists. Whereas implementing higher environmental or social standards normally increases costs, attracting the competition to follow suit levels the playing field.[162] At least in theory, industry and cross-industry standards inhibit companies from competing with each other. In their absence, firms would engage in a "race to the bottom" by adopting less rigorous protections for employees or the environment.[163] Similarly, civil regulations help companies to assist each other in establishing best practices.[164] They also assist with communication and implementation of operational upgrades recommended by civil society.[165] It is noteworthy that NGOs' participation in civil regulations accords a higher degree of legitimacy than obtained by codes of conduct authored by individual companies.[166]

This partnership increases the credibility of a company's commitments to corporate social responsibility.[167] Moreover, transnational enterprises often follow their industry peers to implement comparable procedures and norms.[168] This "follow the leader" dynamic spreads managerial protocols, global CSR undertakings being among them.[169] Hence, if an industry leader consents to a code of practices, its industry peers typically follow suit.[170] This trend also works across sectors.[171] Indeed, the rise of civil regulations among global companies and industries has provided its own impetus as market participants wish to avoid losing reputation capital.[172]

Lastly, even ill-intended modifications in standards often have a substantial and lasting impact on business practices.[173] CSR-type initiatives that originate as mere symbolic gestures or efforts at appeasement may well acquire legitimacy among global civil society.[174] In today's increasingly transparent global economy, staffing a CSR office, sending out an annual CSR report, combining forces with NGOs, signing on to voluntary industry codes, and having a chief reputation officer are all becoming standard operating practices for management at global companies that attract high visibility.[175]

Coregulation and Multistakeholder Partnerships

Together with self-regulation instruments, transnational firms are increasingly implementing various CSR mechanisms and civil regulations geared to a number of collaborative regulatory arrangements.[176] They arise out of crossbreed devices originating with civil society bodies and business associations.[177] One of the motivations for collaborative governance is the ability to provide public goods through alliances.[178] For example, some civil regulations and civil regulatory bodies have been instituted with the backing of trade unions, interstate organizations, or governments.[179] Nevertheless, nation-states have not insisted on enforcing the regulations, which, after all, are not compulsory.[180] Instead, states have mainly played the role of intermediaries.[181] They help companies and, in some instances, NGOs and labor unions, to reach a consensus on mutual standards.[182] Such multistakeholder initiatives amount to public-private systems of coregulation.[183]

Business-NGO cooperative arrangements have emerged in the past several years.[184] There is a significant variety among these cooperative arrangements.[185] In addition, an array of regulatory bodies is undertaking multistakeholder projects such as the Ethical Trading Initiative that seeks to promote compliance with labor guidelines within the context of business supply chains.[186] The growth of these arrangements has given corporations a role in global public policy networks.[187] Global public policy networks are coalitions linking civil society organs, firms, government agencies, international organizations, NGOs, professional associations, and religious groups.[188] Companies that join global public policy networks commit to dialogue with other stakeholders to devise ethical standards.[189] Their objective is to establish monitoring mechanisms for firms, so as to improve accountability.[190] The formation of global public policy networks takes place on three levels: (1) establishment of standards, (2) development of regulatory structures, and (3) creation of assessment and enforcement systems.[191]

For example, the Global Reporting Initiative is a partnership of the Coalition for Environmentally Responsible Economies (CERES) and the United Nations Environmental Program (UNEP), linking firms, governments, the media, NGOs, and professional associations in order to establish uniform reporting standards to assess the organizations' environmental and social impact.[192] Signatory firms agree to observe CERES principles and to preserve and protect the environment at levels exceeding what local law mandates.[193] Every five years, CERES conducts an independent audit to certify that signatory companies are in compliance with the principles.[194]

As for Western NGOs, many of them deem coregulation initiatives an effective way to influence trends in transnational corporate conduct.[195] Altering procurement protocols of corporate giants can arguably obtain more substantial environmental and social results than enacting even massive quantities of national regulations.[196] Although some NGOs stress strategies that "name and shame" multinational corporations, others opt to combine forces with companies and industry associations to establish voluntary standards and take an active part in their enforcement.[197] The NGOs' forming of coalitions with transnational companies has been instrumental to the creation, legitimacy, and efficacy of civil regulations.[198] A number of Western governments, particularly those in Europe, are supporting civil regulations. The European Union has offered substantial support for global CSR.[199] Some European governments implicitly endorse CSR by demanding that firms trading on their stock exchanges distribute annual reports detailing environmental and social performance.[200] Additionally, public pension funds are either encouraged or, at times, required to take firms' environmental and social track records into account in choosing investments.[201] Moreover, some governments grant preferences for privately certified merchandise pursuant to their procurement policies.[202] Various features of civil regulation resemble characteristically European attitudes toward business regulation. That is, the European Union, along with a number of European governments, lean heavily on voluntary agreements and soft law, often turning to nonstate actors to formulate regulatory standards.[203] In the eyes of some European governmental authorities, endorsing global civil regulations is a convenient way of assuaging home-country activists and trade unions that may well be antagonistic to globalization and the immense political sway held by multinational companies.[204] This, however, does not grant nation-states sole regulatory authority over firms operating in their territories.

Thus one notable benefit of civil regulations as a mechanism of global business regulation is that their terms are outside the World Trade Organization's (WTO) purview, as the WTO's regulations have force only if accepted by national governments.[205] Whereas the WTO deems government-mandated eco-labels to constitute potential trade barriers, private product certifications and labels do not have that status.[206] Similarly, whereas companies could require global suppliers' compliance with environmental rules and labor standards as a prerequisite for transacting business, governments typically may not condition market access upon such requirements.[207]

In the case of coregulation and multistakeholder partnerships, CSR's focus shifts away from voluntariness and toward accountability backed by enforcement mechanisms.[208] Accordingly, public accountability mechanisms for private actors constitute a centerpiece of the emerging global governance paradigm.[209] As illustrated below, such emerging governance networks are "held in orbit" around the notion of reputation capital. Reputational sanctions and rewards linked to global firms' most valuable asset (reputation capital) therefore constitute an emerging mode of accountability in global governance.[210] Global firms utilize corporate legitimacy management to shift the role of businesses in society at large.[211] Meanwhile, multistakeholder initiatives provide the forum for a dialogue between business and society—a dialogue required for accountability mechanisms to work.[212] Moreover, involvement in coregulation and enforcement of multistakeholder devices is connected with the new idea of corporate citizenship, or what has been termed "political activism."[213] Through these devices, citizens can participate in dialogue with, and can influence, the conduct of businesses in the environmental and social spheres.[214]

Safeguarding Reputations

In large part, the growth and influence of civil regulations is attributable to the rise of global brands. The pervasiveness of branding means that companies are vulnerable to attacks on their reputations in consumer, labor, and financial markets. Moreover, firms' reputations are susceptible to technological advancements in communication via broadband Internet, coupled with the advent of decentralized and globally available media, such as Facebook, You-Tube, and Twitter, as well as the proliferation of inexpensive voice and text communication via wireless handheld devices.[215] Such technologies subject companies to attack by blogs, spoofs, e-mail campaigns, parasites, and other protest campaigns. This technology has made it easier for activists to obtain and disseminate information concerning business conduct at the speed of light around the globe.[216] The inability to hide, literally and figuratively, in a distant part of the world has made reputation a valuable commodity.

Consequently, the bulk of civil regulations emerge as a result of citizen campaigns aimed at specific business behavior, enterprises, or industry sectors.[217] The number of such campaigns has gradually increased in the past two decades.[218] They address workplace conditions, fair wages, child labor, agricultural worker compensation, sustainable forestry practices, corruption, environmental preservation, and human rights.[219] Campaigns to "name and shame" corporate character target prominent companies. The assault on corporate character through modern media, reaching audiences globally, pressures transnational companies to behave with increased responsibility.[220]

The combination of two trends, in CSR and firms' building and preservation of their reputation capital, has manifested in a nascent framework of global governance. The movement has led companies to develop environmental and social standards and to formulate strategies that impact their supply chains.[221] Additionally, companies have begun to reconfigure as "relational corporations," from "vertical" to "flat" and from domestic to international.[222] They have also begun to transition away from managing relationships and toward building relationships.[223] Moreover, in cooperation with civil society actors, firms continue to implement settled transnational, environmental, and social regulation standards, which substantially impact the firms' reputations.[224]

Reputation Accountability Devices

As a result of major industry scandals, coupled with the recent global financial meltdown, and motivated by accountability principles, corporate management is implementing ethical, transparency, and disclosure standards.[225] The following discussion aims to highlight the need for global corporate governance to recognize the crucial role of the rule of reputation. The need to adopt voluntary civil regulations is especially strong for firms operating in the global environment. The traditional concept of legal accountability is distinguishable from the emerging concept of reputation accountability. As will be shown, the latter is especially intricate since it entails multifaceted components of accountability. This section will illustrate how the reputation capital model of corporate governance influences managerial decision making—namely, how managers seek to accommodate the burgeoning demands for reputation accountability under the emerging regime of civil regulations.

Legal Accountability

Legal accountability simply means that normative regulatory standards are enforceable.[226] Compliance with black-letter legal rules creates a presumption of validity in the eyes of judicial tribunals or quasi-judicial forums.[227] The notion of legal accountability stems from the rule of law maxim.[228] A vast body of civil and criminal law has developed to hold non- and for-profit institutions legally accountable.[229] In the international arena, the WTO Dispute Settlement System, the Hague International Criminal Tribunal for the Former Yugoslavia, the International Criminal Tribunal for Rwanda, and the International Criminal Court are just some of the institutions that enforce "hard" international law.[230] Of course, an actor's failure to comply with law will typically trigger reputational sanctions as well, and compliance may provide for its own reputational rewards.[231] Similar to the early international law phenomena, civil regulations, absent hard enforcement mechanisms, function as mere normative standards and are intended to persuade compliance.[232] Corporations comply with soft law in order to protect their intangible assets; it is not that they are deterred by enforcement sanctions.[233] Arguably, a regime of global civil regulations and the accompanying rule of reputation comprise an integral part of both the domestic and international rule of law. They are, however, often ignored by commentators because they are only backed by reputational sanctions, the nature and extent of which are not always fully appreciated.[234] To fully account for the ontology of civil regulation and actors' compliance internationally, the concept of reputation capital must be incorporated into our current thinking about corporate governance. A deeper inquiry into the various sources of soft law, however, reveals its intricacy and complexity. Global civil regulations embody a compromise among private and public entities. Rather than imposing cost of compliance with formal regulation, civil regulations encourage corporations to examine their conduct and guide it by means of voluntary self-regulation.[235] Global civil regulations are continually undergoing an organic evolution, yet national law depends on its institutions to act, which takes longer.[236]

Reputation Accountability

From the standpoint of the conventional rule of law maxim and its experience, voluntary CSR seems utterly inadequate. That is, CSR is decentralized, it carries conflicting norms, it is run by bureaucrats,[237] and there are no hard sanctions for noncompliance.[238] The concept of reputation accountability offers an explanation for how the enforcement of civil regulations makes global firms more accountable. Accountability means that actors may ensure that other actors also follow standards, and may apply sanctions for noncompliance with those standards.[239] In the context of global corporate governance, civil regulations that impact a firm's reputation capital arguably represent the strongest sanctions, as a firm's most valuable, albeit intangible, asset is its reputation.[240]

Components of Reputation Accountability

The process of corporate reputation accountability involves the following three components.[241] First, reputation accountability presupposes the existence of civil regulations that hold companies accountable; thus, compliance is expected.[242] Similar to the maxim that the law must be knowable—that is, that it must be published by the state so that citizens can discover what rights and responsibilities are given or imposed on them by law—civil regulations must also be a matter of common knowledge.[243] Second, reputation accountability requires that "enforcement agents" possess relevant information about firms' actions to evaluate compliance with applicable civil regulations.[244] Thus, on the one hand, to be held accountable, firms must be aware of the expectations.[245] On the other hand, enforcement agents must know by what standards to render an assessment of business conduct.[246] Because accurate information is essential, some measure of transparency and dialogue among stakeholders appears to be a prerequisite for reputation accountability.[247] Third, reputation accountability depends on the existence of incentives for compliance.[248] That is, enforcement agents must be able to impose reputational sanctions or reputational rewards.[249] Of course, no worldwide government, democratic or otherwise, exists to provide wholesale regulation.[250] Consequently, demands for corporate accountability are decentralized and, thus, diffused.

Enforcing the Rule of Reputation

Whereas the concept of legal accountability derives its central meaning from the notion of the rule of law (ultimately upheld by courts), the concept of reputation accountability may be understood in terms of the rule of reputation. The rule of reputation is upheld by market participants that evaluate business conduct within several forums. For instance, the "forum of key constituents" is especially significant for business enterprises.[251] "Key constituents" are firms' customers, employees, and investors, whose authority and control are exerted in transactions occurring in consumer, labor, and capital markets respectively.[252] For example, individual investors as well as mutual funds may cease investing in companies whose practices or policies they find objectionable.[253] Some pension funds shun securities of certain companies, often on the basis of criteria determined by their beneficiaries.[254] Alternatively, investors may require higher interest rates on corporate bonds.[255] Further, customers may decline to purchase the products produced by firms struck by negative publicity stemming from human rights violations, unfair labor practices, or environmental violations.[256] It has been shown that consumers are willing to incur added costs, such as the cost of traveling greater distances, in order to punish retailers whose conduct they find egregiously unfair.[257] Finally, those in employment markets may select among competing job offers on the basis of the prospective employer's publicity and reputation.[258]

Business partners and associates make up another type of forum for the evaluation of conduct. This forum functions as a peer-driven reputation accountability network powered by the process of business partners' reciprocal appraisals.[259] Institutional lenders, for instance, use caution in scrutinizing their borrowers' creditworthiness as well as that of their partners' borrowers.[260] Business enterprises that are rated low by their peers are less likely to find willing business partners among them.[261] These businesses find themselves in a strategic disadvantage and therefore tend to stagnate.[262]

Next is the forum of public opinion, or the proverbial "court of public opinion."[263] Public reputation accountability means that members of civil society penalize companies by promulgating negative publicity.[264] Lawmakers, courts, government regulators, fiscal watchdogs, journalists, competitors, licensing boards, rating agencies, and markets all render judgments about the reputations of market participants. In fact, reputation constitutes a type of "soft power," which has been characterized as "the ability to shape the preferences of others."[265] Companies with tarnished reputations find it hard to establish relationships, assert authority, or attract loyalty from others.[266]

The Royal Dutch Shell scandal involving the Brent Spar and the Ogoni in Nigeria presents a vivid example of a company experiencing a reputation crisis as a result of its failure to comply with public social expectations and its neglect of both environmental and human rights standards.[267] In 1995, Shell made plans to sink a large decommissioned oil buoy storage rig in the North Sea. It conducted an environmental impact assessment and gained approval from the government of Great Britain.[268] Greenpeace activists challenged the proposed deep-sea dumping and alleged that Shell's sinking the rig would cause serious environmental damage.[269] Shell disputed the claim on scientific grounds and maintained that sinking was the best available option.[270] Since Shell refused to abandon its plans, Greenpeace, acting in front of television crews, surrounded the rig with small boats and even occupied it.[271] Protests erupted throughout Europe. In response to Greenpeace's pressure and the boycotts, Shell abandoned its sinking strategy and towed the rig to a Norwegian fiord.[272]

Reversing its original plan cost Shell considerable expense.[273] In addition, when Shell failed in the same year to intercede to stop the execution of Ken Saro-Wiwa in Nigeria, voices worldwide expressed indignation. Saro-Wiwa, a writer, businessman, and political journalist, had organized the Movement for the Survival of the Ogoni People to take a stand against mounting problems with Shell and the government of Nigeria. Saro-Wiwa, along with nine others, was tried for the murder of four Nigerian officials, a fabricated accusation. Saro-Wiwa was not tried by a traditional court, but rather a special tribunal that refused to admit evidence of innocence.[274] As the defendants were found guilty and sentenced to death, Shell stated that political issues were not their concern.[275] Magazines and newspapers roundly called for punishment of Nigeria and Shell, the Sierra Club initiated a massive boycott campaign against the company, and celebrities advocated a U.S. oil embargo.[276] Shell's subsequent efforts to revive its reputation in the aftermath of the Spar and Nigerian scandals, while very expensive, were successful at averting a public relations crisis, which, like the one BP has undergone from the Gulf of Mexico oil spill, could have been relentless.[277] By contrast, companies that achieve superior reputations within each of the above forums, enjoy a host of advantages. In that sense, reputation account-ability involves not just punishing firms but also rewarding them for their compliance with civil regulations and commitment to CSR.

Reputation Accountability Networks

Reputation accountability in global economic governance is multifaceted. Global companies operate within networks of continuous relationships. Firms are linked with their customers, suppliers, and even rivals via strate-gic alliances. When companies enter into arrangements with various parties, such as government regulators and special interest groups, they are in effect establishing "reputation networks." These networks form a variety of chan-nels of accountability, which are divided by and cover a range of topical areas. Relationships involving international organizations typically establish sequenc-es of accountability.[278] In addition, multiple intersecting accountability relation-ships exist when different groups of market participants, with potentially di-verse interests, set out to hold other agents accountable for their behavior.[279]

In the modern business environment, companies confront manifold and frequently incompatible or contradictory reputation accountability demands.[280] Often it is not sufficient to meet the demands of sharehold-ers and credit markets.[281] Moreover, it is not enough to comply with legal rules as law often lags behind rapidly evolving social norms.[282] Businesses, however, must remain mindful of their constituencies'—peers, the media, and advocacy groups—reactions to their actions. Various calls for reputa-tion accountability concerning a firm's conduct reveal conflicting expec-tations of outside observers.[283] A reputation crisis can also rapidly spread to infect an extensive network. The uncovering of accounting irregularities at the Indian outsourcing firm Satyam Computer Services, Ltd. led to im-mediate suspicion about the firm's global auditor, PriceWaterhouseCoopers, and prompted a group of its clients, including Cigna, Citigroup, Coca-Cola, GlaxoSmithKline, Merrill Lynch, Nissan, Novartis, Pfizer, and State Farm Insurance, to move their business away from the firm.[284]

Dynamic Aspect

Mandates for reputation accountability undergo a constant process of change as activist campaigns are impermanent and public interest and attention are constantly shifting; in general, however, the bar continues to rise.[285] Only a few decades ago, controversy regarding environmental and labor conditions was almost nonexistent, whereas today it is front and center.[286] Those unable to forecast these shifts tend to lag behind the current norms.[287] So far as reputation accountability is concerned, such lag may cause strategic problems.[288] New laws and regulations may be enacted, the ire of civil society activists raised, or reputations sullied before managers implement remedial measures. Thus, a key motivation for companies to become industry leaders in building reputation capital is the need for additional insurance against reputational harm from negative publicity and pressures that may be detrimental to the company.[289] In such instances, having a superior reputation may turn out to be a global company's most valuable asset, albeit an invisible and elusive one.[290]

Implications for Global Operations

To integrate the considerations of reputation capital into global corporate governance is to recognize the corporation's reputation as a productive asset that generates capital, not only for the firm's shareholders but also, ultimately, for a broad range of constituents. Of course, reputation capital goes unrecorded on corporate balance sheets. But creating shareholder value extends beyond capitalization on traditional balance sheet assets; it also entails leveraging value from the company's reputation capital. A firm will realize competitive advantage by correctly forecasting "new waves" of civil society's expectations for responsible corporate conduct. Corporate officers must develop the ability to effectively reach consensus with key decision makers regarding new waves of demand for CSR.[291] To become industry leaders in terms of CSR standards, corporations must implement internal ethical standards and focus on their visions, developing strategies to beat the competition. Having to define accountability requirements imposes a burden and diverts managers from profit-creating activity.[292] If firms fail to comply with reputation accountability requirements, however, they may eventually face reputational sanctions. Still, over time, industry as a whole seeks to catch up with its leaders and innovators.[293] At this point, no special advantage comes from compliance with the new norms. Nevertheless, the emerging global civil regulations function as signposts for corporations. Following their trends, firms may institutionalize norms to respond to their demands.

Criticisms and Replies

On the one hand, the advent of global civil regulation and CSR has been hailed as a panacea to the unhealthy symptoms caused by the inability of nation-states to regulate internationally.[294] For example, laws are often outpaced by rapidly developing technology. This often happens in technical fields, such as the supervision and regulation of risk in the banking industry. In this context, international industry leaders call for allowing institutions' own risk models to participate in financial regulation. On the other hand, while acknowledging the numerous positive aspects of self-regulation, critics contend that voluntary business regulations are intrinsically unable to provide a comprehensive regulatory landscape, especially because transnational firms may evade regulation by relocating.[295] Moreover, critics allege that civil regulations are *too* soft when it comes to regulating conduct as compared to the hard rule of law.[296] After all, absent any adjudicative institution with multinational or international jurisdiction, it is difficult to obtain redress for human rights violations if the victim's home state does not provide the same.[297]

In addition, conceptual difficulties arise to the extent that civil regulations amount to self-regulation and are voluntary codes that merely codify firms' or their primary subjects' responsibilities.[298] A potential drawback is the perception that compliance with the codes is undertaken on a purely voluntary or discretionary basis.[299] Nevertheless, logic dictates that responsibility for human rights, in their broad sense, stems from the fundamental maxim grounded in invisible law that people possess a bundle of human rights that may not be transgressed. Acknowledging the universality of the human rights principle that was established earlier in Chapter 5 negates the notion that firms' human rights responsibilities are purely voluntary or discretionary. Rather, the universal maxim of human rights imposes overriding obligations on transnational firms. Human rights norms fall squarely within the category of hypernorms. Therefore, any CSR initiative that seeks to comply with human rights hypernorms should be viewed as mandatory, rather than discretionary. The Integrative Social Contract Theory, however, fails to account for why corporations commit their resources to advancing human rights. While detailing the firms' decision-making processes, the ISCT focuses on mechanisms for resolving conflicts between authentic norms and hypernorms. The theory does not address the businesses' economic motivations, resources, or competencies. Under the ISCT, a firm's decision to act responsibly with respect to human rights remains discretionary, or within "moral free space." This, however, betrays the nondiscretionary nature of human rights. An alternative theory is necessary, namely, the theory of reputational capital. The latter best accounts for how firms, recognizing the mandatory nature of human rights obligations, can expect support from civil society while proactively advancing them, thus improving their financial and social standing.

While the practical impact of civil regulations is slight, it is nevertheless palpable. The scores of intergovernmental treaties and agreements have been ineffective, at least in the area of ecological preservation.[300] Civil regulations provide greater influence than intergovernmental treaties with respect to human rights, workplace conditions, and forestry practices as they reach beyond national borders.[301] Yet in the absence of universally accepted criteria for assessing such impact, it is difficult to draw solid conclusions.

But the reputational pressure is on. In order to effectuate positive change in businesses' environmental and socioeconomic practices in the developing world, activists in the West make public demands on well-reputed, high-profile transnational companies based in Europe and the United States.[302] These demands and pressures often obviate the need for governmental involvement in the sphere that is left unchecked due to governments' limitations.[303] The main aim in this process is to transfer the more demanding regulatory guidelines from the developed world to businesses, industries, and markets in the developing world.[304] In doing so, civil regulations cause the "California effect"—the export of higher standards through international trade.[305]

Of course, international civil regulations are arguably more effective than the human rights, environmental, and labor standards originating from the developing world.[306] Indeed, civil regulations are almost the exclusive source of effective business regulation for many developing countries.[307] Global civil regulations have led to greater levels of compliance with human rights, workplace, and environmental standards by Western companies or their affiliates operating in a developing region.[308] However, some would deny this claim or discount its significance.[309] Indeed, the traditional regimes of hard law and the emerging regimes of soft law are capable of working together.[310] They are not mutually exclusive vehicles for corporate governance. While civil regulations offset some deficiencies in governmental regulation, they need not completely replace or substitute the hard regulation that originates in domestic, regional, or global arenas. The continuing success of private global business regulation hinges on the degree to which its standards and its instrumentalities for accountability can be successfully incorporated into, and strengthened by, regulatory procedures backed by both traditional legal sanctions and emergent reputational sanctions at domestic, regional, and transnational levels.[311]

Another criticism is that manufacturers in the developing world consider the Western civil regulations to be a burden on their development.[312] Critics point out that compliance with Western codes elevates business costs.[313] Consequently, companies in developing countries are tempted to follow the bare minimum in terms of compliance with requirements foisted upon them by Western contractors.[314] Their relationships with private inspectors and ethics auditors often turn hostile and even involve instances of deception.[315] Similar criticisms are leveled at Western companies as well. Critics contend that Western firms adopt civil regulations merely as public relations ploys to divert attention away from wrongdoing, or as marketing strategies, or in reaction to public and peer influences.[316] For example, the Global Compact is accused of "blue washing."[317] It permits member-companies to exhibit the blue logo of the United Nations, while ignoring their failure to file annual reports and their mere token efforts to comply with the Compact's standards.[318] In the face of this, critics contend that the corporations become free-riders.[319] Some companies have even been accused of violating the Compact's principles.[320] Nevertheless, not all CSR initiatives lack genuine commitment. Arguably, those with genuine respect for civil regulations, as opposed to their mere instrumental value for good business, are most likely to reap long-term reputational and financial rewards. The public, in the long run, is able to discern which firms exhibit a genuine commitment to CSR.[321] Indeed, the critics' assertions that many corporations act insincerely presuppose that it is possible to distinguish disingenuous public relations ploys from sincere moral commitments. In other words, the skeptic's argument assumes what it wants to deny—that corporations are behaving wrongly when they use CSR superficially instead of honoring environmental and social standards for their own sake. If it were true that all corporations always act insincerely, meaning, therefore, that they are incapable of acting otherwise, then what would be the point of drawing our attention to, and condemning, such behavior?

In addition, critics doubt whether firms that proactively comply with civil regulations in order to merely enhance profitability can ultimately grow reputational capital.[322] In other words, critics insist that the pure profit motivation necessarily taints any purported ethical act. Addressing this important objection requires reflection on two fundamental points. First, wealth creation is itself a source of public good. Second, while getting reputational rewards from CSR most likely requires genuine commitment, it is unnecessary and likely impossible to gauge the degree of its authenticity, as the motives for corporate compliance with CSR are notoriously complex.[323] The public, however, deplores corporate marketing and public relations campaigns masquerading as citizenship and social responsibility initiatives, especially when used to divert attention from a firm's own misconduct.[324] As has been shown, activists have been quick to expose firms that engage in disingenuous image-laundering tactics.[325] Any attempt to deceive the public, in today's age of far-reaching, decentralized media, will itself quickly cause reputational harm.

In other words, reputational capital is generated from CSR backed by genuine intention. A company will find it difficult to capitalize on compliance with civil regulations unless it has explicitly declared its moral commitment. Companies that exhibit the "it pays to be ethical" attitude will be undermining their efforts in the long run. From a purely financial standpoint, it arguably pays to appreciate the intrinsic value of good business conduct. Executives of multinational corporations should guide their organizations' actions by this premise.

Finally, some critics contend that the bulk of global CSR practices resemble corporate philanthropic efforts in the sense that they are situated at the outer margins rather than at the core of firms' business strategies.[326] Thus, critics see the CSR practices more as constituting inoculation against public denunciation than as an effort at long-term competitive advantage. On the other hand, such companies as Johnson & Johnson, Seventh Generation, Starbucks, Timberland, and Whole Foods make CSR commitments a vital component of their brands and their core business policies.[327] As it is commonly suggested in order to debunk the widespread misconception that costly Madison Avenue advertising campaigns do not really work: If that were really true, then why would companies continue to spend so much on them?

Conclusion

This chapter has attempted to delineate the transformative trends in global governance that are backed by reputation capital. This change is taking place through emerging civil regulations enforced by reputation accountability mechanisms established by global civil society to impose responsibility on firms for environmental, social, and financial outcomes. Several factors have caused the emergence of CSR, including economic globalization, the development of global civil society, and the role multinational enterprises have begun to play as private authorities. The efforts of businesses to advance human rights and to promote ethical, responsible, and sustainable practices continue to mature, manifesting in the advent of civil regulations and the emergence of a regime of global economic governance.

The rise of CSR is also the result of firms—pressured by the corporate accountability movement—seeking to address the social and ecological byproducts, and in the wake of the economic crisis, the financial impact as well, of their conduct. A set of self-regulating norms and mechanisms, along with multistakeholder initiatives and coregulation, guide CSR. Although accountability is about power, as positivist portrayals are keen to stress, it concerns a good deal more than just power. The global corporate governance paradigm continues to be shaped by the pursuit of greater moral accountability for business.

Chapter 9

Theme and Variations

It is not easy to see moral ideals change. The alteration of assumptions is too subtle, the shifting foundations of guilt and pride too nearly invisible. But when the moral life moves—like a deer in snow-bound woods—it leaves tracks, and we can know where it has been even if we do not see the thing itself.
—Michael Schudson

OVER TIME, JUDGMENTS issuing from stakeholders about what is right and what is wrong change. Sage business leaders must remain keenly attuned to the alterations. Of course, it goes without saying that the principles upon which the voices of stakeholders are raised are not necessarily sacrosanct. They might fail the hypernorm test. We often forget that some stakeholder groups are just special-interest groups. While some of their voices sing sweet melodies wrought from virtue, others bellow Sirens' songs borne of greed, nastiness, or naïveté.

Regardless of the origins and legitimacy of these stakeholder voices, they often undergo revision by cultural influences and informal sources, ending up as new imperatives proclaimed by global civil society according to the conception of polyphonic governance given in Chapter 8. This chapter builds on that discussion by turning our attention toward the complexities of "listening to" or paying heed not only to received "themes"—traditional guideposts for corporate governance (like "firms may vigorously pursue profits to advance the interests of shareholders, so long as they remain within the bounds of settled legal standards")—but also to permutations they undergo, all the while seeking coherence in the way it plays out. Drawing on the musical metaphor, we might consider how moral standards undergo canonical mutation in ways similar to how composers construct thematic variations, as J. S. Bach famously did in *Fourteen Canons on the First Eight Notes of the Goldberg Ground BWV 1087.* For example, a variation known as a retrograde canon is established by moving an original voice backward. A moral counterpart of this can be seen in the flipping of interpretations about the legal, ethical, and social responsibilities of business in an opposite direction. An original theme or "voice" such as that sung by Milton Friedman—"the only social responsibility of business is to maximize profits for shareholders"—in retrograde becomes the song of Davos: "Business is responsible for the wider community of stakeholders." An implicit attitude like "humanity serves business" is inverted to "business serves humanity." The idea that businesses may "freely plunder raw materials from the Earth in manufacturing processes" gets turned around into a commitment by businesses to "securing intergenerational quality of life and restoring the environment," and the notion of product liability of retailers once limited to a "duty of due care" within the scope of "privity of contract" gets turned on its head to spell product liability all the way down to manufacturers even for "strict liability" (liability without fault).

Looking at a more specific example, many firms, heeding what they took to be the call for maximizing their bottom line by simply complying with extant law, might have concluded that it is perfectly permissible to reincorporate offshore to reduce their worldwide tax liability. But over time, the court of public opinion had gradually revamped the theme into a newer, more subtly nuanced variation, so that firms got faulted for singing the same old song. This particular circumstance will be further elaborated in a subsequent section. Before doing so, let us reflect for a moment on the cultural progressions at play in generating such variations on earlier themes.

Normative Standpoints and Transgressive Developments

The concept of a normative interpretive standpoint was introduced in Chapter 6. Normative standpoints make up a part of the economic culture of any society. Such viewpoints are embodied in "hard" legal modes such as legislation and court rulings, and they are also expressed in formal policies such as the multitude of those the Federal Reserve establishes.[1] As well, normative standpoints are signaled in market indicia, such as stock price, currency valuations, exchange rates, and leading economic indicators (employment rate, and so on). However, normative standpoints also arise out of personal attitudes both concerning business and concerning individual matters, such as sexuality, religion, and the pursuit of the good life. There is a plethora of sources for such viewpoints, ranging from "high" culture to mass culture, and from distant historical origins to contemporary discourse, from local influences to global trends. This listing is meant to be merely illustrative, not nearly exhaustive:

- *High Culture:* Arthur Miller's *Death of a Salesman;* Theodore Dreiser's *The Financier;* Charles Dickens's *A Christmas Carol* (Scrooge); the "Western canon"
- *Mid-Culture: The Wizard of Oz* (qua allegory of the Federal Reserve and post-stock market crash "new world order"); Ayn Rand's *The Fountainhead*
- *Mass Culture:* reality television; media coverage of "Octomom"; A&E's *Flip This House; The Apprentice*
- *Modern Discourse:* Twitter and blogs on the Internet; Burrough and Helyar's *Barbarians at the Gate;* McLean and Elkind's *Smartest Guys in the Room*
- *Intellectual History:* Adam Smith's *Wealth of Nations* and *Theory of Moral Sentiments;* Thorstein Veblen's *The Theory of the Leisure Class;* Karl Marx's *Capital;* Max Weber's *The Protestant Ethic and the Spirit of Capitalism*
- *Local Influences:* religion (mosques, temples, synagogues, churches), the family, ancient caste systems, tribal customs, festivals and celebrations
- *Global Influences:* collapse of Berlin Wall; Globish;[2] *Magna Carta;* CNN; Thomas Friedman's *Hot, Flat and Crowded*

Obviously there is no end to items that may be included within each of the above categories; nor do the categories denote rigid boundaries. I make no pretense to offering the complete and definitive guide here. The point is that all of the above sources, together with countless others, play a background role in shaping moral opinions within economic culture. Referring back to an idea from ancient thought that we explored earlier in Chapter 1, it matters what sort of music we listen to, since it instills rhythmic, harmonic, and melodic

Table 9.1   Illustrative Transgressive Developments

Music and Art		
Original Meaning	Transgressive Meaning	Problematization
Opera: Performers and directors remain faithful to realizing the artistic vision of the composer.	"Reggie Opera": the director decides what the opera will signify, e.g., contemporary social critique.	Director usurps composer's aesthetic meaning, yet "piggybacks" on the composer's good name to motivate audience to attend performance.
Harmonic structures with tonal centers; listeners can discern progression of the composer's melodic and harmonic "argument."	Atonal concoctions of "sound laboratories."	Audience cannot discern or follow any "argument" within the incomprehensible harmonic sequences.
Paintings, sculptures aimed at expressing beauty.	"Shock art."	Cannot find any expression of beauty; Arthur Danto claims beauty is opposed to the aim of modern art.

movements into our souls. Much the same is true of the myriad of other elements of culture to which we are exposed and in which we participate. These cultural sources are normative and are connected to economic life and our commercial society—the "ecology" of the marketplace. Such sources influence attitudes about whether a free-enterprise economy constitutes a fundamentally reliable system for coordinating commercial life and also attitudes about the desirability or not of globalization as a shaping force in the economy of today. However, these kinds of sources are not authoritative decisions or regulatory policies made by government officials. Insofar as writings, mass media displays, and other cultural phenomena have an objective reality, they represent distinct "oughts" in the sense that each of these cultural elements tends to impart a vision of either, on the one hand, a more sacred, enlightened, humane, and sustainable economy or, on the other hand, a more secularized, vulgar, dehumanized, and dysfunctional economy.

The normative standpoints serve as a basis for constructing arguments concerning whether, from a cultural outlook on market phenomena, certain

Table 9.1   Illustrative Transgressive Developments (continued)

Law		
Original Meaning	*Transgressive Meaning*	*Problematization*
Bill of Rights: natural rights that serve as limitations on power of the government.	Some rights, such as privacy, are not even specified within the Bill of Rights, yet are interpreted as "emanations of penumbras" (*Griswold v. Connecticut, Roe v. Wade*).	Increasing level of judicial activism; unelected, unaccountable elite justices are deciding controversial issues of political morality.
Law is an ordinance of human reason, ordained to the common good (Aquinas).	Regulations and laws are proposed as holding solutions to every problem.	Transition toward a litigation-frenzied culture; impossible to know what the law is because it has been overwritten and is too complex.
Traditional Marriage: Legal recognition of sacred bond between man and woman.	Civil Union: Legal recognition of joining together of same-sex partners.	Mutated as such, marital relationships no longer are expressive of the full human complementarity embodied in male-female dichotomy, and become inherently nonprocreative, hence moving away from a fundamental feature of human nature.

business conduct is considered ethical or unethical, fair or unfair, rational or irrational. As such, shifting currents from the broader culture can and do influence market ecology, including official economic pronouncements within that ecology (for example, the Fed's decision to keep the fed-funds rate extremely low for a prolonged time period), and become embedded in such decisions. Such currents also influence countless decisions and habits displayed by market participants: consumer purchases, investments, and other transactions, which collectively constitute the marketplace of morality.[3] Sometimes a transgressive development takes place, whereby original meanings established within some cultural standpoint get transformed into something much different, as illustrated in Table 9.1, which showcases examples in music and art, law, and business.

Table 9.1   Illustrative Transgressive Developments (continued)

Business and Economics

Original Meaning	Transgressive Meaning	Problematization
Banks: institutions for borrowers and savers	Banks are casino-like institutions; "too big to fail"	Federal Reserve's government-engineered, taxpayer-funded bailout is elitist treatment that guarantees the largest firms they will be assisted; offends sense of fair play; establishes system of enormous yet fragile banks; institutions should fail if their bad decisions make them insolvent and they cannot compete in the market. Pretending otherwise weakens the foundations of the economic system.
House: place to live and raise a family	Houses become investment opportunities for "flipping"	Contributing cause of sub-prime mortgage crash, leading to financial crisis; rise in speculative culture.
Corporation: formed for specific purposes in order to serve the common good	Corporation acquires a moral personality; sometimes named after a purely fictitious person	Corporate "person" cannot be trusted; eclipses human person as moral agent
Economy: *oikos*, household	Economy is globalized, and dominated by multinational corporations	World economy becoming increasingly chaotic, characterized by boom-bust cycles carrying transnational ripple effects
Mortgages, loans	Collateralized Debt Obligations (CDOs) and other complex instruments	Harder and harder to determine economic value of underlying asset

Table 9.1   Illustrative Transgressive Developments (continued)

Business and Economics (continued)		
Original Meaning	*Transgressive Meaning*	*Problematization*
Money: a unit of weight for a commodity, gold or silver.[4] Money originates in a nonmonetary commodity, which is gradually chosen by the market to be an ever-more general medium of exchange.	"Fiat money," whose value is not fixed by any objective standard.	The supply of money is controlled, regulated, manipulated, and created by the government at will.
Trading: exchanges of goods and services in an "arms-length" transaction between buyer and seller. A shareholder "owns" stock in a company.	Ultra-fast stock trades with computers processing thousands of buy and sell orders within microseconds; emergence of "virtual property" in internet transactions.	Fundamental shifts in traditional notions of shareholder accountability, ownership, and responsibility. In what sense are shares in a firm "owned?"

The moral-economic culture of a complex society has an almost contrapuntal texture, revealing sometimes interwoven, sometimes mutating, sometimes conflicting viewpoints. There are issues for which no unitary gauge of economic morality exists, at times producing substantial cultural dissonance. Debates about the morality of welfare programs, the ethics of outsourcing, the legitimacy of affirmative action initiatives, and the proper scope of privacy in employment, are examples. For other issues, the cultural scheme of economic morality is comparatively determinate and harmonious. The use of slave labor, for instance, is clearly deemed unjust by contemporary cultural norms, at least in most developed countries.

So suppose we were to agree that human nature has not essentially changed since the time of Aristotle. Regardless, it is clear that enough other things have changed to warrant our condemnation of, say, Aristotle's peculiar views on women and slavery. Aristotle himself saw ethical progress emerging from the process of dialectic that was introduced earlier in Chapter 5. If what I argued there about how procedural invisible law guides us into conducting an ongoing moral conversation and guides us in adjusting our principles and judgments in particular cases, while we need not allow that human nature changes, we are well advised to remain open to the possibility that some of our moral standards will. Although I have argued that there is an objective foundation for morality, the flip side is that we sometimes cannot be sure exactly what is foundational and what is alterable. It is conceded that the foundation itself can be perplexingly vague.

In the context of culture, consider traditional views about women, marriage, the family, and sexual behavior. On the whole, we might say, they have kept us in good stead. Nevertheless, particularly in the face of globalization, they are changing, sometimes for good reasons and sometimes not, around the edges. At what point, we may wonder, might some of the central traditional views become obsolete? And if so, what would it mean to declare them obsolete?

Similar questions arise within the context of business, but here, in the midst of what Simon Zadek terms the "New Economy,"[5] many things are moving faster and thus inviting confusion. Over a very long period of time we have come to see, as Locke did, that private property is a crucial notion and that it provides the basis for some fundamental rights.[6] But how do traditional interpretations of private property rights transfer to the cases of newly evolved modes of virtual ownership, and for distributive issues regarding intellectual property rights over new technologies vis-à-vis developed and developing countries? Keeping our moral compasses oriented in the midst of the extraordinary pace and magnitude of these changes is a challenge to those who want to make both our economic system and our moral system work, and work together.

Suppose we distinguish two propositions.[7] The first proposition, consistent with our brand of moral realism, allows us to assert:

(P1) there are cultural changes that cause us to reconsider what virtue requires, and to modify our interpretations regarding what sorts of moral norms we ought to honor.

But the second proposition, urged by moral skeptics and nihilists, purports to claim something else, something altogether much stronger, namely:

(P2) we should stop talking about virtue and cease talking about right and wrong altogether.

So, in the face of widespread cultural transformations, we would do well to make sure we keep (P1) and (P2) separate, and not make the mistake of supposing that (P2) logically follows from (P1).

Shifts in Moral Opinion

What happens where a standard is set where none existed before, or merely a vaguely applicable standard was in place? Sometimes a scandal arises, centered on corporate behaviors that most people were seemingly clueless about, for example, market timing and late trading in the mutual fund industry. The publicity of the scandal operates as a "wake-up call." Granted a legal authority (here, Attorney General Spitzer and the SEC) or the news media may act to apparently bring about the general acceptance of a new rule. The legal authorities' or journalists' powers often consist more in their ability to bring about the general acceptance of moral rules, the justification and legitimate authority of which rests on grounds independent from any purely legal position.

The shift of moral opinion that came about several years ago in connection with corporations playing share-price games, I suggest, is most plausibly construed as having the effect of a piece of invisible legislation; that is, as a case in which the general acceptance of a new rule itself alters the normative position of members of the society in question, making an action wrong that, without the general acceptance of the rule, either would be permissible or would have an unclear and ill-defined normative status. It is the analogue of legislation that serves to deal with an accumulative harm by setting a standard of wrongfulness where either no standard or only a vaguely applicable standard existed before (for example, pre-Enron, World-Com, Adelphia, Andersen, Tyco, Parmalat).

The notion of *Accumulative Harm* refers to circumstances wherein there are some actions that are relatively harmless, maybe even outright beneficial, if done by a few firms, but harmful when done by too many. (See Table 9.2.)

Taking short-cuts across the grass when it is inconvenient to use the sidewalk—if done by one or a few in circumstances where no one else is tempted to do likewise—is an example of an action that is harmless or even slightly beneficial. Individual negligible contributions to pollution are another example. It may not matter at all if a few people engage in some littering action,

Table 9.2   Accumulative Harm Model

Assume: Firms A, B, C, D.

A hunts down a loophole in the law, taking ethically dubious, yet minor harm-causing action Y; A gets competitive advantage. Public is not aware of A doing Y. A rationalizes behavior: "Oh well, no real harm done."

B and C join in, so the public starts to notice the pattern and disapproves of it. This triggers regulatory response, banning practice Y, citing the (now) widespread harm it causes.

D, out of the loop, unwittingly commits Y. D now suffers *major legal sanction* and takes a big reputational hit for engaging in conduct that, if considered by itself, is actually a trivial harm.

---

but if many do it, a threshold of positive harm comes about. A type of action may become polluting, or it may become socially abrasive, precisely because there are a whole lot of people who are inclined to do it. Yet another example is the use of creative accounting and other earnings manipulation tricks that corporations use to boost their stock price. If a massive number of firms do it, the effect is to bring about at least two huge negative events: (1) the bursting of the stock market's bubble; (2) a significant undermining of investor confidence.

Let us consider an alternative construal. On a different account, the shift in public opinion is taken to be a recognition of wrongness, a "waking up" to the fact that what companies had been doing in playing the share-price game was already wrong independently of signing on to any new rule. One possibility is that it is virtually never consistent with the basic duty to do good to engineer earnings; that the duty to be honest and transparent with investors is almost always greater than the value of satisfying the desires of CEOs to profit from boosting stock prices, the value of companies attempting to satisfy expectations for meeting earnings expectations in the short-term, and so on. This possibility is to be taken seriously if investor confidence has already been considerably reduced, if not endangered. But it is much less plausible if that has not yet happened. Indeed, if our concern is to have a strong economy and stable companies, the moderate thinning out of some companies when a bubble bursts might actually do positive good.

Another possibility is that for some ratio macro*P/E, which represents an aggregate of what, on the microlevel, function as p/e ratios (for example, price-earnings ratios, considered with regard to a single firm), it is the case that after a certain point is reached, where an excessive amount of capital is not in the market anymore, we have what is colloquially termed a "bubble" (though nobody, not even economists, ever has bothered to give a precise definition of this concept). At some critical tipping point, the bubble will burst. Thus, in a given market, macro*P/E represents the theoretical economic threshold above which manufactured earnings becomes a bad, no fatal, practice. There is too much capital; it is in surplus. The excess capital did not go through the production cycle; together, a large number of companies took a short cut; they took advantage of a systemic inefficiency. Like a persistent stream of students, all of them deciding to take a short cut across the campus lawn instead of using the sidewalk, perhaps due to intense time pressures to get across campus (say, the teachers are starting to penalize them for arriving late to class), which leads to a path getting etched in the lawn. It's not that any one person cutting across the lawn is committing a major moral crime, but everybody doing it eventually mars the lawn. Even though the threshold point at which macro*P/E turns into a "bubble" may be a ratio that no one can discern with any precision.

Teachings and judgments based on responses to accumulative harms have several functions that are analogous to those of enacted laws. To illustrate, let us first look at the form of the visible legal dimension. The salient features arising in law are: (1) a threshold of harm arises from joint and successive contributions of numerous firms; (2) considered in isolation, each contribution seems harmless, except that it moves the overall state of affairs closer to the threshold of harm; (3) when the threshold is reached, the accumulation constitutes a serious public harm, negatively impacting widely shared vital interests; (4) the activities producing these contributions are so beneficial in other ways that, prevented entirely, the resulting harm would be as great as the harm they now produce; and (5) legislation narrowly tailored to regulating or prohibiting the appropriate activities creates a standard of wrongfulness where none existed before, at least not visibly.

Especially in situations where such public accumulative harm takes place, practices of moral judgment about corporate wrongdoing function, like law, to erect a standard of wrongful behavior. Such practices consist in a general agreement about the sort of conduct to be deemed wrong, a consensus supported by an underlying rationale. It is a kind of coordinated response that may be only one of several alternative responses that would have solved the problem. Thus there appears to be nothing inherently wrong about a firm reincorporating in an offshore tax haven or shifting its manufacturing base or customer service operations abroad. But if too many such "corporate inversions" have caused substantial harm to the tax base or to the domestic labor market, respectively, and, to deal with this problem, new teachings about the evils of reincorporations and "exporting of America" have started to spring up, then a firm may be wrong in making the move, even if its behavior, considered by itself will have no material effects for the public problem, and even if its noncompliance would stay secret and have no damaging effects on public coordination to correct the problem. The creation of a moral standard of wrongfulness as a way of dealing with public accumulative harms is often masked by the existence of legislation.

But the establishment of general agreement need not be the result of legislation or governmental policy. It can arise gradually from moral debate and the consensus that crystallizes around it. A firm will realize competitive advantage by correctly forecasting the "new wave" of accumulative harm forming and proactively opting out of the conventional behavior. Being able to persuade key audiences within the firm's governance network that the wave is forming—and will inevitably lead to a crystallized standard of wrongfulness—is a critical task of visionary corporate governance.

Accumulative Expectation is the flip side, or inverse, of accumulative harm. (See Table 9.3.)

There are some actions undertaken by a few firms as supererogatory measures, above and beyond the call of duty, often with no expectation of financial reward at all. Yet, over time, increasingly larger numbers of firms adopt the same behavior until an initial threshold point is reached where the conduct becomes expected. There is a crucial element of timing involved. If firms can discern the emerging standard early enough—see that there is an element of positive satisfaction by investors, consumers, or employees that arises out of following the new rule—they will receive competitive advantage by complying with the standard. However, over time, and with a substantial number of firms adopting the practice, there comes a second threshold point at which no special advantage comes from compliance with the new rule; indeed, noncompliance will be met with reputational sanctions, as with rules established from accumulative harms as outlined above.

(1) A threshold of a higher standard is reached through joint and successive contributions of numerous parties; (2) each contribution is merely discretionary or "permissive" (as opposed to mandatory) in itself, except that

Table 9.3   Accumulative Expectation Model

Assume: Firms A, B, C, D.

A proactively goes beyond law, taking socially responsible action X; gets reputational boost by being first-mover. Public approves of A doing X.

B and C join in, seeking public approval too. D remains in a dither.

Later on, once doing X is the customary norm, D, unawares, gets slammed for not following the norm.

it moves the overall state of affairs closer to the threshold of heightened *expectations*; (3) when the threshold is reached, the accumulation constitutes a perceived *public entitlement* in that it is seen to promote widely shared vital interests (for example, clean environment, social justice, philanthropy, human rights); and (4) the firms that can discern the requirements of new standard *early* and implement it into its operations in a cost-effective way will attain a competitive advantage relative to other firms in its industry. In other words, the first-mover advantage here is a payoff for quickly seizing the opportunities for "doing the right thing." The resulting invisible "legislation" mandating the appropriate activities creates a standard of "business ethics" where none existed before. Visionary corporate governance means seizing opportunities in a timely way. By the time "everybody's doing it," there is nothing especially noteworthy about compliance with the new standards. And it may be quite costly to play the game of catching up.

Conflicts Among Rules

Conflicts arise between rules of invisible law, whether they are rules generated by accumulative harm or accumulative expectation. Thus accumulative expectations can create a standard to do both X and not-X: a CEO may be held to both play the share-price game (boost stock price in the short term by manufacturing earnings), and to refrain from playing it (give unpolished numbers, be transparent, generate long-term value for the firm). Likewise standards from accumulated expectations may transform rapidly into accumulative harms, as when widespread adoption of the share-price game leads to a market bubble poised to burst at any moment.

Rules of Corporate Obligation: Moral Versus Legal

Our ordinary thinking distinguishes what is merely desirable from what is obligatory—our duties as persons. But what does it mean for a rule to impose an obligation on a firm, a business entity? Does it matter whether it's a moral rather than a legal obligation being imposed?

According to H. L. A. Hart, with obligation-imposing rules, a "general demand for conformity is insistent and the social pressure brought to bear upon those who deviate or threaten to deviate is great." Whether we classify a rule of obligation as a legal or a moral one, he says, depends mainly on the nature of the sanctions wielded to secure conformity. These ideas provide a starting point. But when we are dealing with moral standards, should we accord such a tight connection between obligation and sanctions as this? Some fairly ordinary moral obligations—returning favors and keeping appointments—are not backed by severe or extreme social pressure. Plus, sanction accounts of obligation misleadingly suggest that it's the presence or likelihood of penalties that provides corporations with their reasons for performing their obligations, reasons that, presumably, would otherwise be insufficient.

Among the characteristic features of obligation is the idea that performing an obligation is a matter of legitimate interest and concern of others, whether members of some immediate group or community, or of humanity at large. This legitimate interest is reflected in an attitude that it is alright to exert pressure to exact performance. Often, this pressure is not thought to be limited to those who have an immediate interest in the performance of the obligation, but is appropriately exerted by others who assume the role of legitimate defenders of society's interests in the obligation at hand. Sometimes the pressure is exerted in the form of moral teaching, which might generate guilty or remorseful feelings.

A prevailing rule of obligation, therefore, is connected with an attitude about applying pressure, whether official sanctions, informal opinion, or feelings of indignation and guilt. The mildest kind of sanction comes in the form of beliefs or opinions that failure to perform the obligation is at least the business of others; failure to perform the obligation is not just something undesirable in the abstract.

Areas of corporate behavior most advantageously governed by public, collective moral rules are areas in which: (1) firms and the people working in them are especially likely to be tempted by interests that come into conflict, not only with impersonal good, but with the interests of other firms and individuals. (2) It is important to have a single public criterion applying to all in order to make inquiries more efficient and to forestall rationalization. (3) Where it is important to elevate judgments to the level of public discussion, pressure, and collective sanctions, the appropriateness of which can be efficiently decided in public moral debate. Paradigm cases of corporate behavior needing to be governed by such rules would thus be those involving the using and holding of other people's property, injury of other persons, and gaining unfair advantage. (4) Collective strategies wherein the efficacy of some rules, such as those imposing environmental controls and insider-trading regulations, requires that all firms obey them; they operate as a constraint on maximizing behavior.

Reincorporation: Offshore and Out-of-tune

Corporate leaders frequently must provide answers to questions that are either new, or newly troubling. Many would deem it wrong (at least questionable) for a person, say, an American citizen, to establish a bogus address in a foreign country and to relinquish his citizenship purely to avoid having to pay any income tax on money earned within the United States, where he continues to live. (President Clinton supported legislation forbidding such practices.) But what about when a *corporation* uses a similar ploy? Stanley Works, along with other companies such as Halliburton, reincorporated in offshore locations such as Bermuda, with just a postal drop, to cut their worldwide tax bill. Critics hammered the firm, claiming it was an unpatriotic move. Is it wrong for a corporation to do this?

It might seem that the only question about wrongness that matters for corporate governance is the legal question. A firm is interested in knowing whether reincorporating to avoid taxes will lead to liability in a court of law. As a legal question, the thought runs, it will be decided authoritatively in a legal forum. As a moral question, it is idle. No doubt it is true that the bulk of whatever attention this question gets will be focused on its likely legal resolution. Indeed, Congress was prompted to hold hearings to reconsider applicable tax law on this matter. But this should not obscure the moral analogues to the legal questions. If the question has not yet been resolved in the courts or in revised tax legislation, corporate leaders need to reflect on what is morally right; that is, on the kinds of rules and practices they ought to adopt, and the moral teaching and example to guide corporate behavior. Even if the question has been resolved in the legislature and the courts, and the resulting legal rule is reasonable, reasons may remain for thinking of certain things as morally wrong even though legally permitted. Perhaps the actions of the reincorporating company are legal from a taxation perspective, yet seen as wrong from the standpoint of patriotic obligations that are not so neatly defined as tax obligations.

One way to get answers to questions like these is to engage in moral analysis and debate. Out of such a debate additional rules will emerge defining the boundaries of corporate tax responsibilities. But there are disadvantages. The debate needs at least to be a national one, given the importance of nationally recognized tax obligations, and such a debate would be virtually impossible to carry on with any resolution. If tax "rules of the game" are indeed necessary, we would no doubt rely on the legislative action of the U.S. Congress to settle, not just the legal disputes that are likely to appear before the courts of the land, but some of the moral issues as well. Our reliance on the law to develop a legal rule would be especially appropriate if the need to have some rule or other was at least as important as having a good rule.

Let us consider an objection. It would seem that the way moral norms get changed is by individual companies acting separately. A company sees that an existing moral norm is unacceptable, and it just starts acting as it sees fit (or profitable). It does not wait for any collective corporate consensus to develop. But if there is a norm in place, then to act for the best would seem to constitute a violation of the authority of the existing norms of the corporate community. Consequently, the dilemma for those companies that accept the authority of the existing norm is either to reject the existing norm, or to wait for the needed new consensus to develop. But waiting is impractical for large groups of firms and imposes hardships in coordinating moral opinion around a new norm.

The offshore incorporation example provides a good illustration and test case. The behavior of the firm may constitute just the kind of actions that, although wrong given the de facto standards in force at the time, come to be regarded as permissible under newly revised rules. (Another possibility is that the rightness or wrongness of this kind of offshore reincorporation is still unsettled and indeterminate; that it is important that there be some generally accepted rule about this, though it is not clear which would be best.) Suppose that is what Stanley Works did: their action was wrong according to then-prevailing standards, although permissible by the standards that came to be accepted in the wake of the rule's violation.

There are several questions. First, in such a case, do corporations simply act on their own best judgment of what the best rule would require or of which action would produce the best results in the circumstances? The firm concerned about doing the right thing, it would seem, will consult the generally accepted rules about such behavior. If it is well understood that a certain type of tax-reducing behavior lies well over the accepted borderline, and in the area of offshore reincorporations, that fact ought to be taken seriously, even though, on a different and better drawing of the boundaries, the behavior would not count as an unpatriotic gesture or as an instance of wrongly evading tax obligations. This accepted borderline will be viewed, not as a generally useful guide to the sorts of actions that are right on act-utilitarian grounds, but as a standard of right behavior that excludes some of the normally relevant considerations about promoting overall good. Above all, in considering what is actually accepted or has potential acceptance, a company is not simply acting alone. A company does not simply follow the course of self-maximizing behavior, attempting to act in a way that has the best consequences.

Secondly, if the prevailing rule is then violated, does that amount to a wrongdoing that defies the authority of the prevailing rule? It may. It might be both a wrongdoing and something about which we can, in retrospect, be grateful that happened. Perhaps it was wrong for that offshore reincorporation to have taken place. We need understood boundaries of responsible corporate behavior concerning global tax obligations, and those were the understood boundaries at that time. Stanley Works did wrong in not respecting the boundaries, but, as a consequence, some beneficial changes have been brought about. Now, one reason why it might be difficult to think of such an action as wrong is that it did (according to one interpretation) produce more overall good. (Another interpretation would claim that some shareholders were harmed by having large capital gains increases that would increase their individual tax liability.) Because the action did produce a beneficial revision in accepted boundaries, it would seem to be the kind of action that is right and to be encouraged, not the opposite. Moreover, if the action is wrong, that would seem to imply that the most typical route to bringing about improvements in prevailing morality is one that involves wrongdoing. Presumably we want to encourage corporations to bring about beneficial changes, but if we do so, we would be encouraging wrongdoing. If we do not, we must settle for the status quo.

Actually this is a false dilemma. We do not need to worry about being stuck with the status quo morality. Not every firm is going to be so respectful of existing rules. Violations will happen. The violations will help bring about the benefits of an improved morality. Indeed, it might be collectively rational for a group of corporations in a given industry to agree on and then teach and otherwise reinforce a standard or right behavior, knowing that (1) the standard might turn out to be imperfect and open to improvement, and (2) the standard should not itself include exceptions for violations aimed at its improvement. Again, the reason for (2) might be that to authorize and encourage such behavior would be self-defeating and that, anyway, there will be quite enough violations and disrespect for the rule to perform the function of allowing for change. But even this grants too much. It overstates the case for bringing about changes in the de facto morality through deliberate violations of that morality. There are many other ways in which an accepted rule can be challenged without acts of defiance. For what the rule requires is that corporations act (or not act) in certain ways.

Many of the best-publicized debates in business crop up because of putative violations of accepted standards. There is, however, no necessity in this. Established standards are sometimes debated even when no violations are taking place. Moral opinion can undergo a shift as a result of the debate. This is the analogue of an "advisory opinion" being given by a court even when there is no actual case or controversy. Maybe this kind of public moral deliberation should take place more frequently. Perhaps we ought not to have waited until the case of Stanley Works's Bermuda reincorporation to reflect on what public opinion ought to be on the question of worldwide tax responsibilities, and whether the public has a sufficiently important and legitimate interest in where corporations are headquartered and incorporated in such cases.

Finally, if a firm is in such a position, ought the firm to violate this code, doing wrong in order to bring about an improved moral code? The way the question is proposed gives it an air of paradox. Companies should not do wrong; yet it is equally true that companies should do good by bringing about improvements in the moral code, and breaking the code may be the only way an improved code will result. We should first notice that situations like this are unlikely. In many cases the rule, understood in light of its justifying rationale, will clearly prohibit companies avoiding having to pay any taxes from any jurisdiction, but will be at least unclear if not silent about the case of setting up a postal-drop location in order to reduce, though not eliminate altogether, its taxes worldwide. But even if reincorporating in Bermuda really is a violation of a firm's generally understood duty to pay a fair share of taxes, it still does not follow that those firms that fail to meet that obligation ought to have done as they did, nor that we ought to encourage them to do as they did. In retrospect we might be correct in judging that (1) given the situation before the fact, the action ought not to have been done; (2) the action was and remains wrong; but (3) it all turned out well in the end; so (4) those who did it ought not to be blamed, or at least, not blamed severely, for what they did. In short, with respect to some wrongs, we can in retrospect be glad they occurred. This helps to dispel the air of paradox. It seems strange that wrongdoing can benefit society and its moral code, but it is true.

Nor does the judgment that the action was or would be wrong entail that its agent is in any way an immoral corporation. An immoral firm is one whose inclination to do the right thing is defective. A company that knowingly does wrong, or is indifferent about whether its actions might be wrong, is an immoral firm, especially if these deficiencies comprise a consistent pattern put in action. But a particular instance of knowing wrongdoing does not amount to immorality. If the sincere purpose behind it is to bring about improvements in prevailing corporate practices, it may be evidence of an especially deep concern for morality and the right. This is not to say that the knowing wrongdoing itself adds anything good to the company's character, or that by itself it reflects positively on the firm. It is rather that, given the larger context—that the action arises out of a deep concern to do good by improving moral opinion—the action tends to confirm, rather than disconfirm, what we knew already: that the agent is a highly moral company motivated to do good.

Hedge-fund Hubris

From the late 1990s until December 2008, the hedge-fund industry enjoyed a reputational competitive advantage. Professionally, hedge-fund employees were believed to be the most talented and best compensated. Large-asset management firms would consistently lose their best talent to hedge funds. Hedge funds were able to compensate above industry averages because they charged their investors higher management and performance-based fees. The standard for hedge-fund fees was a 2 percent management fee and a 20 percent performance fee. Compared to traditional equity investments in mutual-fund-like products, these fees were far more than what investors were used to paying. Historically, professional investors, including high-net-worth individuals, pension funds, endowments, foundations, and corporations paid these relatively high hedge-fund fees because hedge funds offered investors the opportunity to diversify their portfolios and capture absolute, as opposed to relative, returns. As absolute-return investments, investments in hedge funds were believed to be uncorrelated to other equity investments and indices, such as the S&P 500. The impressive past returns of hedge-fund investments often caused asset-allocation committee members and plan sponsors to overlook the risks of the asset class, complex due diligence needed, and the high fees. In 2008, with the Bernard Madoff scandal, the hedge-fund industry, as everyone knew it, changed.

On December 11, Bernard Madoff was arrested and charged with securities fraud. On March 12, 2009, Madoff pleaded guilty to eleven federal crimes, including securities fraud, wire fraud, mail fraud, money laundering, perjury, and making false filings with the SEC. Madoff admitted to defrauding thousands of investors of billions and was convicted of operating a Ponzi scheme that has been called the largest investor fraud ever committed by a single person. Estimated client losses were US$65 billion. On June 29, 2009, he was sentenced to 150 years in prison, the maximum allowed. In part because of the Madoff scandal, the amount of hedge-fund managers in the world was cut in half and total estimated hedge-fund industry assets dropped to around US$1 trillion, down from a peak of US$2.8 trillion.

The reputation of the hedge-fund industry was a productive asset prior to the Madoff scandal. Assets in the industry continued to increase and hedge funds, as a percentage of total assets within an investor's portfolio, were growing significantly. For example, coming into 2008, 20 percent of all endowments and foundations in the United States were using hedge funds, up from 15 percent in 2007. Madoff and many hedge funds received the benefit of being in an expanding industry. What most firms didn't realize was how interconnected everyone in the industry was and how one firm can hurt the competitiveness of an industry. Corporate leaders must pay attention to the expectations of key constituencies and keep abreast of the changing perceptions and interpretations of these constituencies.

In the wake of the Madoff scandal, there has been widespread redemption pressure from hedge-fund allocators, or constituents. Also, hedge-fund allocators are demanding increased transparency on their portfolios and lower management and performance fees. Some hedge funds are paying attention to what matters to allocators and adapting to the new allocating environment, for example, by developing transparency reports that allow investors to have a better understanding of the makeup of their portfolio. Also, some hedge funds have revised their offering terms (fees) to better align themselves with investor demand. Like Ford did when it proactively announced problems with their SUVs, some hedge funds have begun to lay a new foundation of trust, and these recent improvements will assist the funds in raising their assets.

The reputation of the hedge-fund industry not only was a productive asset for the hedge-fund industry, but also it was a source of competitive advantage.

The hedge-fund industry was put on a high pedestal, and it was acceptable to be a "closed door" to outside investors. Due diligence on hedge-fund firms was historically minimal and charging high fees was acceptable. This was all made possible because of the great reputation hedge funds had. The hedge-fund industry, which had become celebrity-like, had become vulnerable. The hedge-fund industry had not, and still has not, collectively committed to pro-actively managing its own reputation. Madoff ruined the competitive advantage the hedge-fund industry had built on its reputation by making it clear that even the most respected hedge-fund managers and firms can pull off a fraud. Investors no longer believe that the hedge-fund industry has plenty of best practices and regulations. To date, the industry has been either unwilling or incapable of standardizing forms of regulation and adopting a comprehensive plan that protects investors, and this has limited the amount of credibility and trust with which outsiders view the hedge-fund industry.

Another related area within the hedge-fund industry worth noting is whether to allow investors to take their money out of hedge funds. "Gating" investors, a practice not often used prior to 2008, is the legal act of blocking investors from redeeming their investment in a hedge fund. Hedge funds have gates in place in order to protect their franchise as well as the overall client's investments should their hedge fund be forced to liquidate. Although certainly related to Madoff and his impact on redemptions in hedge funds, this issue is also the result of the economic crisis and the associated stock market performance in 2008. Investors need liquidity more than ever as many of their investments and businesses are struggling. As a hedge fund, if your investors want to pull out their money, you are allowed to gate them. Gating restrictions typically are set at 20 percent, and can either be set at the overall fund level or at the investor level. Hedge funds are not forced to act consistently when their 20 percent gates are triggered because they can decide to either allow their investors to redeem more than 20 percent or gate the investor and not allow them to redeem. If hedge funds allow investors to redeem past the gated level, the hedge fund knowingly can be hurting the remaining investors in the fund. The remaining investors may be hurt by staying in because hedge funds are often forced to sell the most liquid assets into a falling market at below-market prices. A lot of the volatility in November and December 2008 was the result of redemption selling as hedge funds were force to liquidate equities and debt so that investors could withdraw funds. In addition to suffering poor performance from forced selling at below-market prices, the remaining investors can be left with the most illiquid securities. However, the fund can tell their investors they can't take their money out and hold all the investors funds until it is a more stable time to sell.

The issue of gating in the hedge-fund industry highlights the ethical dimension. A utilitarian approach would say that the greater good is not accomplished by allowing only certain investors out of the fund and leaving the remaining investors with poor performance and an illiquid portfolio. The greatest good would be accomplished by gating all investors and waiting until there is an appropriate time to return capital. What is interesting about this issue is that hedge funds are being accused of being egoists because gating investors allows the hedge fund to stay in business longer by locking their investors into paying fees. Some hedge funds that could have used a gate on investors, however, chose not to use the gate and paid out cash to all investors who wanted to redeem. This gave them a great marketing pitch to use with future investors, telling them that they didn't use their gate and gave back to investors the money that was rightly theirs. Those hedge funds using a highly liquid strategy were able to pay out redemptions without adversely affecting remaining investors.

The debate within the hedge-fund industry, and what has been angering hedge-fund investors, is that the choice to gate and the definition of adversely affecting investors is *not a science but instead an art*. A hedge fund that is faced with redemptions can decide themselves if giving money back is the right thing to do. Often, if a hedge fund gives money back, they themselves may be forced to go out of business. Many hedge funds today are said to be abusing their decision-making authority and claiming that using their gate is good for all investors when it is really only allowing the hedge fund to buy more time and stay in business.

Arguably, the ethical issues highlighted above, as well as others, are changing the hedge-fund industry for the better in the long term. There will be some short-term pain as investors reexamine their hedge-fund exposure and allocate to safer and more liquid types of strategies. However, hedge funds that survived 2009 have a competitive advantage and story to tell investors about how they adapted to change and successfully adapted to a changing industry. From a regulatory standpoint, today there is still no clear set of rules and hedge funds can voluntarily register with the SEC (not that registration with the SEC has equated to safety—Madoff was registered). Most funds still provide limited transparency to investors, but given the events surrounding Madoff, the level of regulation on hedge funds will likely increase. Also, increased investor due diligence is a good thing; it will highlight the strongest firms. Only the best hedge funds will survive.

Conclusion

The same age, which produces great philosophers and politicians, renowned generals and poets, usually abounds with skillful weavers, and ship-carpenters. We cannot reasonably expect that a piece of woolen cloth will be wrought to perfection in a nation, which is ignorant of astronomy, or where ethics are neglected. The spirit of the age affects all the arts.
—David Hume

Everything you do is music and everywhere is the best seat.
—John Cage

CONTEMPORARY MARKET ECONOMIES across the globe have attained significant success thanks to their ability to establish the rule of law, free trade, and technological innovation. Yet these accomplishments, worthy as they are, are inadequate for generating deeper human associations and shared meanings necessary for the ecology of the market to be sustained. What is required is a viewpoint on the meaning of human existence compelling enough to rise above the nihilistic detractors of postmodern culture, which threaten the foundations of the free-market economy.

Moral strength is the foundation of all human accomplishments. Yet such strength depends on there being shared meanings that can be imparted to people from their culture. In this sense, culture can be seen as a storehouse of moral knowledge. To the extent that our cultural inheritance is permitted to erode, to diminish in terms of the value that we attach to it, our civilization will be so much the worse and will be vulnerable in the face of those forces around the world that are bent on destroying it.

To some extent, our culture—shaped by its artistic, literary, musical, and philosophical achievements—is necessarily framed by good judgment, and the ability to render such judgment is closely intertwined with moral knowledge. Hence, the perpetuation of culture from one generation to the next requires instilling the right patterns or practices of making sound judgments in the youth upon whom the future rests. Thus, given the interdependence between morality and economics, on the one hand, and the strong interplay between culture and morality, on the other hand, it would appear that a healthy commercial society and the market around which it functions requires a healthy culture.

But culture is more than a collection of facts, and more than a set of theories. Moreover, cultural knowledge is not coextensive with technical training. Nevertheless, culture is an embodiment of moral knowledge in the broadest sense, which encompasses one's vision of the good life. A civilization's culture, manifested in its art, literature, music, and philosophy, provides a means by which that civilization becomes conscious of itself and equips it to craft its vision of reality and human life.

To be sure, there is a continual replenishment that occurs as new works of art, literature, and music come on the scene. However, not all creations will stand as enduring masterpieces but will instead pass into oblivion. The same dynamic holds for our moral heritage. In fact, the cultural inheritance of a civilization contributes significantly to its stock of moral capital. Just as the treasured works of art, music, and literature of a culture stand as archetypes and often become a source of inspiration for originators in successive generations, the moral accomplishments of our ancestors can hold up a similar standard of excellence for us and for our descendents.

For virtuosity to take hold as a higher standard for business and professional life there must be some intrinsic appreciation of objective moral ideals. That kind of moral knowledge, which is not simply intellectual but also emotional, is passed on to us, or withheld from us as the case may be, from our culture. Some measure of piety with respect to goodness, truth, and beauty needs to be in place, surpassing any merely utilitarian value they may come to be associated with. Significantly, the lack of reverence for such ideals needs to be attached to a sense of genuine shame. A feeling of remorse must attend the awareness that I have not lived up to the highest standards of which my human nature is capable. Perhaps I have discredited truth by twisting logic or concealing facts. Maybe I have failed to act with an eye to benefiting those impacted by my conduct, or desecrated the beautiful in some way. In all such instances, my culture must teach me, not simply what is legal and illegal, and what is right and what is wrong, but to feel shame, and to feel it whether anyone else happens to find out or not; regardless of whether I happen to get caught by the authorities.

Consider the conduct of those working in the financial services industry who knowingly and willfully engage in questionable practices that are abusive to their clients. Or ponder the brazen behavior of swindlers such as Allen Stratford or Bernard Madoff. Our culture must instruct us to regard their conduct not simply as illegal, or as imprudent or damaging to their careers, but as morally shameful, as shrinking them from what they ought to be as human beings. Reading of their misdeeds in the morning newspaper we might remark, "How on earth could they have done that?" Yet all the while we know exactly how. Dedication to reason, adoration of beauty, and love of goodness do not represent a source of direction for their life, do not figure deep into their moral identity, regardless of the way they might try to spin it. Such people lack virtue, no matter how high their level of mastery of technical business skills may be. Bernard Madoff is reported to remain unrepentant about his US$65 billion Ponzi scheme, as revealed in his remark, "f— my victims, I carried them for twenty years, and now I'm doing 150 years."[1]

There is a big difference between a culture that encourages one to be ashamed of wrongdoing—a culture of virtue—and a culture that only pragmatically judges good or bad consequences resulting from the exercise of self-interest. Such a utilitarian-minded culture only pities the corporate crook for misfortune of getting caught, prosecuted, and sentenced to do jail time. What this signals is that we desperately need to retain the right to designate those individuals who are not good persons as just that. A person lacking moral virtue, with no functioning conscience, is in reality neither good nor authentic, despite the confused messages our culture sends us to the effect that no one has the right to judge anyone else. Culture needs to stand behind virtue, providing support for the moral life. Developing cultures of virtue, economic communities of objective moral comprehension appear to be the solution to our present predicament. This appears to be the only thing able to redeem business and the economy. The potential for objective moral insight is more universal and less relativistic than many business ethicists assume.

As was demonstrated in earlier chapters, for Aristotle, just as there is an ideal of excellence for any given craft or occupation, there is an excellence we can attain simply as human beings. We can conduct our lives as a whole so that they can be pronounced not just as excellent in this respect or in that occupation but as excellent, pure and simple. Only when we cultivate our authentic human capacities sufficiently to accomplish this human excellence, in a word, to attain virtuosity, will we have lives blessed with happiness in the deepest sense.

There is a human nature. Its characteristics are evident and have not fundamentally changed from the time they were elucidated by Aristotle, Socrates, and Plato. No doubt the inculcation of moral knowledge into business culture requires a community of intellectuals and professionals dedicated to that pursuit over an extensive time period.

It is necessary to raise a disquieting possibility. Could it be that the dwindling of the life of virtue on the part of both individuals and organizations that we are witnessing throughout the business world stems from an erosion of the canon of moral knowledge not just from economic society but from the wider culture as well? Can any plausible account be given today of what a morally educated businessperson is? Even in the midst of all the attention paid to "ethics training" in the companies we work in we do not permit ourselves to speak about matters such as this. Is it possible to cultivate and safeguard the moral life inside of business culture and throughout the wider culture if no agreed-upon corpus of moral knowledge exists?

The disciples of ethical noncognitivism have a pervasive presence throughout our popular culture and within academic institutions today, even though its seminal crass articulation as the emotivist theory has been generally repudiated for some time. Instead of proceeding from a foundation of the human capacity to know truth, some theories of business ethics have instead accentuated the manner in which that ability is restricted and conditioned.

Consequently, this current of thought has nurtured various versions of postmodernism and relativism, gussied up as serious scholarship, yet unable to provide a foundation for visionary moral leadership. The manifestation of such a clueless standpoint in the economic world was the utter incomprehensibility of complex financial instruments, even in the eyes of specially trained experts. Professional rating agencies did not hesitate to render seemingly authoritative opinions that seemed to have had no basis in truth at all. For such a skeptical view, truth is stripped of its exclusive character. Everything comes down to mere subjective opinion. As a result, there is a pervasive sense of anxiety and uncertainty.

My contention, which has been stressed throughout this book, is that there are canons of objective moral knowledge that can be accessed by reasonable people. Such moral knowledge is anchored in intuition, in self-knowledge aimed at intention and character. Like our grasp of logic, basic moral knowledge is direct. This point is emphasized in Jacques Maritain's writings concerning connatural knowledge of the virtues. As he states:

> If we are asked a question about fortitude, we shall give the right an-swer, no longer through science, but through intuition, by looking at and consulting what we are and the inner bents or propensities of our own being. A virtuous man may possibly be utterly ignorant in moral philosophy, and know as well—probably better—everything about virtues, through connaturality.
>
> In this knowledge through union or inclination, connaturality or congeniality, the intellect is at play not alone, but together with affective inclinations and the dispositions of the will, and is guided and directed by them. It is not rational knowledge, knowledge through the con-ceptual, logical and discursive exercise of Reason. But it is really and genuinely knowledge, though obscure and perhaps incapable of giving account of itself, or of being translated into words.[2]

Although throughout much of our business culture and the broader culture there is a sense that objective moral knowledge is absent, we cannot thereby conclude that such knowledge does not in fact exist. The problem is not that there is no objective moral order. Nor is the problem that we have no ca-pability to know it. The problem is that the knowledge is not commonly acknowledged, systematically received and adequately integrated into our educational institutions and into our commercial society. Making matters worse there is a lack of appreciation for how taking a moral perspective on business life requires a contemplative disposition.

If we genuinely believe that objective morality exists, then that convic-tion will inexorably affect our personal choices and economic behavior. Our faith in an objective moral order will influence how we frame our economic concepts and design our business institutions. In that case, quarantining morality from our economic life cannot promote the common good. It comes down to enthroning the unreal while fleeing from reality.

The fact that truth, goodness, and beauty stand as philosophical ide-als does not mean that they are somehow unimportant for the practical economic sphere in which people participate in the day-to-day task of building wealth. Such ideals are grasped by human reason. Yet, owing to their "invisible" status, there is a persistent temptation to treat them as abstract and distant notions lacking any bearing or significance in the "real world." Nevertheless, the emergence of social entrepreneurship business models suggests that the wellsprings of human compassion and the virtue of generosity are not, and need not be, decoupled from hard-nosed business decisions and actions. The successful entrepreneurs, business leaders, and CEOs of tomorrow will need to find imaginative ways to incorporate the commandment of love of neighbor and the responsibility to live in truth into business life.

What are the practical implications of this? It means that, regardless of how brutal the competition may get, one is not entitled to treat others merely as stepping-stones to advance one's career or to treat customers, employees, and peers simply as a means to maximizing profits. Not only does this follow from basic considerations of maintaining a reputation, but it also reflects the awareness that such business constituencies are persons made in the image of their creator and, as such, are deserving of human dignity.

One is worthy of assuming a leadership role in business in much the same way one earns the status of master conductor of an orchestra: by displaying a true passion and an exceptional knack for bringing out the best in others in such a way as to make the entire collective perform the very best it can, to the glory of the greater good of humankind.

Virtuosity's attention to fundamentals like virtue, beauty, and truth has profound significance for the operation of the free-market economy. Of the utmost urgency for a healthy market ecology is the extent to which business conduct and commercial transactions of all kinds are anchored in moral truth. Absent internal structures that embody human dignity and mutual trust, the free market is unable to adequately play its appropriate economic role. Nowhere has this been more clearly demonstrated than in the events surrounding the global financial crisis. For example, as was pointed out in Chapter 7, the subprime mortgage imbroglio came about in part as a consequence of legions of people making material misrepresentations of fact in filling out mortgage applications. It should come as no surprise that a massive disregard for the moral imperative of truth telling engenders debilitating economic outcomes.

Disregard for moral value leads to destruction of economic value. The market and the businesses that operate in it are essentially bound up with human endeavors. In opposition to ethical relativism, I would counter that healthy free-market economies need to be supported by allegiance to fundamental moral goods as well as adherence to the primacy and inherent worth and dignity of human persons. These components need to be in place for the economy to be sustainable and efficient, for it to advance instead of inhibit the common good of humankind. In other words, preserving market ecology requires business ethics. But this is not to say that any sort of business ethics will suffice. The attention we are paying in this book to the vital linkages between economic value and moral values, between financial capital and the cultural and reputational capital that breathe life into it, between virtue and character on the one hand, and profitability and excellence in business performance on the other, all goes to show that business ethics must be human-centered. Humans comprise the very core of a free economy. Against utilitarian approaches to business ethics I would stress that individuals whose inclinations are captured by a culture of hedonism will remain bound to render hedonistic economic decisions that support hedonistic life styles. What this means is that the market as such is not the determinant of moral versus immoral conduct. Again, as was demonstrated in Chapter 7, what is of equal importance is the moral culture within which the free market operates.

Many of today's economic troubles reveal a profound and widespread moral contamination of our civilization. Indeed, the financial calamities of recent years offer all of us strong evidence that there is such a thing as immorality in our markets and that it is very destructive. So long as we ignore this correlation between moral-cultural dysfunction and commercial life, all of the proposed alterations in business conduct and economic policy, all of the calls for stepped-up regulations and issuances of new ethics rules, although some are necessary, are bound to offer incomplete remedies.

This moral malaise is not limited to Western culture. Within contemporary China, for instance, instead of any fundamental democratic rule of law there is a centralized regime that dispenses arbitrary administrative edicts. Much of its population is trapped within a post-Cultural Revolution moral void that can be traced to many sources: the weakening of Confucianism that was occasioned by the government of Mao Zedong after Nationalists left the mainland of China for Taiwan in 1949, the official repression of religious freedom, and the rise of consumerism in tandem with an explosive rise in economic development. However, there are discernable currents of change from the other direction, such as evidence of China's concern for environmental sustainability; so although things are very far from morally satisfactory there, some of its developments are widely hailed as moral progress.

It is important to underscore that the world we inhabit today is fraught with a great deal of moral confusion. This is not to say that earlier times witnessed anything close to moral perfection (we may recall Plato's complaint that the youth of his day weren't as respectful of their elders as they used to be).[3] And it must be granted that, as was seen in our examination of global civil society's rising concern with corporate social responsibility in Chapter 8, many around the world today harbor a genuine concern for a number of social and ecological problems for which previous generations were not particularly attuned. As well, the world has fewer wars, fewer famines, and much more concern about human rights than it did a century ago.

Nevertheless, we must guard against the temptation to be in a state of denial about the persistent threat of genuine moral decay. The point is captured in the musings of Cormac McCarthy's character of an aging sheriff in *No Country for Old Men*:

> I read in the papers here a while back some teachers come across a survey that was sent out back in the thirties to a number of schools around the country. Had this questionnaire about what was the problems with teachin in the schools. And they come across these forms, they'd been filled out and sent in from around the country answerin these questions. And the biggest problems they could name was things like talking in class and runnin in the hallways. Chewin gum. Copyin homework. Things of that nature. So they got one of them forms that was blank and printed up a bunch of em and sent em back out to the same schools. Forty years later. Well, here come the answers back. Rape, arson, murder. Drugs. Suicide. So I think about that. Because a lot of the time ever when I say anything about how the world is goin to hell in a handbasket people will just sort of smile and tell me I'm getting old. That it's one of the symptoms. But my feelin about that is that anybody that can't tell the difference between rapin and murderin people and chewin gum has got a whole lot bigger problem than what I've got.[4]

What we see from the recent financial crisis is that there is a pronounced neglect, not only in business but also in the wider culture for matters like trust and character and basic honesty. There is a widespread desertion regarding elemental concepts of right and wrong. When such moral cornerstones are dislodged, our economic and social structures are deeply imperiled.

This book has shown that we discover, and in part also create, an invisible moral law of the market economy from two primary sources. The first source is virtuous conduct. The second source is the multitude of norms comprising the broader moral law of humankind as such. So conceived, the invisible law of the free market is like the footprints left behind by alternating steps of virtue and law walking a path toward wisdom.

We would do well to bear in mind that this same pathway, which is oriented toward truth, beauty, justice, and the good may be discerned in traditions crossing cultures throughout history, in different parts of the world. Woven into the work of Aristotle and Plato, the epics of Homer, the dramas of Sophocles, the reflections of Lao-Tse, Buddha, or Confucius, the sacred scriptures of the Upanishads, one finds the same elemental concerns, what for Charles Ives all came down to the "unanswered question" at the core of human existence. Of course, while tradition bequeaths us pearls of wisdom, it also bequeaths us a fair share of gimcrackery, along with some attitudes that are no longer appropriate. It is hard enough to figure out what tradition teaches us today; far harder it is to figure out what valuable lessons tradition has for tomorrow. At any rate, we should not allow the quest for material success to eclipse our eternal promptings for authenticity and spiritual well-being.

Instead, we ought to consider how we might revivify that tradition of reverence for human wisdom in the service of sustaining the ecology of the free market and the pricelessness of our civilization, rather than discarding it as if it had been hopelessly shattered by moral skeptics, nihilists, and antagonists of our higher spirit. Let's hope that posterity can summon the virtuosity it will need to carry on the good work. *Ars longa vita brevis est.*[5]

Notes

Introduction

1. "It is not just that freedom is part of the act of faith: it is absolutely required. Indeed, it is faith that allows individuals to give consummate expression to their own freedom. Put differently, freedom is not realized in decisions made against God. For how could it be an exercise of true freedom to refuse to be open to the very reality which enables our self-realization? Men and women can accomplish no more important act in their lives than the act of faith; it is here that freedom reaches the certainty of truth and chooses to live in that truth" (John Paul II, *Fides et Ratio* ¶13).

2. Plato's dialogue, *Phaedrus,* employs an allegory to depict the moral soul as a triad composed of reason (charioteer), noble spirit (good horse), and irrational emotion (bad horse). The charioteer symbolizes intellect, reason, or the part of the soul that must guide the soul to truth. The good horse symbolizes rational moral impulse and the positive side of our passionate nature. The bad horse, by contrast, represents irrational passions and appetites. The charioteer guides the chariot, preventing the horses from going in different directions, to advance toward the enlightenment of truth (Plato, *Six Great Dialogues*, Benjamin Jowett, trans. [2007]).

3. David Hume, *A Treatise of Human Nature* (1739), 415.

Chapter 1

1. James Legge, *The Confucian Analects, The Great Learning and the Doctrine of the Mean* (1971), 356–59.

2. Lao Tse, *Tao Te Ching*, Steven Mitchell, trans. (1988), ch. 54.

3. Ibid., ch. 49.

4. Aristotle, *Nicomachean Ethics*, bk. I, ch. 1, 1094a 1–2, 935.

5. Ibid., bk. I, ch. 8, 1098b 30–1099a6, 944.

6. Ibid., bk. I, ch. 2, 1094a 17–24, 935.

7. Aristotle, *Politics*, bk. I, ch. 2, 1253a 25–32, 1130.

8. Aristotle, *Nicomachean Ethics*, bk. I, ch. 5, 1095b 14–19, 938.

9. Ibid., bk. I, ch. 5, 1095b 19–22, 938. In Greek legend, Sardanapallus was an especially hedonistic and licentious Assyrian potentate.

10. Paul Nystrom, *Economics of Fashion* 68 (1928). See also David Barsamian and Noam Chomsky, *Propaganda and the Public Mind: Conversations with Noam Chomsky* (2001), 151.

11. Aristotle, *Nicomachean Ethics*, bk. I, ch. 5, 1095b 22–24, 938.

12. Ibid., bk. X, ch. 6, 1176b 32–33, 1103.

13. Ibid., bk. X, ch. 6, 1176b 33–36, 1103.

14. Ibid., bk. I, ch. 5, 1095b 22–30, 938.

15. Ibid., bk. X, ch. 7, 1177a 11–19, 1104.

16. Lao Tse, *Tao Te Ching*, ch. 15.

17. Jean-Marie Tasset, "Fernando Botero: Life and Work Within the Century," available at http://karaart.com/botero/tasset/life.html.

18. Aristotle, *Nicomachean Ethics*, bk. I, ch. 5, 1096a 5–7, 939.

19. Aristotle, *Politics*, bk. I, ch. 9, 1258a 13–14, 1140.

20. Ibid., 1257b 38–1258a 3, 1139.

21. Ibid., 1257b 33–38, 1139.

22. Ibid., 1257a 8–16, 1138.

23. Ibid., bk. I, ch. 10, 1258a 38–1258b 2, 1141.

24. Ibid., 1258b 2–8, 1141.

25. Ibid., bk I, ch. 13, 1102a 5–16, 950.

26. Aristotle, *Nicomachean Ethics*, bk. VI, ch. 1, 1139a 4–a14, 1023.

27. Ibid., bk. I, ch. 7, 1098a 6–18, 943.

28. Ibid., bk. I, ch. 8, 1099b 1–9, 945.

29. Ibid., bk. I, ch. 8, 1099a 12–16, 945.

30. Ibid., bk. I, ch. 10, 1100b 22–32, 948.

31. Ibid., 1100a 5–7, 946.

32. Ibid., 1101a 9–13, 948.

33. Ibid., 1100b 12–21, 947.

34. Cf. Hermann Hesse's optimistic view: "I have always believed, and I still believe, that whatever good or bad fortune may come our way we can always give it meaning and transform it into something of value."

35. The term *cardinal* is derived from the Latin word "cardo," which means "hinge-point." The idea here is that everything hinges on these four virtues. If they are absent, no other virtues can be properly developed and put into play.

36. Aristotle, *Nicomachean Ethics*, bk. I, ch. 13, 1103a 3–10, 952.

37. Aristotle, *Nicomachean Ethics*, bk. II, ch. 1, 1103a 32–1103b 1–2, 952.

38. Ibid., bk. II, ch. 1, 1103b 24–26, 953.

39. Ibid., bk. X, ch. 9, 1179b 32–1180a 3, 1109.

40. Ibid., 1180a 3–4.

41. Ibid., 1180a 5–13.

42. Ibid., bk. VI, ch. 5, 1140a 25–32, 1026.

43. Ibid., 1140b8–11.

44. See, generally, Robert Solomon, "Aristotle, Ethics, and Business Organizations," 25(6) *Org. Studies* (2006), 1021–43; Chris Lowney, *Heroic Leadership: Best Practices from a 450-Year-Old Company that Changed the World* (2003); Larry C. Spears, ed., *Insights on Leadership: Service, Stewardship, Spirit, and Servant-Leadership* (1998).

45. Aristotle, *Nicomachean Ethics*, bk. VI, ch. 6, 1141a 16–19, 1027–28.

46. Jan Adkins, *Thomas Edison* (2009), provides an account of the wide range of Edison's technological innovations—stock ticker, telegraph, typewriter, light bulb, kinetoscope, phonograph—as well as a description of the collaborative efforts and mutual admiration that Ford and Edison had for one another.

47. The argument against typical CEO remuneration in the United States is buttressed by the observation that American CEO's pull down significantly more pay than their counterparts in countries such as Canada, Great Britain, Japan, Spain, and other developed nations. See, e.g., Nuno Fernandes et al., "The Pay Divide: (Why) Are U.S. Top Executives Paid More?" 25 (Feb. 12, 2009), available at http://ssrn.com/abstract=1341639 (compiling data showing that U.S. executives pull down higher compensation than counterparts in Europe and Asia, while taking into account a broad array of firm, industry, governance, and CEO characteristics).

48. See "The Pay at the Top," *N. Y. Times*, available at http://projects.nytimes.com/executive_compensation?ref=business; Matteo Tonello, "Overseeing Risk Management and Executive Compensation: 'Pressure Points' for Corporate Directors," The Conference Board: Executive Action Series, Dec. 2008, available at http://ssrn.com/abstract=1325028 (showing that in the past two decades executive compensation grew substantially faster than corporate earnings and reporting a study from the *Wall Street Journal* and the Economic Research Institute showing that in 2007 the median salary of top executives among the Standard & Poor's 500 increased 20.5 percent over the preceding year).

49. Kim Dixon, "More CEOs Got Pay Hike than Pay Cuts in '08," Apr. 14, 2009 (a study of 946 companies in the Russell 3000 index indicated that more than half of the CEOs got raises in 2008).

50. In 2008, despite the economic downturn, the total direct compensation to CEOs of nearly two hundred Fortune 500 companies decreased only 2 percent. See Towers Watson, "2009 Proxy Statements Highlight the New Realities in Executive Compensation," *Dec.* 2009, available at http://www.towerswatson.com/research/641.

Information collected by Equilar reveals that for SEC-reporting companies filing proxy statements by March 27 and attaining minimum revenues of US$6.3 billion, their average executive compensation declined by 5.1 percent for 2008, not as sharp a decline as the drop in shareholder values. See Kathryn Jones, "Who Moved My Bonus?

Executive Pay Makes a U-Turn," *N. Y. Times*, Apr. 5, 2009, B1 (reporting that, prior to 2008, executive pay had increased every year up to the bursting of the technology bubble in 2001–2 . Even while the recession hammered corporate profits and shareholder return, the average total compensation among CEOs at these companies in 2008 was US$10.8 million. See "AFL-CIO 2009 Executive PayWatch," available at http://www.aflcio.org/corporatewatch/paywatch/.

Executives of some of the most financially imperiled investment houses remained immune from the turmoil of the economic crisis. Merrill Lynch paid eleven of its top executives more than US$11 million in 2008, and the brokerage house paid another one hundred forty-nine of their executives more than US$3 million. See "Merrill's $10 Million Dollar Men: Top 10 Earners Made $209 Million in 2008 as Firm Floundered," *Wall St. J.*, Mar. 4, 2009, A1. The remuneration of directors at three hundred of the Fortune 500 companies climbed upward during the financial crisis, increasing 4.7 percent from 2007 to 2008. See "Non-Employee Director Pay Climbs 4.7 percent to 182K," Equilar Press Release, May 5, 2009, available at http://equilar.com/press_20090505_1.php.

51. See "The Pay at the Top," *N.Y. Times*, June 13, 2009, available at http://projects.nytimes.com/executive_compensation?ref=business.

52. Ibid.

53. Ibid.

54. Ibid.

55. See Greg Hitt and Aaron Lucchetti, "House Passes Bonus Tax Bill: 90% Hit Would Affect Major Banks; Senate Mulls Similar Action Amid AIG Furor," *Wall St. J.*, Mar. 20, 2009, A1.

56. Helen Kennedy, "Not So Fast on Those Bonuses, You AIG Hot Shots," *Daily News* (New York), Oct. 23, 2008, 2.

57. See "Senior Executives: Cuomo Clawing Compensation," *Westlaw Bus. Legal Currents*, Feb. 24, 2009 (reporting New York State Attorney General Andrew Cuomo's investigation of bonus payments by Bank of America, which acquired Merrill Lynch).

58. Martin Kady II, "Grassley on AIG Execs: Quit or Suicide," *Politico*, Mar. 16, 2009, available at http://www.politico.com/news/stories/0309/20083.html.

59. See "Bonuses for Bozos," *New York Post*, Mar. 17, 2009, 24. See also Deborah Solomon and Laura Meckler, "Strict Executive Pay Caps Planned: Latest Salvo From Obama Administration Aims to Rein In Firms Receiving Federal Aid," *Wall St. J.*, Feb. 4, 2009, A3.

60. See Yin Wilczek, "Lawmakers Ask Regulators for Details on Merrill Bonuses, Use of TARP Funds," 41 *Sec. Reg. L. Rep.* 654 (Apr. 13, 2009).

61. Ibid.

62. Ibid.

63. Some CEO portraits assembled in the gallery of the gluttonous herein I have rendered from a collection of exquisite models showcased in Kenneth R. Davis,

"Taking Stock—Salary and Options Too: The Looting of Corporate America," 69(3) *Maryland L. Rev.* (2010) 419, 420–22.

64. H.R. Rep. No. 111–236, 7 (2009).

65. Ibid.

66. Total real compensation reflects adjustments for increases in price levels.

67. Xavier Gaibaix and Augustin Landier, "Why Has CEO Pay Increased So Much?" MIT Department of Economics Working Paper No. 06-13.

68. Cynthia E. Devers, Albert A. Cannella Jr., Gregory P. Reilly, and Michele E. Yoder, "Executive Compensation: A Multidisciplinary Review of Recent Developments," 33 *J. of Mgt.* (2007), 1016–72.

69. Michael C. Jensen and Kevin J. Murphy, "Performance Pay and Top Management Incentives," 98 *J. of Political Econ.* (1990), 225–64.

70. See Gaibaix and Landier, note 67 supra.

71. The NBC Symphony was created for Toscanini by RCA's David Sarnoff. Toscanini was the conductor of it from 1937 to 1954. See Joseph Horowitz, *Understanding Toscanini* (1987).

72. "The American taxpayers are tired of paying for Wall Street's mistake, our government guaranteeing their obligations. They see something manifestly and fundamentally wrong with the casino environment in which high rollers pocket the profits, often measured in millions if not billions of dollars, while the taxpayers pay off the losses." Bachus Statement During Systemic Risk Hearing, U.S. House of Representatives Doc. (Sept. 24, 2009).

73. Aristotle, *Politics*, bk. III, ch. 9, 1280a 8–23, 1187.

74. Ibid., bk. III, ch. 12, 1282b 32–1283a 3, 1193.

75. See Michael Maccoby, *Narcissistic Leaders: Who Succeeds and Who Fails* (2007). Narcissistic leaders, among whom Maccoby includes Andy Grove (Intel), Larry Ellison (Oracle), Jack Welch (GE), Bill Gates (Microsoft), Jeff Bezos (Amazon.com), and Steve Jobs (Apple), are typically "more interested in controlling others than in knowing and disciplining themselves." They also tend be poor listeners, hypersensitive to criticism, devoid of empathy, and "relentless and ruthless in their pursuit of victory." Michael Maccoby, "Narcissistic Leaders: The Incredible Pros, the Inevitable Cons," *Harv. Bus. Rev.* (Jan.-Feb. 2000).

76. See New Economics Foundation, *A Bit Rich: Calculating the Real Value to Society of Different Professions* (2009).

77. See note 24, supra.

78. Eleanor O'Higgins, "After the Fall: The Ethics of Bankers' Bonuses" (paper presented for the 2010 Transatlantic Business Ethics Conference, York University).

79. Samuel Brittan, "Thoughts on the Troubles of Banks," *Fin. Times*, Aug. 12, 2010, 9 (cited in O'Higgins, note 78 supra).

80. Shumeet Banerji, "Solving Moral Hazard in Banking," *strategy+business*, June 7, 2010.

81. Aristotle, *Nicomachean Ethics*, bk. IV, ch. 2 1123a 18–27, 990–91.

82. Ibid., 1123a 27–32, 991.

83. Ibid., bk. IV, ch. 2, 1123a 6–9, 990.

84. Lauren Beale, "Foreclosure Auction of Nicolas Cage's Mansion Is a Flop," *L. A. Times* (Apr. 8, 2010), B1.

85. "Nigeria; The Shame of a Nation," *Africa News* (June 4, 2009).

86. Aristotle, *Nicomachean Ethics*, bk, X, ch. 8 1178a 10–21, 1106.

87. Ibid., bk. II, ch. 3, 1104b 4–11, 954.

88. Ibid., bk. VI, ch. 13, 1144b 30–2, 1036.

89. See Terence H. Irwin, "Aristotle on Reason, Desire, and Virtue," 72 *J. of Phil.* (1975), 567–78; and John M. Cooper, "Some Remarks on Aristotle's Moral Psychology," 27 *S. J. of Phil.*, Supplement (1988), 25–42.

90. See David Wiggins, "Deliberation and Practical Reason," in A. O. Rorty, ed., *Essays on Aristotle's Ethics* (1980), 221–40; and John McDowell, "Deliberation and Moral Development in Aristotle's Ethics," in S. Engstrom and J. Whiting, eds., *Aristotle, Kant, and the Stoics—Rethinking Happiness and Duty* (1996), 19–35.

91. Cf., for Kant, the virtues of character inhere in moderation. For Philippa Foot, and others (such as Christine Korsgaard) the virtues of character amount to correctives for deficiencies in our human nature.

92. Babbit, who is in the real estate business, is described by Lewis early on in the novel as making "nothing in particular, neither butter nor shoes nor poetry," yet is nevertheless "nimble in the calling of selling houses for more than people could afford to pay." Reflecting on his way of life, Babbit states that it is "mechanical" and that his occupation amounts to a "mechanical business—a brisk selling of badly built houses."

93. Aristotle, *Nicomachean Ethics*, bk. III, ch. 3, 1112b 5–6, 969.

94. Ibid., 1112b 8.

95. Ibid., 1112b 7–8.

96. Aristotle, *Nicomachean Ethics*, bk. IX, ch. 4, 1166b 15–22, 1082.

97. See, generally, Jamie James, *The Music of the Spheres: Music, Science, and the Natural Order of the Universe* (1995).

98. Aristotle, *Politics*, bk. VIII, ch. 5, 1340a 16–24, 1311.

99. Plato, *The Republic*, Benjamin Jowett, trans. (1888), 88.

100. David Dubal, *Evenings with Horowitz: A Personal Portrait* (1991). "No matter the extent of the 'virtuosity,' however, it is his control, his very coolness that is so exciting." Ibid., 299.

101. See, generally, Aristotle, *Politics*, bk. VIII.

102. See Plato, *The Republic*, 443d–444.

103. Aristotle, *Nicomachean Ethics*, bk. III, ch. 5 1113b 34–1114b 4, 972.

104. Ibid., bk. VIII, ch. 3, 1146b 31–34, 1040.

105. See Thomas M. Jones, "Ethical Decision Making by Individuals in Organizations: An Issue-Contingent Model," 16 *Acad. Mgmt. Rev.* (Feb. 1991), 366–95, 372.

106. Michael J. de la Merced and Andrew Ross Sorkin, "Report Details How Lehman Hid Its Woes," *N. Y. Times*, Mar. 11, 2010.

Chapter 2

1. The hypothetical scenario is inspired by a somewhat similar moral dilemma framed by Joseph L. Badaracco Jr. in *Defining Moments: When Managers Must Choose Between Right and Right* (1997), 1–2.

2. For instance, under a virtue-oriented approach, a person's "character is the sum of his or her virtues and vices. A person who habitually tends to act as he morally should has a good character. If he resists strong temptation, he has a strong character. If he habitually acts immorally, he has a morally bad character. If despite good intentions he frequently succumbs to temptation, he has a weak character" (Richard T. De George, *Business Ethics* 5th ed. [1999], 123).

3. The Sartrean perspective presented here is from his early writings, with special emphasis on *Being and Nothingness*. Nevertheless, Hazel Barnes identifies a number of instances in which a fundamental continuity exists linking Sartre's early and later work. See Hazel E. Barnes, *Existentialist Ethics* (1978). Thus, Professor Barnes points out that Sartre's terminology "free choice of being" found in early writings, together with the phrase "lived experience" appearing in later works, are alike in that both of them "represent man as internalizing and structuring the significance and meaning of the situation in which he finds himself" (ibid., 28).

4. The analysis provided throughout this chapter is limited to Sartre's early thought. In later writings, Sartre sought to expand his existentialist perspective into Marxism. However promising it might be, relating Sartre's later work to business ethics would involve a much larger project than can be provided in the present book and must be deferred for the time being.

5. Jean Paul Sartre, *Being and Nothingness: A Phenomenological Essay on Ontology*, H. E. Barnes, trans. (1984), 559.

6. Ibid., 560.

7. Ibid.

8. Ibid., 561.

9. Sartre's technical terms "being-for-itself" and "being-in-itself" require special explanation. Humans are made up of a duality of these factors. "Being-in-itself" refers to the sense in which a person exists with objective properties, such as being blond or six feet tall. "Being-for-itself," by contrast, refers to the sense in which we exist as a human consciousness, which is not what it is in the same way that a chair is a chair. We are not, for Sartre, investment bankers, or waiters, or aggressive in the same way that we are six feet tall or blond. Sartre, note 5 supra, 131.

10. Ibid., 562.

11. Ibid., 563.

12. Ibid., 564.

13. Such reasons for and against outsourcing are laid out, in the context of the case of the cell-phone manufacturing industry, in E. Porter, "The Bright Side of Sending Jobs Overseas," *N. Y. Times,* Feb. 15, 2004, 3.

14. Sartre, note 5 supra, 565.

15. Badaracco, note 1 supra; Robert Solomon, *A Better Way to Think About Business: How Personal Integrity Leads to Corporate Success* (1999); Robert Solomon, *Ethics and Excellence* (1992).

16. According to Welch, "many of my basic management beliefs, things like competing hard to win, facing reality, motivating people by alternately hugging and kicking them, setting stretch goals, and relentlessly following up on people to make sure things get done, can be traced to [my mother]. The insights she drilled into me never faded. She always insisted on facing the facts of a situation. One of her favorite expressions was 'Don't kid yourself. That's the way it is'" (Jack Welch and John A. Byme, *Straight from the Gut* [2001], 4).

17. Donald J. Trump and Tony Schwartz, *Trump: The Art of the Deal* (1989).

18. Rudolph W. Giuliani and Ken Kurson, *Leadership* (2002).

19. Sartre, note 5 supra, 575.

20. Ibid.

21. Ibid., 575–76.

22. Ibid., 577.

23. Ibid., 578.

24. Ibid., 577.

25. Ibid., 578.

26. Ibid.

27. Ibid., 579.

28. Ibid.

29. Ibid., 581.

30. Ibid.

31. Ibid., 585.

32. Ibid., 586.

33. Ibid., 587.

34. Ibid.

35. Ibid.

36. Ibid., 597.

37. Ibid.

38. Ibid., 598.

39. Ibid., 615.

40. Ibid., 626.

41. Ibid., 640.

42. Ibid., 641.

43. Ibid.

44. The following passage is illustrative: "I've always been a manic guy. Not manic-depressive, just manic. Fired-up. Ready. Everybody in the business knew I was shot out of a cannon each morning. I was always first to arrive at 85 Broad Street, the headquarters of Goldman Sachs, gleefully turning the lights of the 28th floor on, hating it if anyone got in before me. It was no different when I left Goldman four years later to start my fund. In the first years of the hedge fund, I couldn't even wait till my wife would come in at 7:00 A.M. I left our Brooklyn Heights apartment seventy minutes before she did" (James J. Cramer, *Confessions of a Street Addict* [2002], 92). One can find similar examples of taking one's character as a "given" everywhere. Consider the following passage, somewhat arbitrarily selected from legendary hedge-fund investor Jim Rogers's popular book about his adventures around the world via motorcycle: "I'm told that one of the many fatal flaws in my character is that when anyone pushes me, I push back. Back home in Alabama, we were brought up properly and played by the rules. I never had any reason to push anybody. But once I moved to New York I met people who broke the rules, and I've become far more assertive" (Jim Rogers, *Investment Biker* [1994], 219).

45. Sartre, note 5 supra, 705.

46. Ibid., 702.

47. Ibid., 578.

48. Ibid., 76.

49. Robert Solomon, *A Better Way to Think About Business: How Personal Integrity Leads to Corporate Success* (1999).

50. W. Eugene Hedley, *Freedom, Inquiry and Language* (1968), 31.

51. Jean Paul Sartre, *Nausea* (1964), 39.

52. Walter Kaufmann, *Existentialism from Dostoevsky to Sartre* (1956), 44.

53. Sartre, note 5 supra, 99.

54. Ibid., 110.

55. Hazel E. Barnes, "Translator's Introduction," in Jean Paul Sartre, *Being and Nothingness*, H. E. Barnes, trans. (1984), xxxviii–xxxvix.

56. Jean Paul Sartre, "Existentialism is a Humanism," in W. Kaufmann, ed., *Existentialism from Dostoevsky to Sartre* (1956), 305.

57. Jeremy Bentham, *An Introduction to the Principles of Morals and Legislation* (1781); John Stuart Mill, *Utilitarianism* (1863).

58. Richard Brandt, *A Theory of the Good and the Right* (1979).

59. Immanuel Kant, *Foundations of the Metaphysics of Morals* (1785); William D. Ross, *The Right and the Good* (1930).

60. James W. Nickel, *Making Sense of Human Rights: Philosophical Reflections on the Universal Declaration of Human Rights* (1987).

61. Robert Nozick, *Anarchy, State and Utopia* (1974); John Rawls, *A Theory of Justice* (1971).

62. Thomas Donaldson and Thomas Dunfee, *Ties that Bind: A Social Contract Approach to Business Ethics* (1999).

63. Max B. E. Clarkson, ed., *The Corporation and Its Stakeholders: Classic and Contemporary Readings* (1998); R. Edward Freeman, *Strategic Management: A Stakeholder Approach* (1984).

64. Miguel Alzola, "Character and Environment: The Status of Virtues in Organizations," 78 *J. of Bus. Ethics* (Mar. 2008), 343–57; Robert Solomon, "Aristotle, Ethics, and Business Organizations," 25(6) *Org. Studies* (2006), 1021–43.

65. John Dewey, *Democracy and Education* (1944), 364.

66. Mark Johnson, *Moral Imagination: Implications of Cognitive Science for Ethics* (1993).

67. Lynn S. Paine, *Value Shift: Wily Companies Must Merge Social and Financial Imperatives* (2003).

68. William Greider, "Crime in the Suites," 4 *The Nation* (Feb. 2002), 11–14.

69. John A. Byrne, "After Enron: The Ideal Corporation," *Bus. Wk.*, Aug. 26, 2002, 68–74.

70. Archie B. Carroll, "Ethical Challenges for Business in the New Millennium: Corporate Social Responsibility and Models of Management Morality," 10(1) *Bus. Ethics Q.* (2000), 33–42.

71. Jean Paul Sartre, "Existentialism Is a Humanism," in W. Kaufmann, ed., *Existentialism from Dostoevsky to Sartre* (1956), 304.

72. Tenzin Gyatso and Fabien Ouaki, *Imagine All the People: A Conversation with the Dalai Lama on Money, Politics, and Life as it Could Be* (1999).

73. Nel Noddings, *Starting at Home* (2002); Nel Noddings, *Caring* (1984); Joan C. Tronto, *Moral Boundaries* (1993).

74. Consider, for instance, the following passage from Adam Smith, himself a moral philosopher and founder of modern capitalism: "How selfish soever man may be supposed, there are evidently some principles in his nature, which interest him in the fortune of others, and render their happiness necessary to him, though he derives nothing from it, except the pleasure of seeing it. Of this kind is pity or compassion, the emotion which we feel for the misery of others, when we either see it, or are made to conceive it in a very lively manner" (Adam Smith, in D. D. Raphael and A. L. Macfie, eds., *The Theory of Moral Sentiments* [1759; 1976], 9).

75. Daniel Goleman, *Emotional Intelligence: Why It Can Matter More than IQ* (1997).

76. John A. Byrne, *Chainsaw: The Notorious Career of Al Dunlap in the Era of Profit-at-Any-Price* (1999); Albert J. Dunlap, *Mean Business: How I Save Bad Companies and Make Good Companies Great* (1996).

77. Richard Bayer, "Termination with Dignity," *Bus. Horizons* (Sept./Oct. 2000), 4–10.

78. Simon de Beauvoir, *The Ethics of Ambiguity*, B. Frechtman, trans. (1997).

79. M. L. Johnson Abercrombie, *The Anatomy of Judgment* (1969); William G. Perry, *Forms of Intellectual and Ethical Development in the College Years* (1968).

80. R. Edward Freeman, *Strategic Management: A Stakeholder Approach* (1984);

Kenneth E. Goodpaster, "Business Ethics and Stakeholder Analysis," 1(1) *Bus. Ethics Q.* (1991), 53–73.

81. Archie B. Carroll, "A Three-Dimensional Conceptual Model of Corporate Performance," 4 *Acad. Mgmt. Rev.* (1979), 497–505.

82. Sartre, "Existentialism Is a Humanism," in B. Frechtman, trans., *Existentialism and Human Emotions* (1957), 24–29.

83. Roles are general cultural descriptions or refer to a professional category (e.g., lawyer) or social status (e.g., parenthood) applicable to those who occupy the role. See David Luban, *Lawyers and Justice* (1988). All of us have a number of overlapping roles, which are subject to change over time. Such roles impose a variety of demands and expectations; sometimes they function to shape ideals, such as the ideal baseball player. See Michael O. Hardimon, "Role Obligations," 91 *J. of Phil.* (1994), 333–63. When a person decides to take on a particular role, he or she assumes various rights and obligations. Accordingly, accompanying various roles are the moral demands specified by such roles, which make up what is termed role morality. See Judith Andre, "Role Morality as a Complex Instance of Ordinary Morality," 28 *Amer. Phil. Q.* (1991), 73–80.

84. Joseph L. Badaracco Jr., *Defining Moments: When Managers Must Choose Between Right and Right* (1997), 25–37. However, Badaracco's recommended solutions point to a genre of Aristotelian virtue ethics, which Sartre would reject as ultimately grounded in bad faith. It should also be noted that Badaracco does reference Sartre in his book, but only with regard to the idea of "dirty hands" from the play with that title. The insight Badaracco relates to business ethics with the "dirty hands" image is that "men and women who have power over the lives and livelihoods of others must almost inevitably get their hands dirty—not in the sense of rolling up their sleeves and working hard, but in the sense of losing their moral innocence" (3).

85. Sartre, note 5, supra, 581.

86. Sartre, note 82 supra, 28.

87. Robert Jackall, *Moral Mazes: The World of Corporate Managers* (1988).

88. Phillip G. Zimbardo, "The Human Choice: Individuation, Reason, and Order Versus Deindividuation, Impulse, and Chaos," in W. J. Arnold and D. Levine, eds., *1969 Nebraska Symposium on Motivation* (1970), 237–307.

89. Laura Nash, "The Real Truth About Corporate 'Values'" 2(2) *Public Relations Strategist* (summer 1995), 7–13.

90. Linda K. Treviño and Katherine A. Nelson, *Managing Business Ethics: Straight Talk About How to Do It Right* (2004), 166–70.

91. Solomon, note 49 supra.

92. Keith H. Hammonds, "The Secret Life of the CEO: Do They Even Know Right from Wrong?" in P. E. Murphy, ed., *Fast Company Business Ethics* (2004), 124–27.

93. The separation thesis holds that economics and ethics constitute two distinct kinds of discourse for depicting managerial decision making and business practices.

R. Edward Freeman, "The Politics of Stakeholder Theory: Some Future Directions," 4 *Bus. Ethics Q.* (1994), 409–22.

94. For Sartre, the "spirit of seriousness" considers humans as objects subordinated to the world. It sees values as having an absolute existence independently of human life.

95. Kevin T. Jackson, *Building Reputational Capital: Strategies for Integrity and Fair Play that Improve the Bottom Line* (2004), 129.

96. Lynn S. Paine, *Value Shift: Why Companies Must Merge Social and Financial Imperatives* (2003), 26.

97. Milton Friedman, *Capitalism and Freedom* (1962).

98. Friedrich A. Hayek, *The Road to Serfdom* (1944).

99. Thomas Aquinas, *On the Power of God, Third Book* (1934), Q. 10, Art. 2, 186.

100. Plato, *Symposium*, in Benjamin Jowett, trans., *Selected Dialogues of Plato* (2000), 204e–205b, 251.

101. Joseph Pieper, *Happiness and Contemplation*, Richard Winston and Clara Winston, trans. (1998), 85.

Chapter 3

1. See "People in the News," *Facts on File World News Digest*, Dec. 21, 2006, 988A1.

2. Helen Coster, "The Biggest CEO Outrages of 2009: This Year's C-Suite Hall of Shame," Forbes.com, Nov. 25, 2009.

3. As will be seen, I include not only performative, but also composition- and conductor-related (in the case of music) and entrepreneurial- and executive-related (in the case of business) aspects of virtuosity.

4. Nevertheless, it is interesting to note the bizarre case of Joyce Hatto, the now deceased concert pianist who, either on her own or with the complicity of her husband, William Barrington-Coupe, fraudulently produced well over one hundred recordings of other pianists' renditions, passing them off in the recording industry as her own. In such a situation, the moral dimension naturally figures in to one's assessment of her "forged virtuosity." Ironically, she was purported to be "a good pianist, if not an extraordinary one." See Esther Bintliff, "Grand Theft Piano," *Newsweek*, May 28, 2007, 60–62.

5. Eliot Clark, "Goldman Sachs and Legality Vs. Morality," May 20, 2010, The CSR Blog, Forbes.com.

6. Cf. Alasdair MacIntyre's concept of a "practice," which he defines in the context of a more general discussion of the role of the virtues in moral life as follows: "Any coherent and complex form of socially established cooperative human activity through which goods internal to that form of activity are realized in the course of trying to achieve those standards of excellence which are appropriate to, and partially definitive of, that form of activity, with the result that human powers to achieve excellence, and human conceptions of the ends and goods involved,

are systematically extended" (Alasdair MacIntyre, *After Virtue: A Study in Moral Theory* [1984] 187).

7. Ibid., 194.

8. "New U.S. Consumer Survey Shows High Distrusts of Financial Services Companies," *Bus. Wire* (Jan. 20, 2009), available at http://findarticles.com/p/articles/mi_mOEIN/is_2009_jan_20/ai_n31202849/, accessed Mar. 12, 2010.

9. François Duc de la Rochefoucauld, *Maxims*, Leonard Tancock, trans. (1959), 65 (Maxim 218).

10. Alexis de Tocqueville, *Democracy in America*, vol. 2, J. P. Mayer, ed., trans., G. Lawrence, trans. (1994), 527.

11. Ibid.

12. James C. Collins and Jerry I. Porras, *Built to Last: Successful Habits of Visionary Companies* (1994).

13. Ibid., 54.

14. See HDFC (A) Harvard Business School Case No. 9–301–093 (2000).

15. See Sealed Air Corporation: Globalization and Corporate Culture (A), (B), Harvard Business School Case Nos. 9–398–096, 9–398–097 (1998).

16. See AES Honeycomb (A), Harvard Business School Case No. 9–395–132 (1994).

17. James C. Collins and Jerry I. Porras, *Built to Last: Successful Habits of Visionary Companies* (1994), 75.

18. Ibid., 8.

19. In this regard, Collins and Porras, drawing a comparison between visionary companies, such as Hewlett-Packard and purely profit-driving companies such as Texas Instruments, quote the words of James Young, former CEO of Hewlett-Packard: "Maximizing shareholder wealth has always been way down the list. Yes, profit is a cornerstone of what we do—it is a measure of our contribution and a means of self-financed growth—but it has never been the *point* in and of itself. The point, in fact, is to *win*, and winning is judged in the eyes of the customer and by doing something you can be proud of. There is symmetry of logic in this. If we provide real satisfaction to real customers—we will be profitable" (James C. Collins and Jerry I. Porras, *Built to Last: Successful Habits of Visionary Companies* [1994], 57).

20. Deepak Chopra, *The Seven Spiritual Laws of Success* (1994), 83.

21. Proverbs 29:18.

22. Here I intend to use "education" in the broad sense, which encompasses not only what is taught in schools but also in churches, temples, synagogues, and mosques, and other associations.

23. A recognition of the vital importance of the family institution is expressed in the following passage: "It is surprising to see that humanity's oldest institution, the one making it possible for people to live a harmonious and balanced life, and the very origin or society, is the target of ideological attacks. The family, not the individual is the basis of society, since the latter can't fully develop itself on its own: it's not self-sufficient and is

naturally family orientated" (Nuria Chinchilla and Maruja Moragas, *Masters of Our Destiny* [2008], 120).

24. See the application of this aspect of Adam Smith's view to the economic crisis provided below in Chapter 7.

25. George W. Merck, Speech at the Medical College of Virginia at Richmond, Dec. 1, 1950; qtd. in Collins and Porras, 48.

26. Those who may think I am laying too much stress on the ameliorative side of business should turn to Chapter 7 where the dark side is amply revealed in connection with the financial crisis.

27. Bach assumed directorship of the *Collegium* in the spring of 1729. In the winter, the ensemble performed on Friday nights (6pm to 8pm) in Zimmermann's coffee house on the Catherine Strasse, located near the Marktplatz. During the warmer season, the music moved outdoors, to the coffee garden, with performances on Wednesdays (4pm to 6pm).

28. Stephen A. Crist, "The Question of Parody in Bach's Cantata *Preise dein Glück, gesegnetes Sachsen,* BWV 215," in Russell Stinson, ed., *Bach Perspectives* (1995), 161.

29. Ibid., 136.

30. For speculation about improprieties associated with Johann Tost's mysterious activities with regard to the way he handled some of Haydn's symphonies and string quartets entrusted to him for placement with a publisher, see Melvin Berger, *Guide to Chamber Music* (2001), 202.

31. Debbie Galante Block, "Kenny G Plays on the Soundtrack of People's Lives," *Billboard,* Sept. 14, 2002, 30.

32. Charlotte Moscheles, *Recent Music and Musicians: As Described in the Diaries and Correspondence of Ignatz Moscheles* (2009), 87.

33. Harold C. Schonberg, *The Great Pianists* (2006), 52.

34. David Ewen, *Composers of Yesterday* (1937), 105.

35. Harold C. Schonberg, *The Great Pianists* (2006), 54.

36. Ibid., 52.

37. Sandra P. Rosenblum, *Performance Practices in Classic Piano Music: Their Principles and Applications* (1991), 25.

38. See, e.g., Henry Cowell and Sidney Cowell, *Charles Ives and His Music* (1969); J. Peter Burkholder, ed., *Charles Ives and His World* (1996); Jan Swafford, *Charles Ives: A Life with Music* (1996); Vivian Perlis, *Charles Ives Remembered: An Oral History* (1976); Frank R. Rossiter, *Charles Ives and His America* (1975); Stuart Feder, *The Life of Charles Ives* (1999).

39. Ranier Maria Rilke, *Letters to a Young Poet*, Stephen Mitchell, trans. (1986).

40. "Life Insurance Just Philanthropy," *N. Y. Times,* Oct. 11, 1905, 2; qtd. in Michael Broyles, "Charles Ives and the American Democratic Tradition," in J. Peter Burkholder, ed., *Charles Ives and His World* (1996), 141–42.

41. Michael Broyles, "Charles Ives and the American Democratic Tradition," in J. Peter Burkholder, ed., *Charles Ives and His World* (1996), 142. The author points out,

however, that McCurdy's comments were met with laughter and derision by members of the committee.

42. Charles Ives, *Essays Before a Sonata and Other Writings*, Howard Boatright, ed. (1970), 95–96.

43. "We are all embarked upon a heroic personal voyage of growth and discovery that is part of the upward passage of all humanity. And music, Ives believed, plays an essential role in these expeditions. Whether music issues from a symphonic orchestra, a marching band, or a ragtime piano, the essence is the same, so long as it is earnest and authentic. External sound is the imperfect manifestation of the eternal inward spirit. 'Music is life'" (Charles Ives and Harmony Twichell, *Uncollected Letters,* from the collection of John Kirkpatrick, qtd. in Jan Swafford, *Charles Ives: A Life with Music* [1996], 238. See also ibid., 263: "When Ives wrote *music is life*, he wrote what Thoreau and his father had taught him. Thoreau taught him as well to see silence and the sounds of nature as a higher, eternal music: 'Music is the sound of the circulation in nature's veins'. . . ." quoting Henry David Thoreau, *The Journal of Henry D. Thoreau*, vol. 1 [1962], 251).

44. Charles Ives, *The Amount to Carry—Measuring the Prospect*, Ives and Myrick Publication, Salesmanship ed., (1920), qtd. in Jan Swafford, *Charles Ives: A Life With Music* (1996), 203.

45. Ibid., 209.

46. Vivian Perlis, *Charles Ives Remembered: An Oral History* (1976), 56.

47. Jan Swafford, *Charles Ives: A Life with Music* (1996), 209.

48. Henry Cowell and Sidney Cowell, *Charles Ives and His Music* (1969), 96–97.

Chapter 4

1. Plato, *Republic* 443c, 221.

2. This understanding of justice was adopted by Ulpian in his digest of Roman Law.

3. Among the many depictions of justice, Plato likens it to musical harmony: "The just man will not allow the three elements which make up his inward self to trespass on each other's functions or interfere with each other, but, by keeping all three in tune, like the notes of a scale (high, middle, and low, and any others there be), will in the truest sense set his house to rights, attain self-mastery and order, and live on good terms with himself" (*Republic,* 443d, 221).

4. Karl Moore and David Lewis, *Birth of the Multinational: 2000 Years of Ancient Business History—From Ashur to Augustus* (1999), cited in Mira Wilkins, "Multinational Enterprises to 1930," in Alfred D. Chandler Jr. and Bruce Mazlish, eds., *Leviathans: Multinational Corporations and the New Global History* (2005), 45–47.

5. Such an inference can be drawn from archaeological findings such as the famous discovery by Robert D. Ballard (who discovered the Titanic) of two

Phoenician shipwrecks off the coast of Israel in the Mediterranean Sea dating back to 750 B.C.. One of the ships was estimated to be sixty feet in length, the largest ancient sailing vessel ever found. The other ship, found about two miles away, was approximately forty-five feet long. The ships had been transporting a huge number of ceramic amphorae, found intact. Ballard suggests they were en route from the Phoenician port of Tyre to Egypt or Carthage when they sank due to a violent storm. J. M. Lawrence, "Ocean Explorers Find Phoenician Treasure," *Bos. Herald,* June 24, 1999, 2.

6. Larry Soderquist, Linda Smiddy, A. A. Sommer Jr., and Pat Chew, *Corporate Law and Practice,* 2d ed. (1999), 11.

7. *Dartmouth College v. Woodard,* 4 Wheat. 518, 636 (1819).

8. Qtd. in John Poynder, *Literary Extracts,* vol. I (1844), 2.

9. See, e.g., Meir Dan-Cohen, *Rights, Persons, and Organizations* (1986); Thomas Donaldson, *Corporations and Morality* (1982); Joel Feinberg, "Collective Responsibility," in Joel Feinberg, *Doing and Deserving: Essays in the Theory of Responsibility* (1970), 222–51; Larry May, *The Morality of Groups* (1987); Virginia Held, "Can a Random Collective Be Morally Responsible?" 67 *J. of Phil.* (1970), 471–81; Michael Keeley, "Organizations as Non-persons," 15 *J. of Val. Inquiry* (1981), 149–55; John Ladd, "Corporate Mythology and Individual Responsibility," 2(1) *Int'l J. of Applied Phil.* (spring 1984).

10. Peter A. French, *Corporate Ethics* (1995).

11. Peter A. French, "The Corporation as a Moral Person," 16 *Am. Phil. Q.* (July 1979), 207–15.

12. Kenneth Goodpaster and John Matthews, "Can a Corporation Have a Conscience?" 60 *Harv. Bus. Rev.* (Jan.–Feb. 1982), 132–41.

13. Thomas Donaldson, *Corporations and Morality* 10 (1982).

14. Manuel Velasquez, "Why Corporations Are Not Morally Responsible for Anything They Do," 2 *Bus. and Prof. Ethics J.* (spring 1983). In another article, Velasquez extends his argument further, identifying mistakes he assigns to collectivists who argue that corporate organizations are morally responsible for their actions. Velasquez says that one such fallacy can be seen in the following argument: (1) If X has properties that cannot be attributed to its individual members, then X is a real individual entity distinct from its members. (2) But corporate organizations have properties that cannot be attributed to their members. (3) So the corporate organization is a real individual entity distinct from its members. The argument's initial premise, Velasquez contends, commits a logical mistake known as the "fallacy of division." Any collection of objects, regardless of their degree of unrelatedness, has properties properly attributable only to the entire collection, rather than to its individual members, and vice versa. Whereas it might be that a pile of sand is big, we cannot thereby conclude that every particle of sand in it is big. Velasquez argues that another fallacy is seen in the following collectivist argument: "1. An agent is morally responsible for an act or event when the agent both (1) is causally responsible for the act or event, and (2) had the intention to so act. 2. Now sometimes corporate

organizations (1) are causally responsible for acts and events, and (2) have intentions to so act. 3. Consequently, corporate organizations are sometimes morally responsible for an act or event." The big mistake, Velasquez avers, occurs in the second premise, with the assertion that organizations are causally responsible for certain actions or occurrences and that they hold intentions. Moreover, Velasquez contends that collectivists err in the course of making what he terms "prescriptive" attributions of "as if" intentionality. See Manuel Velasquez, "Debunking Corporate Moral Responsibility," 13 *Bus. Ethics Q.* (Oct. 2003).

15. See John Searle, "Intrinsic Intentionality: Reply to Criticisms of Minds, Brains, and Programs," 3 *Behavioral and Brain Sciences* (1980), 450–56; see also John Searle, *The Rediscovery of the Mind* (1992), 78; John Searle, *Mind, Language, and Society* (1999), 93.

16. These justifications for the doctrine of strict liability are elaborated in Richard T. De George, *Bus. Ethics*, 6th ed. (2006), 284–86.

17. *The Corporation* (Big Picture Media Corporation, 2003).

18. The Conoco Conscience, *Inhouse Booklet on Moral Standards* (1976), excerpted in Kenneth Goodpaster and John B. Matthews Jr., "Can a Corporation Have a Conscience?" 60 *Harv. Bus. Rev.* (Jan.–Feb. 1982), 132, 141; emphasis in original.

19. See Jeffrey Seglin, "A Safer World for Mea Culpas," *N. Y. Times*, Mar. 21, 1999, sec. 3, 4.

20. Brian Jacobs and Patrick Kain, *Essays on Kant's Anthropology* (2003).

21. James R. Hagerty, "Distressed Homeowners Ponder Whether to Stay or Go," *Wall St. J.*, Nov. 25, 2009.

22. See Morton Horwitz, *The Transformation of American Law: 1780–1860* (1977).

23. Thus, virtually all accounts of the prerequisites for solid economic growth stress the significance of property rights. Governments should avoid dampening an expectancy of reliability with crass expropriation or through monetary experimentalism. In the absence of legal security, or where the legitimacy and stability of the political system are crippled by pervasive corruption, would-be entrepreneurs lack confidence that their property rights will be honored, and they will shy away from entrepreneurial ventures.

24. Robert Jackall, *Moral Mazes: The World of Corporate Managers* (1988), 204.

25. Ibid.

26. Wilhelm Röpke, *A Humane Economy: The Social Framework of the Free Market* (1998).

27. See Gareth Chadwick, "Profit with a Conscience; Corporate Social Responsibility Is Not Only Essential, It Pays Off," *The Independent* (London), Mar. 21, 2005, 6–7.

28. Doug Steiner, "Bernie, I Hardly Knew Ya," *The Globe and Mail* (Canada), Feb. 27, 2009, Report on Business Magazine, 50.

29. My claim is not that all activist efforts are irresponsible and hence illegitimate, only that some of them are. Arguably, an example of irresponsible activism would be Greenpeace's exaggerated misportrayal of the threat posed by Shell's attempted

disposal of the Brent Spar oil rig into the North Sea. As a consequence, the final disposal turned out to be more harmful to the environment, more wasteful, and more hazardous for workers than Shell's initial plan would have been. See, e.g., Jon Entine, "Shell, Greenpeace, and Brent Spar: The Politics of Dialogue," in Chris Megone and Simon J. Robinson, eds., *Case Histories in Business Ethics* (2002), 59–95. It is a conceptual blunder to assail all CSR as a coercive appropriation of corporate assets from their owners.

30. By "conventional business ethics" Sternberg means to include all approaches that "claim that businesses, and people in their business capacities, must pursue some objective other than owner value in order to be moral." She faults such approaches for their tendency to "identify extraneous responsibilities that businesses allegedly owe to others" (Elaine Sternberg, "The Need for Realism in Business Ethics," 31 *Reason Papers*, May 2010, 1, available at http://reasonpapers.com/pdf/31/rp_31_2.pdf).

31. Ibid., 41.

32. David Gardner, "BP Oil Leak Could Last for Months," *Daily Mail,* May 31, 2010.

33. We will return to a deeper consideration of this question in the context of the financial crisis in Chapter 7, and in the context of global corporate governance in Chapter 8.

34. Editorial, *The Economist,* June 24, 1995.

35. See HBS Case No. 9–301–093.

36. See HBS Case Nos. 9–395–132, 9–395–122.

37. See HBS Case Nos. 9–398–101, 9–398–102, 0–398–162.

38. See HBS Case Nos. 9–399–111, 9–399–112, 9–399–116.

Chapter 5

1. The dialectical process is scrupulously studied and related to John Rawls's notion of reflective equilibrium in Edwin M. Hartman, "Socratic Questions and Aristotelian Answers: A Virtue-Based Approach to Business Ethics," 78 *J. of Bus. Ethics* (2008), 320–21.

2. Sophocles, *Antigone,* lines 453–57.

3. Donald Jay Grout, *A History of Western Music* (1960), 7.

4. William Ebenstein and Alan Ebenstein, *Great Political Thinkers: From Plato to the Present* (2000), 133.

5. Martin Luther King Jr., "Letter from a Birmingham Jail," Apr. 16, 1963, available at http://www.sas.upenn.edu/African_Studies/Articles_Gen/Letter_Birmingham.html. According to Aquinas: "Human law is law inasmuch as it is in conformity with right reason and thus derives from the eternal law. But when law is contrary to reason, it is called an unjust law; but in this case it ceases to be a law and becomes instead an act of

violence. . . . Every law made by man can be called a law insofar as it derives from the natural law. But if it is somehow opposed to the natural law, then it is really not a law but rather a corruption of the law" (Thomas Aquinas, *Summa Theologica*, I-II Q. 95, art. 2).

6. By contrast, the narrower sense of "corporate governance" is limited to actions of a firm's board of directors, addressing specifically the relationship between a firm and its board.

7. James Nickel, *Making Sense of Human Rights: Philosophical Reflections on the Universal Declaration of Human Rights* (1987).

8. According to Simone Weil, it is from the act of creation that the divine being permitted something besides itself to exist. So through a renunciation of the self, a person recognizes their unity with the divine. As Weil expresses it, "God created me as non-being appearing to exist, so that, by renouncing through love this apparent existence, I may be annihilated in the fullness of being" Simone Weil, *La Connaissance Surnaturelle* (1950). She refers to this renunciation of the "I" as "decreation." Christopher Frost and Rebecca Bell-Metereau, *Simone Weil: On Politics, Religion and Society* (1998), 104–10, 107.

9. See Thomas Donaldson, *The Ethics of International Business* (1989), 81–94.

10. See George Brenkert, "Google, Human Rights, and Moral Compromise," 85(4) *J. of Bus. Ethics* (2009), 453–78.

11. See Thomas Donaldson and Thomas Dunfee, *Ties that Bind: A Social Contracts Approach to Business Ethics* (1999).

12. See Henry Shue, *Basic Rights: Subsistence, Affluence, and U.S. Foreign Policy* (1980).

13. See James Nickel, *Making Sense of Human Rights: Philosophical Reflections on the Universal Declaration of Human Rights* (1987).

14. See Wesley Cragg, "Human Rights and Business Ethics: Fashioning a New Social Contract," 27 *J. of Bus. Ethics* (2000), 205–14.

15. See John G. Ruggie, "Business and Human Rights: The Evolving International Agenda," 101 *Amer. J. of Int'l. L.* (2007), 819; John G. Ruggie, "Report of the Special Representative of the Secretary-General on the Issue of Human Rights and Transnational Corporations and Other Business Enterprises," UN Doc. A/HRC/8/5 (Apr. 7, 2008).

16. "Being in the image of God the human individual possesses the dignity of a person, who is not just something, but someone. He is capable of self-knowledge, of self-possession and of freely giving himself and entering into communion with other persons. And he is called by grace to a covenant with his Creator, to offer him a response of faith and love that no other creature can give in his stead" (*Catechism of the Catholic Church* ¶ 357). "The human person, created in the image of God, is a being at once corporeal and spiritual" (ibid., ¶ 362). "The unity of soul and body is so profound that one has to consider the soul to be the "form" of the body: it is because of its spiritual soul that the body made of matter becomes a living, human body; spirit

and matter, in man, are not two natures united, but rather their union forms a single nature" (ibid., ¶ 365).

17. See John Finnis, *Natural Law and Natural Rights* (1980), ch. 3–5.

18. *Leviathan*, ch. 8.

19. Kenneth E. Goodpaster, *Conscience and Corporate Culture* (2007), 28.

20. Robert P. George, "Natural Law," 52 *Amer. J. of Juris.* (2007), 55, 69–70.

21. Thomas Donaldson, *The Ethics of International Business* (1989); George Brenkert, "Can We Afford International Human Rights?" 11 *J. of Bus. Ethics* (1992), 515–21; Kevin T. Jackson, "Global Distributive Justice and the Corporate Duty to Aid," 12 *J. of Bus. Ethics* (1993), 547–51.

22. Other ancient Chinese thinkers, among them Shang Yang (390–338 B.C.) who earned the label "legalists," emphasized keeping the kingdom strong by disciplining the people and ordering the economy by the government with *fa* (normally translated as "law").

23. David Hume, *A Treatise of Human Nature* (1739), ii. iii. 3.

24. John Finnis, *Natural Law and Natural Rights* (1980).

25. According to Aristotle, "There really is, as everyone to some extent divines, a natural justice and injustice." In this passage the word "divines" may be translated as "perceives" or as knowing by inclination. In other words, one knows what is naturally just or unjust by way of inclination. This does not preclude knowing what is just or unjust by means of rationality, only that one's knowledge of natural law happens by means of inclination prior to being known by reason. See Yves R. Simon, *The Tradition of Natural Law: A Philosopher's Reflections,* Vukan Kuic, ed. (1965), 132.

26. *Summa Theologica* I-II, 51, 1.

27. For instance, although David Hume is ordinarily attributed with repudiating natural law, e.g., by presenting the "fact-value" distinction that prevents inferring values from facts, and showing reason to be slave to the passions (since supposedly only emotions can establish human ends), it is possible to interpret his thought as actually resting upon natural law. Thus, Professor Hesselberg shows how Hume needed to inject natural law premises into his social philosophy, particularly in his account of justice. According to Hesselberg, Hume "recognized and accepted that the social . . . order is an indispensable prerequisite to man's well-being and happiness: and that this is a statement of fact." The social order, therefore, *must* be maintained by man. Hesselberg further argues as follows: "But a social order is not possible unless man is able to conceive what it is, and what its advantages are, and also conceive those norms of conduct which are necessary to its establishment and preservation, namely, respect for another's person and for his rightful possessions, which is the substance of justice. . . . But justice is the product of reason, not the passions. And justice is the necessary support of the social order; and the social order is necessary to man's well-being and happiness. If this is so, the norms of justice must control and regulate the passions, and not *vice versa*" (A. Kenneth Hesselberg, "Hume, Natural Law and Justice," *Duquesne Review* [spring 1961], 46–47).

In conclusion, Hesselberg avers, "Hume's original 'primacy of the passions' thesis is seen to be utterly untenable for his social and political theory, and . . . he is compelled to reintroduce reason as a cognitive-normative factor in human social relations" (ibid.)

28. Duane Windsor, "Defining the Ethical Obligations of the Multinational Enterprise," in W. M. Hoffman et al., eds., *Ethics and the Multinational Enterprise* (1986).

29. Thomas Donaldson, *The Ethics of International Business* (1989).

30. See Andrew C. Wicks, R. Edward Freeman, Patricia H. Werhane, and Kirsten E. Martin, *Business Ethics: A Managerial Approach* (2010), 100.

31. Thus, it has been argued that moral realism postulates the existence of a kind of "moral fact," which is nonmaterial and does not appear to be accessible to the scientific method. See, e.g., Gilbert Harman, *The Nature of Morality: An Introduction to Ethics* (1977), I.1. In response, I would contend, first, that science itself sometimes assumes the existence of the nonmaterial (as in the case of some psychological accounts of human consciousness) and second, that this criticism wrongly assumes that that the scientific method is the only path to knowledge and explanation.

32. See, e.g., David Luban, *Legal Modernism* (1994); Alasdair MacIntyre, *After Virtue* (1981); Arthur Lef, "Unspeakable Ethics, Unnatural Law," 1979 *Duke L. J.* (1979), 1229; Henry Mather, "Natural Law and Right Answers," 38 *Amer. J. of Juris.* (1993), 297. The critical legal studies movement takes this view as a starting point for its critique of law and legal systems. For countervailing arguments that there are objective normative truths (or at least that we should act as if there were), see John Finnis, *Natural Law and Natural Rights* (1980); William A. Galston, *Liberal Purposes: Goods, Virtues and Diversity in the Liberal State* (1991), 158; Michael S. Moore, "Moral Reality Revisited," 90 *Mich. L. Rev.* (1992), 2424; Ernest J. Weinreb, "Legal Formalism: On the Immanent Rationality of Law," 97 *Yale L. J.* (1988), 949.

33. See Robert Nozick, *Anarchy, State and Utopia* (1974).

34. See John Rawls, *A Theory of Justice* (1971).

Chapter 6

Note to epigraph: If the quote is rendered in its entirety, and understood in the context of her book, Anne Morrow Lindbergh's reflections beautifully express her impressions of the special challenges facing women as they seek to balance conflicting demands of multiple "stakeholders" such as children, husband, career, and so on. My selective use of her quotation is not meant to obstruct her original meaning, but rather to attempt to relate her fundamental insight to the business context.

1. Rhys Blakely, "Millions of Indian Children Must Labour as Slaves for Loans They Can Never Repay," *The Times* (London), Apr. 23, 2009, 37.

2. Martin Hickman, "Blood, Sweat and Tears: The Truth About How Your Sportswear Is Made," *The Independent* (London), Oct. 1, 2010, 18.

3. The idea of a normative matrix is loosely based on Thomas Kuhn's concept of a "disciplinary matrix" in the philosophy of science. For Kuhn, a disciplinary matrix unifies knowledge of science. Disciplinary matrixes are made up of symbolic generalizations (for example, laws or theories), shared exemplars (for example, equations, experimental designs, and calculational procedures). Such matrixes are shared components that explain the relatively unproblematic character of professional opinion within a scientific community. Thomas S. Kuhn, *The Structure of Scientific Revolutions* 2d ed. (1970).

4. See Daniel J. Levitin, *This Is Your Brain on Music* (2006), 39–40.

5. Donald Jay Grout, *A History of Western Music* (1960), 644.

6. Extending the musical comparison with law and morality further, it may be noted that the tritone was considered "Diabolus in Musica" (the devil in music). According to a (dubious) legend, the interval was considered so diabolical that the church threatened excommunication as punishment to anyone using it.

7. There is greater disagreement in decisions about whether a given business activity should be dealt with by one normative process mode instead of another. It is contestable whether the airline industry should be deregulated and hence guided by free-market forces—that is, handled mainly by contract—or regulated and thus guided more by managerial control and direction.

8. Similarly, many traditional theories of jurisprudence have connected a definition of law to a particular institution of law, such as legislation, sovereignty or adjudication. However, when faced with new phenomena (for example, international law) that share many of the familiar attributes, though not the purportedly central ones, such theories relegate those phenomena to the category of "nonlegal."

9. A similar legal principle appears in Section 90 of the ALI's Restatement of Contracts. Such a respect for the process of business custom as a norm-creating source is reminiscent of the reverence Blackstone had for custom in judicial interpretation. Blackstone believed that judges should follow custom unless it was patently unreasonable to do so: "Though their reason be not obvious at first view, yet we owe such a deference to former times as not to suppose that they acted wholly without consideration" (William Blackstone 1962, *Commentaries on the Laws of England* [originally published 1771–72] [1962], 70).

10. See Thomas Donaldson, *The Ethics of International Business* (1989), 47–64.

11. Bernardo M. Cremades and Steven L. Plehn, "The New Lex Mercatoria and the Harmonization of the Laws of International Commercial Transactions," 2 *B. U. Int'l L. J.* (1984), 317–48.

12. Courts of appeal sometimes review arbitrator's decisions that deny due process rights. See Kenneth R. Davis, "The Arbitration Claws: Unconscionability in the Securities Industry," 78 *B. U. L. Rev.* (1998), 255.

13. The term *specification* refers to the spelling out of various conditions ("what, where, when, why, how") for norm application. Henry Richardson, "Specifying Norms as a Way to Resolve Concrete Ethical Problems," *Philosophy and Public Affairs* (1991), 279–310.

14. A manager that consults only the nonspecific norm "it is wrong not to pursue a company's interests by all lawful means" may feel justified in using bankruptcy strategy in the face of massive debt to enable her firm to lawfully start a new, more successful, venture. After all, that norm was followed in the Manville and A. H. Robins bankruptcy filings. See Rogene A. Buchholtz, William Evans, and Robert Wagley, *Management Responses to Public Issues: Concepts and Cases in Strategy Formulation* 3d ed. (1994). However, since Manville used bankruptcy to avoid liability to plaintiffs injured from asbestos, and Robins used bankruptcy to thwart liability for personal injury from the Dalkon Shield, it may be assumed that the corporations would have decided differently had they followed a differently specified norm "it is wrong not to pursue their company's interest by all means that are *both* lawful *and ethical*." Additional norms could be specified as entailments of the above norm that would assist deliberators in bankruptcy situations posing ethical problems. Two ethical norms that would help deliberators in concrete bankruptcy problems are: "It is wrong for a manager to use fraudulent conveyances—sales of assets to favored noncreditor parties (such as family and friends) prior to filing for bankruptcy—to cheat creditors," and "it is wrong for a manager to arrange preferential transfers (treating certain unsecured creditors better than others) before filing for bankruptcy." John D. Ayer, "How to Think About Bankruptcy Ethics," *Amer. Bkrptcy L. J.* (fall 1986), 355–98.

15. Classical accounts of jurisprudence advise that norms promulgated in legislation should be: general, published, nonretroactive, clear and comprehensible, capable of being obeyed (not impossible to perform), consistent with norms as actually administered and enforced, given with impersonal direction and free of "Solomonic" (compromise) solutions. An interpretive issue arises as to whether "checkerboard" codes of ethics would be appropriate. Suppose that at Acme Corporation, a nonunion company, there is a split of opinion about whether workers should be free to associate with union representatives on company premises. Could Acme author a code of conduct that tried a compromise solution, along the lines of a "checkerboard" statute, reflecting the internal disagreement in viewpoint? For instance employees are allowed to associate with union organizers on company premises on alternate workdays. The problem is that, although it may be advisable to give every point of view a voice in the process of norm creating, the collective decision must aim to settle on a coherent principle whose scope extends to the natural boundaries of its authority. For considerations in establishing international codes of conduct, see Kevin T. Jackson, "Globalizing Corporate Ethics Programs: Problems and Prospects," 16 *J. of Bus. Ethics* (1997), 1227–35.

16. United Nations Special Representative of the Secretary-General on the Issue of Human Rights and Transnational Corporations and Other Business Enterprises, "Protect, Respect and Remedy: A Framework for Business and Human Rights," *U.N. Doc. A/HRC/8/5* (Apr. 7, 2008); Richard T. De George, *Competing with Integrity in International Business* (1993); William Frederick, "The Moral Authority of Transnational Corporate Codes," 10 *J. of Bus. Ethics* (1991), 165–77.

17. De George, note 16 supra 90.

18. Norman Bowie and Stefanie Ann Lenway, "Resistol Sales in Central America" (Case Prepared at Carlson School of Management, University of Minnesota).

19. Diana B. Henriques, "Black Mark for a 'Good Citizen,'" *N. Y. Times* (Nov. 25, 1995), 1.

20. See Child Labor Coalition, *Child Labor Around the World*, available at http://www.stopchildlabor.org/ internationalchildlabor/claroundworld.htm; see also Milton Meltzer, *Cheap Raw Material* (1994).

21. In the corporate sphere, custom is embodied in a firm's culture. "Corporate culture" refers to the formal and informal norms that people in a corporation habitually follow. Linda Treviño and Katherine Nelson, *Managing Business Ethics: Straight Talk About How to Do It Right* (2003).

22. Thomas Donaldson and Thomas Dunfee, "Toward a Unified Conception of Business Ethics: Integrative Social Contracts Theory," 19 *Academy of Management Review* (1994), 252–79. See the analysis of ISCT given in Chapter 8 of this book.

23. Donald McCabe, "Grievance Processing: Non-Union Setting—Peer Review Systems and Internal Corporate Tribunals: A Procedural Analysis," *Labor L. J.* (1988), 496–502.

24. Evelyn Iritani, "Senator Feinstein Opposes Myanmar Ban," *L. A. Times* (Feb. 6, 1997).

25. Paul Blustein, "Burma Campaign Has Business Fighting Trend Toward Sanctions," *Wash. Post* (Mar. 4, 1997).

26. "Unocal Won't Study Costs of Opposition to Burma Investment" *Dow Jones News Service*, June 2, 1997.

27. Tiffany Danitz, "Burmese Government-in-Exile Takes U.S. Company to Court," 13(10) *Insight Magazine* (1997).

28. 630 F.2d 876 (2d Cir. 1980), *remanded,* 577 F. Supp. 860.

29. See "Multinational Corporations in Apartheid-Era South Africa: The Issue of Reparations," HBS Case No. 9–804–027 (2005).

30. Ibid.

31. See, generally, Robert C. Thompson, Anita Ramasastry, and Mark B. Taylor, "Transnational Corporate Responsibility for the 21ˢᵗ Century: Translating UNOCAL: The Expanding Liability for Business Entities Implicated in International Crimes," 40 *Geo. Wash. Int'l L. Rev.* (2009), 841.

32. Sheri Prasso, and Larry Armstrong, "A Company Without a Country?" *Bus. Wk.* (May 5, 1997).

33. Ibid.

34. H. L. A. Hart, *The Concept of Law* (1961). Open texture refers to the "fringe of vagueness" that surrounds legal rules. Ibid., 123.

35. Ronald Dworkin, *Law's Empire* (1986). For Dworkin, the "plain fact" view holds that "the law is only a matter of what legal institutions, like legislatures and city councils and courts, have decided in the past" (ibid., 7).

36. See United Nations Special Representative of the Secretary General on the Issue of Human Rights and Transnational Corporations and Other Business Enterprises, "Promotion and Protection of Human Rights," *United Nations Doc. E/CN.4/2006/97*, Feb. 22, 2006, 8; United Nations Commission on Human Rights, "Human Rights Resolution 2005/69: Human Rights and Transnational Corporations and Other Business Enterprises," Apr. 20, 2005, *E/CN.4/RES/2005/69*; United Nations Special Representative of the Secretary-General on the Issue of Human Rights and Transnational Corporations and Other Business Enterprises, "Protect, Respect and Remedy: A Framework for Business and Human Rights," *United Nations Doc. A/HRC/8/5*, Apr. 7, 2008, 4; David Weissbrodt and Muria Kruger, "Norms on the Responsibilities of Transnational Corporations and Other Business Enterprises with Regard to Human Rights," 97 *Amer. J. of Int'l L.* (2003), 901–22.

37. Generally courts have held that arbitrators are not obligated to follow otherwise applicable norms in resolving issues unless explicitly directed to by the arbitration agreement. Arbitrators are not strictly bound by the force of precedents, *Shearson/American Express, Inc. v. McMahon*, 482 U.S. 220 (1987). Instead, arbitrators should select the most appropriate norms for a given situation. Soia Mentschikoff, "Commercial Arbitration," 61 *Columbia L. Rev.* (1961), 846–67.

38. Edward M. Morgan, "Contract Theory and the Sources of Rights: An Approach to the Arbitrability Question," 10 *J. of Bus. Ethics* (1987), 519–26.

39. Arbitration is used in antitrust cases, *Aimcee Wholesale Corporation v. Tomar Products, Inc.* 237 N.E. 2d 223 (1968); 10(b) Exchange Act claims, *Scherk v. Alberto-Culver Co.*, 417 U.S. 506 (1973); RICO matters, *Shearson/American Express, Inc. v. McMahon*, 482 U.S. 242 (1986); and in cases of age discrimination, *Gilmer v. Interstate/Johnson Lane Corporation*, 500 U.S. 20 (1991).

40. A 1988 SEC study found brokerage firms using arbitration agreements in 95 percent of option accounts, 94 percent of margin accounts, and 39 percent of cash accounts. Constantine N. Katsoris, "SICA: The First Twenty Years," 23 *Fordham Urban L. J.* (1996), 483.

41. Constantine N. Katsoris, "The Arbitration of a Public Securities Dispute," 3 *Fordham L. Rev.* (1984), 279–84.

42. See Archie B. Carroll, *Business and Society: Ethics and Stakeholder Management* (1989); R. Edward Freeman, "The Politics of Stakeholder Theory: Some Future Directions," 4 *Bus. Ethics Q.* (1984), 409–21; Jamshid C. Hosseini and Steven N. Brenner, "The Stakeholder Theory of the Firm: A Methodology to Generate Value Matrix Weights," 2 *Bus. Ethics Q.* (1992), 99–119; Martin B. Meznar, James J. Chrisman, and Archie B. Carroll, "Social Responsibility and Strategic Management: Toward an Enterprise Strategy Classification," *Acad. Mgmt. Best Paper Proc.* (1990), 332–36; Lee E. Preston and Harry J. Sapienza, "Stakeholder Management and Corporate Performance," *J. of Behavioral Econ.* (1990), 361–75.

43. Having a "strong sense" of discretion means that a deliberator is not strictly bound by preexisting standards. Ronald Dworkin has studied the notion of discretion

in the context of legal reasoning. For Dworkin, a sergeant that is directed to select "any five soldiers" for duty patrol would be in a similar position to that of a judge deciding a case without the benefit of existing legal standards. Dworkin argues that, because law and morality join to make principles and policies available in rendering judgment in hard cases, judges only have discretion in a weak sense. Although judges often have to make difficult decisions with vague standards, they are constrained by preexisting principles of law. Thus, a sergeant would only have discretion in the weak sense if ordered to choose "the five soldiers *with the most experience*" (Ronald Dworkin, *Taking Rights Seriously* [1977]).

44. Deon Rossouw, *Business Ethics: A Southern African Perspective* (1994).

45. Lon Fuller, "The Forms and Limits of Adjudication," in Kenneth. Winston, ed., *The Principles of Social Order* (1981).

46. Thomas Donaldson, *The Ethics of International Business* (1989).

47. Ronald Green, *The Ethical Manager: A New Method for Business Ethics* (1994).

48. Chaim Perelman, *Justice, Law and Argumentation: Essays on Moral and Legal Reasoning* (1980); Aulis Aarnio, *The Rational as Reasonable: A Treatise on Legal Justification* (1987).

49. Richard T. De George, *Competing with Integrity in International Business* (1993); Ronald Green, *The Ethical Manager: A New Method for Business Ethics* (1994).

50. George Brenkert, "Private Corporations and Public Welfare," 6 *Public Affairs Q.* (1992), 155–68.

51. Thomas Donaldson, "The Perils of Multinationals' Largesse," 4 *Bus. Ethics Q.* (1994), 367–71.

52. George Brenkert, "Private Corporations and Public Welfare," 6 *Public Affairs Q.* (1992), 155–68.

53. See discussion of *determinatio* in Chapter 5 (in the section called "Modes of Derivation and Discernment").

54. See Nien-hê Hsieh, "The Obligations of Transnational Corporations: Rawlsian Justice and the Duty of Assistance," 14(4) *Bus. Ethics Q.* (2004), 643–61; Kevin T. Jackson, "Global Distributive Justice and the Corporate Duty to Aid," 12 *J. of Bus. Ethics* (1993), 547–51; Thomas Donaldson, "The Perils of Multinationals' Largesse," 4 *Bus. Ethics Q.* (1994), 367–71.

55. The deliberator might be, say, an idealized account manager, arbitrator, auditor, broker-dealer, director, entrepreneur, executive, salesperson, or realtor. The particular role occupied by the deliberator depends on the case at hand.

56. Chaim Perelman, *Justice, Law and Argumentation: Essays on Moral and Legal Reasoning* (1980); Aulis Aarnio, *The Rational as Reasonable: A Treatise on Legal Justification* (1987).

57. Statements S connect to the various exemplars of ordering. So a statement about a company's nepotism norms might be based on custom, formal norm promulgation, or both of these.

58. The array of statements A is a part of what Wittgenstein terms a "form of life."

Wittgenstein writes, "What I hold fast to is not *one* proposition but a nest of proposi-tions. " Ludwig Wittgenstein, *On Certainty*, G. E. M. Anscombe and G. H. von Wright, eds. (1969), 30e. Using a metaphor of a rope, the binding part is not one individual strand, but a whole twine of strands between which a new strand, that is, a statement at issue, will be attached. The nest of statements is fused into the foundations of our language games. This nest forms the frame for all our considerations about truth and falsity, as well as rightness and wrongness. Ludwig Wittgenstein, *Philosophical Inves-tigations*, G. E. M. Anscombe, trans. (1958).

59. Regarding nondeductive practical judgment, see Charles Taylor, *Sources of the Self: The Making of Modern Identity* (1989).

60. Law and philosophy have something important in common: both pursue ra-tional argumentation valid for the human community at large. These fields attempt to frame arguments that could be proposed to what Chaim Perelman terms a "universal audience." See Perelman, note 56 supra. However, Aulis Aarnio maintains that the notion of the universal audience is an ambiguous concept. In some respects, the audi-ence is ideal and universal, yet in other ways it is culturally and socially determined. The makeup of the universal audience depends, in part, on contingent facts. Several distinctions serve to clarify how a universal audience might be interpreted: concrete versus ideal audience, and universal versus particular ideal audience. A concrete au-dience is made up of real, exiting persons with a finite membership. The makeup of a concrete audience in its universal aspect would be all the people in the world at a given time, without regard for what other particular properties they have. A particu-lar concrete audience has some restriction in its membership based on characteristics like similarity in professional training, or shared interests. One cannot assume that the acceptability of arguments addressed to such an audience will be rationally based. Nonrational elements (acceptance of the speaker's authority as final, or a coercive ele-ment) may influence the audience's acceptance of an interpretive position. A particu-lar concrete audience does not provide a sufficient foundation for the rational accept-ability of an interpretive point of view. The ideal audience is comprised only of rational individuals. Members of a universal audience, in its ideal aspect, might converge in their views even though, antecedent to their discourse, they might have had conflict-ing positions. Aarnio does not wish to assume any objective "cognitive value theory" behind the universal audience in the ideal sense. Accordingly, he advocates taking the universal audience as a particular ideal audience. See Aarnio, note 56 supra.

Chapter 7

1. Although written in the midst of the rise of totalitarian regimes posing a threat to free institutions, the following words sound equally germane to the present global financial crisis: "We are ready to accept almost any explanation of the present crisis of our civilization except one: that the present state of the world may be the result of

genuine error on our own part and that the pursuit of some of our most cherished ideals has apparently produced results utterly different from those which we expected"
(F. A. Hayek, *The Road to Serfdom: Texts and Documents*, Bruce Caldwell, ed. [1944;
2007], 65–66).

2. Dependence modeling with the use of copula functions is commonly used in
financial risk assessment and actuarial analysis—for instance, in the pricing of collateralized debt obligations (CDOs). A methodology of applying the Gaussian copula
to credit derivatives, as formulated by David X. Li, has been cited among factors contributing to the financial crisis. See Felix Salmon, "A Formula for Disaster," *Wired*,
Mar. 2009, 74, 74–75.

3. For instance, consider the term *global contagion*. In the context of economic
analysis, the word "contagion" expresses the effect of financial calamities spreading
from one institution to another. For example, a run on a bank can expand from a few
banks to many others. Similarly, a financial crisis can spread from one country to
another, as in the case of currency crises, sovereign defaults, or stock market crashes
advancing across borders. Another example of medical jargon is "transfusion." In an
online commentary, Boston University's School of Management Dean Louis Lataif
stated that "the public is beginning to see bailouts as 'transfusions,' rather than a closing
of the wound, and is losing patience with them." Posting of Louis Lataif to The Great
Debate, available at http://blogs.reuters.com/great-debate/2009/03/23/transfusions-
dont-stop-the-bleeding/ (Mar. 23, 2009, 14:26 EDT).

4. See "Making It Worse; Government Should Stop Using Credit Card to Post-
pone Financial Day of Reckoning," *The Columbus Dispatch*, Oct. 16, 2008, 8A; An-
gela Charlton and Emma Vandore, "Europe Puts More on the Line for Banks Than
U.S.," USAToday.com, Oct. 13, 2008, available at http://www.usatoday.com/money/
economy/2008–10–13–2102616413_x.htm.

5. Richard Herring and Susan Wachter, "Bubbles in Real Estate Markets" (Zell/
Lurie Real Estate Ctr, Working Paper No. 402, 2002), available at http://realestate.
wharton.upenn.edu/newsletter/bubbles.pdf; Knowledge@Wharton, "Hope, Greed
and Fear: The Psychology behind the Financial Crisis," available at http://knowledge.
wharton.upenn.edu/article.cfm?articleid=2204.

6. Ibid.

7. See William B. Rouse and Nancy M. Morris, "On Looking Into the Black Box:
Prospects and Limits in the Search for Mental Models," 100 *Psy. Bull.* 349 (1986), 349–
63; Patricia H. Werhane, "Exporting Mental Models: Global Capitalism in the 21st
Century," 10 *Bus. Ethics Q.* (2000), 353, 354.

8. Of course, many other mental models exist and represent important perspectives from which to address the financial crisis. For instance, the mental model of
the politician looks for the most expeditious way of getting through public matters.
Consider the account of Federal Reserve Chairman Ben Bernanke (both an economist
and a politician) in February 2008: "I expect there will be some failures," but "among
the largest banks, ratios are solid." "Fed Chairman: Some Small US Banks May Go

Under," CNBC, Feb. 28, 2008, available at http://www.cnbc.com/id/23390252/. Seven months later, in a dramatic meeting in September 2008, Bernanke, along with Treasury Secretary Henry Paulson, met with key legislators. In Bernanke's alarming words, "If we don't do this, we may not have an economy on Monday." Joe Nocera, "36 Hours of Alarm and Action as Crisis Spiraled," *N. Y. Times*, Oct. 2, 2008, A1. The purpose of this depiction was political expediency—to pressure Congress into approving a US$700 billion emergency bailout. The rhetoric worked. Within a month, on October 3, 2008, the Emergency Economic Stabilization Act created the Troubled Asset Relief Program (TARP). Pub. L. No. 110–343, 122 Stat. 3765 (2008).

The fatal limitation of the politician's mental model is that it is ill equipped to capture any sense of the common good. Narrow special interests are stronger and more vocal, and there is a paralyzing lack of consensus regarding national priorities. Politicians normally operate on a confrontational basis, as reflected in the opposition of labor versus management, business versus government, and environmentalism versus economic growth. Political rhetoric is characteristically framed in terms of "battles" and "wins or loses," as if a win for one group is always a loss for another. Special interest groups, such as the American Medical Association, the National Rifle Association, the National Education Association, feminists, pro-choice groups and pro-life groups, gather to push for their narrow objectives. The problem, then, in the context of the financial crisis, is that the discourse of contemporary politicians based on expediency and confrontation tends to foster poor communication, distrust, and cynicism at a time when listening, cooperation, and compromise would be more conducive to moral leadership.

9. See, e.g., Eugene A. Ludwig, "Act 3 of Crisis Is Over. Get Set for Act 4," *Am. Banker*, Dec. 18, 2009, 9; Robert J. Samuelson, "Economists Undone by Their Ignorance of History," *Toronto Star*, July 15, 2009, A19.

10. See Kevin G. Hall, "Not Another Real-Estate Crisis: Commercial Mortgages Next?" *McClatchy*, Apr. 30, 2009.

11. "The Intersection of Main and Wall," *Globe and Mail* (Canada), Oct. 1, 2008, A20.

12. See Nick Onnembo, "U.S. Financial System: Can it Collapse?" *Telegram and Gazette* (Mass.), June 13, 2008, 8.

13. See William Poole, "Causes and Consequences of the Financial Crisis of 2007–2008," 33 *Harv. J. L. and Pub. Pol'y* (2010), 6.

14. Paul Krugman, *The Return of Depression Economics* (2009), 158.

15. Kenneth Howe, "A Year on, and Lehman Fallout Still Being Felt Around the World," *S. China Morning Post*, Sept. 14, 2009, 1.

16. Alan Greenspan, "We Need a Better Cushion Against Risk," *Fin. Times*, Mar. 27, 2009, 11.

17. Rick Newman, "The Private Sector Gets Another Chance," *U.S. News.Com*, Nov. 2, 2009, available at http://www.usnews.com/money/blogs/flowchart/2009/11/02/the-private-sector-gets-another-chance.

18. Tom Petruno, "Mortgage Forgiveness May Be Next," *L. A. Times*, June 27, 2009, B1.

19. See Irwin Stelzer, "Weak Housing Threatens to Slow Economy," *Sun. Times* (London), Mar. 25, 2007, B4.

20. Peter S. Goodman, "Taking the Pulse of An America That Has Always Felt Lucky: Populist Anger Amid Crisis May Sharpen Appetite for More Regulatory Oversight," *Int'l Herald Trib.*, Sept. 21, 2009, 18.

21. Vikram Khanna, "Sub-Prime: Six Lessons, and Counting," *Bus. Times Sing.*, Mar. 7, 2008.

22. Andrea Fuller, "House Backs Limits on Pay to Executives," *N. Y. Times*, Aug. 1, 2009, B1.

23. Richard Northedge, "Make Banking Boring to Avoid Boom and Bust," *Indep. on Sunday* (London), Mar. 15, 2009, 82; see also Krugman, supra note 14, 163.

24. Irwin Stelzer, "If a Bank Is too Big to Fail, It Must Be Broken Up: None of the Planned Banking Reforms Protects the Financial System," *Daily Telegraph* (London), July 29, 2009, 19.

25. David Prosser, "The Question Obama Can't Quite Face," *Indep.* (London), Sept. 15, 2009, 34.

26. David Ignatius, Editorial, "The View from the Eye of the Storm," *Wash. Post*, July 18, 2008, A17.

27. Boyd Erman, "Europe, U.S. at Odds Over Bank Capital Ratios; Split Emerges over How Much More Is Needed; European Banks Could Be Less Competitive," *Globe and Mail* (Canada), Sept. 24, 2009, B4.

28. See "Reforming America's Financial System," *Int'l Herald Trib.*, Sept. 15, 2009, 6.

29. Of course, not *all* economists, management theorists, and legal experts operate with the mental models herein diagnosed.

30. See Thomas S. Kuhn, *The Structure of Scientific Revolutions* 175 (2d ed. 1970). Professor Kuhn uses the term "paradigm" to explain how fields of knowledge are based upon shared systems of belief that are defined by a common vocabulary and a set of accepted problems and agreed-upon solutions. Thus, on the one hand, a paradigm defines a community of belief; on the other hand, communities of belief do not exist but for the shared beliefs, acknowledged problems, and recognized solutions that constitute a paradigm. Although Kuhn's book was aimed at the history of changes in the physical or "hard" sciences, John Kenneth Galbraith articulated a similar idea that is closer to the context of the present discussion: "The first requirement for an understanding of contemporary economic and social life is a clear view of the relation between events and the ideas which interpret them" (John Kenneth Galbraith, *The Affluent Society* 4th ed. [1984], 6).

31. Interestingly, Wilhelm Röpke makes a similar observation: "A few months before the beginning of the greatest economic crisis in history, in the spring of 1929, the most distinguished American economists were talking about the happily secure equilibrium of

an economy running in top gear." Wilhelm Röpke, *A Humane Economy* (1960), 250–51. One magazine article stated that economist Nouriel Roubini had presaged the economic downturn as far back as September 2006, but added that the field of economics is not well equipped to foretell a recession. Stephen Mihm, "Dr. Doom," *N. Y. Times* (Magazine), Aug. 17, 2008, 26; see also Emma Brockes, "He Told Us So," *Guardian* (London), Jan. 24, 2009, 24. For other accounts of experts providing signals of an impending crisis, see "Recession in America," *Economist*, Nov. 17, 2007, 385; and Kabir Chibber, "Goldman Sees Subprime Cutting \$2 Trillion in Lending," *Bloomberg*, Nov. 16, 2007, available at http://www.bloomberg.com/apps/news?pid=newsarchive&sid=aXHulkIznCr0/.

32. See, e.g., Frank Rich, Op-Ed., "The Other Plot to Wreck America," *N. Y. Times*, Jan. 10, 2010, WK10.

33. This critique of the mathematization of economics has been advanced by such thinkers as Friedrich Hayek, Robert Heilbroner, and John Maynard Keynes.

34. See R. Edward Freeman and David Newkirk, "Business as a Human Enterprise: Implications for Education," in Samuel Gregg and James R. Stoner Jr., eds., *Rethinking Business Management: Examining the Foundations of Business Education* (2008), 131, 139–43.

35. See, e.g., Paul Anthony Samuelson, *Foundations of Economic Analysis* (1947), 5–6.

36. As Röpke puts it, "When one tries to read an economic journal nowadays, often enough one wonders whether one has not inadvertently picked up a journal of chemistry or hydraulics" (Röpke, supra note 31, 247).

37. As Nobel Prize economist Myron Scholes stated, "There are models, and there are those who use the models," referring to the distinction between "ivory tower" economists who concoct models and financial engineers who apply the models to the actual business world ("Efficiency and Beyond," *Economist*, July 18, 2009, 368). Of course, a number of economists who embrace the efficient markets hypothesis posit some modifications to it as a consequence of their readiness to accept findings from other fields of study, such as psychology, in an effort to account for seemingly irrational economic behavior on the part of both individuals and institutions. See ibid.

38. Röpke, supra note 31, 247.

39. Ibid.

40. See Freeman and Newkirk, supra note 34, 138.

41. Rakesh Khurana, *From Higher Aims to Hired Hands: The Social Transformation of American Business Schools and the Unfulfilled Promise of Management as a Profession* (2007).

42. Ibid., 176–92.

43. Pablo Triana, "Why Business Schools Are to Blame for the Crisis," July 13, 2009, *Bus. Wk. Online*, available at http://www.businessweek.com/bschools/content/jul2009/bs20090713_635092.htm.

44. See John R. Boatright, *Ethics in Finance* (1999), 176; R. H. Coase, "The Nature of the Firm," 4 *Economica* (1937), 388, 391–93.

45. Kelley Holland, "Is it Time to Retrain B-Schools?" *N. Y. Times*, Mar. 15, 2009, BU1.

46. But see Christopher Avery, Judith A. Chevalier, and Scott Schaefer, "Why Do Managers Undertake Acquisitions? An Analysis of Internal and External Rewards for Acquisitiveness," 14(1) *J. of L. Econ. and Org.* (1998), 24, 24; they argue that executives pursue prestige in the business community rather than extra compensation.

47. Sumantra Ghoshal, "Bad Management Theories Are Destroying Good Management Practices," 4 *Acad. Mgmt. Learning and Educ.* (2005), 75, 75; citations omitted.

48. John Rolfe and Peter Troob, *Monkey Business: Swinging Through the Wall Street Jungle* (2000), 8–9.

49. George Anders, "Business Schools Forgetting Missions?" *Wall St. J.*, Sept. 26, 2007, A2.

50. See Milton Friedman, *Capitalism and Freedom* (1962), 133–34.

51. See *Business as a Humanity*, Thomas J. Donaldson and R. Edward Freeman, eds. (1994).

52. Throughout the history of Western civilization, one repeatedly finds business ventures embodying humanitarian endeavors. Monasteries dating back to the Middle Ages were, in effect, incipient institutions of economic activity, in which *ora* (culture) and *labora* (work) were coupled. Likewise, as far back as the fifteenth century, the Franciscans had established the *Montes Pietatis*, precursors of modern banks, which grew up not directly seeking profit, but instead trying to battle usury and provide the impoverished with new beginnings in the wake of economic hardship. The nineteenth century also provided for a merging of economic and humanitarian objectives as the bulk of European welfare establishments and hospitals emerged out of spiritual associations. Luigino Bruni and Amelia J. Uelmen, "Religious Values and Corporate Decision Making: The Economy of Communion Project," 11 *Fordham J. Corp. and Fin. L.* (2006), 645, 657–58.

53. Research indicates that donors themselves experience a tremendous amount of benefit from giving. Indeed, economists and psychologists have found that charitable giving makes people healthier, happier, and even more financially successful. Giving is, in and of itself, a source of value for those who donate to charity. See Arthur C. Brooks, *Who Really Cares: The Surprising Truth About Compassionate Conservatism* (2006); Stephen Post and Jill Neimark, *Why Good Things Happen to Good People* (2007).

54. See Samuel Gregg, *The Commercial Society: Foundations and Challenges in a Global Age* (2007), 9.

55. See ibid., 3.

56. See, e.g., Vikas Bajaj, "Senate Questioning on Mortgages Put Regulators on the Defensive," *N. Y. Times*, Mar. 23, 2007, C4.

57. "Politically Driven Post-crisis Legislation Must Be Avoided," *Banker*, Apr. 7, 2008, available at http://www.thebanker.com/news/fullstory.php/aid/5663/Politically_driven_post-crisis_legislation_must_be_avoided.html.

58. For Michael Novak, the innovative spirit becomes the hallmark of capitalism. Criticizing Max Weber who holds "economic rationality" to be the essence of capitalism, and drawing from Hayek, Schumpeter, Kirzner, and others, Novak states, "The heart of capitalism . . . lies in discovery, innovation, and invention. Its fundamental activity is insight into what needs to be done to provide a new good or service. The distinctive materials of capitalism are not numbers already assembled for calculation by the logic of the past. On the contrary, its distinctive materials are new possibilities glimpsed by surprise through enterprising imagination" (Michael Novak, *The Catholic Ethic and the Spirit of Capitalism* [1993], 10).

59. Steven Malanga, "Whatever Happened to the Work Ethic?" 19 *City J.* (2009), 36, 36–45. The existence of easy credit, along with the belief that home prices would keep on appreciating, persuaded legions of subprime borrowers to assume adjustable-rate mortgages. The financial institutions that offered these products lured homebuyers with below market interest rates for preestablished terms, followed by market interest rates for the rest of the mortgage's term. Unable to afford increased payments at the end of the initial grace period, many borrowers attempted to refinance. But refinancing proved difficult as housing prices started to drop across the United States. Borrowers found themselves incapable of avoiding heftier monthly payments by refinancing and started to default. Patrice Hill, "Treasury Seeks To Stem Second Wave of Foreclosures," *Wash. Times*, Feb. 13, 2008, A1; Kathleen M. Howley, "Plummeting Home Values Sinking American Dream," *Detroit Free Press*, Nov. 22, 2009, 2.

60. Malanga, supra note 59, 36–45.

61. See Khanna, supra note 21.

62. See ibid., arguing that credit agencies failed in their role as "gatekeepers" to the financial system.

63. See Charles R. Schwab, "Restore the Uptick Rule, Restore Confidence," *Wall St. J.*, Dec. 9, 2008, A17, describing the harm caused by "manipulative short sellers."

64. Press Release, "U.S. Dep't of the Treasury, Statement by Treasury Secretary Timothy Geithner on Compensation" (June 10, 2009), available at http://www.treas.gov/press/releases/tg163.htm.

65. A recent study found that it is "quite easy for a hedge fund manager to 'fake' high performance over an extended period of time without getting caught." Dean P. Foster and H. Peyton Young, "Hedge Fund Wizards," *Economist's Voice* Feb. 2008, 1, 1. Hedge-fund managers sometimes make risky speculative moves by investing in transactions that may yield higher-than-average returns because of the minute yet real risk that the whole venture may blow up. Ibid. This kind of arrangement, dubbed a "Taleb distribution," has a strong likelihood of producing moderate gains and only a slight chance of resulting in huge losses in a given period. Martin Wolf, "Why Today's Hedge Fund Industry May Not Survive," *Fin. Times*, Mar. 19, 2008, 15. Thus, even if the probability of suffering a large loss is one in ten, the fund manager might stand ready to assume the risk because, after all, his own money is not on the line, and he is likely to pull down a tidy profit for years to come. For instance, although the manager will

likely be ousted should that one-chance-in-ten risk occur, the investment might nevertheless produce sufficiently large returns for the fund manger to get large returns, reap a "2 and 20" commission, and satisfy his clients along the way. To his clients, the fund manager will seem to have immense talent. The problem is that his clients have no way of suspecting that the manager is basically gambling their money away. See Thomas Donaldson, "Hedge Fund Ethics," 18 *Bus. Ethics Q.* (2008), 405, 409.

66.   In a recent editorial Professor Michael Jacobs describes how failures related to board oversight, executive rewards, and agency costs, which contributed to the financial meltdown, were not even on the radar screens of America's business schools. In his words, "Most B-schools paper over the topic [of corporate governance] by requiring first-year students to take a compulsory ethics class, which is necessary, but not sufficient" (Michael Jacobs, "How Business Schools Have Failed Business," *Wall St. J.*, Apr. 24, 2009, A13). Jacobs continues his critique by posing two rhetorical questions: "Would Bernie Madoff have acted differently if he had aced his ethics final? Could we have avoided most of the economic problems we now face if we had a generation of business leaders who were trained in designing compensation systems that promote long-term value?" (ibid.)

67.   For a detailed explanation of why the attitude "if it's legal, then it's morally okay" is insufficient, particularly in the intensively regulated field of finance, see Boatright, supra note 44, 9–10.

68.   There is probably no better exposition of the moral relativism that pervades our age than the one given by Alasdair MacIntyre. He shows how contemporary moral fragmentation, in the form of emotivist and utilitarian culture, is connected to the loss of Aristotelian ethics together with the inability of the Enlightenment to supply any suitable substitution for it. See Alasdair MacIntyre, *After Virtue: A Study in Moral Theory* (1984), 22–61.

69.   See, e.g., Joe W. (Chip) Pitts III, "Corporate Social Responsibility: Current Status and Future Evolution," 6 *Rutgers J. L. and Pub. Pol'y* (2009), 334, 374.

70.   Enron's mission statement listed the following values: respect, integrity, communication, and excellence. In addition, it proclaimed that all business dealings were to be "open and fair." Chris Penttila, "Missed Mission: Watch Out! If Your Mission Statement Is a Joke, Enron May Be the Punchline," *Entrepreneur*, May 2002, 73, 73. Almost all Fortune 500 companies have a mission statement. Within the text of nearly every mission statement there appears some statement of the firm's commitment to moral values. Yet it is evident that legions of senior executives behave contrary to such pronouncements. For discussion of how misalignment of formal and informal messages sent out by firms to their employees poses challenges for developing ethical corporate culture, see Linda Klebe Treviño and Katherine A. Nelson, *Managing Business Ethics* 4th ed. (2007).

71.   See Edwin M. Epstein, "The Good Company: Rhetoric or Reality? Corporate Social Responsibility and Business Ethics Redux," 44 *Amer. Bus. L. J.* (2007), 207, 212–14.

72. For a more detailed look at such tendencies to overregulate the business world, see Catherine Crier, *The Case Against Lawyers* (2002); Philip K. Howard, *The Death of Common Sense: How Law Is Suffocating America* (1994).

73. Aristotle, *The Nicomachean Ethics,* in Richard McKeon, ed., *The Basic Works of Aristotle* (1941).

74. Ibid., bk. VI, ch. 7, 1141a 17–19 at 1027–28; 1141b 3 1028.

75. Ibid., bk. II, ch. 6, 1107a 1–8 959.

76. Ibid.

77. Ibid., bk. IV, ch. 1 1119b 20– 1122a 17.

78. Ibid., bk. III, ch. 5 1115a 3–6.

79. See Jared D. Harris and Philip Bromiley, "Incentives to Cheat: The Influence of Executive Compensation and Firm Performance on Financial Misrepresentation," 18 *Org. Sci.* (2007), 350; Jared D. Harris, "What's Wrong with Executive Compensation?" 85 *J. of Bus. Ethics* (2009), 147.

80. Aristotle notes that this trait can be found in a certain class of people: "Others . . . exceed in respect of taking by taking anything and from any source, e.g., those who ply sordid trades, pimps and all such people, and those who lend small sums and at high rates. For all of these take more than they ought and from wrong sources. What is common to them is evidently sordid love of gain; they all put up with a bad name for the sake of gain, and little gain at that. For those who make great gains but from wrong sources, and not the right gains, e.g. despots when they sack cities and spoil temples, we do not call mean but rather wicked, impious, and unjust. But the gamester and the footpad [and the highwayman] belong to the class of the mean, since they have a sordid love of gain. For it is for gain that both of them ply their craft and endure the disgrace of it, and the one faces the greatest dangers for the sake of the booty, while the other makes gain from his friends, to whom he ought to be giving. Both, then, since they are willing to make gain from wrong sources, are sordid lovers of gain; therefore all such forms of taking are mean" (Aristotle, supra note 73, bk. IV, ch. 1, 1121b 30– 1122a 12 988).

81. *Catechism of the Catholic Church* ¶¶ 355–84; Second Vatican Ecumenical Council, Declaration on Religious Freedom, *Dignitatis Humanae* ¶¶ 2, 9 (Dec. 7, 1965); Second Vatican Ecumenical Council, Pastoral Constitution on the Church in the Modern World, *Gaudium et Spes* ¶¶ 12–24 (Dec. 7, 1965) [hereinafter *Gaudium et Spes*]; Second Vatican Ecumenical Council, Declaration on the Relationship of the Church to non-Christian Religions, *Nostra Aetate* (Oct. 28, 1965); Pope Pius XII, Encyclical Letter, *Humani Generis* (Aug. 12, 1950); Pope John Paul II, Encyclical Letter, *Redemptor Hominis* (Mar. 4, 1979); Pope John Paul II, Encyclical Letter, *Veritatis Splendor* (Aug. 6, 1993). All referenced documents are available on the Vatican Web site.

82. Immanuel Kant, *The Moral Law: Kant's Groundwork of the Metaphysic of Morals,* H. J. Paton, trans. (1785; 1961), 95–96.

83. Mark Brown, "Countrywide Wasn't Really on Your Side; Mortgage Crisis Comes Down to Plain Old Consumer Fraud," *Chi. Sun Times,* June 26, 2008, 8.

84. David Novak, "Natural Law, Human Dignity, and the Protection of Human Property," in Samuel Gregg and James Stoner, eds., *Profit, Prudence and Virtue* (2009), 42, 47, 51–52.

85. See Michael Novak, *Free Persons and the Common Good* (1989), 175–88.

86. Vatican II defined the common good similarly as "the sum of those conditions of the social life whereby men, families and associations more adequately and readily may attain their own perfection." *Gaudium et Spes*, supra note 81, ¶ 74.

87. See the analysis in Chapter 2 concerning how such a notion of authenticity and self-actualization drawn from the existentialist philosophy of Jean-Paul Sartre applies to a variety of the moral dilemmas one confronts in the world of business.

88. Pope John Paul II, Encyclical Letter, *Centesimus Annus* ¶ 17 (May 1, 1991).

89. The reference to "proper proportion" refers us back to Aristotle's idea of virtue as a mean between extremes. Aristotle, supra note 73.

90. See Harold James, Op-Ed., "A Financial Crisis Letting Us Unmask Deceit; But Whose Deceit?" *Daily Star* (Lebanon), June 8, 2009, available at http://www.dailystar.com/lb/article.asp?edition_ID=10&article_ID=102752&categ_ID=5.

91. *Wall Street* (20th Century Fox 1987).

92. See Robert H. Bork, "Thomas More for Our Season," *First Things*, June/July 1999, 17.

93. See ibid., 17–18.

94. See Thorstein Veblen, *The Theory of Business Enterprise* (1904), 41–42.

95. See ibid., 27–29; comparing a businessman whose "end is pecuniary gain" to a "speculator in grain futures."

96. Victor Niederhoffer, *The Education of a Speculator* (1997), 327–34.

97. Ibid., Back Cover.

98. In general, "flipping" refers to the practice of buying an asset and quickly reselling it for profit. Although flipping can apply to any asset, the term most often refers to real estate and initial public offerings.

99. The phrase was coined by HCL Finance to designate one of its financial products. Edward Chancellor, "Ponzi Nation," *Institutional Investor*, Feb. 2007, 56. The phrase is a play on words on two levels: first, as an acronym; second, as a signal that NINJA loans frequently end up in default, with the borrower vanishing into thin air like a ninja.

100. Darrin W. Snyder Belousek, "Greenspan's Folly: The Demise of the Cult of Self-Interest," *America*, Mar. 30–Apr. 6, 2009, 10, 10–12. Belousek is restating Ayn Rand's philosophy of egoism as expressed in Ayn Rand, *The Virtue of Selfishness: A New Concept of Freedom* (1964).

101. Belousek, supra note 100, at 12.

102. Ibid.

103. Letter from Benjamin Franklin to Abbots Chalet and Arnaud (Apr. 17, 1787), in 11 *The Works of Benjamin Franklin*, John Bigelow, ed. (1904), 318.

104. See John Finnis, *Aquinas: Moral, Political, and Legal Theory* (1998), 266–74; John Finnis, *Natural Law and Natural Rights* (1980), 281–90.

105. See Adam Smith, *An Inquiry Into the Nature and Causes of the Wealth of Nations,* R. H. Campbell and Andrew S. Skinner, eds. (1776; 1976), 456.

106. For an extended analysis of Smith's argument for the necessity of beneficence to a well-functioning marketplace, see Ryan Patrick Hanley, *Adam Smith and the Character of Virtue* (2009).

107. Adam Smith, *The Theory of Moral Sentiments,* D. D. Raphael and A. L. Macfie, eds. (1759; 1976).

108. Ibid., 184–85; "The rich . . . consume little more than the poor, and in spite of their natural selfishness and rapacity, though they mean only their own conveniency, though the sole end which they propose from the labours of all the thousands whom they employ, be the gratification of their own vain and insatiable desires, they divide with the poor the produce of all their improvements. They are led by an invisible hand to make nearly the same distribution of the necessaries of life, which would have been made, had the earth been divided into equal portions among all its inhabitants."

109. Friedrich A. Hayek, *The Fatal Conceit: The Errors of Socialism,* W. W. Bartley III, ed. (1988), 102.

110. Ibid., 73.

111. Ibid., 84.

112. Ibid., 83.

113. Ibid., 7; "The main point of my argument is . . . that the conflict between, on one hand, advocates of the spontaneous extended human order created by a competitive market, and on the other hand those who demand a deliberate arrangement of human interaction by central authority based on collective command over available resources is due to a factual error by the latter about how knowledge of these resources is and can be generated and utilised." See also Friedrich A. Hayek, *The Road to Serfdom* (1944).

114. Hayek, supra note 109, 84–85.

115. See Francis Fukuyama, *Trust: The Social Virtues and the Creation of Prosperity* (1995).

116. See the discussion of this point in Chapter 8.

117. See, e.g., Valerie P. Hans, *Business on Trial: The Civil Jury and Corporate Responsibility* (2000), 120–21.

118. See Lynn Sharp Paine, *Value Shift: Why Companies Must Merge Social and Financial Imperatives to Achieve Superior Performance* (2003), 112.

119. The concept of reputational capital refers to the intangible long-term strategic assets of a businessman or a business organization. Reputational capital is a hybrid of economic values and moral values. See Kevin T. Jackson, *Building Reputational Capital: Strategies for Integrity and Fair Play that Improve the Bottom Line* (2004).

120. The concept of social capital refers to intangible assets encompassing features

such as personal aptitudes, social cohesion, and competency in problem-solving—
traits that are entrenched in and conveyed by cultures. See *Democracies in Flux: The
Evolution of Social Capital in Contemporary Society,* Robert D. Putnam, ed. (2002).
Francis Fukuyama, one of the earliest scholars of social capital, notes "the improbable
power of culture in the making of economic society" (Fukuyama, supra note 115, at 1).
Fukuyama further explains that the notion of social capital "has to do with people's
ability to associate with each other," which is vital "not only to economic life but to
virtually every other aspect of social existence as well" (ibid., 10).

121. In the United States, the legal roots of the shareholder-centered view extend
back to the landmark case of *Dodge v. Ford Motor Co.*, in which the Michigan Supreme
Court held that a business corporation is organized primarily for the profit of the
stockholders, rather than for the good of the community or its employees. 170 N.W.
668, 684 (Mich. 1919). ("A business corporation is organized and carried on primarily
for the profit of the stockholders. The powers of the directors are to be employed for
that end. The discretion of directors is to be exercised in the choice of means to attain
that end, and does not extend to a change in the end itself, to the reduction of profits,
or to the non-distribution of profits among stockholders in order to devote them to
other purposes.")

122. See generally Jackson, supra note 119.

123. Fukuyama, supra note 115, 26.

124. Ibid.

125. See Jackson, supra note 119, 49–50.

Chapter 8

1. See, generally, Gareth Morgan, "Paradigms, Metaphors and Problem Solving
in Organization Theory," 25 *Admin. Sci. Q.* (1980), 605, 616; Morgan provides a critique of the metaphors that have "imprisoned" organization theory.

2. See Richard Holme and Philip Watts, *Corporate Social Responsibility: Making
Good Business Sense* (2000), 20; see also Jan Aart Scholte, "Globalization, Governance
and Corporate Citizenship," 1 *J. Corp. Citizenship* (2001), 15, 15–23. The analysis of
"soft law" in this chapter draws upon my article, "Global Corporate Governance: Soft
Law and Reputational Accountability," 35(1) *Brooklyn J. Int'l. L.* (2010), 41–106.

3. See, generally, Cynthia Day Wallace, *Legal Control of the Multinational Enterprise* (1982), 23; providing examples and discussing distinctions among various forms
of regulation.

4. See ibid., 295–96; see also Scholte, supra note 2, 19–21.

5. See Thomas W. Dunfee, "Business Ethics and Extant Social Contracts," 1 *Bus.
Ethics Q.* (1991), 23, 24.

6. See John Braithwaite and Peter Drahos, *Global Business Regulation* (2000),
18. The G-20 summit convened in Pittsburgh during September 2009 represented a

dramatic escalation in the push for global governance of corporate financial affairs. The body's efforts to promote international economic teamwork not only attempted to curb excesses and set executive pay in accordance with the long-term plans of a firm, but also it weighed in on issues as varied as sustainability, food policy, and corporate social responsibility. In this regard, it should be noted that although the G-20 largely deploys moral suasion against nation-states deemed noncompliant with their edicts, there has nevertheless been chatter in some circles suggesting the possibility of stepped-up sanction authorization.

7. See Simon Zadek, *The Civil Corporation: The New Economy of Corporate Citizenship* rev. ed. (2007), 91. See, generally, *Corporate Social Responsibility: Readings and Cases in Global Context* 1, Andrew CraneDirk Matten, and Laura Spence, eds. (2008).

8. See, generally, Archie Carroll, "Corporate Social Responsibility: Evolution of a Definitional Construct," 38 *Bus. and Soc'y* (1999), 268, 268; Dirk Matten and Andrew Crane, "Corporate Citizenship: Toward an Extended Theoretical Conceptualization," 30 *Acad. Mgmt. Rev.* (2005), 166, 166.

9. See, generally, Andreas Georg Scherer and Guido Palazzo, "Toward a Political Conception of Corporate Responsibility: Business and Society Seen from a Habermasian Perspective," 32 *Acad. Mgmt. Rev.* (2007), 1096, 1096–120.

10. Alasdair Ross, "Reputation: Risk of Risks," *The Economist Intelligence Unit*, Dec. 2005, 2; see Robert O. Keohane, "Complex Accountability and Power in Global Governance: Issues for Global Business," 8 *Corp. Governance* (2008), 361, 365.

11. In its original sense, the term "corporate governance" referred to the "structure and functioning of the corporate polity" (Richard Eells, *The Meaning of Modern Business: An Introduction to the Philosophy of Large Corporate Enterprise* [1960], 108).

12. See Jean Jacques Servan-Schreiber, *Le Défi américain* [*The American Challenge*] 1 (1968) (Fr.); providing a provocative angle on America-style management, business, and ethics; and Raymond Vernon, *Sovereignty at Bay* 1 (1971), which is a seminal book that was widely acclaimed to be "no more than the tip of an iceberg."

13. See Richard Barnet and Ronald Mueller, *Global Reach: The Power of Multinational Corporations* (1974), 113.

14. See Paul M. Minus, "Introduction" to *The Ethics of Business in a Global Economy*, Paul M. Minus, ed. (1993), 1, 1; Robert C. Solomon, *The New World of Business: Ethics and Free Enterprise in the Global 1990s* (1994), 167. See, generally, Theodore H. Moran, *Multinational Corporations: The Political Economy of Foreign Direct Investment* (1985), 1; Moran presents an extensive and a thorough discussion of the sociopolitical developments resulting from the spread of multinational corporations.

15. Arlene I. Broadhurst, "Corporations and the Ethics of Social Responsibility: An Emerging Regime of Expansion and Compliance," 9 *Bus. Ethics: A Euro. Rev.* (2000), 86, 88.

16. Noteworthy examples are the Bhopal disaster involving leakage of deadly MIC gas from one of Union Carbide's industrial plants, and the widespread calls for

disinvestment of U.S.-based multinationals from apartheid South Africa. See Cortelyou Kenney, Comment, "Disaster in the Amazon: Dodging 'Boomerang Suits' in Transnational Human Rights Litigation," 97 *Cal. L. Rev.* (2009), 857, 875; see also Kenneth A. Rodman, "Public and Private Sanctions Against South Africa," 109 *Pol. Sci. Q.* (1994), 313, 320.

17. See "European Commission Green Paper on Promoting a European Framework for Corporate Responsibility," *COM* (2001) 366 final (July 18, 2001), available at http://eur-lex.europa.eu/LexUriServ/site/en/com/2001/com2001_0366en01.pdf.

18. See, generally, Milton Friedman, "The Social Responsibility of Business is to Increase its Profits," *N. Y. Times* (Magazine), Sept. 13, 1970.

19. Debora Spar, "The Spotlight and the Bottom Line," *Foreign Aff.* (Mar.–Apr. 1998), 7–9.

20. See Morton Winston, "NGO Strategies for Promoting Corporate Social Responsibility," 16 *Ethics and Int'l Aff.* (2002), 71, 72–73.

21. Ngaire Woods, "Global Governance and Role of Institutions," in David Held and Anthony McGrew eds., *Governing Globalization* (2002), 25, 32.

22. See, generally, John G. Ruggie, "Reconstituting the Global Public Domain: Issues, Actors and Practices," 10 *Eur. J. of Int'l Rel.* (2004), 499, 499–504.

23. *Corporate Social Responsibility: Readings and Cases in Global Context*, supra note 7, 1.

24. See Reuven S. Avi-Yonah, "The Cyclical Transformations of the Corporate Form: A Historical Perspective on Corporate Social Responsibility," 30 *Del. J. Corp. L.* (2005), 767, 767; cf. Eric W. Orts, "The Complexity and Legitimacy of Corporate Law," 50 *Wash. and Lee L. Rev.* (1993), 1565, 1587; Orts is arguing that the "policies underlying corporate law cannot be reduced to a unidimensional value, such as the economic objective of 'maximizing shareholders' wealth.'"

25. See Avi-Yonah, supra note 24, 768–70; Avi-Yonah is delineating the parameters of the debate about the broader role of the corporations.

26. William T. Allen, "Our Schizophrenic Conception of the Business Corporation," 14 *Cardozo L. Rev.* (1992), 261, 264.

27. See Melvin A. Eisenberg, "The Conception that the Corporation Is a Nexus of Contracts, and the Dual Nature of the Firm," 24 *J. of Corp. L.* (1999), 819, 825–26; Michael Klausner, "The Contractarian Theory of Corporate Law: A Generation Later," 31 *J. of Corp. L.* (2006), 779, 782–84.

28. David S. Allen, "The First Amendment and the Doctrine of Corporate Personhood: Collapsing the Press-Corporation Distinction," 2 *Journalism* (2001), 255, 259–60.

29. See Kent Greenfield, "The Place of Workers in Corporate Law," 39 *B. C. L. Rev.* (1998), 283, 294.

30. See, e.g., Greenfield, ibid., 304. Scholarly commentary has also focused on the property rights justifications for the notion of the shareholder primacy. See Oliver

Hart and John Moore, "Property Rights and the Nature of the Firm," 98 *J. of Pol. Econ.* (1990), 1119, 1119.

31. See, generally, Kent Greenfield, "There's a Forest in Those Trees: Teaching About the Role of Corporations in Society," 34 *Ga. L. Rev.* (2000), 1011, 1011; Ronen Shamir, "The Age of Responsibilization: On Market-Embedded Morality," 37 *Econ. and Soc'y* (2008), 1, 1.

32. See, generally, Kent Greenfield, "New Principles for Corporate Law," 1 *Hastings Bus. L. J.* (2005), 87, 117; Lawrence E. Mitchell, "A Theoretical and Practical Framework for Enforcing Corporate Constituency Statutes," 70 *Tex. L. Rev.* (1992), 579, 590.

33. See Kent Greenfield, *The Failure of Corporate Law: Fundamental Flaws and Progressive Possibilities* (2006), 29. See, generally, Margaret M. Blair and Lynn A. Stout, "A Team Production Theory of Corporate Law," 85 *Va. L. Rev.* (1999), 247, 247; building on the presumption that corporate managers owe a duty beyond that which they owe to the shareholders.

34. For example, corporate law professors Henry Hansmann and Reinier Kraakman argue that "the recent dominance of a shareholder-centered ideology of corporate law among the business, government, and legal elites in key commercial jurisdictions" has left no serious contenders to this view of a corporation. Henry Hansmann and Reinier Kraakman, "The End of History for Corporate Law," 89 *Geo. L. J.* (2001), 439, 439; see also John C. Coffee Jr., "The Future as History: The Prospects for Global Convergence in Corporate Governance and Its Implications," 93 *NW. U. L Rev.* (1999), 641, 650; Ronald J. Gilson, "Globalizing Corporate Governance: Convergence of Form or Function," 49 *Amer. J. of Comp. L.* (2001), 329, 333. For a critique of Hansmann's and Kraakman's position decrying their perspective as "Americanocentric," see Douglas M. Branson, "The Very Uncertain Prospect of 'Global' Convergence in Corporate Governance," 34 *Cornell Int'l L. J.* (2001), 321, 331.

35. See, e.g., Michael Bradley, Cindy A. Schipani, Anant K. Sundaram, and James P. Walsh, "The Purposes and Accountability of the Corporation in Contemporary Society: Corporate Governance at a Crossroads," *Law and Contemp. Probs.* (summer 1999), 9.

36. See, generally, Craig Mackenzie, "Boards, Incentives and Corporate Social Responsibility: The Case for a Change of Emphasis," 15 *Corp. Governance Int'l Rev.* (2007), 935.

37. See Lyman P. Q. Johnson and David Millon, "Recalling Why Corporate Officers Are Fiduciaries," 46 *Wm. and Mary L. Rev.* (2005), 1597, 1600–1601.

38. See Adam Winkler, "Corporate Law or the Law of Business?: Stakeholders and Corporate Governance at the End of History," *Law and Contemp. Probs.* (autumn 2004), 109, 110.

39. See, e.g., Thomas W. Joo, "A Trip Through the Maze of 'Corporate Democracy': Shareholder Voice and Management Composition," 77 *St. John's L. Rev.* (2003), 735, 754; see also Adam J. Sulkowski and Kent Greenfield, "A Bridle, a Prod and a Big Stick: An

Evaluation of Class Actions, Shareholder Proposals and the Ultra Vires Doctrine as Methods for Controlling Corporate Behavior," 79 *St. John's L. Rev.* (2005), 929, 938.

40. See Craig Deegan, "The Legitimizing Effect of Social and Environmental Disclosures: A Theoretical Foundation," 15 *Acct. Auditing and Accountability J.* (2002), 282, 283–86; see also Reggy Hooghiemstra, "Corporate Communication and Impression Management: New Perspectives Why Companies Engage in Social Reporting," 27 *J. of Bus. Ethics* (2000), 55, 55; Ans Kolk, "Sustainability, Accountability and Corporate Governance: Exploring Multinationals' Reporting Practices," 18 *Bus. Strategy and Env't* (2008), 1, 3.

41. See, generally, Lawrence E. Mitchell, "The Board as a Path Toward Corporate Social Responsibility," in Doreen McBarnet, Aurora Voiculescu, and Tom Campbell, eds., *The New Corporate Accountability: Corporate Social Responsibility and the Law* (2007), 279, 302; Mitchell is proposing several remedial measures.

42. See Arthur R. Pinto, "Globalization and the Study of Comparative Corporate Governance," 23 *Wis. Int'l L. J.* (2005), 477, 479. See, generally, Yadong Luo, *Global Dimensions of Corporate Governance* (2007), 131.

43. See William C. Frederick, "From CSR-1 to CSR-2: The Maturing of Business- and- Society Thought," 33 *Bus. and Soc'y* (1994), 150, 150–54 [hereinafter "CSR-1 to CSR-2"]; see also Barry M. Mitnick, "Systematics and CSR: The Theory and Processes of Normative Referencing," 34 *Bus. and Soc'y* (1995), 5, 6.

44. See Edwin M. Epstein, "The Corporate Social Policy Process and the Process of Corporate Governance," 25 *Amer. Bus. L. J.* (1987), 361, 374.

45. See Archie B. Carroll, "A Three-Dimensional Conceptual Model of Corporate Social Performance," 4 *Acad. Mgmt. Rev.* (1979), 497, 503.

46. Peter Drucker elaborates this point of view as follows: economic performance is the *first* responsibility of business. A business that does not show a profit at least equal to its cost of capital is socially irresponsible. It wastes society's resources. Economic performance is the basis; without it, a business cannot discharge any other responsibilities, cannot be a good employer, a good citizen, a good neighbor. But economic performance is not the sole responsibility of business (Peter F. Drucker, *Post-Capitalist Society* [1993], 101).

47. See, generally, John R. Boatright, *Ethics and the Conduct of Business* 4th ed. (2003), 1.

48. For instance, legal responsibilities imposed by FDA, FTC, OSHA, CPSC, EPA, EEOC, and SEC regulations, to name but a handful from the morass of U.S. regulatory agencies. See ibid., 111, 210, 264, 272, 306–11, 339.

49. See ibid., 369.

50. See Carroll, supra note 45, 500.

51. Ibid., 502–4.

52. Ibid., 500.

53. Ibid.

54. See Robert Ackerman and Raymond Bauer, *Corporate Social Responsiveness: The Modern Dilemma* (1976), 6–7.

55. See ibid., 6.

56. Ibid.

57. Ibid.

58. See "CSR-1 to CSR-2," supra note 43, 154; see also Edwin M. Epstein, "The Corporate Social Policy Process: Beyond Business Ethics, Corporate Social Responsibility and Corporate Social Responsiveness," 29 *Cal. Mgmt. Rev.* (1987), 99, 104.

59. Boatright, supra note 47, 370, discussing the difference between responsibility and responsiveness.

60. Archie B. Carroll, "The Pyramid of Corporate Social Responsibility: Toward the Moral Management of Organizational Stakeholders," *Bus. Horizons* (July–Aug. 1991), 42.

61. Barbara Russano Hanning, *Concise History of Western Music* 1st ed. (1998), 44.

62. Depending on disciplinary context, the various designations have included: "communitarian versus contractarian," "Berle versus Dodd debate," "shareholder paradox," "separation fallacy," "separation thesis," and "monotonic versus pluralist" and "unidimensional versus multidimensional."

63. But see Timothy L. Fort and Cindy A. Schipani, "Corporate Governance in a Global Environment: A Search for the Best of all Worlds," 33 *Vand. J. Transnat'l L.* (2000), 829, 838–42; they are arguing that differing corporate governance structures in Europe, Japan, and the United States restrict the extent to which transnational firms may permit stakeholder influences.

64. Curiously, the same conflict is embodied in the Company Law of the People's Republic of China, which sets out a legal framework for the organization and operation of private stock enterprises. See Michael Irl Nikkel, Note, "'Chinese Characteristics' in Corporate Clothing: Questions of Fiduciary Duty in China's Company Law," 80 *Minn. L. Rev.* (1995), 503, 523. (Whereas Article 102 states that shareholders "shall be the organ of authority" of the firm, Article 14 maintains that business enterprises must "strengthen the establishment of a socialist spiritual civilization, and accept the supervision of the government and the public.")

65. See, generally, William W. Bratton Jr., "The 'Nexus of Contracts' Corporation: A Critical Appraisal," 74 *Cornell L. Rev.* (1989), 407, 407; Ronald M. Green, "Shareholders as Stakeholders: Changing Metaphors of Corporate Governance," 50 *Wash. and Lee L. Rev.* (1993), 1409, 1409; Lyman Johnson, "The Delaware Judiciary and the Meaning of Corporate Life and Corporate Law," 68 *Tex. L. Rev.* (1990), 865, 865; David Millon, "Redefining Corporate Law," 24 *Ind. L. Rev.* (1991), 223, 223; David Millon, "Theories of the Corporation," *Duke L. J.* (1990), 201, 210; Stephen M. Bainbridge, "Community and Statism: A Conservative Contractuarian Critique of Progressive Corporate Law Scholarship," 82 *Cornell L. Rev.* (1997), 856, 856; reviewing *Progressive Corporate Law,* Lawrence E. Mitchell, ed. (1995).

66. See Judd F. Sneirson, "Doing Well by Doing Good: Leveraging Due Care for

Better, More Socially Responsible Corporate Decision Making," 3 *Corp. Governance L. Rev.* (2007), 438, 439–40.

67. *Dodge v. Ford Motor Co.,* 170 N.W. 668, 684 (Mich. 1919).

68. Ibid. The *Dodge* Court reasoned: "A business corporation is organized and carried on primarily for the profit of the stockholders. The powers of the directors are to be employed for that end. The discretion of directors is to be exercised in the choice of means to attain that end and does not extend to a change in the end itself, to the reduction of profits or to the nondistribution of profits among stockholders in order to devote them to other purposes" (ibid.). Later, the debate resurfaced in the context of corporate mergers and acquisitions during the 1980s. The Delaware Supreme Court held that the interests of nonshareholders could be taken into account by managers and directors when assessing the implications of the takeover bids. Cf. *Unocal Corp. v. Mesa Petroleum Co.,* 493 A.2d 946, 949 (Del. 1985) (finding a duty to evaluate the threat to the corporate enterprise as a whole).

69. See Adolf A. Berle Jr., "For Whom Corporate Managers Are Trustees," 45 *Harv. L. Rev.* (1932), 1365, 1365–66; see also Adolf A. Berle Jr., "Corporate Powers as Powers in Trust," 44 *Harv. L. Rev.* (1931), 1049, 1049; E. Merrick Dodd Jr., "For Whom are Corporate Managers Trustees?" 45 *Harv. L. Rev.* (1932), 1145, 1145–53; A. A. Sommer Jr., "Whom Should the Corporation Serve? The Berle-Dodd Debate Revisited Sixty Years Later," 16 *Del. J. Corp. L.* (1991), 33, 36–38; C. A. Harwell Wells, "The Cycles of Corporate Social Responsibility: An Historical Retrospective for the Twenty-First Century," 51 *U. Kan. L. Rev.* (2002), 77, 77–89, 89 note 4.

70. See, generally, Adolf A. Berle Jr. and Gardiner C. Means, *The Modern Corporation and Private Property* rev. ed. (1967), 125–26.

71. See Henry Hansmann and Reinier Kraakman, "Agency Problems and Legal Strategies," in Reinier Kraakman et al. eds., *The Anatomy of Corporate Law: A Comparative and Functional Approach* (2004), 21, 21.

72. See Michael C. Jensen and William H. Meckling, "Theory of the Firm: Managerial Behavior, Agency Costs and Ownership Structure," 3 *J. of Fin. Econ.* (1976), 305, 308; see also Steven M. H. Wallman, "Understanding the Purpose of a Corporation: An Introduction," 24 *J. of Corp. L.* (1999), 807, 808–9; cf. D. Gordon Smith, "The Shareholder Primacy Norm," 23 *J. of Corp. L.* (1998), 277, 279.

73. See Harold Demsetz and Kenneth Lehn, "The Structure of Corporate Ownership: Causes and Consequences," 93 *J. of Pol. Econ.* (1985), 1155, 1155–56; see also Frank H. Easterbrook and Daniel R. Fischel, *The Economic Structure of Corporate Law* (1991), 4–5, 17, 38, 70.

74. See Lynne L. Dallas, *Law and Public Policy: A Socioeconomic Approach* (2005), 483.

75. See Michael E. DeBow and Dwight R. Lee, "Shareholders, Nonshareholders and Corporate Law: Communitarianism and Resource Allocation," 18 *Del. J. of Corp. L.* (1993), 393, 398; see, generally, Stephen M. Bainbridge, "In Defense of the

Shareholder Wealth Maximization Norm: A Reply to Professor Green," 50 *Wash. and Lee L. Rev.* (1993), 1423, 1423–25.

76. See Milton Friedman, *Capitalism and Freedom* (1962), 133; see also "Willa Johnson, Freedom and Philanthropy: An Interview with Milton Friedman," 71 *Bus. and Soc. Rev.* (1989), 11, 14. Friedman also offered this decidedly monophonic account of corporate governance: "In a free-enterprise, private-property system, a corporate executive is an employee of the owners of the business. He has direct responsibility to his employers. That responsibility is to conduct the business in accordance with their desires, which generally will be to make as much money as possible while conforming to the basic rules of the society, both those embodied in law and those embodied in ethical custom" (Friedman, supra note 18, 32).

77. R. Edward Freeman, "The Politics of Stakeholder Theory: Some Future Directions," 4 *Bus. Ethics Q.* (1994), 409, 412.

78. See Friedman, supra note 76, 133; arguing that a corporation's social responsibility is to "increase profits."

79. See ibid., 133, implying that social responsibility is distracting and restrains corporate activity.

80. Cf. ibid., 133–36.

81. See, generally, Joseph M. Lozano, "Towards the Relational Corporation: From Managing Stakeholder Relationships to Building Stakeholder Relationships (Waiting for Copernicus)," 5(2) *Corp. Governance* (2005), 60, 60; Lozano discusses relations among stakeholders and shareholders.

82. David Millon, "Communitarians, Contractarians, and the Crisis in Corporate Law," 50 *Wash. and Lee L. Rev.* (1993), 1373, 1378–79.

83. See Norman E. Bowie, *Business Ethics: A Kantian Perspective* (1999), 142.

84. See ibid., 142.

85. Ross, supra note 10, 7–8; Spar, supra note 19, 7–9.

86. See Thomas Donaldson, "'Ethical Blowback': The Missing Piece in the Corporate Governance Puzzle—The Risks to a Company Which Fails to Understand and Respect Its Social Contract," 7 *Corp. Governance* (2007), 534, 536.

87. See Robert C. Solomon, *Ethics and Excellence: Cooperation and Integrity in Business* (1992), 45.

88. See Amartya Sen, "Economics, Business Principles, and Moral Sentiments," 7 *Bus. Ethics Q.* (1997), 5, 5. "In contrast, moral sentiments are seen to be quite *complex* (involving different types of ethical systems), but it is assumed, that at least in economic matters, they have a very *narrow reach* (indeed, it is often presumed that such sentiments have no real influence on economic behavior)" (ibid.).

89. See Boatright, supra note 47, 368; see also Donaldson, *The Ethics of International Business* (1989), 45.

90. See Boatright, supra note 47, 370 (noting that CSR requires "responsiveness"); R. Edward Freeman and Daniel R. Gilbert Jr., *Corporate Strategy and the*

Search for Ethics (1988), 104–5; "CSR-1 to CSR-2," supra note 43, 152; Mitnick, supra note 43, 6.

91. Donaldson, supra note 89, 45–46. Thomas Donaldson writes that "despite its important insights, the stakeholder model has serious problems. The two most obvious are its inability to provide standards for assigning relative weights to the interests of the various constituencies, and its failure to contain within itself, or make references to, a normative justificatory foundation" (ibid.; see also Thomas W. Dunfee and Thomas Donaldson, "Contractarian Business Ethics: Current Status and Next Steps," 5 *Bus. Ethics Q.* [1995], 173, 175). The stakeholder model has also been challenged on the ground that it does not provide sufficiently rigorous criteria for settling disputes about who or what qualifies as a legitimate stakeholder, as in the case of child laborers working for a multinational corporation's supplier when the firm is in the process of a merger with another multinational firm. See Bert van de Ven, "Human Rights as a Normative Basis for Stakeholder Legitimacy," 5(2) *Corp. Governance* (2005), 48, 55–56.

92. See Donaldson and Dunfee, *Ties that Bind: A Social Contracts Approach to Business Ethics* (1999), 235–36; Thomas Donaldson and Thomas W. Dunfee, "Integrative Social Contracts Theory: A Communitarian Conception of Economic Ethics," 11 *Econ. and Phil.* (1995), 85, 85–86; see also Thomas Donaldson and Thomas W. Dunfee, "Toward a Unified Conception of Business Ethics: Integrative Social Contracts Theory," 19 *Acad. Mgmt. Rev.* (1994), 252, 252 [hereinafter "Toward a Unified Conception"].

93. Donaldson and Dunfee, *Ties that Bind*, 222.

94. Ibid.

95. Ibid., 74–81.

96. Ibid., 49–52.

97. Ibid., 222.

98. Ibid., 40.

99. Ibid., 222.

100. Ibid., 38.

101. Ibid., 46.

102. Ibid., 43.

103. Most members of community C approve of compliance with N in recurrent situation S, most members of C disapprove of deviance from N in S, a substantial percentage (well over 50 percent) of members of C comply with N when facing S. See "Toward a Unified Conception," supra note 92, 263–64.

104. Ibid., 265.

105. Ibid., 254.

106. See Donaldson and Dunfee, *Ties that Bind*, 235–36.

107. Ibid., 49. In circumstances lacking dominant or well-established norms, firms remain in the area of moral free space. Ibid., 85. It should be noted that, according to ISCT, all of firms' activities must comply with extant and applicable hypernorms. See

Donaldson and Dunfee, *Ties that Bind*, 89; see also "Toward a Unified Conception," supra note 92, 268–69.

108. See, for example, Robert C. Ellickson, "Law and Economics Discovers Social Norms," 27 *J. Legal Stud.* (1998), 537, 546; and Richard H. McAdams, "The Origin, Development, and Regulation of Norms," 96 *Mich. L. Rev.* (1997), 338, 338, for a discussion of the concept of social norms.

109. See, generally, Donaldson and Dunfee, *Ties that Bind*, 25, discussing social contract and global civil regulations.

110. Thomas Dunfee, "Challenges to Corporate Governance: Corporate Governance in a Market with Morality," *Law and Contemp. Probs.* (summer 1999), 129, 145.

111. See Donaldson and Dunfee, *Ties that Bind*, 97; the graphic table sets out the dynamics that occur in the "moral free space."

112. See, e.g., William C. Frederick, *The Moral Authority of Transnational Corporate Codes*, 10 *J. of Bus. Ethics* (1991), 165, 165.

113. Joel Bakan, *The Corporation: The Pathological Pursuit of Profit and Power* (2004), 27.

114. See S. Prakash Sethi and Linda M. Sama, "Ethical Behavior as a Strategic Choice by Large Corporations: The Interactive Effect of Marketplace Competition, Industry Structure and Firm Resources," 1 *Bus. Ethics Q.* (1998), 85, 95–98.

115. See Kenneth E. Goodpaster, "Business Ethics and Stakeholder Analysis," 1 *Bus. Ethics Q.* (1991), 53, 57–58.

116. See Donaldson, supra note 86, 534–36.

117. "Reputation capital" denotes a firm's intangible long-term strategic assets calculated to generate profits. The reputation capital of a corporation is a hybrid of economic values and moral values. See Grahame Dowling, *Creating Corporate Reputations: Identity, Image, and Performance* (2001), 23; see also Charles J. Fombrun and Cees B. M. Van Riel, *Fame and Fortune: How Successful Companies Build Winning Reputations* (2004), 32–35; discussing "perceptual and social assets." See, generally, Ronald J. Alsop, *The 18 Immutable Laws of Corporate Reputation* (2004), 17; Charles J. Fomburn, *Reputation: Realizing Value From the Corporate Image* (1996), 1.

118. See Kevin Jackson, *Building Reputational Capital* (2004), 25–35.

119. Ross, supra note 10, 8.

120. See Edwin Epstein, Commentary, "The Good Company: Rhetoric or Reality? Corporate Social Responsibility and Business Ethics Redux," 44 *Amer. Bus. L. J.* (2007), 207, 214, 219.

121. See Thomas J. Biersteker, "The 'Triumph' of Neoclassical Economics in the Developing World," in James N. Rosenau and Ernst-Otto Czempiel, eds., *Governance Without Government: Order and Change in World Politics* (1992), 102, 110–11; James N. Rosenau, "Governance in the Twenty-First Century," 1 *Global Governance* (1995), 13, 13; Scholte, supra note 2, 15–23; cf. Robert W. Cox, "Structural Issues of Global Governance: Implications for Europe," in *Approaches to World Order* (1996), 237; Cox

is examining diminishing political authority of the European nation-states who are members of the European Union and its impact on its regulatory landscape.

122. Cf. Christoph Knill and Dirk Lehmkuhl, "Private Actors and the State: Internationalization and Changing Patterns of Governance," 15 *Governance* (2002), 41, 44–45. See, generally, R. Edward Freeman, Andrew C. Wicks, and Bidhan Parmar, "Stakeholder Theory and the 'Corporate Objective Revisited,'" 15 *Organization Science* (2004), 364, 364; R. Edward Freeman, supra note 77, 409–22.

123. See Lester M. Salaman, "The New Governance and the Tools of Public Action: An Introduction," in Lester M. Salaman and Odus V. Elliott, eds., *The Tools of Government: A Guide to the New Governance* (2002), 8, 11–14.

124. Cf. Yuval Feldman and Orly Lobel, "Decentralized Enforcement in Organizations: An Experimental Approach," 2 *Reg. and Governance* (2008), 165–92; they conclude that social and cultural norms dominate state regulation and its policy making as far as civil enforcement.

125. See, generally, Orly Lobel, "Setting the Agenda for New Governance Research," 89 *Minn. L. Rev.* (2004), 498, 498; Lobel is discussing employment disputes, organizational compliance, financial regulation, and employee misconduct.

126. See, e.g., David Hess, "Social Reporting and New Governance Regulation: The Prospects of Achieving Corporate Accountability through Transparency," 17 *Bus. Ethics Q.* (2007), 453, 455; see also Orly Lobel, "The Renew Deal: The Fall of Regulation and the Rise of Governance in Contemporary Legal Thought," 89 *Minn. L. Rev.* (2004), 342, 371–76.

127. See Bruce L. Benson, "The Spontaneous Evolution of Commercial Law," 55 *S. Econ. J.* (1989), 644, 658.

128. See, e.g., Mary Ellen O'Connell, "The Role of Soft Law in a Global Order," in *Commitment and Compliance: The Role of Non-Binding Norms in the International Legal System* (2000), 100, 110; Leon E. Trakman, *The Law Merchant: The Evolution of Commercial Law* (1983), 39; Trakman delineates historical development of transnational business litigation.

129. See Feldman and Lobel, supra note 124, 165 (2008).

130. See A. Claire Cutler, Virginia Haufler, and Tony Porter, "Private Authority and International Affairs," in *Private Authority and International Affairs* (1999), 3; Scholte, supra note 2, 19.

131. See sources cited supra note 130.

132. See sources cited supra note 130.

133. See Cutler, Haufler and Porter, supra note 130, 4–18; Scholte, supra note 2, 19.

134. See Robert W. Cox, "Structural Issues of Global Governance: Implications for Europe," in *Approaches to World Order* (1996), 237, 237; Cox is discussing the shift of authority away from the states in the European Union.

135. See Virginia Haufler, "Globalization and Industry Self-Regulation," in Miles Kahler and David A. Lake eds., *Governance in a Global Economy: Political Authority in Transition* (2003), 226, 226.

136. "Soft law" generally refers to nonbinding, quasi-legal instruments, or to mechanisms whose binding force is relatively weaker than conventional legal instruments. See David Kinley and Junko Tadaki, "From Talk to Walk: The Emergence of Human Rights Responsibilities for Corporations at International Law," 44 *Va. J. Int'l L.* (2004), 931, 960; see also Alan C. Neal, "Corporate Social Responsibility: Governance Gain or Laissez-Faire Figleaf?" 29 *Comp. Lab. L. and Pol'y J.* (2008), 459, 464. From the standpoint of the international law nomenclature, "soft law" refers to international agreements not concluded as treaties and thus not yet binding. See, e.g., Mary Ellen O'Connell, "The Role of Soft Law in a Global Order," in Dinah Shelton, ed., *Commitment and Compliance: The Role of Non-Binding Norms in the International Legal System* (2000), 100, 113–14; Antonio Vives, "Corporate Social Responsibility: The Role of Law and Markets and the Case of Developing Countries," 83 *Chi.-Kent L. Rev.* (2008), 199, 216. In addition, "soft law" denotes a self-contained set of obligations arising out of the occasional preference of nation-states to reach *non*binding agreements and to pattern relations in ways that avoid application of treaty or customary law. See Hartmut Hillgenberg, "A Fresh Look at Soft Law," 10 *Eur. J. Int'l L.* (1999), 499, 501; discussing the nature of the transnational self-regulatory and coregulatory structures; see also Rebecca Kathleen Atkins, "Multinational Enterprises and Workplace Reproductive Health: Extending Corporate Social Responsibility," 40 *Vand. J. Transnat'l L.* (2007), 233, 239; Ilias Bantekas, "Corporate Social Responsibility in International Law," 22 *B. U. Int'l L. J.* (2004), 309, 317; Ronen Shamir, "Between Self-Regulation and the Alien Tort Claims Act: On the Contested Concept of Corporate Social Responsibility," 38 *Law and Soc'y Rev.* (2004), 635, 645.

137. See John J. Kirton and Michael J. Trebilock, "Introduction: Hard Choices and Soft Law in Sustainable Global Commerce," in John J. Kirton and Michael J. Trebilock, eds., *Hard Choices, Soft Law: Voluntary Standards in Global Trade, Environment and Social Governance* (2004), 3, 6, 11. See, generally, *Soft Law in Governance and Regulation,* Ulrika Moth ed. (2004); Kenneth Abbott and Duncan Snidal, "Hard and Soft Law in International Governance," 54 *Int'l Org.* (2000), 421, 434–50.

138. See Haufler, supra note 135, 226–27.

139. See Virginia Haufler, *The Public Role for the Private Sector: Industry Self-Regulation in a Global Economy* (2001), 12–15; see also Rodney Bruce Hall and Thomas J. Biersteker, "The Emergence of Private Authority in the International System," in *The Emergence of Private Authority in Global Governance* (2002), 3–4.

140. See Ruggie, supra note 22, 519.

141. See Kenneth W. Abbott and Duncan Snidal, "The Governance Triangle: Regulatory Standards, Institutions and the Shadow of the State," in *The Politics of Global Regulation* (2009), 44–50.

142. See Linda Cornett and James A. Caporaso, "'And Still It Moves' State Interests and Social Forces in the European Community," in James N. Rosenau and Ernst-Otto Czempiel, eds., *Governance Without Government: Order and Change in World Politics* (1992), 219, 228 note 21.

143. R. A. W. Rhodes, "The New Governance: Governing Without Government," 44 *Pol. Stud.* (1996), 652, 660.

144. Lawrence S. Finkelstein, "What Is Global Governance?" 1 *Global Governance* (1995), 367, 369.

145. See James N. Rosenau, "Citizenship in a Changing Global Order," in James N. Rosenau and Ernst-Otto Czempiel, eds., *Governance Without Government: Order and Change in World Politics* (1992), 272, 286–87.

146. See Laura Albareda, "Corporate Responsibility, Governance and Accountability: From Self-Regulation to Co-Regulation," 8 *Corp. Governance* (2008), 430, 430.

147. See, e.g., Gene R. Laczniak and Jacob Naor, "Global Ethics: Wrestling with the Corporate Conscience," *Bus.*, July—Sept. 1985, 7; discussing the examples of Allis Chalmers, Caterpillar Tractor, Chiquita Brands International, Medtronic, and S. C. Johnson. While there are firms that do not have comprehensive codes addressing their international operations, many adopt codes that include sections that speak to foreign practices. Ibid. For instance, Northrop Grumman Corporation's "Standards of Business Conduct" contains an "International" segment. Northrop Grumman Corporation, Standards of Business Conduct, 10, available at http://www.northropgrumman.com/pdf/noc_standards_conduct.pdf. The section reads, in relevant part: "Employees and consultants or agents representing the company abroad or working on international business in the United States should be aware that the company's Values and Standards of Conduct apply to them anywhere in the world. Less than strict adherence to laws and regulations that apply to the company's conduct of international business would be considered a compromise of our Values and Standards of Conduct" (ibid.).

148. See The Sullivan Foundation, "The Global Sullivan Principles," available at http://www.thesullivanfoundation.org/about/global_sullivan_principles.

149. The objectives of the Principles are to support economic, social, and political justice by firms wherever they conduct operations; to advance human rights and to promote equality of opportunity at all levels of employment, including racial and gender diversity on decision-making committees and boards; and to train and advance disadvantaged workers for technical, supervisory, and management opportunities. Ibid.

150. See, e.g., Gordon Leslie Clark and Tessa Hebb, "Why Do They Care? The Market for Corporate Global Responsibility and the Role of Institutional Investors" (June 16, 2004), 17–23 (unpublished paper presented at the Using Pensions for Social Control of Capitalist Investment conference, *available at* http://www.community-wealth.org/_pdfs/articles-publications/state-local/paper-clark.pdf) (noting that CalPERS' may withhold investment in companies that do not meet the Sullivan Principles, thus creating the risk of reputational harm).

151. See Lynn Paine, Rohit Deshpandé, Joshua D. Margolis and Kim Eric Bettcher, "Up to Code: Does Your Company's Conduct Meet World-Class Standards?" *Harv. Bus. Rev.*, Dec. 2005, 122.

152. Ibid., 124–25.

153. Ibid., 125.

154. See, generally, *Global Codes of Conduct: An Idea Whose Time Has Come,* Oliver F. Williams ed. (2000); Raymond J. Waldmann, *Regulating International Business Through Codes of Conduct* (1980), 21.

155. Waldmann, supra note 154, 65; discussing the need to emphasize profit); James E. Post, "Global Codes of Conduct: Activists, Lawyers, and Managers in Search of a Solution," in *Global Codes of Conduct: An Idea Whose Time Has Come,* Oliver F. Williams, ed., 2000), 103, 111; expanding on the lack of enforcement criticism.

156. Broadhurst, supra note 15, 89.

157. Such business associations include: Business in the Community, Business for Social Responsibility, Caux Round Table, CSR Europe, Forum Empresa, International Business Leaders Forum, the International Chamber of Commerce (ICC) and World Business Council for Sustainable Development (WBCSD).

158. For example, Business for Social Responsibility runs programs including business ethics, the workplace, the marketplace, the community, the environment, and the global economy. See "BSR, How We Work," available at http://www.bsr.org/about/how-we-work.cfm.

159. For example, the Caux Round Table, headquartered in Switzerland, has adopted an international code for multinational firms in Europe, North America, and Japan. The Code identifies five basic principles, which, as statements of aspirations for business leaders worldwide, extend far beyond those embodied in earlier codes. The principles cover: (1) stakeholder responsibility, (2) social justice, (3) mutual support, (4) environmental concern, and (5) avoidance of illicit operations and corrupt practices. Caux Round Table, Principles For Business, available at http://www.cauxroundtable.org/index.cfm?&menuid=8.

160. For example, the "WBCSD defended a voluntary approach before the United Nations; CSR Europe did the same before the European Commission, [the executive branch of the European Union], and individual European governments, and BSR has done the same with the United States government" (ibid., 435).

161. Although typically underwritten by corporate contributions, inter-firm initiatives sometimes obtain financial backing from international organizations (ibid., 436); noting contributions from European Union, various national governments, and the United States.

162. See Sethi and Sama, supra note 114, 89.

163. Debora Spar and David Yaffe, "Multinational Enterprises and the Prospects for Justice," 52 *J. of Int'l Aff.* (1999), 557, 557.

164. See Broadhurst, supra note 15, 95–96.

165. See ibid., 97.

166. See Dara O'Rourke, "Market Movements: Nongovernmental Organization Strategies to Influence Global Production and Consumption," *J. of Indus. Ecology* (winter/spring 2005), 115, 122; see also Sethi and Sama, supra note 114, 99–100.

167. See O'Rourke, supra note 166, 125.

168. See, generally, Marvin B. Lieberman and Shigeru Asaba, "Why Do Firms Imitate Each Other?" 31 *Acad. Mgmt. Rev.* (2006), 366, 366–75.

169. Ibid., 366.

170. See Broadhurst, supra note 15, 97.

171. Ibid.

172. See Alison Maitland, "Industries Seek Safety in Numbers," *Fin. Times* (Special Report), Nov. 25, 2005, 1. The headline by the author here is ostensibly intended as a quip.

173. See Lieberman and Asaba, supra note 168, 366.

174. See Claire Moore Dickerson, "Human Rights: The Emerging Norm of Corporate Social Responsibility," 76 *Tul. L. Rev.* (2002), 1431, 1440 [hereinafter "Emerging Norm"]; see also Claire Moore Dickerson, "Transnational Codes of Conduct Through Dialogue: Leveling the Playing Field for Developing-Country Workers," 53 *U. Fla. L. Rev.* (2001), 611, 613.

175. See, generally, "Emerging Norm," supra note 174, 1431, discussing the relationship between corporate social responsibility and human rights movement.

176. See Albareda, supra note 146, 435–36.

177. See ibid., 435–36.

178. Simon Zadek, "The Logic of Collaborative Governance: Corporate Responsibility, Accountability, and the Social Contract" (Corporate Soc. Responsibility Initiative, Working Paper No. 17, 2006), 4; available at http://www.hks.harvard.edu/mrcbg/CSRI/publications/workingpaper _17_zadek.pdf. See, generally, Ruggie, supra note 22, 499–531.

179. The United Nations Environmental Program, for instance, assisted in setting up the Electronics Industry Code of Conduct. Similarly, the governments of the United States and the United Kingdom assisted companies in extractive industries in assembling Voluntary Principles on Security and Human Rights. In addition, the government of Austria helped underwrite the Forest Stewardship Council.

180. See, generally, Mary Ellen O'Connell, "The Role of Soft Law in a Global Order," in *Commitment and Compliance: The Role of Non-Binding Norms in the International Legal System* (2000), 100, 110.

181. See, e.g., John Braithwaite and Peter Drahos, *Global Business Regulation* (2000), 198–200.

182. See, e.g., ibid.

183. See, e.g., ibid.

184. See Peter Utting, "Corporate Responsibility and the Movement of Business," 15 *Dev. Practice* (2005), 375, 384–85.

185. Various NGOs—such as Amnesty International, the Clean Clothes Campaign, the Council on Economic Priorities, Greenpeace, Oxfam, and the World Wildlife Fund—have partnered with trade associations active in the areas of apparel, cocoa, chemicals, coffee, electronics, mining, and toys, as well as trade unions, and other organizations, such as the International Textile Workers

Association and the International Standards Organization. See Tim Bartley, "Institutional Emergence in an Era of Globalization: The Rise of Transnational Private Regulation of Labor and Environmental Conditions," 113 *Amer. J. of Soc.* (2007), 297, 335; Bartley discusses in detail case studies of the codes' development in the apparel and timber sectors [hereinafter "Institutional Emergence in an Era of Globalization"]; see also Tim Bartley, "Certifying Forests and Factories: States, Social Movements, and the Rise of Private Regulation in the Apparel and Forest Products Fields," 3 *Pol. and Soc'y* (2003), 433, 434–35; Lars H. Gulbrandsen, "Overlapping Public and Private Governance: Can Forest Certification Fill the Gaps in the Global Forest Regime?" 4 *Global Envtl. Pol.* (2004), 75, 81.

186. Other multistakeholder initiatives are the Forest Stewardship Council, the Global Reporting Initiative, the Marine Stewardship Council, and the United Nations Global Compact. See, e.g., "GRI Portal, About GRI," available at http://www.globalreporting.org/AboutGRI.

187. See, generally, David Antony Detomasi, "The Multinational Corporation and Global Governance: Modeling Global Public Policy Networks," 71 *J. of Bus. Ethics* (2007), 321, 321.

188. See Wolfgang H. Reinicke, "The Other World Wide Web: Global Public Policy Networks," *Foreign Pol'y* (winter 1999), 44. See, generally, Wolfgang H. Reinicke, *Global Public Policy: Governing Without Government* (1998), 228.

189. See, e.g., Braithwaite and Drahos, supra note 6, 159–60.

190. See, e.g., ibid., 168–69.

191. See, generally, ibid., 550.

192. See "Global Reporting Initiative, History," available at http://www.globalreporting.org/AboutGRI/WhatIsGRI/History.

193. Ibid.

194. Ibid.

195. See David Vogel, "Private Global Business Regulation," 11 *Ann. Rev. Pol. Sci.* (2008), 261, 267.

196. Philipp Pattberg, "The Institutionalization of Private Governance: How Business and Nonprofit Organizations Agree on Transnational Rules," 18 *Governance* (2005), 589, 590.

197. See "Institutional Emergence in an Era of Globalization," supra note 185, 299–300.

198. See Pattberg, supra note 196 at 589–610 (2005); Gary Gereffi, Ronie Garcia-Johnson and Erika Sasser, "The NGO-Industrial Complex," *Foreign Pol'y* (July/Aug. 2001), 56, 61; Dennis A. Rondinelli and Ted London, "How Corporations and Environmental Groups Cooperate: Assessing Cross-sector Alliances and Collaborations," 1 *Acad. Mgmt. Exec.* (2003), 61, 62–76.

199. Kristina Herrmann, "Corporate Social Responsibility and Sustainable Development: The European Union Initiative as a Case Study," *Ind. J. Global Legal Stud.* (summer 2004), 205, 227.

200. See "Institutional Emergence in an Era of Globalization," supra note 185, 302–3.

201. Ibid., 336.

202. Ibid., 337.

203. See, e.g., Michelle Egan, *Constructing a European Market* (2001), 263; Christopher Ansell and David Vogel, "The Contested Governance of European Food Safety Regulation," in Christopher Ansell and David Vogel, eds., *What's the Beef?: The Contested Governance of European Food Safety* (2006), 8–9; Jan Willem Biekart, "Negotiated Agreements in EU Environmental Policy," in Jonathan Golub, ed., *New Instruments for Environmental Policy in the EU* 166 (1998); Olivier Borraz, Julien Besançon, and Christophe Clergeau, "Is It Just About Trust? The Partial Reform of French Food Safety Regulation," in Christopher Ansell and David Vogel, eds., *What's the Beef?: The Contested Governance of European Food Safety* (2006), 137–39; Jonathan Golub, "New Instruments for Environmental Policy in the EU: Introduction and Overview," in Jonathan Golub, ed., *New Instruments for Environmental Policy in the EU* (1998) 5, 13–15; Karl-Heinz Ladeur, "Towards a Legal Concept of the Network in European Standard-Setting," in Christian Joerges and Ellen Vos, eds., *EU Committees: Social Regulation, Law and Politics* (1999), 151, 156–59; Stephen Tindale and Chris Hewett, "New Environmental Policy Instruments in the UK," in Jonathan Golub, ed., *New Instruments for Environmental Policy in the EU* (1998), 52–53; Frans van Waarden, "Taste, Traditions, and Transactions: The Public and Private Regulation of Food," in Christopher Ansell and David Vogel, eds., *What's the Beef?: The Contested Governance of European Food Safety* (2006), 56–57.

204. See "Institutional Emergence in an Era of Globalization," supra note 185, 337.

205. See Steven Bernstein and Erin Hannah, "Non-State Global Standard Setting and the WTO: Legitimacy and the Need for Regulatory Space," 11 *J. of Int'l Econ. L.* (2008), 575, 575–608.

206. See Organisation for Economic Co-operation and Development [OECD], "Informing Consumers of CSR in International Trade," ¶¶ 44–46, June 28, 2006.

207. See Vogel, supra note 195, 264–65.

208. See Utting, supra note 184, 381.

209. Ibid., 383–86.

210. Ibid., 384; discussing the relationship between rewards and penalties on accountability and performance; Ross, supra note 10, 8; arguing that managing reputation requires awareness of stakeholder's opinion and the capacity to respond.

211. See Beverly Kracher and Kelly D. Martin, "A Moral Evaluation of Online Business Protest Tactics and Implications for Stakeholder Management," 114 *Bus. and Soc'y Rev.* (2009), 59, 61–64; they discuss businesses' managing corporate image in response to activists' using the internet to protest "objectionable business practices."

212. See Guido Palazzo and Andreas Georg Scherer, "Corporate Legitimacy as Deliberation: A Communicative Framework," 66 *J. of Bus. Ethics* (2006), 71, 77, 82.

213. See, generally, Virginia Haufler, "Self-Regulations and Business Norms:

Political Risk, Political Activism," in A. Claire Cutler, Virginia Haufler, and Tony Porter, eds., *Private Authority and International Affairs* (1999), 199, 199; she is arguing that corporate behavior is guided by principles and norms beyond profit maximization.

214. See Dirk Matten and Andrew Crane, "Corporate Citizenship: Towards an Extended Theoretical Conceptualization," 30 *Acad. Mgmt. Rev.* (2005), 166, 172–173.

215. See Kracher and Martin, supra note 211, 62–64; cf. Ross, supra note 10, 7.

216. See Kracher and Martin, supra note 211, 62–64; cf. Ross, supra note 10, 7–8.

217. See Tim Bartley and Curtis Child, "Shaming the Corporation: Reputation, Globalization, and the Dynamics of Anti-Corporate Movements" 2 (Aug. 11, 2007) (unpublished manuscript, available at http://www.Indiana.edu/~tbsoc/SM-corps-sub.pdf); see also O'Rourke, supra note 166, 115. See, generally, Naomi Klein, *No Logo* (2001); providing a vivid discussion of the resulting dynamics triggered by activists and their effect on the global brands and international business.

218. Vogel, supra note 195, 268.

219. See, generally, supra notes 213–17 and accompanying text.

220. See Kracher and Martin, supra note 211, 59; see also O'Rourke, supra note 166, 121–22, 124; discussing the role of the media in successful campaigns by NGOs against companies, specifically by the foreign press and international NGOs in the antisweatshop market campaign against Nike.

221. See Vogel, supra note 195, 268; see also Scholte, supra note 2, 19.

222. See Lozano, supra note 81, 60–63.

223. Ibid.

224. See Zadek, supra note 7, 66.

225. Some of the well-known names embroiled in the scandals are Nicholas Leeson on behalf of the British Barings Bank, as well as the infamous Enron, WorldCom, Adelphia, Arthur Anderson, and Tyco. See Diana E. Murphy, "The Federal Sentencing Guidelines for Organizations: A Decade of Promoting Compliance and Ethics," 87 *Iowa L. Rev.* (2002), 697, 707; see also Note, "The Good, the Bad, and Their Corporate Codes of Ethics: Enron, Sarbanes-Oxley, and the Problems with Legislating Good Behavior," 116 *Harv. L. Rev.* (2003), 2123, 2126; Brian A. Warwick, Commentary, "Reinventing the Wheel: Firestone and the Role of Ethics in the Corporation," 54 *Ala. L. Rev.* (2003), 1455, 1466–71.

226. See Ruth W. Grant and Robert O. Keohane, "Accountability and Abuses of Power in World Politics," 99 *Am. Pol. Sci. Rev.* (2005), 29, 36.

227. Cf. Hans Kelsen, *Pure Theory of Law* 11 (1967); discussing validity of norms and noting that if a norm is not obeyed, it is thus not valid; H. L. A. Hart, *The Concept of Law* (1961), 197, noting that if the "system is fair," it "may gain and retain allegiance."

228. Throughout the latter part of the twentieth century, one of the central topics addressed by legal philosophers was the nature of the rule of law. See Robert P. George, Reason, Freedom, and the Rule of Law: Their Significance in the Natural Law Tradition, 46 *Amer. J. of Juris.* (2001), 249, 249. Arguably one reason for the keen attention

extended to the concept was the rise and decline of totalitarian governments. See ibid. "In the aftermath of the defeat of Nazism, legal philosophers of every religious persuasion tested their legal theories by asking, for example, whether the Nazi regime constituted a legal system in any meaningful sense" (ibid.). Following the collapse of communism throughout Europe, scholars of jurisprudence sought to account for the manner in which legal institutions and procedures foster respectable democracies. See ibid. Today, the rise of global civil regulations for business leads to the analogous question of whether, and to what extent, such initiatives embody the rule of law. On this point, reference to the fundamental components of legality is illuminating. See, e.g., Lon L. Fuller, *The Morality of Law* rev. ed. (1964). (Basic elements constituting the "internal morality" of law are: nonretroactivity, amenability to compliance, promulgation, clarity, coherence, temporal constancy, generality, and congruence between official behavior and rules.) Arguably, global business civil regulations display many if not all of these characteristics.

229. See Christine Parker, "Meta-Regulation: Legal Accountability to Corporate Social Responsibility," *The New Corporate Accountability: Corporate Social Responsibility and the Law* (2007), 207–17; see also Alnoor Ebrahim, "Making Sense of Accountability: Conceptual Perspectives for Northern and Southern Nonprofits," 14 *Nonprofit Mgmt. and Leadership* (2003), 191, 194–95.

230. Concerning violence and nation-states, enormous changes have come about in relevant international standards, practices, and institutions. War crimes tribunals and the International Criminal Court were established in order to make accountable, to the point of incarceration, chiefs of states that deploy violence aimed at their own populace. These developments represent a tremendous departure from customary norms governing the principle of national sovereignty. That principle extended immunity to heads of states from legal petitions for accountability, save from members of their own principalities. Indeed, an inaugural precept of the nation-state system, observed all the way from Westphalia in 1648 to Nuremberg in 1946, dictated that heads of states enjoyed immunity from prosecution. See Geoffrey Robertson, "Ending Impunity: How International Criminal Law Can Put Tyrants on Trial," 38 *Cornell Int'l L. J.* (2005), 649, 650.

231. See Ross, supra note 10, 11.

232. Cf. Terry Nardin, "Theorizing the International Rule of Law," 34 *Rev. Int'l Stud.* (2008), 385, 389; noting that compliance with international law is a result of a desire for legitimacy.

233. See Göran Ahrne and Nils Brunsson, "Soft Regulation from an Organizational Perspective," in Ulrika Mörth, ed., *Soft Law in Governance and Regulation* (2004), 171, 187–89.

234. Cf. Andrew T. Guzman and Timothy L. Meyer, "International Common Law: The Soft Law of International Tribunals," 9 *Chi. J. of Int'l L.* (2009), 515, 519, 522–23; arguing that the reputational impacts of following or forgoing soft law is difficult to anticipate and remains a puzzle.

235. See Ian Maitland, "The Limits of Business Self-Regulation," 27 *Cal. Mgmt. Rev.* (1985), 132, 132.

236. The sources of law applied and enforced by courts of law are generally understood by both legal practitioners and scholars. But what sources of "soft law" are applied by reputational accountability-holders? Consider the famous dictum that the task of jurists is to prophesize what courts will do. See Oliver Wendell Holmes, "The Path of the Law," 10 *Harv. L. Rev.* (1897), 457, 457–58. This so-called predictive theory of law helps us understand the nature of the "soft law" of accountability holders. "The idea is that the law [of soft law] resides in the actual judgment given, not in any crisp preexisting formulation in a statute or case precedent." Jackson, supra note 118, 38. The challenge for firms is to forecast what these (nonlegal and unelected) accountability-holders expect (ibid.).

237. From this standpoint, the rise of global governance raises questions about the legitimacy of the actors attempting to hold transnational firms accountable. The theory of rent seeking proceeds from the hypothesis that the priority of typical bureaucrats are to advance their own self-interest. Consequently, if restraints of accountability and election are removed, bureaucrats become owners of rents, with the power to potentially raise these rents at the cost of those for whom the resources are supposed to benefit. Rosemary Righter argues that United Nations institutions provide substantial income for the politicians and bureaucrats that control them, and that the objectives for which they were set up are absorbing ever smaller portions of their internal budgets. See, generally, Rosemary Righter, *Utopia Lost: The United Nations and the World Order* (1995), 56–63.

238. See Cyrus Mehri, Andrea Giampetro-Meyer, and Michael B. Runnels, "One Nation, Indivisible: The Use of Diversity Report Cards to Promote Transparency, Accountability, and Workplace Fairness," 9 *Fordham J. of Corp. and Fin. L.* (2004), 395, 400–401.

239. See Grant and Keohane, supra note 226, 29.

240. Cf. Jonathan M. Karpoff and John R. Lott Jr., "The Reputational Penalty Firms Bear from Committing Criminal Fraud," 36 *J. of L. and Econ.* (1993), 757, 758–59; noting that majority of falling stock price in the wake of corporate malfeasance, whether proven, is attributable to reputational loss, whereas anticipated legal sanctions, including fines and damage awards comprise only 6 percent of the decline in share value.

241. This analysis builds on the discussion by Robert O. Keohane, illustrating the power dimensions of accountability demands. See Keohane, supra note 10, 362.

242. Cf. ibid., 362.

243. See infra note 248 and accompanying text.

244. Keohane, supra note 10, 362, 366.

245. See Ross, supra note 10, 11.

246. See ibid., 5.

247. See, generally, Pamela Stapleton and David Woodward, "Stakeholder

Reporting: The Role of Intermediaries," 114 *Bus. and Soc'y Rev.* (2009), 183, 184; not-ing the important role of the dialogue with and among stakeholders.

248. According to Robert Keohane, the notion of accountability involves both sharing of information regarding actions, decisions, or behavior of some kind and the exercise of sanctions. See Robert O. Keohane, "The Concept of Accountability in World Politics and the Use of Force," 24 *Mich. J. of Int'l L.* (2003), 1121, 1123–24.

249. See Jackson, supra note 118, 150–52.

250. In the eyes of one commentator, what we are witnessing is a worldwide dif-fraction of traditional forms of representative democracy, alongside an overall mis-trust of politics. See Pierre Rosanvallon, *Democracy Past and Future,* Samuel Moyn, ed., (2006), 192–93. Replacing procedural representation by means of elections, alter-native modes of representation are becoming prevalent within civil society, such as functional representation by experts, and ethical representation, asserted by social groups and NGOs. Such developments increase the number of political players, dif-fusing political legitimacy. "We are moving bit by bit to more disseminated forms of civil democracy" (ibid., 235), an "indirect democracy," created by "whole conge-ries of efforts—through informal social movements but institutions too—intended to compensate for the erosion of trust by institutionalizing distrust" (ibid., 238). Indirect democracy is engaged in the deployment of "mechanisms of oversight, the creation of independent institutions, and the formation of powers of rejection" (ibid., 239).

251. Jackson, supra note 118, 36.

252. See ibid., 106–8.

253. The Council on Economic Priorities reports that there are three key factors accounting for escalation in social and ethical investing: (1) the existence of more reliable and more sophisticated data regarding corporate social performance than previously; (2) investment firms utilizing social criteria have a demonstrated track record, and it is not necessary for investors to sacrifice gains for principles; and (3) the socially conscious generation of the 1960s is currently engaged in rendering investment decisions. See, e.g., "First Affirmative Financial Network, LLC, Socially Responsible Investing (SRI) In the United States," available at http://www.firstaffir-mative.com/news/sriArticle.jsp; see also Samuel B. Graves and Sandra A. Waddock, "Institutional Owners and Corporate Social Performance," 37 *Acad. Mgmt. J.* (1994), 1034, 1034.

254. See R. Bruce Hutton, Louis D'Antonio and Tommi Johnsen, "Socially Respon-sible Investing: Growing Issues and New Opportunities," 37 *Bus. and Soc.* (1998), 281, 288.

255. Layna Mosley, *Global Capital and National Governments* (2003), 18.

256. Spar, supra note 19, 9.

257. See Daniel Kahneman, Jack L. Knetsch, and Richard Thaler, "Fairness as a Constraint on Profit Seeking: Entitlements in the Market," 76 *Am. Econ. Rev.* (1986), 718, 735–36.

258. Jackson, supra note 118, 13.

259. Grant and Keohane, supra note 226, 35. "When standards are not legalized,

we would expect accountability to operate chiefly through reputation and peer pressures, rather than in more formal ways" (ibid.)

260. Jackson, supra note 118, 13.

261. Ibid., 14.

262. Ibid.

263. Ibid., 36.

264. "Reputation risk is the current and prospective impact on earnings and capital arising from negative public opinion." Steven Herz, Antonio La Vida, and Jonathan Sohn, *Development Without Conflict: The Business Case for Community Consent,* Jonathan Sohn, ed. (2007), 14; available at http://www.wri.org/publication/development-without-conflict.

265. Joseph S. Nye Jr., *Soft Power: The Means to Success in World Politics* (2004), 5.

266. See Jackson, supra note 118, 15, 36.

267. See, generally, Joshua P. Eaton, Note, "The Nigerian Tragedy, Environmental Regulation of Transnational Corporations, and the Human Right to a Healthy Environment," 15 *B. U. Int'l L. J.* (1997), 261, 261; see also Scott Greathead, "The Multinational and the 'New Stakeholder': Examining the Business Case for Human Rights," 35 *Vand. J. of Transnat'l L.* (2002), 719, 724.

268. See Graeme Smith, "Precedent Feared as Shell Saves £34m: Atlantic Grave Approved for Giant Oil Installation," *Herald* (Glasgow), Feb. 17, 1995, 9.

269. Ibid., 9.

270. See, generally, "Greenpeace Admits Error Against Shell," *L.A. Times,* Sept. 6, 1995, D2.

271. See "Shell Oil Platform to Become a Pier," *Houston Chronicle,* Jan. 30, 1998, Business 1.

272. Ibid.

273. In January 1998, after assessing a range of proposals, Shell opted to cut up the rig and turn it into a pier in Norway, costing the company approximately US$42 million, over twice the cost of dumping the rig into the sea. See ibid.

274. See Paul Lewis, "Nigeria Rulers Back Hanging of 9 Members of Opposition," *N. Y. Times,* Nov. 9, 1995, A9.

275. See Paul Lewis, "Rights Groups Say Shell Oil Shares Blame," *N. Y. Times,* Nov. 11, 1995, A6.

276. Christopher S. Wren, "U.S. is Seeking Further Ways to Punish Nigeria for Executions," *N. Y. Times,* Dec. 17, 1995, 1.11.

277. See Eaton, supra note 267, 270–71.

278. In a common accountability sequence, an agent will be authorized by a given accountability relationship, and yet another such relationship will restrict it. Thus, the International Accounting Standards Board holds companies responsible for accounting practices, yet is itself accountable to the entities granting authority to it, namely the G-7 Finance Ministers and Central Bank Governors and the International Organization of Securities Commissions. See Keohane, supra note 10, 364.

279. Thus, the World Trade Organization (WTO) and the Trade-Related Aspects of Intellectual Property Rights Agreement, both attempt to hold multinational pharmaceutical companies accountable, yet the shareholders of the pharmaceutical companies also hold the firms accountable. See Stephanie A. Barbosa, Note, "Implementation of the DOHA Declaration: Its Impact on American Pharmaceuticals," 36 *Rutgers L. J.* (2004), 205, 207–11; citing "Agreement on Trade-Related Aspects of Intellectual Property Rights," *opened for signature* Apr. 15, 1994, "Marrakesh Agreement Establishing the World Trade Organization," Annex 1C, 1869 *U.N.T.S.* 299; 33 *I.L.M.* 1197 (1994).

280. See Ross, supra note 10, 8, 11–13.

281. Ibid., 7–8.

282. Archie B. Carroll and Ann K. Buchholtz, *Business and Society: Ethics and Stakeholder Management* 7th ed. (2009), 41.

283. See, generally, Jackson, supra note 118. For example, when U.S. West contributed to the Boy Scouts of America they were criticized by gay-rights activists (ibid., 109). Yet when Levi-Strauss ceased its funding of the Boy Scouts, they were attacked by many religious leaders (ibid.). Similarly, the retailer Dayton-Hudson donated to Planned Parenthood (ibid.). This led to antiabortion demonstrators outside of the company's stores (ibid.). The company reversed its stance and began contributing to anti-abortion groups instead. This move was met by pro-choice protesters' denouncing the company for abandoning their cause (ibid.).

284. Sarah Johnson, "No Way Out?" *CFO*, Mar. 2009, 73; Lison Joseph, "Customer Desertion Could Lower Valuations of Satyam: iGate," *Livemint.Com*, Mar. 17, 2009, http://www.livemint.com/2009/03/17225447/Customer-desertion-could-lower.html.

285. See Carroll and Buchholtz, supra note 282, 15–16.

286. See, generally, "Institutional Emergence in an Era of Globalization," supra note 185, 297.

287. See, generally, Michael D. Watkins and Max H. Bazerman, "Predictable Surprises: The Disasters You Should Have Seen Coming," *Harv. Bus. Rev.* (Mar. 2003), 72, 74.

288. For example, in the *Financial Times* 1997 annual survey of Europe's most respected corporations, the Times cited the public criticism of Shell's ethical behavior in connection with environmental and human rights issues as the main cause of the firm's precipitous fall in ranking ("BP Steals the Limelight from Shell," *Fin. Times,* Surveys edition [Sept. 24, 1997], I-II).

289. See, generally, Joe Marconi, *Crisis Marketing: When Bad Things Happen to Good Companies* 2d ed. (1997), 26.

290. As one scholar writes, "Companies that have built up a stock of reputational capital may enjoy an extra measure of goodwill in times of difficulty or crisis. This goodwill can cash out in varied and sometimes surprising ways—as other parties refrain from using their superior bargaining power, remain willing to forego costly and time-consuming formalities, or tolerate mistakes they would otherwise challenge"

(Lynn S. Paine, *Value Shift: Why Companies Must Merge Social and Financial Imperatives to Achieve Superior Performance* [2003], 49).

291. See Sharon H. Garrison, *The Financial Impact of Corporate Events on Corporate Stakeholders* (1990), 3–6; Ian I. Mitroff and Mural C. Alpaslan, "Preparing for Evil," *Harv. Bus. Rev.* (Apr. 2003), 109, 115; see also Ian I. Mitroff, "Crisis Management and Environmentalism: A Natural Fit," *Cal. Mgmt. Rev.* (winter 1994), 101, 101–2.

292. See F. A. Hayek, "The Corporation in a Democratic Society: In Whose Interest Ought It and Will It Be Run?" in H. Igor Ansoff, ed., *Business Strategy* (1969), 225, 225–26; arguing that such activities place the corporation beyond what must be considered its "sole task" of generating capital; see also Keith Davis, "The Case for and Against Business Assumption of Social Responsibilities," 16 *Acad. Mgmt. J.* (1973), 312, 318–19.

293. See, generally, Jim Collins and Jerry I. Porras, *Built to Last: Successful Habits of Visionary Companies* (2002), 93, 181; discussing the example of the Boeing Company.

294. See Andrew Savitz, *The Triple Bottom Line: How Today's Best-Run Companies Are Achieving Economic, Social, and Environmental Success–And How You Can Too* (2006), 193–94.

295. See Ronnie D. Lipschutz and James K. Rowe, *Globalization, Governmentality and Global Politics: Regulation for the Rest of Us?* (2005), 154, 167.

296. See, e.g., Organisation for Economic Cooperation and Development, *Voluntary Approaches for Environmental Policy: An Assessment* (1999); see also Madhu Khanna, "The U.S. 33/50 Voluntary Program: Its Design and Effectiveness," in Richard D. Morgenstern and William A. Pizer, eds., *Reality Check: The Nature and Performance of Voluntary Environmental Program in the U.S., Europe, and Japan* (2007), 15, 15. See, generally, Michael J. Lenox and Jennifer Nash, "Industry Self-Regulation and Adverse Selection: A Comparison Across Four Trade Association Programs," 12 *Bus. Strategy and Env't* (2003), 343, 343.

297. See Prudence E. Taylor, "From Environmental to Ecological Human Rights: A New Dynamic in International Law?" 10 *Geo. Int'l Envtl. L. Rev.* (1998), 309, 359.

298. See Khanna, supra note 296, at 15, 35.

299. Ibid., 15, 31–32.

300. See, generally, *The Implementation and Effectiveness of International Environmental Commitments: Theory and Practice*, David G. Victor, Kal Raustiala, and Eugene B. Skolnikoff, eds. (1998).

301. See Winston, supra note 20, 71–72.

302. Ibid., 81.

303. See Virginia Haufler, "Global Governance and the Private Sector," in Christopher May, ed., *Global Corporate Power* (2006), 85, 90, 92; Oran R. Young, "The Effectiveness of International Institutions: Hard Cases and Critical Variables," in James N. Rosenau and Ernst-Otto Czempiel, eds., *Governance Without Government* (1992), 160, 170–71, as an example, discussing the whaling industry; see also Robert Falkner,

"Private Environmental Governance and International Relations: Exploring the Links," *Global Environ. Pol.* (May 2003), 72, 79.

304. See John Gerard Ruggie, "Taking Embedded Liberalism Global: The Corporate Connection," in David Held and Mathias Koenig-Archibugi, eds., *Taming Globalization: Frontiers of Governance* (2003), 93, 106–8.

305. David Vogel, *Trading Up: Consumer and Environmental Regulation in the Global Economy* (1995), 748.

306. See Winston, supra note 20, 76.

307. Ibid., 72–73.

308. See, e.g., A. Claire Cutler, "Transnational Business Civilization, Corporations, and the Privatization of Global Governance," in Christopher May, ed., *Global Corporate Power* (2006), 199, 199–200; Thomas Risse and Kathryn Sikkink, "The Socialization of International Human Rights Norms into Domestic Practices: Introduction," in Thomas Risse, Stephen C. Ropp, and Kathryn Sikkink, eds., *The Power of Human Rights: International Norms and Domestic Change* (1999), 39, 39. See, generally, Aseem Prakash and Matthew Potoski, *The Voluntary Environmentalists: Green Clubs, ISO 14001, and Voluntary Environmental Regulations* (2006); Jean-Philippe Thérien and Vincent Pouliot, "The Global Compact: Shifting the Politics of International Development," 12 *Global Governance* (2006), 55, 55; they are discussing the example of the UN Global Compact.

309. See, e.g., Don Wells, "Too Weak for the Job: Corporate Codes of Conduct, Nongovernmental Organizations and the Regulation of International Labour Standards," 7 *Global Soc. Pol'y* (2007), 51, 73. See, generally, Jill Esbenshade, *Monitoring Sweatshops: Workers, Consumers, and the Global Apparel Industry* (2004).

310. Lorne Sossin and Charles W. Smith, "Hard Choices and Soft Law: Ethical Codes, Policy Guidelines and the Role of the Courts in Regulating Government," 40 *Alta. L. Rev.* 867, 869 note 5; they note that relationship between "soft" and "hard" law "is analogous" to the relationship between a computer's software and hardware.

311. See, e.g., Halina Ward, *Public Sector Roles in Strengthening Corporate Social Responsibility: Taking Stock* (2004), 381; see also Corporate Social Responsibility Initiative, *Leadership, Accountability and Partnership: Critical Trends and Issues in Corporate Social Responsibility* (2004).

312. See, e.g., Orly Lobel. "Sustainable Capitalism or Ethical Transnationalism: Offshore Production and Economic Development," 17 *J. of Asian Econ.* (2006), 56, 56. See, generally, David Henderson, Misguided Virtue: False Notions of Corporate Social Responsibility (2001), 58; David Vogel, *The Market for Virtue: The Potential and Limits of Corporate Social Responsibility* (2005).

313. See Lobel, supra note 312, 56. See, generally, Henderson, supra note 312, 58.

314. See Lobel, supra note 312, 56.

315. For an insightful documentary into factories' working conditions, see *A Decent Factory* (First Run/Icarus Films 2004). *See* Dexter Roberts and Pete Engardio, "Secrets, Lies and Sweatshops," *Bus. Wk.*, Nov. 27, 2006, 50, 50–58.

316. See Surya Deva, "Global Compact: A Critique of the U.N.'s 'Public-Private' Partnership for Promoting Corporate Citizenship," 34 *Syracuse J. of Int'l L. and Com.* (2006), 107, 147.

317. Ralph Nader, "Corporations and the U.N.: Nike and Others 'Bluewash' Their Images," *San Francisco Bay Guardian*, available at www.commondreams.org/views/091900-103.htm.

318. See Deva, supra note 316, 147–48; see also Evaristus Oshionebo, "The U.N. Global Compact and Accountability of Transnational Corporations: Separating Myth from Realities," 19 *Fla. J. of Int'l L.* (2007), 1, 36–37.

319. See Pete Engardio, Commentary, "Global Compact, Little Impact," *Bus. Wk.*, July 12, 2004, 86, 86–87; Oliver F. Williams, "The UN Global Compact: The Challenge and the Promise," 14 *Bus. Ethics Q.* (2004), 755, 757.

320. Among those criticized were Aventis, Bayer, BHP, Nestle, Nike, Norsk Hydro, Rio Tinto, Shell, Unilever, and the International Chamber of Commerce. See David M. Bigge, "Bring on the Bluewash: A Social Constructivist Argument Against Using *Nike v. Kasky* to Attack the UN Global Compact," *Int'l Legal Persp.* (spring 2004), 6, 12–13.

321. See Winston, supra note 20, 86–87.

322. Ella Joseph and John Parkinson, "Confronting the Critics" (Jan. 18, 2002), 10; unpublished manuscript, available at http://www.ippr.org.uk/uploadedFiles/events/confrontingcritics.pdf.

323. One author identifies four ways in which companies respond to demands placed by CSR, arguing that taken together they establish a business case for CSR. Zadek, supra note 7, at 64. The four approaches are distinguished as follows: (1) defensive approach, intended to alleviate pain; (2) traditional cost-benefit approach holding that firms commit to activities for which they can see direct benefits exceeding costs; (3) strategic approach, according to which firms recognize the changing environment and thus engage with CSR as part of a conscious emergent strategy; and (4) innovation and learning approach, where active engagement with CSR both provides fresh opportunities to understand the marketplace and enhances organizational learning, all of which fosters competitive advantage. Ibid.

324. See, e.g., Janet E. Kerr, "The Creative Capitalism Spectrum: Evaluating Corporate Social Responsibility Through a Legal Lens," 81 *Temp. L. Rev.* (2008), 831, 854.

325. See Deva, supra note 316, 148.

326. See, e.g., Michael E. Porter and Mark R. Kramer, "Strategy and Society: The Link Between Competitive Advantage and Corporate Social Responsibility," *Harv. Bus. Rev.* (Dec. 2006), 78–92.

327. See, generally, Ruth V. Aguilera et al., "Putting the S Back in Corporate Social Change in Organizations" U. Ill. College of Bus., Working Paper No. 04–0107 (2004), 5–6; Rimmy Malhotra, "Corporate Social Responsibility Done Right," *The Motley Fool*, Oct. 3, 2007, available at http://www.fool.com/investing/value/2007/10/03/corporate-social-responsibility-done-right.aspx.

Chapter 9

1. The Fed has extensive regulatory reach with authority over bank holding companies; state chartered banks; foreign branches of member banks; edge and agreement corporations; United States state-licensed branches, agencies, and representative offices of foreign banks; nonbanking activities of foreign banks; national banks; savings banks; nonbank subsidiaries of bank holding companies; thrift holding companies; financial reporting; accounting policies of banks; business continuity in case of economic emergency; consumer-protection laws; securities dealings of banks; information technology used by banks; foreign investments of banks; foreign lending by banks; branch banking; bank mergers and acquisitions; who may own a bank; capital adequacy standards; extensions of credit for the purchase of securities; equal-opportunity lending; mortgage disclosure information; reserve requirements; electronic-funds transfers; interbank liabilities; Community Reinvestment Act subprime lending requirements; all international banking operations; consumer leasing; privacy of consumer financial information; payments on demand deposits; fair credit reporting; transactions between member banks and their affiliates; truth in lending; and truth in savings. See http://www.federalreserve.gov.

2. See Robert McCrum, *Globish, How English Became the World's Language* (2010).

3. As Pope Benedict expresses in the Encyclical *Caritas in Veritate,* "every economic decision has a moral consequence."

4. The term *dollar* referred to an ounce of silver, coined in the sixteenth century by the Bohemian, Count Schlick, who lived in Joachimsthal. His highly reputed coins were called "Joachimsthalers," which later was simplified as "'Thalers" or "dollars." The dollar remained a unit of weight specie up until 1933, when the United States went off of the gold standard.

5. According to Zadek, the New Economy is characterized by "the acceleration of every aspect of social life; the collapse of geographical distance as a basis for defining and sustaining difference; and the growing significance of knowledge and innovation as the primary source of business competition and economic value" (Simon Zadek, *The Civil Corporation* [2007], 35).

6. See Edward Feser, *Locke* (2007), 123–34.

7. I am indebted to Edwin Hartman for bringing out this distinction.

Conclusion

Note to epigraph: David Hume, *Essays, Moral, Political and Literary*, part II, essay II, no. 4 (1742), 32.

1. Steve Fishman, "Bernie Madoff, Free at Last; In Prison He Doesn't Have to

Hide His Lack of Conscience. In Fact, He's a Hero for It," *New York Magazine*, June 14, 2010.

2. Jacques Maritain, *The Range of Reason* (1952), 23.

3. "What is happening to our young people? They disrespect their elders, they disobey their parents. They ignore the law. They riot in the streets inflamed with wild notions. Their morals are decaying. What is to become of them?"

4. Cormac McCarthy, *No Country for Old Men* (2005), 196. While it may be comforting to dismiss the ruminations of this character as mere urban legend, it is in fact an accurate portrayal of cold-blooded reality. Consider the case of Samuel Hengel, a fifteen-year-old Marinette, Wisconsin, high school student who fatally shot himself November 30, 2010, after holding his teacher and classmates at gunpoint for five hours ("School Gunman Dies of Self-Inflicted Wound," *Wall St. J.*, Dec.1, 2010, A6).

5. Art endures, life is short.

Index

Acknowledgments

THANKS TO MY editor, Erin Graham, for her kindness and sage advice throughout the process of developing this book, from its inception to completion. I also am grateful for the extensive and expert contributions of Tim Roberts with final manuscript preparation. As well, I wish to extend my appreciation to Edwin Hartman and Georges Enderle for their superb efforts in reading and commenting on earlier drafts and revisions.

I am appreciative of the support and encouragement of many colleagues and friends, not only those who offered comments on the manuscript, but also those who provided valuable input and recommendations on previous presentations and papers that led up to it. Thanks to Miguel Alzola, Sherri Anderson, Daniel Arenas, John Boatright, George Brenkert, Boris Brownstein, Carlos Cavalle, Christopher Cowton, Wesley Cragg, Andrew Crane, Jeanne Davis, Kenneth Davis, Thomas Donaldson, Laszlo Fekete, Robert George, Amy Goodman, Joseph Heath, Martin Hilb, Knut Ims, Harold James, Garrett MacSweeney, Hilary Martin, Dirk Matten, Gary Miller, Fr. Martin Miller, Geoff Moore, Wayne Norman, David Oakley, Eleanor O'Higgins, Darryl Reed, Mark Schwartz, Laura Spence, Luis Tellez, Antonio Tencati, David Weitzner, Cynthia Williams, Brad Wilson, and Michael Windle.

I am deeply grateful to Zhenni, Wenlan, and Brendan for their abiding love, and for the inspiration and encouragement they provide. To them I dedicate this book.

DATE DUE	RETURNED